BRIGHT EARTH

Philip Ball is a freelance writer and a consultant
editor for the world's leading science journal
Nature. He is a regular commentator on the
interactions between science, art, history and
culture. His previous books include *Bright Earth:
The Invention of Colour*, *H2O: A Biography of
Water* and *Critical Mass: How One Thing Leads
To Another*, which won the 2005 Aventis Prize
for Science Books. He lives in London with his
wife and daughter.

ALSO BY PHILIP BALL

The Devil's Doctor: Paracelus and the World of Renaissance Magic and Science

Elegant Solutions: Ten Beautiful Experiments in Chemistry

Critical Mass: How One Thing Leads to Another

The Elements: A Very Short Introduction

Molecules: A Very Short Introduction

H2O: A Biography of Water

The Self-made Tapestry: Pattern Formation in Nature

Made to Measure: New Materials for the 21st Century

Designing the Molecular World: Chemistry at the Frontier

PHILIP BALL

Bright Earth

The Invention of Colour

VINTAGE BOOKS
London

Published by Vintage 2009

12

Copyright © Philip Ball 2001

Philip Ball has asserted his right under the Copyright, Designs
and Patents Act, 1988 to be identified as the author of this work

This book is sold subject to the condition that it shall not,
by way of trade or otherwise, be lent, resold, hired out,
or otherwise circulated without the publisher's prior
consent in any form of binding or cover other than that
in which it is published and without a similar condition,
including this condition, being imposed on the
subsequent purchaser

Excerpts from *Ways of Seeing* by John Berger (Penguin Books, 1972)
Copyright © John Berger 1972

First published in Great Britain by Viking in 2001

Published by Penguin Books 2002

Vintage
Random House, 20 Vauxhall Bridge Road,
London SW1V 2SA

www.vintage-books.co.uk

Addresses for companies within The Random House Group Limited
can be found at: www.randomhouse.co.uk/offices.htm

The Random House Group Limited Reg. No. 954009

A CIP catalogue record for this book
is available from the British Library

ISBN 9780099507130

Penguin Random House is committed to a sustainable future for
our business, our readers and our planet. This book is made from
Forest Stewardship Council® certified paper.

Printed and bound in Great Britain by Clays Ltd, Elcograf S.p.A.

Contents

List of Illustrations   vii

Preface   xii

1. The Eye of the Beholder   1
   THE SCIENTIST IN THE STUDIO

2. Plucking the Rainbow   25
   THE PHYSICS AND CHEMISTRY OF COLOUR

3. The Forge of Vulcan   55
   COLOUR TECHNOLOGY IN ANTIQUITY

4. Secret Recipes   80
   ALCHEMY'S ARTISTIC LEGACY

5. Masters of Light and Shadow   116
   THE GLORY OF THE RENAISSANCE

6. Old Gold   143
   THE REVIVAL OF AN AUSTERE PALETTE

7. The Prismatic Metals   165
   SYNTHETIC PIGMENTS AND THE DAWN OF
   COLOUR CHEMISTRY

8. The Reign of Light   189
   IMPRESSIONISM'S BRIGHT IMPACT

9. A Passion for Purple   222
   DYES AND THE INDUSTRIALIZATION OF COLOUR

10. Shades of Midnight   260
    THE PROBLEM OF BLUE

11. Time as Painter   283
    THE EVER-CHANGING CANVAS

12. Capturing Colour   306
    HOW ART APPEARS IN REPRODUCTION

13. Mind over Matter   343
    COLOUR AS FORM IN MODERNISM

14. **Art for Art's Sake**   360
    NEW MATERIALS, NEW HORIZONS

Notes   386

Bibliography   408

Index   417

Illustrations

Text Figures

2.1 How the rainbow is formed   30
2.2 Microscopic ribs on a butterfly's wing (Dee Breger,
     Lamont-Doherty Earth Observatory, New York)   31
2.3 Isaac Newton's colour wheel   42
2.4 Nineteenth-century colour stars   43
2.5 The visual system of the human eye   48
4.1 An alchemist at work   82
4.2 A painter saved by an image of the Virgin Mary
     (Cantigas de Santa Maria, folio 109r: Patrimonio
     Nacional, Madrid)   96
8.1 Ogden Rood's colour wheel   199
9.1 Synthetic organic colourants   258
11.1 Tura's *Allegorical Figure*, after cleaning but before
     restoration (National Gallery, London)   289
11.2 A painting illuminated by raking light (Tate Gallery,
     London)   295
12.1 Ugo da Carpi, *Saturn* (1604) (Victoria and Albert
     Museum, London)   310
12.2 A nineteenth-century photographer and the equipment
     needed to make daguerreotypes   323
12.3 Photographic film   329
12.4 The spectra of printing inks   333
12.5 The colour gamut of TV phosphors, and how to treat
     colours outside the gamut   337

Inset Plates

1.1   Anish Kapoor, *As If to Celebrate, I Discovered a Mountain Blooming with Red Flowers* (1981) (Tate Gallery, London)

1.2   Wassily Kandinsky, *Yellow Accompaniment* (1924) (Guggenheim Museum, New York)

2.1   Michel-Eugène Chevreul's colour wheel (1864)

2.2   The CIE chromaticity diagram

2.3   Albert Munsell's colour atlas (Victoria and Albert Museum, London)

3.1   Cave art from Altamira, Spain, dating from *c.* 15000 BC (Art Resource, New York)

3.2   Egyptian faience (*c.* 1290 BC) (British Museum, London)

3.3   Egyptian wall painting, probably from the tomb of Nebamun (*c.* 1350 BC) (British Museum, London)

3.4   The 'Alexander' mosaic from the House of the Faun, Pompeii (before AD 79) (Museo Archeologica Nazionale, Naples)

3.5   The Villa of Mysteries, Pompeii (*c.* 50 BC) (Art Resource, New York)

4.1   Attributed to Masaccio and Masolino, *Saints Jerome and John the Baptist* (*c.* 1423–8) (National Gallery, London)

4.2   The female painter Thamar, with an assistant (taken from an illuminated manuscript of 1403, ms 12.420, folio 86: Bibliothèque Nationale, Paris; Art Resource, New York)

4.3   Giotto, the Arena Chapel in Padua (*c.* 1305) (Art Resource, New York)

4.4   The Master of Saint Bartholomew, *Saints Peter and Dorothy* (*c.* 1505–10) (National Gallery, London)

4.5   Giovanni del Ponte, *The Ascension of St John the Evangelist* (*c.* 1410–20) (National Gallery, London)

5.1   Giotto, *The Betrayal of Christ* (*c.* 1305) (Arena Chapel, Padua; Alinari/Art Resource, New York)

5.2   Nardo di Cione, *St John the Baptist with St John the Evangelist(?) and St James* (*c.* 1365) (National Gallery, London)

5.3 Leonardo da Vinci, *The Virgin of the Rocks* (c. 1508) (National Gallery, London)

5.4 Raphael, *The Madonna del Granduca* (c. 1505) (Palazzo Pitti, Florence; Art Resource, New York)

5.5 Jan van Eyck, *The Portrait of Giovanni Arnolfini and His Wife* (*The Arnolfini Marriage*) (1434) (National Gallery, London)

5.6 Carlo Crivelli, *Annunciation, with St Emidius* (1486) (National Gallery, London)

5.7 Titian, *Bacchus and Ariadne* (1523) (National Gallery, London)

5.8 Titian, *Portrait of a Man* (c. 1512) (National Gallery, London)

6.1 Anthony van Dyck, *Equestrian Portrait of Charles I* (c. 1637–8) (National Gallery, London)

6.2 Paolo Veronese, *Adoration of the Kings* (1573) (National Gallery, London)

6.3 Tintoretto, *St George and the Dragon* (c. 1560) (National Gallery, London)

6.4 Peter Paul Rubens, *Samson and Delilah* (c. 1609) (National Gallery, London)

6.5 Anthony van Dyck, *Charity* (c. 1627–8) (National Gallery, London)

6.6 Rembrandt, *Portrait of Hendrickje Stoffels* (c. 1654–6) (National Gallery, London)

7.1 J. M. W. Turner, *Ulysses Deriding Polyphemus* (1829) (National Gallery, London)

7.2 William Holman Hunt, *Valentine Rescuing Sylvia from Proteus* (1850–51) (Birmingham Museums and Art Gallery)

8.1 Eugène Delacroix, *Algerian Women in Their Apartment* (1834) (Louvre, Paris. © Photo RMN)

8.2 William Holman Hunt, *Our English Coasts* (later *Strayed Sheep*) (1852) (Tate Gallery, London)

8.3 Claude Monet, *Regatta at Argenteuil* (1872) (Musée d'Orsay, Paris. © Photo RMN/H. Lewandowski, S. Hubert; ADAGP, Paris, and DACS, London, 2001)

8.4 The Impressionist palette (National Gallery, London)

8.5   Auguste Renoir, *Boating on the Seine* (1879–80) (National Gallery, London)

8.6   Claude Monet, *Lavacourt under Snow* (*c.* 1879) (National Gallery, London)

8.7   Georges Seurat, *Sunday Afternoon on the Island of La Grande Jatte* (1884–5) (Art Institute of Chicago)

8.8   Paul Cézanne, *Hillside in Provence* (*c.* 1885) (National Gallery, London)

8.9   Paul Sérusier, *The Talisman* (1888) (Musée d'Orsay, Paris. © Photo RMN/Jean Schormans)

8.10   Vincent van Gogh, *The Night Café* (1888) (Yale University Art Gallery)

9.1   Jan van Eyck, *The Virgin with Chancellor Rolin* (*c.* 1437) (Louvre, Paris. © Photo RMN/Hervé Lewandowski)

9.2   Arthur Hughes, *April Love* (1856) (Tate Gallery, London)

9.3   A silk dress from *c.* 1862 dyed with Perkin's mauve (Science Museum/Science & Society Picture Library, London)

10.1   Lapis lazuli (Natural History Museum, London)

10.2   Duccio, *The Virgin and Child with Saints* (*c.* 1315) (National Gallery, London)

10.3   Titian, *Madonna and Child with Saints John the Baptist and Catherine of Alexandria* (*c.* 1530) (National Gallery, London)

10.4   Anish Kapoor, *A Wing at the Heart of Things* (1990) (National Gallery, London)

10.5   Yves Klein, *IKB 79* (1959) (Tate Gallery, London)

10.6   Yves Klein, *Ex Voto for the Shrine of St Rita* (1961) (Cascia Convent; David Bordes. © ADAGP, Paris, and DACS, London)

11.1   Titian, *Bacchus and Ariadne* before cleaning (National Gallery, London)

11.2   Cosimo Tura, *Allegorical Figure* (*c.* 1459–63) (National Gallery, London)

11.3   A cross-section through a paint layer from Gerard David, *Canon Bernadinus de Salviatis and Three Saints* (after 1501) (National Gallery, London)

11.4   Follower of Campin, *The Virgin and Child before a Firescreen* (*c.* 1440) (National Gallery, London)

11.5   Antonio del Pollaiuolo, *Apollo and Daphne* (*c.* 1470–80) (National Gallery, London)

11.6   Jan van Huysum, *Flowers in a Terracotta Vase* (1736) (National Gallery, London)

12.1   Jacob Le Blon, colour print of a woman's head (*c.* 1722) (Victoria and Albert Museum, London)

12.2   George Baxter, *Hollyhocks* (1857) (Victoria and Albert Museum, London)

12.3   Jan Vermeer, *View of Delft*, digitally reproduced using different 'cluts' (Original: Art Resource, New York. Images digitally prepared by Anne Morgan Spalter, Brown University)

13.1   André Derain, *The Pool of London* (1906) (Tate Gallery, London)

14.1   Patrick Caulfield, *Pottery* (1969) (Tate Gallery, London)

14.2   Mark Rothko, *Ochre and Red on Red* (1954) (Phillips Collection, Washington, DC)

14.3   Morris Louis, *VAV* (1960) (Tate Gallery, London)

14.4   Kenneth Noland, *Drought* (1962) (Tate Gallery, London)

14.5   Frank Stella, *Six Mile Bottom* (1960) (Tate Gallery, London)

14.6   Frank Stella, *Guadalupe Island* (1979) (Tate Gallery, London)

Preface

For the past two years I have been learning to speak a new language. Or rather, not so much to speak it as to think it, for painterly colour is a language that words struggle to convey. Here, for example, is German art critic Lorenz Dittmann on Jean-François Millet's *The Gleaners* (1857):

The unusually restrained colours . . . follow a closely-stepped sequence: reddish tones in the central figure, based around copper-reddish, brownish and bright carmine; delicate nuances of colourful greys in the standing figure to the right: silvery bright blue-grey, dove-grey, blue and turquoise greys . . . the barely definable, shimmering brownish tone of the field in the middle distance takes on a slender pink-violet tone against the grey-scale of the figure at the back, which is echoed again in the slightly darkened foreground.

Do you see the image? Of course not, although the words begin to paint a picture of their own. Colour, like music, takes a short cut to our senses and our emotions. The Church understood this in the Middle Ages; so have the greatest painters, as well as propagandists, advertisers and designers. No wonder philosophers and linguists so love to debate colour – it tempts, teases and eludes them, at the same time as it promises wonders and deep secrets.

Well then, where does one start to learn this language? I am quite sure that there is no best answer. I have approached it through the *substance* of colour; and if that is partly because I have trained as a chemist, it is also because I relish paint and pigments as materials, with appearances, smells, textures and names that entice and intoxicate. Here is one language of colour that I can interpret already: phthalocyanine speaks to me of chlorophyll and blood, vermilion conjures up the sulphur and mercury of the alchemists. Yet the painter's use of colour has not only its unique chemistry but also its historical traditions, its psychology, its prejudices, its religiosity and mysticism.

I imagine that, were I ever to acquire fluency in a foreign language, I would, on entering the country in which it is spoken, experience something of what I felt after revisiting the National Gallery several months into this project. Through the agency of colour I could begin to understand, or at least to catch fragments of, what was being said on the walls all around. Where before there were two-dimensional images in gilded frames, there was now a living world. Each picture seemed as though it had just left the artist's workshop or studio, the paint's transition from palette to panel or canvas visible in the brush-marks. Of course, time too has left its mark: paintings often need more decoding than the artist intended, as greens darken to black and reds fade to pink. In the end, the language of colour is really about learning to see.

I have been deeply fortunate to benefit, in this learning process, from the advice of people who have far greater fluency in the language of colour than I shall ever attain. My thanks go to Tom Learner at the Tate Gallery, Jo Kirby at the National Gallery, John Gage at the University of Cambridge, Martin Kemp at the University of Oxford, Helen Skelton and David Lewis at the University of Leeds, and most of all to Joyce Townsend at the Tate, who not only helped with materials and information but read the entire draft manuscript diligently. I am indebted to the Royal College of Art for the use of its splendid Colour Reference Library, and to my editors Andrew Kidd and John Glusman for helping the book find its shape. The sustaining interest and enthusiasm of many friends and colleagues are, of course, the nutrition that every writer needs, and can never adequately acknowledge.

Philip Ball
London, 2001

Note: I have often used the masculine third person to denote a generic painter until the twentieth century. This is simply an attempt to be consistent with the historical record: female painters were usually such rare exceptions that 'his or her' would jar with the context. We can deplore the inequities of earlier ages without trying to deny them. But, as Plate 4.2 shows, some women were able to become painters even in the most chauvinistic of times.

1. The Eye of the Beholder

THE SCIENTIST IN THE STUDIO

The starting point is the study of colour and its effects on men.

Wassily Kandinsky, *Concerning the Spiritual in Art* (1912)

Then the man in the blue suit reaches into his pocket and takes out a large sheet of paper, which he carefully unfolds and hands to me. It is covered with Picasso's handwriting – less spasmodic, more studied than usual. At first sight, it resembles a poem. Twenty or so verses are assembled in a column, surrounded by broad white margins. Each verse is prolonged with a dash, occasionally a very long one. But it is not a poem; it is Picasso's most recent order for colours . . .

For once, all the anonymous heroes of Picasso's palette trooped forth from the shadows, with Permanent White at their head. Each had distinguished himself in some great battle – the Blue Period, the Rose Period, Cubism, 'Guernica' . . . Each could say: 'I too, I was there . . .' And Picasso, reviewing his old comrades-in-arms, gives to each of them a sweep of his pen, a long dash that seems a fraternal salute: 'Welcome Persian red! Welcome emerald green! Cerulean blue, ivory black, cobalt violet, clear and deep, welcome! Welcome!'

Brassaï, *Conversations avec Picasso* (1964)

'I believe that in future, people will start painting pictures in one single colour, and nothing else but colour.' The French artist Yves Klein said this in 1954, before embarking on a 'monochrome' period in which each work was composed from just a single glorious hue. This adventure culminated in Klein's collaboration with Paris paint retailer Edouard Adam in 1955 to make a new blue paint of unnerving vibrancy. In 1957 he launched his manifesto with an exhibition, 'Proclamation of the Blue Epoch', that contained eleven paintings in Klein's new blue.

By saying that Yves Klein's monochrome art was the offspring of chemical technology, I mean something more than that his paint was a modern chemical product. The very *concept* of this art was technologically inspired. Klein did not just want to show us pure colour; he wanted to display the glory of *new* colour, to revel in its materiality. His striking oranges and yellows are synthetic colours, inventions of the twentieth century. Klein's blue was ultramarine, but not the natural, mineral-based ultramarine of the Middle Ages: it was a product of the chemical industry, and Klein and Adam experimented for a year to turn it into a paint with the mesmerizing quality the artist was seeking. By patenting this new colour, Klein was not simply protecting his commercial interests but hallmarking the authenticity of a creative idea. One could say that the patent was a part of his art.

Yves Klein's use of colour became possible only when chemical technology had reached a certain level of maturity. But this was nothing new. For as long as painters have fashioned their visions and dreams into images, they have relied on technical knowledge and skill to supply their materials. With the blossoming of the chemical sciences in the early nineteenth century it became impossible to overlook this fact: chemistry was laid out there on the artist's palette. And the artist rejoiced in it: 'Praise be to the palette for the delights it offers . . . it is itself a "work", more beautiful, indeed, than many a work,' said Wassily Kandinsky in 1913. The Impressionist Camille Pissarro made the point forcefully in his *Palette with a Landscape* (1878), a pastoral scene constructed directly on his palette by pulling down the bright colours dotted around its edges.

The Impressionists and their descendants – van Gogh, Matisse, Gauguin, Kandinsky – explored the new chromatic dimensions opened up by chemistry with a vitality that has arguably not been equalled since. Their audiences were shocked not only by the breaking of the rules – the deviation from 'naturalistic' colouration – but by the sight of colours never before seen on canvas: glowing orange, velvety purples, vibrant new greens. Van Gogh dispatched his brother to acquire some of the brightest and most striking of the new pigments available, and wrought them into disturbing compositions whose strident tones are almost painful to behold. Many were dumbfounded or outraged by this new visual language: the conservative French painter Jean-Georges Vibert rebuked the Impressionists for painting 'only with intense colours'.

It was a complaint that echoes back through the ages, to be heard whenever chemistry (or foreign trade, which also broadens a culture's repertoire of materials) has made new or superior colours available to painters. When Titian, Henry James's 'prince of colourists', took advantage of having the first pick of the pigments brought to the thriving ports of Venice to cover his canvases with sumptuous reds, blues, pinks and violets, Michelangelo remarked sniffily that it was a pity the Venetians were not taught to draw better. Pliny bemoaned the influx of bright new pigments from the East that corrupted the austere colouring scheme Rome had inherited from Classical Greece: 'Now India contributes the ooze of her rivers and the blood of dragons and of elephants.'

That the invention and availability of new chemical pigments influenced the use of colour in art is indisputable. As art historian Ernst Gombrich says, the artist 'cannot transcribe what he sees; he can only translate it into the terms of his medium. He, too, is strictly tied to the range of tones which his medium will yield.'[1] So it is surprising that little attention has been given to the matter of how artists obtained their colours, as opposed to how they used them. This neglect of the material aspect of the artist's craft is perhaps a consequence of a cultural tendency in the West to separate inspiration from substance. Art historian John Gage confesses that 'One of the least studied aspects of the history of art is art's tools.' Anthea Callen, a specialist in the techniques of the Impressionists, makes a stronger criticism:

Ironically, people who write on art frequently overlook the practical side of their craft, often concentrating solely on stylistic, literary or formal qualities in their discussion of painting. As a result, unnecessary errors and misunderstandings have grown up in art history, only to be reiterated by succeeding generations of writers. Any work of art is determined first and foremost by the materials available to the artist, and by the artist's ability to manipulate those materials. Thus only when the limitations imposed by artists' materials and social conditions are taken fully into account can aesthetic preoccupations, and the place of art in history, be adequately understood.[2]

One might expect the 'craft' aspects of art to suffer less neglect when the use of colour is under discussion – for surely the nature of materials should then come naturally to the fore? But it is not always so. Faber Birren admits in his classic *History of Color in Painting* that 'the choice of colours for a palette or palettes is not in any way concerned with chemistry, or with permanence, transparency, opacity or any of the *material* aspects of art'. This extraordinary omission of the substantial dimension of colour is surely the precondition for such absurdities as Birren's assigning cobalt blue to the palette of Rubens and his contemporaries, almost two centuries before its invention.[3] In view of the attention that Birren gives to the hues required for a 'balanced palette', it is indeed odd how little concerned he is with whether artists of different eras had access to them.

Paint and the painter

Every painter must confront the question: what is colour *for*? Bridget Riley, one of the modern artists most concerned with colour relationships, has expressed the dilemma very clearly:

For painters, colour is not only all those things which we all see but also, most extraordinarily, the pigments spread out on the palette, and there, quite uniquely, they are simply and solely colour. This is the first important fact of the painter's art to be grasped. These bright and shining pigments will not, however, continue to lie there on the palette as pristine colours in themselves but will be put to use – for the painter paints a picture, so the use of colour has to be conditioned by this function of picture making . . . The painter has two quite distinct systems of colour to deal with – one provided by nature, the other required by art – perceptual colour and pictorial colour. Both will be present and the painter's work depends upon the emphasis they place first upon the one and then upon the other.[4]

This is not a contemporary conundrum, but one that has confronted artists of all eras. And yet there is something missing from Riley's formulation of the artist's situation. Pigments are not 'simply and solely colour', but substances with specific properties and attributes, not least amongst them cost. How is your desire for blue affected if you have just paid more for it than for the equivalent weight in gold? That yellow looks glorious, but what if its traces on your fingertips could poison you at your supper table? This orange tempts like distilled sunlight, but how do you know that it will not have faded to dirty brown by next year? What, in short, is your relationship with the materials?

Raw colour supplies more than a physical medium from which artists can construct their images. 'Materials influence form,' said American artist Morris Louis in the 1950s; but 'influence' is too weak a word when we are faced with the explosive vibrancy of Titian's *Bacchus and Ariadne* (1523), Ingres's *Odalisque with a Slave* (1839–40) or Matisse's *Red Studio* (1911). This is art that follows directly from the impact of colour – from possibilities delimited by the prevailing chemical technology.

But although technology made Yves Klein's monochromes possible for the first time, it would be meaningless to suggest that Rubens did not paint them because those colours were not available to him. It is equally absurd to suppose that, but for a technical knowledge of anatomy and perspective and the chemical prowess to extend the range of pigments, the ancient Egyptians would have painted in the style of Titian. Use of colour in art is determined at least as much by the artist's personal inclinations and cultural context as by the materials to hand.

So it would be a mistake to assume that the history of colour in art is an accumulation of possibilities proportional to the accumulation of pigments. Every choice an artist makes is an act of exclusion as well as inclusion. Before we can gain a clear understanding of where technological considerations enter the decision, we must appreciate the social and cultural factors at work on the artist's attitudes. In the end, each artist makes his or her own contract with the colours of the time.

Leonardo's quest

Ernst Gombrich asserts that 'art is altogether different from science', but the reason he gives will bring a rueful smile to the lips of many a scientist: 'art itself can hardly be said to progress in the way in which science progresses. Each discovery in one direction creates a new difficulty somewhere else.' One can see that Gombrich never dabbled in science.

Exploring the link between art and science is back in fashion; but the debate is dominated by the supposition of cognate ideas and sources of inspiration. Artists of all persuasions today may be found mining the rich seam of association that crystallizes from our genetic inheritance, just as one can draw analogies between relativity and Cubism, between quantum mechanics and the works of Virginia Woolf.

This is all well and good in so far as it speaks of the much-needed cultural assimilation of scientific ideas (albeit commonly in a distorted or half-digested form). But it appears that we are happier in the realm of the intellectual than that of the tangible.

Yet this Cartesian-like division of material and mind has not always reflected the attitude of the practising artist. It is only in the past half-century or so that every conceivable subdivision and admixture of the rainbow has been available in off-the-shelf tubes. Until the eighteenth century, most artists ground and mixed their own pigments, or at least had this process conducted in their studios. The almost sensual pleasure in the material component of colour evinced by medieval craftsmen like the Italian Cennino Cennini demonstrates that artists of his time were on intimate terms with their paints, and possessed some considerable skill as practical chemists.

Moreover, before the Age of Reason the distinction between 'art' and 'science' was not synonymous with that between intuition and rationality. In medieval times, men of science were chroniclers of antique knowledge and theory – a practice that did not necessarily require an inquiring mind. 'Art', on the other hand, implied technical or manual skill, and a chemist was as much an artist as was a painter. The artist was valued not for his imagination, passion or inventiveness, but for his ability to do a workmanlike job.

This was the world in which Leonardo da Vinci lived and worked. Vladimir Nabokov once said that he would be more interested in C. P. Snow's famous 'Two Cultures' debate if their disjunction did not seem to him more of a ditch than an abyss. Leonardo barely seemed to notice so much as a ditch. The ease with which he passed between his roles as artist, technologist and natural philosopher remains remarkable even when we remember that these distinctions were by no means as rigid during the Renaissance as they are today.

Scholarly circles in Leonardo's fifteenth-century Florence were alive with discussion about the role of reason, geometry and mathematics in art. Leonardo himself was a firm advocate of the need for the artist to imitate nature as exactly as possible, which entailed learning the mathematical rules that governed nature: 'Those who devote themselves to [artistic] practice without science are like sailors who put to sea without a rudder or compass and who can never be certain where they are going.'[5] Yet how readily we see Leonardo's boundary-straddling through modern eyes. In stressing the importance of science in art, Leonardo had an agenda that was very much a product of its time. By emphasizing the role of mathematics, he attempted to elevate the status of painting to a Liberal Art, alongside geometry, music, rhetoric and astronomy. These Arts were those deemed worthy of serious intellectual study at the universities, whereas painting had been regarded since the Middle Ages as a craft, a lowly manual skill. Such activities in the classical past had often been performed by slaves, and painters of Leonardo's time were desperate to throw off this stigma. By arguing for the acceptance of painting as a Liberal Art, they sought to advance their own social standing.

Artists would plead their cause by pointing out that many great men of antiquity had shared their trade, and that kings and (more recently) popes had conferred favour upon them. In his book *Della Pittura (On Painting)* (1435), the Florentine architect and artist Leon Battista Alberti (1404–72) reminded his readers that

The number of painters and sculptors was enormous in those days, when princes and people, and learned and unlearned alike delighted in painting . . . Eventually Paulus Aemilius and many other Roman citizens taught their sons painting among the Liberal Arts in the pursuit of the good and happy life. The excellent custom was especially observed among the Greeks that free-born and liberally educated young people were also taught the art of painting together with letters, geometry and music.[6]

Leonardo, Alberti and their fellow painters questioned how poetry could be accepted as a Liberal Art while the creation of beautiful images in paint rather than in words was not. 'Write up in one place the name of God,' said Leonardo, 'and put a figure representing him opposite, and see which will be the more reverenced.'[7]

The artist's cause demanded that artists dissociated themselves from craftsmen, and allied their skills with mathematics and abstract thought. 'Painting', said Alberti, 'was honoured by our ancestors with this special distinction that, whereas all other artists were called craftsmen, the painter alone was not counted among their number.'[8] This could not but have encouraged artists to downplay the material aspects of painting, such as the creation and grinding of pigments. In turn, this surely contributed to the desire of the Florentine painters to emphasize drawing and line (*disegno*) above the use of colour (*colore*), initiating a dispute that lasted for centuries. Dismissive comments such as those of Equicola in the sixteenth century could only have egged them on: 'Painting has no other concern except with copying nature with various appropriately chosen colours.'

By the late fifteenth century Leonardo and his fellow painters had largely won their battle – but at the cost of simply reinforcing the bigotry that they inherited from Classical times. Nowhere does Leonardo challenge the underlying hierarchy that values the intellectual over the manual. Instead, he seeks to relocate the craft of the medieval painter on an abstract plane. Thus did art begin to fragment into the 'pure' and the 'applied', a distinction not seriously challenged until the nineteenth century. In *The Two Paths* (1859), John Ruskin deplored art's own 'two cultures' and argued that decorative art and craft should not be regarded as 'a degraded or separate kind of art'. With William Morris and others, Ruskin tried to reunite the craftsperson with the fine artist in the Arts and Crafts movement. It is not clear that they enjoyed much success: Art Nouveau came and went, but artistic elitism remains.

Chemistry and art

The relation of painting to the Liberal Arts in Leonardo's time was wholly analogous to the standing of chemistry in relation to natural philosophy, or what we would now call science. Those who pursued the chemical arts, who dwelt in smoky laboratories and wrought useful things, were excluded from the lofty halls of academic science. Science historian Lawrence Principe says of this pre-scientific chemistry or 'chymistry':

> It has long been recognized that one of the 'problems' of chymistry before the eighteenth century was its status as a practical or technical art rather than as a branch of natural philosophy. The low status of chymistry as determined by its use amongst low technical appliers militated against its acceptance by many natural philosophers.[9]

Thus the Anglo-Irish chemist Robert Boyle, in his polemical *Sceptical Chymist* (1665), denounces the ignorance of the 'vulgar chymists', including not only the out-and-out cheats who sought to profit from faked alchemical transformations but also the 'laborants' such as the dyers, distillers and apothecaries who lacked theoretical knowledge. Leonardo had nothing at all to gain by aligning his cause with such a crowd, and so there is good reason for him to gloss over the chemical aspects of art.

That cannot, however, excuse the persistent perception of unseemliness in the idea that science provides art not only with concepts but with materials. The snobbery and ignorance apparent in the words of the Bauhaus architect Le Corbusier (Charles-Edouard Jeanneret) and his collaborator Amédée Ozenfant in 1920 are breathtaking:

> . . . it is form which comes first, and everything else should be subordinated to it . . . Cézanne's imitators were quite right to see the error of their master, who accepted without examination the attractive offer of the colour-vendor, in a period marked by a fad for colour-chemistry, a science with no possible effect on great painting. Let us leave to the clothes-dyers the sensory jubilations of the paint tube.[10]

Let's not be too distracted by the absurdity of the suggestion that Cézanne – not the Impressionists or the Fauves, but Cézanne! – was an undiscerning dauber of raw colour. What is more telling is the way that Le Corbusier denigrates manual skills and delight in substance, in favour of 'form' and abstract space. This passage could almost have been written by the most bigoted of late-sixteenth-century Italian scholars praising *disegno* over *colore*. To deny that colour chemistry can have any possible effect on 'great painting' is, in the end, to claim that great art is all in the head, and cheapened by the sad necessity to reconstruct it from mere matter.

The connection to chemistry was perhaps deemed less distasteful in the nineteenth century, when chemists enjoyed unrivalled respectability (even Goethe used their metaphors). An anonymous writer on artistic technique in 1810 says cautiously: 'Chemistry is to painting what anatomy is to drawing. The artist should be acquainted with them, but not bestow too much time on either.' Yet even this much may be seen as a swan-song to the era when the painter was of necessity something of a chemist, when a training in art required at least as great an attention to the mechanical and practical aspects as to the aesthetic and intellectual. By the end of the nineteenth century, the artist was wholly reliant on scientifically adept professionals – 'colourmen' – to attend to the chemical aspects of their profession. One consequence of this rift is that the colours of some works of that period have weathered less well than the jewel-like fifteenth-century paintings of Jan van Eyck.

Chemistry is a topic that strikes fear into many a heart, and there seems little point in seeking to evade that fact. Unusually among artists, students of ceramics are one group who still have to learn some real chemistry – the whole package: balanced equations, the Periodic Table, atomic weights and so forth. In my experience, this does not make them feel any better about it. There appears to be something intimidating about the dizzying varieties in which matter is composed from elemental blends; and if we are honest about it, something vaguely ominous and unsettling about the grey metallic minarets and pipelines within which these blends are industrially concocted today. It is a challenge to the imagination to connect these ugly factories and alien or unsettling names – cadmium, arsenic, antimony – with the stuff that, smeared over canvas, leaves us breathless in art galleries. Can such a villain (and the chemical industry's transgressions are not at all imaginary) be responsible for this beauty?

The truth – a dirty truth, if you will – is that new colours for artists have long been a by-product of industrial chemical processes that reach out to a much wider market. Without the engine of commerce to drive it, the manufacture of these new pigments would simply have not been viable. Artificial copper blues or 'verditers', the principal cheap alternatives to expensive blue pigments from the fifteenth to the eighteenth century, were a side-product of silver mining. They were largely replaced by Prussian blue, produced primarily for the massive textile dyeing industry rather than for the tiny market in artists' colours. The Mars colours (artificial iron oxides) could not have been made without the availability of cheap sulphuric acid, which was manufactured primarily as a textile bleach. The pigment known as patent yellow was an offshoot of the soda industry, while the manufacture of chrome yellow was stimulated by its use in cotton printing. Textile dyeing also led to a better understanding of the use of metals for the fixing (mordanting) of dyes, which then drove improvements in the preparation of 'lake' pigments in the early nineteenth century. The almost ubiquitous white pigment of the twentieth century, titanium dioxide, is produced almost entirely for commercial paints – the amount diverted to artists' materials is trivial.

Might it be exciting to see not only an art history but also an art that reflects these connections? The commercial aspects of colour manufacture have indeed influenced some twentieth-century artists. But aren't naked pigments already works of art – the products of skill and creativity, and substances of glorious elegance and splendour? The Anglo-Indian artist Anish Kapoor thinks so (Plate 1.1), and Yves Klein did too.

It is commonly asserted that the interaction between art and science is a one-way street; but the relationship between chemistry and art has been to their mutual benefit. The modern chemicals industry was spawned and nurtured largely by the demand for colour. Important advances in synthetic chemistry in the nineteenth century were stimulated by the quest for artificial colours. Many of the world's major chemicals companies – BASF, Bayer, Hoechst, Ciba-Geigy – began as manufacturers of synthetic dyes. And the reproduction of art and colour in photography and printing has given rise to major technological companies such as Xerox and Kodak.

There is, meanwhile, ample precedent for the collaboration between art and chemistry personified in Klein and Adam. Michael Faraday advised J. M. W. Turner on his pigments. The German chemistry Nobel Laureate Wilhelm Ostwald worked with the German paint industry in the 1920s, and his theory of colour was hotly debated at the Bauhaus where Klee and Kandinsky taught. In more distant times, painters consorted with alchemists to procure their colours. In this story about science, technology, culture and society, there are no chickens and no eggs. Chemical science and technology and the use of colour in art have always existed in a symbiotic relationship that has shaped both their courses throughout history. By tracing their co-evolution, we shall see both how art is more of a science, and science more of an art, than is commonly appreciated on either side of the fence.[11]

Fear and loathing of colour

Yves Klein invites us to engage with the beauty of raw colour. This goes against our training. What is brightly coloured? Children's toys, the Land of Oz. And so colour threatens us with regression, with infantilism. Cultural theorist Julia Kristeva claims that 'the chromatic experience constitutes a menace to the "self" . . . Colour is the shattering of unity.'[12] What else is coloured? Vulgar things, vulgar people. Colour speaks of heightened emotions, even linguistically, and of eroticism. Pliny is not alone in xenophobically attributing strong colour to a kind of decadent Orientalism. Le Corbusier asserted that colour was 'suited to simple races, peasants, and savages'. Needless to say, he found it in abundance in his 'journey to the East', and was repelled: 'What shimmering silks, what fancy, glittering marbles, what opulent bronzes and golds . . . Let's have done with it . . . It is time to crusade for whitewash and Diogenes'[13] – which is to say, for cool reason over all this unseemly passion.

The nineteenth-century art theorist Charles Blanc (what's in a name?) insisted that 'design must maintain its preponderance over colour. Otherwise painting speeds to its ruin: it will fall through colour just as mankind fell through Eve.'[14] Here, then, is another reason to distrust colour: it is feminine. Contemporary artist David Batchelor argues that a fear of colour – chromophobia – pervades Western culture.[15] 'Man', said Yves Klein, 'is exiled far from his coloured soul.'[16]

But perhaps chemists, who are on intimate terms with the materiality of colour, who have seen the majestic rainbow progression of manganese through its different states of oxidation, who have watched the royal, clear blue of ammoniacal copper sulphate emerge from the pale, opaque blue of its alkaline precipitate – perhaps they are especially attuned to and appreciative of unadulterated colour. Oliver Sacks recalls the allure of chemistry's liquid colours in his childhood:

My father had his surgery in the house, with all sorts of medicines, lotions, and elixirs in the dispensary – it looked like an old-fashioned chemist's shop in miniature – and a small lab with a spirit lamp, test tubes, and reagents for testing patients' urine, like the bright-blue Fehling's solution, which turned yellow when there was sugar in the urine. There were potions and cordials in cherry red and golden yellow and colourful liniments like gentian violet and malachite green.[17]

To the chemist, colour is a bountiful clue to composition and, if measured carefully enough, can reveal delicate truths about molecular structure. It takes a particular turn of mind to see chromatic beauty lurking in the molecular structures of alizarin and indigo, to sense the rich hues within the stark, schematic depictions of these dye molecules. The Italian chemist and writer Primo Levi intimates how this relation between colour and constitution broadens the chemist's sensitivity to colour:

I find myself richer than other writers because for me words like 'bright', 'dark', 'heavy', 'light', and 'blue' have a more extensive and more concrete gamut of meanings. For me 'blue' is not only the blue of the sky. I have five or six blues at my disposal.[18]

Naming colours

Before we can adequately explore what colour means to the artist, we must ask what we mean by colour itself. This might seem uncontentious enough. In spite of the old solipsism that I can never know if my experience of 'red' is the same as yours, we both agree when the term is appropriate and when it is not. Yet there are hordes of 'lower-level' colour terms in most modern languages over which the scope for dispute is limitless: when does puce become russet, burgundy, rust-red? This is partly a matter for perceptual psychology; but the language of colour reveals much about the way we conceptualize the world. Linguistic considerations are often central to an interpretation of the historical use of colour in art.

Pliny claims that the painter in Classical Greece used only four colours: black, white, red and yellow. This noble and restrained palette, he said, is the proper choice for all sober-minded painters. After all, didn't Apelles, the most famous painter of that golden age, choose to limit himself within this austere range?

We cannot check the accuracy of this claim, for all of Apelles' works are lost, along with almost every other painting his culture produced. Yet we do know that the Greeks possessed a considerably wider range of pigments than these four. As for the Romans, no fewer than twenty-nine pigments have been identified in the ruins of Pompeii. Might Pliny have exaggerated the paucity of Apelles' palette? And if so, why? In part, the reason might be metaphysical: four 'primary' colours equate neatly with the Aristotelian quartet of elements: earth, air, fire, water. But the breadth of colour use in classical painting may also be obscured by linguistics. In interpreting archaic writings on the use of colour in art, there is for example ample scope for confusion of red and green. The medieval term *sinople* – derived from Pliny's *sinopis*, which in turn stemmed from the geographical source of a red earth pigment at Sinope on the

Black Sea – could refer to either red or green until at least the fifteenth century. The Latin *caeruleum* carries a similar ambiguity between yellow and blue (its root is the Greek *kuanos*, which can in some contexts denote the dark-green colour of the sea). There is no Latin word for brown or grey, but this does not imply that the Roman artists did not recognize or use brown earth pigments.

How could red and green ever be conflated? From a modern-day perspective this appears absurd, because we have in our minds Isaac Newton's rainbow spectrum and its corresponding colour terminology, with its seven bands firmly delineated. The Greeks saw a different spectrum, with white at one end and black at the other – or more properly, light and dark. All the colours lay along the scale between these two extremes, being admixtures of light and dark in different degrees. Yellow was towards the light end (it appears the brightest of colours for physiological reasons). Red and green were both considered median colours, midway between light and dark – and so in some sense equivalent. The reliance of medieval scholars on Classical Greek texts ensured that this colour scale was perpetuated for centuries after the temples of Athens stood in ruins. In the tenth century AD, the monk Heraclius still classified all colours as black, white and 'intermediate'.

The confusion of blue and yellow may have been purely linguistic, or it may have its origin in the naming of colours after the materials that supplied them (see page 264). For reasons that are far from clear, blue and yellow are categorized together in many languages and cultures, including some Slavic tongues, the Ainu language of northern Japan, the Daza language of East Nigeria and that of the Mechopdo Native Americans in northern California. The Latin *flavus*, meaning yellow, is the etymological root of *blue*, *bleu* and *blau*. The location of blue at the dark end of the scale gives us another reason to be wary of its apparent exclusion from Pliny's list: it was seen as a variant of black, and Greek terms for the two overlap.

Thus whether or not an artist considers two hues to be different colours or variants of the same colour is largely a linguistic issue. The Celtic word *glas* refers to the colour of mountain lakes and straddles the range from a brownish-green to blue. The Japanese *awo* can mean 'green', 'blue' or 'dark', depending on the context;

Vietnamese and Korean also decline to distinguish green from blue. Some languages have only three or four colour terms.

As there are no culture-independent concepts of basic colours, it seems impossible to establish a universal basis for a discussion of colour use. In 1969, however, anthropologists Brent Berlin and Paul Kay attempted to bring some order to the mass of conflicting categories by proposing a kind of colour hierarchy, according to which hues emerge in a universal order as the complexity of a culture's colour terminology increases. First, they said, comes a distinction between light and dark, or white and black. Australian Aboriginals and speakers of the Dugerm Dani tongue of New Guinea have only two colour terms with essentially these meanings. Red is the next colour to be identified as a distinct hue. Then either green or yellow is added to the list, followed by the other of the two. After this comes blue, and gradually the more complex secondaries and tertiaries are included – brown first, then (in any order) purple, orange, pink and grey. So according to Berlin and Kay, there can be no language that has terms for just black, white and green, or just yellow and blue. Colour vocabulary, they said, unfolds in a strict sequence.

The validity of Berlin and Kay's idea, which was based largely on anthropological and linguistic studies of contemporary non-technological cultures, has been much questioned. For example, Hanunoo, which is spoken by a Malayo-Polynesian people in the Philippines, has four colour terms: 'dark' and 'light', which we can equate readily enough with black and white; but also 'fresh' and 'dry' (in so far as they can be matched with English words at all). Some prefer to ally these two with green and red, but they seem to allude to texture as much as to hue. There is no Hanunoo word meaning 'colour'.

Berlin and Kay's synoptic scheme nevertheless affords some foundation for a discussion of what has been meant by 'colour' through the ages, and there seems good reason to regard it as expressing at least a partial truth. A part of the difficulty in applying the theory is that it presupposes the existence of 'basic' colour terms – words for hues that have no dependence on context. This is not always true even in complex modern languages. French *brun*, for instance, is not the strict equivalent of English *brown* but can be supplanted by *marron* or *beige* in certain situations, while implying 'dark', rather than a specific hue, in others.

It is all but impossible to identify basic colour terms, in the sense of Berlin and Kay, in ancient Greek. This has led some commentators to assume that the Greeks had poor colour awareness. In 1921, Maurice Platnauer claimed that 'colours made a much less vivid impression upon their senses . . . or . . . they felt little interest in the qualitative differences of decomposed and partially absorbed light'.[19] Colour technologist Harold Osborne reiterated the point in 1968, saying that the Greeks were 'not given to careful discrimination of colour hue'.

But there is no reason to suppose that our ability to distinguish colours is limited by the structure of our colour vocabulary. We can tell apart hues to which we cannot ascribe names – indeed, the vast majority of distinguishable hues are not named specifically in any language. So we should rather conclude that for the Greeks, 'colour' had a somewhat different meaning (although they had a word – *chroma* or *chroia* – that is usually translated in this way). Since their colours lay on a scale between light and dark, brilliance or lustre, as well as hue, could be valid discriminants. Platnauer suggested that 'it is lustre or superficial effect that struck the Greeks and not what we call colour or tint' – an over-simplification, perhaps, but probably true in essence. He points out that the same word is used in Greek literature to describe darkened blood and a cloud, or the glint of metal and a tree. This is presumably the explanation for Homer's famously puzzling 'wine-dark' sea (*oinopos*) in the *Odyssey*. Wittgenstein voiced the same idea in his *Remarks on Colour*: 'Mightn't shiny black and matt black have different colour names?' (In his black monochromes of the 1960s the American minimalist artist Ad Reinhardt used these two as if they were indeed distinct colours.)

The Greeks certainly possessed colour terms – but none that are obviously 'basic'. 'Red' is generally equated with *eruthos* (to which it is etymologically related); but there is no good case for giving this term primacy over *phoinikous* or *porphurous*, as there is for red over scarlet or crimson. Similarly, green could be rendered as *chloros*, *prasinos* or *poödes*, depending on the context.

Linguist John Lyons suggests it is safest to conclude only that colours 'are the product of language under the influence of culture'. The fluidity of colour terminology led to a frequent reliance on materials, rather than abstract concepts of hue, as the basis of a discussion about artists' use of colour. Pliny's four classical colours were not simply 'black', 'white' and so forth, but 'white from Milos' and 'red from Sinope on the Black Sea' – they were embodied in specific pigments. Without a secure theoretical basis for classification, talk of colour needs to be rooted in the physical substances that provide it. Yet this simply creates fresh scope for ambiguity, for the substance can mutate into a colour term in its own right. Scarlet, for example, was once a kind of medieval dyed cloth, which need not have been red at all.

True colours

It is tempting to regard modern and abstract painters as the first consciously to decide that they would not simply try to paint 'what they saw'. Yet the most casual of glances at any image from the Renaissance or the Baroque period shows how much the work is guided by certain conventions, and at the same time by imagination and interpretation, rather than being an attempt to depict nature as faithfully as possible. Many artists through the ages have talked of painting 'true to nature' – but this means many things, of which the advent of photography has encouraged us to select just one.

For example, until the late nineteenth century, using colour to mimic nature was necessarily an artifice in at least this respect: nearly all paintings were produced in studios with reliance on the painter's judgement about 'proper' composition and contrast. It was only when painting of finished works (as opposed to reference studies) out of doors was pioneered by the French Realists, and later adopted by the Impressionists, that artists began to liberate themselves from academic notions about light and shade, to see the purples and blues in shadows, the yellows and oranges in 'white' sunlight.

Let us nevertheless accept the idea that Western art from antiquity to the advent of abstraction has purported to depict the forms of nature in a basically representational manner. So, then, the artist presumably sought sufficient pigments to permit an accurate translation of his or her visual impressions? Ah, but if only it were so simple! Since (as the ancients believed) the world could be depicted by good drawing alone, was colour not merely superfluous decoration? 'One who haphazardly throws around even the most beautiful colours', said Aristotle, 'cannot delight the eye as one who has drawn a simple figure against a white background.'

Moreover, Classical art was not slavishly imitative, but largely symbolic. Pliny's four-colour scheme was linked more closely to metaphysics than to any relation with the hues of nature, which on a fine day in the hills of Greece would be saturated with the very colours – green and blue – that the scheme omits.

Furthermore, the Greek penchant for idealization and intellectual abstraction led to the notion that mixed colours are inferior both to 'pure' natural pigments and to the 'true' colours of nature. So there was little point in attempting to match artists' colours to nature's by mixing them together. This practice was discouraged by Classical scholars: 'mixing produces conflict,' said Plutarch in the first century AD. It was common to refer to the blending of pigments as 'deflowering': a loss of virginity. Aristotle called colour-mixing a 'passing away'.

But there was also a technical inhibition towards mixing. Because the available pigments were not pure primary colours, mixing resulted in a diminution of tone towards greyness or brownness, and so was indeed a degrading process. This reluctance to mix pigments might explain some of the curious claims about painting made in the Classical literature, which would readily have been disproved by experiment: that red and green could generate yellow, or that (as Aristotle suggested) no pigment mixture could generate violet or green. Greek painters were prepared to glaze a translucent colour over an opaque one, but mixing 'on the palette' was usually restricted to the use of white or black for highlights and shadows.

This self-imposed limitation on the range of available colours is just one of the reasons why it would be incorrect to regard ancient and medieval art as an attempt to render the world naturalistically with an imperfect technique and a constrained palette. As Ernst

Gombrich says, 'The painters of the Middle Ages were no more concerned about the "real" colours of things than they were about their real shapes.' The painter of the early Middle Ages had no difficulty with the concept of proportion; he simply did not regard it as very important. He was typically an anonymous monk whose task it was to illustrate the stories of the Gospels in a way that conveyed devotion and piety. The picture was schematic, even formulaic – a kind of writing in pictures. In the late Middle Ages, beauty and a display of wealth became as important in religious art as they were in all aspects of Holy Rome's domain; but that did not entail any need for naturalism. Quite the contrary – it became desirable to display the most costly and wonderful pigments in flat, unbroken fields of colour: vermilion, ultramarine and gold. These colours had merely to be laid out on the panel to inspire admiration and awe in onlookers.

Thus medieval colour use is seldom complex. The skill lay not in creating subtle gradations of colour, but in arranging raw pigments harmoniously in the scene. This is why a late-medieval craftsman like Cennino Cennini could, in his *Il Libro dell'Arte* (*The Craftsman's Handbook*) (c. 1390), provide the artist not just with practical advice about the preparation of pigments and panels or the techniques of painting *alla fresco* and *a secco*, but with prescriptions for depicting flesh, drapery, water – as if painting was nothing but a mechanical craft. Similarly, Leon Battista Alberti discusses juxtapositions of colour almost as if arranging a series of coloured wooden blocks – or in this case, the robes of a series of nymphs:

If red stands between blue and green, it somehow enhances their beauty as well as its own. White lends gaiety, not only when placed between grey and yellow, but almost to any colour. But dark colours acquire a certain dignity when between light colours, and similarly light colours may be placed with good effect among dark.[20]

There is in this advice a hint of the ideas about colour harmony that were to recur throughout artistic theory from the Renaissance to the twentieth century. But with Alberti it is a question of placing one colour-field next to another, reminiscent of the works of a modernist like Mondrian rather than the blending and contrasting hues of the Venetian Old Masters. Moreover, Alberti betrays an abiding concern with the integrity of the pure pigment – with preserving the raw colour and avoiding practices that would muddy it or degrade its brilliance. Highlight and shadow, he advises, should be rendered simply by adding white and black – and with great restraint, lest the virtue of the colour be degraded:

Those painters who use white immoderately and black carelessly, should be strongly condemned. It would be a good thing if white and black were made from those pearls Cleopatra dissolved in vinegar, so that painters would become as mean as possible with them, for their works would then be both more agreeable and nearer the truth.[21]

Here 'truth' means true to the glory of the materials rather than capturing what nature reveals to the eye. All the same, Alberti's remarks on colour reflect the Humanism of the Renaissance more than the symbolic materialism of the Middle Ages. His book concerns itself only with secular painting, whereas Cennino makes several references to religious works, like a workman describing how to lay the bricks for a church. For Alberti, the use of the finest colours is not to please God but to satisfy the patron who has commissioned the work and who, in all likelihood, contractually specified the pigments to be used.

Leap into the void

At the centre of Alberti's discussion of colour is the question that all painters had to address once the prescriptive approach of the Middle Ages was discarded: how to *organize* colour. The artist of the twentieth century faced the same question, although the rules had changed dramatically. Whereas Renaissance painters disagreed over *how* to paint, they had little dispute over *what* to paint. But in the early twentieth century, painters began first to abandon 'naturalistic' colouring and then to discard naturalistic form.

The consequent problem was analogous to that confronting the contemporaneous atonal composers: if trees can be blue, skies pink, faces yellow, how does one choose the colour at all? Without a 'natural' reference – the mathematical rules of musical harmony, or the hues of nature – how does one escape the incoherence threatened by such multiplicity of choice? What is the appropriate organizational system that apportions colours 'truthfully'?

Arnold Schoenberg found a musical answer in serialism – the twelve-note compositional method. But nothing so general was to emerge for the modern colourist. Wassily Kandinsky (1866–1944) recognized almost with horror the obligation of the abstract artist to discover guiding principles: 'A terrifying abyss of all kinds of questions, a wealth of responsibilities stretched before me. And most important of all: what is to replace the missing object?'[22] His answer was a very personal and subjective one. He sensed that colours have symbolic and spiritual connotations. This belief seems to have been profoundly influenced by the fact that Kandinsky experienced synaesthesia, a perceptual condition in which two sensory sensations are simultaneously triggered by the same stimulus. This is most commonly manifested as 'colour-hearing': the association of specific colours with timbral or pitch sensations. The composer Alexander Scriabin was affected by the same condition: he heard the key of C major as red and D major as yellow, and he composed in colours for a 'keyboard of light' (*clavier à lumière*).

Kandinsky was deeply influenced by Theosophy, a spiritual philosophy derived from Wolfgang von Goethe's simplistic division of the world into polar contrasts. Theosophy appealed also to the Dutch painter Piet Mondrian (1872–1944), whose efforts to arrange rectangles of primary colours on a heavy black grid evoke a kind of mathematical angst. He was an advocate of the Theosophist M. H. J. Schoenmaekers, who argued that all colours except the three primaries were superfluous – providing Mondrian with his own distinctive answer to the problem of colour.

Theosophy's dogmatic categorization is reflected in Kandinsky's conviction that colour acts as a universal language of the soul. Of course, colour *does* speak to our emotions – but not, it seems, in a way that everyone agrees on, independent of cultural conditioning. Yet Kandinsky believed there are concrete, objective colour associations, so that an abstract composition can, through the calculated use of colour, invoke a very particular emotional response. It was simply a matter of cracking the code – or, in a more Kandinskian metaphor, of using colour mechanistically to pluck the strings of the emotions:

Generally speaking, colour directly influences the soul. Colour is the keyboard, the eyes are the hammers, the soul is the piano with many strings. The artist is the hand that plays, touching one key after another purposively, to cause vibrations in the soul.[23]

Kandinsky explained his chromatic language in his book *Concerning the Spiritual in Art* (1912), where we find such claims as this:

Yellow is the typical earthly colour. It can never have profound meaning. An intermixture of blue makes it a sickly colour . . . Vermilion is a red with a feeling of sharpness, like glowing steel which can be cooled by water . . . Orange is like a man, convinced of his own powers . . . Violet is . . . rather sad and ailing.[24]

He attempted to establish these 'meanings' of colours through 'scientific' experiments at the Bauhaus art and design school in Germany. He distributed a thousand test cards to a 'cross-section of the community' on which recipients were asked to match the three primary colours to three geometric shapes – a square, circle and triangle. There was some consensus that the triangle was yellow, but disagreement about whether blue belonged in the square or the circle.

A link between colour and music is not unique to synaesthetics, but has been perceived since the time of ancient Greece. Kandinsky, himself a violinist and cellist, collaborated with Schoenberg and hoped to find a way of incorporating 'dissonance' into existing, 'harmonious' schemes for organizing colour. He felt that a work of art should have a symphonic structure, and his 'colour–music' compositions are generally regarded as some of the first truly abstract paintings, devoid of all reference to recognizable objects (Plate 1.2).

Kandinsky's fruitless search for the emotional language of colour, like the tangles of colour linguistics, reminds us that it is futile to be dogmatic about colour. There can be no consensus about what colours 'mean', nor how to use them 'truthfully'. Colour theories – and we will encounter several later – can assist the construction of good art, but they do not define it. In the end, the modern artist's struggle to find form for colour is an individual quest. To Bridget Riley, it is precisely this that makes colour so powerful a medium of artistic expression:

. . . just because there is *no* guiding principle, *no* firm conceptual basis on which a tradition of colour painting can be reliably founded, this means that each individual artistic sensibility has a chance to discover a unique means of expression.[25]

2. Plucking the Rainbow

THE PHYSICS AND CHEMISTRY OF COLOUR

There is no such thing as colour, only coloured materials.

Jean Dubuffet (1973)

Inorganic nature has only the language of colour. It is by colour alone that a certain stone tells us it is a sapphire or an emerald.

Charles Blanc, *Grammar of Painting and Engraving* (1867)

What is paint after all? Colored dirt.

Philip Guston

Much currency has been made, in the tug-of-war between art and science, of Isaac Newton's 'unweaving the rainbow'. John Keats expresses it thus in *Lamia* (1819), a poetic lament about the detrimental effect (as he perceived it) of scientific knowledge on mystery and wonder in the world. Yet the bright arc's threads remained tangled in art long after Newton had elucidated their prismatic sequence. We can hardly be surprised that an anti-Newtonian like Goethe would rearrange the colours to oppose nature; but even a keen observer of nature like John Constable was known to get the order wrong in the secondary bow (where the sequence is inverted). The Pre-Raphaelite artist John Everett Millais had to correct the same mistake hastily after it was pointed out to him in his *Blind Girl* (1856).

Newton's achievement was not, in any event, to demonstrate that daylight was woven of many hues which the rainbow separates. That much had long been evident in the spectrum prised from sunlight when it passes through glass. Nor was it Newton who showed how sunlight becomes focused into a circular band by refraction inside water droplets in moist air: René Descartes explained the basic science of rainbow formation in 1637. But Newton brought colour to Descartes' white bow by identifying the rainbow's irreducible colours and showing that they are refracted at slightly different angles. In Newton's *experimentum crucis*, conducted in 1665 or '66, he deduced that 'light itself is a heterogeneous mixture of differently refrangible rays', and demonstrated that these rays, separated by their passage through a prism in a darkened room, were 'uncompounded colours' which could not be further split by a second prism. Passed through a lens, they merged back into a beam of white light.

Scientists keen to celebrate Newton's reductionism, and artists eager to decry it, overlook the strong mystical thread in his work – something that seems anomalous today, when the lens of centuries allows us to split science from magic. But it was quite in keeping with the spirit of his age that Newton saw fit to identify seven arbitrary subdivisions of the prismatic spectrum purely in order to establish a consonance with ideas about musical harmony:

Do not several sorts of rays make vibrations of several bignesses, which according to their brightness excite sensations of several colours, much after the manner that the vibrations of air, according to several bignesses excite sensations of several sounds?[1]

And so the Newtonian rainbow acquired its indigo and violet where I defy anyone to see other than a blue deepening to purple.

Colour comes from plucking this rainbow. Newton's analogy with music is misguided in any concrete sense, but useful as a metaphor. Matter sings to many different notes and chords in the chromatic scale. When the resonances are sounded in the glare of the white 'noise' that is sunlight, these notes are absorbed from the multi-pitched stimulus and fall silent in the echo. What we see as colour is the remains, after the material has absorbed its own private and unique chime. A red berry sings to the tune of green and blue, a yellow flower to the strains of blue and red.

Artists have expressed diverse opinions about the value of scientific theories of colour. Some have seen little need to comprehend colour scientifically. Despite its title, *Science de la peinture* (*The Science of Painting*) (1891) by the French artist and Academician Jean-Georges Vibert contains a pungent lampoon on the nineteenth-century scientists who claimed to uncover the 'truth' about colour. Veronese, Rubens and Delacroix are better equipped than any scientist to instruct the artist on colour, says Vibert, because 'with their colours they created a language which speaks to the soul, which communicates emotion and life'.

I think Vibert is probably right. Delacroix showed some interest in the colour theories of his age; but the Old Masters wrought their miracles through an intuitive feeling for colour that the discoveries of Newton do not touch. The Neo-Impressionists Georges Seurat and Paul Signac longed for a thoroughly scientific use of colour in painting but the result, even by Signac's own admission, could turn out 'grey and colourless'. Painters benefit from some instruction about the effective use of colour, but this is tantamount to acquiring rules of thumb which do not require a strong basis in theoretical knowledge of colour physics. Indeed, the tricks employed with informed deliberation by the Impressionists can be found in some works of Renaissance artists, who reached the same conclusions empirically. Trying to paint according to scientific rules of colour, said Paul Klee, 'means renouncing the wealth of the soul'.

Yet there are several reasons why this chapter on the science of colour is indispensable for what follows. Since in this book we shall be concerned primarily with the material rather than the abstract, theoretical role of science in art – with how colour is manufactured – I could leave it as a mystery that copper gives blues and greens, that whites and reds may be had from compounds of lead. But only by appreciating the 'why' can one truly understand the social and technological factors that brought these colours on to the palette. Moreover, some basic facts about colour mixing have a strong bearing on the uses to which painters have put their pure and shining pigments (whether they knew it or not). Lest this sound like an apology from Logos to Eros, I should reprise my assertion that in the end the differentiation between the two is only a relatively

modern idea. I feel sure that Leonardo would have damned any
book that claimed to speak of colour without explaining it.

The many causes of colour

'Colour always answers to the sort or sorts of the Rays whereof the
Light consists, as I have constantly found in whatever Phaenomena
of Colours I have hitherto been able to examine.'[2] By making light
not the activating principle of colour as Aristotle believed, nor the
vehicle of colour as perceived in medieval thought, but the medium
of colour itself, Newton was inviting the inquiry: what, then, is
light?

It was not until another two centuries had passed that the Scottish
physicist James Clerk Maxwell gave the answer. Light, said Maxwell
in the 1870s, is a vibrating electromagnetic field: a combination of
self-supporting electric and magnetic fields oscillating in step but
oriented perpendicular to one another, like two ropes tied to a
pole and shaken vertically and horizontally. The frequency of the
vibrations determines the colour of the light, and increases progressively from the red to the blue end of the visible spectrum.
Electromagnetic radiation with lower frequencies than red light is
infra-red, or, at still lower frequencies, microwaves and radio waves.
High frequencies beyond the blue and violet correspond to ultra-
violet, and then to X-rays and gamma rays.

The wavelength of the vibration is inversely related to the frequency: it declines as frequency increases. Frequency and wavelength are the modern correlates of Newton's 'vibrations of several
bignesses'.

This picture was refined at the beginning of the twentieth century
with the realization that, with that perversity for which quantum
theory is notorious, light is not just wave but particle too. Light
comes in packets or 'quanta', each containing an amount of energy
proportional to the frequency. These quanta of light are called
photons. Albert Einstein proposed this heretical notion in 1905,
and it later won him his Nobel prize.

A substance's colour may be generated by absorption of light, a phenomenon governed by the material's resonant frequencies. Think of an undamped piano wire humming in sympathy with a sung note; in the same way, matter sings along with sunlight. The resonant vibration absorbs the energy of the light at that frequency, and so it strips out a particular colour from the spectrum of the light. Those rays whose frequencies do not correspond with some resonant frequency of the material either pass right through it (if the material is transparent or translucent) or are reflected (if it is opaque). Only these 'rejected' rays reach our eye. So, paradoxically, it is on the basis of their frequencies – their position in the visible spectrum – that we award the material a colour.

For absorption of visible light, these resonances involve the clouds of electrons that surround the tiny, dense nuclei of atoms like bees swarming around the hive. The light may be absorbed if it can boost the electrons from one energy state to another, just as the piano wire's energy is increased when it is stimulated into resonant vibration by sound waves. Because the electrons' energies are governed by the rules of quantum physics and increase in discrete steps like the gear shifts in a car, only rays of certain frequencies have the right energy to stimulate these colour-inducing 'electronic transitions'.

Not all colour is generated in this way. The rainbow's variegated arc, for instance, is not the result of light absorption by the raindrops, but of refraction: the bending of rays of different wavelength through differing angles (Figure 2.1). This is an example of light scattering, which is the major *physical* way in which colour can be produced. Light absorption, in contrast, depends on the *chemical* composition of the substance.

As light enters a raindrop, the ray is bent (refracted). The angle of bending depends on the wavelength of the light, being sharper for shorter wavelengths. So blue light is deflected more than red light, and the various colours in sunlight are unravelled. Each colour reaches your eye from a slightly different region in the rainbow's arc. The scattering of light can therefore separate colours according to their wavelength. The sky is blue because blue light is scattered by the molecules and dust in the atmosphere more strongly than red light, and so seems to come from all directions. Distant hills acquire a blueness for the same reason: the reflected light is

Figure 2.1
How the rainbow is formed. Light of different wavelengths is refracted
by raindrops through different angles, and so beams of white light are
separated into their spectral components.

augmented by the omnidirectional blue before reaching the eye.
(In art this blueing of distant landscape, described by Leonardo, is
called aerial perspective.) As the sun sinks low in the sky, its rays
travel through a thicker slice of the atmosphere before reaching the observer, and the blue component of the light may be
scattered so strongly that it never gets to the eye. Goethe had
but a hazy intimation of this: 'as the sun at last was about to
set . . . its rays, greatly mitigated by the thicker vapours, began
to diffuse a most beautiful red colour over the whole scene around
me'.[3]

Natural pigments obtain their colours by absorption of light. But
some colours in nature result from physical scattering processes. In
particular, no vertebrate animals contain blue pigments: their blue
markings are produced by light scattering. The blues on butterfly
wings are the result of a microscopic ribbed structure of individual
scales on the wing (Figure 2.2). These ridges have a spacing that

induces preferential scattering of blue light. But the scattering, and thus the hue, varies somewhat depending on the angle of reflection (or equivalently, the viewing angle). So the colour is iridescent, seeming to shimmer and shift as the wing moves. The same is true of blue insect cuticle, and of the kaleidoscopic colours of a peacock's tail: the peacock's feathers are laced with a tiny grid of pigmented black bars that scatter light like the ribs of butterfly wing scales. The rainbow-like colour changes of these feathers have long fascinated artists; a Byzantine writer of the seventh century AD asked:

How could anyone who sees the peacock not be amazed at the gold interwoven with sapphire, at the purple and emerald-green feathers, at the composition of the colours of many patterns, all mingled together but not confused with one another?[4]

Figure 2.2
The iridescent blues and greens of a butterfly's wings are formed by light scattering from microscopic ribs on the wing scales.

Alexander Pope's sylphs in *The Rape of the Lock* clearly share with insects an iridescence caused by light scattering:

> While ev'ry beam new transient colour flings,
> Colours that change whene'er they wave their wings.

Light is scattered most strongly when the scattering objects are of comparable size to the wavelength of the radiation. Water droplets in clouds are the right size to scatter all visible light, creating the sky's milky billows. Glass wool and ground glass, made of the same fabric as windows, look white and opaque for the same reason. Ground-up stained glass becomes paler with prolonged grinding: smaller particles have a greater total surface area to scatter from, and so scattering (which is indiscriminate about wavelength across the visible range) dominates over absorption (which picks out certain wavelengths). This is why grinding a coloured powder may affect its hue – a phenomenon exploited by the artists of the Middle Ages, who controlled the shade of a pigment by the degree of grinding.

Colour from the earth

Until the advent of 'modern' synthetic pigments in the nineteenth century, many artists' colours were finely ground minerals: metal-containing compounds pulled from the earth. Their colours are usually determined by the nature of the metal atoms they contain; and this much is true of many of the new synthetic colours too, among which chromium, cobalt and cadmium compounds feature prominently. Strongly coloured minerals commonly contain so-called transition metals, which occupy the centre of the Periodic Table, chemistry's group portrait of the elements.

Ancient and medieval scholars played a fruitless game in trying to assign particular colours to the four Aristotelian 'elements'. We now know that an element's colour depends on its context. Nevertheless, some of them exhibit recurring chromatic themes. Ask a chemist to assign colours to the most common transition metals and he or she will know the game at once. Red is for iron, resplendent in blood and rust and the red ochres daubed by painters since the Stone Age. Copper claims for itself the turquoise shade associated with that mineral and which is echoed in the greenish patina of ageing copperwork. Rich, deep blue stands for cobalt, and nickel takes a sea-green; while chromium provokes some hesitation, an elemental chameleon and named for it too.

These are not rigid identities — copper, for instance, can form rust-red salts, and iron offers greens and yellows, even the dark lustre of Prussian blue. But none the less these metals make chromatic choices that are by no means arbitrary. Why is that?

In inorganic compounds such as crystalline minerals and salts, metal atoms are *ions* – they are deficient in electrons, and so bear a positive electric charge. This is compensated by negative charges on surrounding ions of non-metallic elements – oxygen, chlorine, sulphur, to name a few. These ions are stacked in the crystal with the regularity of apples and oranges in a greengrocer's window display, but with rather more inventiveness. The electrical attraction of opposite charges holds the whole assembly together, providing a glue of great strength. Ionic crystals are robust substances on the whole, and much sweat was shed during their grinding in an artist's workshop.

Transition metals engender colour because their ions tend to have electronic transitions whose resonant frequencies fall in the range of visible light. But the precise wavelength required to stimulate such a transition depends on the atomic-scale environment in which the metal ion sits. The combined electric fields of the surrounding ions – the so-called crystal field – modify the energies of the electrons on the metal ion. Not only the chemical composition of the metal ion's neighbours but even their geometrical arrangement matters. So a metal ion doesn't impart a unique colour – it depends on the other chemical constituents with which it is compounded in the crystal, and on how they are arranged.

Sometimes the variations in crystal field from one substance to another make only a minor difference to the frequency at which a metal ion absorbs light. Copper ions, for instance, usually absorb in the red part of the spectrum, and so copper salts appear bluish-green; but exactly how blue or how green depends on the chemical nature of the other ions. In other cases, differences in the crystal field can impart a striking shift in colour. Chromium impurities colour various gemstones: they are deep red in ruby but sea-green in emerald, because the crystal field is significantly stronger in emerald than in ruby. The host material of rubies and emeralds – aluminium oxide, or corundum – becomes blue sapphire when laced instead with iron and titanium.

Heat may alter the chemical composition or structure of a mineral, and so induce a colour change. Heating blue copper sulphate to drive out water molecules from the crystal lattice turns it almost white. The pigment known as white lead turns red and then yellow when heated. White lead is 'basic' lead carbonate which has water (more precisely, hydroxide ions) locked into its crystal structure. When white lead is heated, water and carbon dioxide (formed from the carbonate ions) are expelled from the crystal as gases, leaving behind the compound lead tetroxide. This 'red lead' is a very ancient pigment. All the lead ions are now surrounded by oxide ions, and this different environment makes them absorb photons in the green and blue parts of the spectrum, leaving red to be reflected. If white lead is heated more gently, however, a different compound – lead monoxide or 'litharge' – is formed. This still contains only lead and oxide ions, but in a different ratio and a different arrangement; so the lead again absorbs light at different frequencies. This substance is yellow, and has in the past afforded another lead-based pigment, once called massicot.

In many metal compounds, the rearrangement of electrons induced by light absorption is confined largely to the metal ions themselves. But in some cases the electrons are shifted more dramatically. Iron's red signature is produced by the movement of an electron on to the metal ion from an adjacent oxygen ion: a so-called charge-transfer process, which in this case diminishes the positive charge on the iron. The same thing, more elaborately staged, is played out in the pigment Prussian blue. Here the crystal lattice contains a mixture of iron ions in two different charged states, interspersed with cyanide ions. Absorption of red light can send an electron across a cyanide 'bridge' between metal ions of different charge.

The colour of some important mineral pigments arises through a very long-ranged rearrangement of electrons: absorption of light liberates electrons entirely from their orbits around particular ions and sets them free to wander through the solid. When this happens, the material becomes more electrically conducting. Semiconductors are substances that need only a little extra energy to boost electrons into such a mobile state. Among them is cadmium sulphide, introduced as a pigment in the nineteenth century. It absorbs violet and blue light, and can range in colour from yellow to orange depending on how it is prepared. The deeper hue of 'cadmium red' is produced by replacing some of the sulphur with selenium. Mercury sulphide, which occurs naturally as the mineral cinnabar, is also a red-tinted semiconductor. A synthetic version corresponds to the renowned pigment vermilion. One hazard of vermilion is that its constituent ions can reshuffle from their usual positions to new locations in a form of the compound called metacinnabar. This absorbs red light as well as blue and green, and so it appears black – fatal, of course, if it happens on the canvas.

In pure metals, such as iron, copper, silver and gold, some electrons are intrinsically mobile; this is why metals are good electrical conductors. The interaction of these mobile electrons with light creates a reflective, metallic sheen. The light is not absorbed but is instead reflected without much scattering, resulting in a mirror-like appearance. But metals like copper and gold do absorb some of the short-wavelength (bluish) rays that strike them, and so they take on a reddish tinge. To medieval artists, this allied pure gold leaf with red pigments.

Organic colour

While rose quartz acquires its colour from titanium or manganese impurities, no such metals tint the rose itself. The colourants in living organisms are organic compounds: discrete molecules containing perhaps several dozen atoms each, with backbones of interlinked carbon atoms. Until the nineteenth century nearly all dyes were 'natural products', which is to say, organic substances derived from animals or plants. As well as being used for colouring textiles, they tinted inks and, fixed to particles of a colourless inorganic powder, were the colouring agents of so-called lake pigments.

Tyrian purple, the imperial colour of Rome, was drawn out of shellfish. Blue indigo was the frothy extract of a weed. Madder red came from a root, cochineal from an insect. Today virtually all dyes are synthetic organic molecules, their carbon skeletons custom-built by industrial chemists. While barely a dozen natural dyestuffs proved stable enough to be useful in the ancient and medieval world, over 4,000 synthetic dyes now bring colour to our industrialized societies.

Nature owes its verdancy to the most abundant of natural pigments: chlorophyll, which imbibes the red and blue of the sun's rays and channels the energy into the biochemical processes of the cell. At the heart of the chlorophyll molecule sits a mag-nesium ion, which undergoes electronic transitions under the glare of the sun. The oxygen-binding part of the haemoglobin molecule in blood has a similar molecular architecture to chloro-phyll's light-harvesting eye, except that iron in all its ruddiness substitutes for magnesium. And much the same structure crops up, studded with a copper ion, in the synthetic blue dye known as monastral blue, familiar from its use on the covers of old Pelican books. No longer do John Donne's words reflect our state of ignorance:

> Why grass is green, or why our blood is red
> Are mysteries which none have reach'd into.

Why roses are red and daffodils yellow is a question of the same order, though the answer must invoke different species of pigment. The yellows, oranges and reds of many flowers, as well as of carrots, tomatoes and sweetcorn, are produced by molecules called carotenoids. Plant pigments called flavonoids are responsible for blues, purples and reds. Carotenoids are also found in some animals. In lobsters these pigments are nearly black; boiling degrades them to redness, as Samuel Butler avers in his satire *Hudibras*:

> And, like a lobster boil'd, the morn
> From black to red began to turn.

Light absorption by organic pigments is fundamentally no different to that by inorganic minerals: it involves a rearrangement of electrons. Often this takes place within floppy electron clouds smeared out across the carbon backbone. This is the case, for example, in the aniline dyes synthesized in the mid-nineteenth century, where the electrons are distributed in doughnut-shaped clouds around 'benzene rings' of six carbon atoms.

The medium matters

That colour is a treacherous thing is a lesson learned in childhood. The pebbles that glittered so richly when plucked from a seaside pool turn to unremarkable greyish lumps when pulled dry from the bag at home.

This change is due to the fact that light is affected by its passage from one transmitting medium – air, say – to another, such as water. Light travels more slowly in water than in air, which is why light rays bend as they pass into limpid rock pools, deceiving us about the depth.[5] This change in speed, characterized by a quantity called the refractive index of the material, determines the strength of light scattering: the greater the change in refractive index, the greater the scattering. So because light passing from air to rock at the surface of a dry pebble experiences a greater change in refractive index than light passing from water to rock when the pebble is wet, more of it is scattered rather than being reflected directly to our eye. This makes the dry pebble look paler and chalkier than the wet pebble.

Sadly, the same effect can undo the bright promise of pigments: glorious as dry powders, they might become dark or semi-transparent when mixed with a binding agent such as linseed oil. This degradation of brilliance when a pigment meets the liquid medium of a paint is what dismayed Yves Klein and led him on his chemical quest for a new binder that honoured the vibrancy of the raw pigment. The principal binding media before the fifteenth century were water (in frescos), gum or egg white (in manuscript illumination) and egg yolk (in tempera painting on panels). When artists began to use oils, which have a higher refractive index, they found that some of their most treasured pigments were no longer so beautiful. Ultramarine is darker, vermilion less opaque, chalk white is almost transparent. Other changes were for the better. In oils, translucent colours such as red lakes become not only more transparent but warmer, and give rich results when glazed in thin layers over other colours.

So the colour of a paint depends not only on the colour of the pigment but also on the fluid binding medium – as well as the reflective properties and absorbency of the surface to which it is applied, the texture of the finish, and the shape and size of the particles themselves, not to mention the effects of ageing (which are discussed in Chapter 11). This is why, although I shall be concerned primarily with the substances that have been dug up, synthesized, pulverized and purified to lend colour to paint, I cannot survey the topic of colour manufacture for painting without also occasionally considering the technology of paints as a whole – including the binder.

Wheels of light

'. . . in the Rays [Colours] are nothing but their Dispositions to propagate this or that Motion into the Sensorium, and in the Sensorium they are Sensations of those Motions under the Forms of Colours'.[6] We can perhaps forgive Newton a little vagueness about how we see colours, given his great achievements in explaining how they are generated. But his detractor Goethe was right to stress that colour is not about light alone. There is also the matter of how we perceive it – and this is the trickiest business of all.

For instance, colour depends on the circumstances under which we look for it. There is a sense in which we can regard leaves as possessing a kind of *latent* greenness, in that they contain a compound (chlorophyll) that absorbs red and blue from white light. But of course green leaves are not 'green' under all circumstances – under starlight, for instance, or viewed through a red filter. Colour is a function of the illumination.

This may seem obvious enough; but it would be thoroughly confusing if, like the ancient Greeks, we were to regard colour as an intrinsic property, requiring light only to activate it like electricity activating a light-bulb. This confusion is apparent in Aristotle's views on the relationship between colour and light:

> things appear different according to whether they are seen in shadow or in sunlight, in a hard or soft light, and according to the angle at which they are seen ... Those which are seen in the light of the fire or the moon, and by the rays of the lamp differ by reason of the light in each case; and also by the mixture of the colours with each other; for in passing through each other they are coloured; for when light falls on another colour, being again mixed by it, it takes on still another mixture of colour.'

He claims, in other words, that colour is a property that does something to light. For Descartes and Newton, colour was equated with the light itself and not the illuminated object. Newton's prism experiments helped to clarify that apparently colourless light contains colour within it.

In the nineteenth century the emphasis shifted again. Strictly speaking, there is no such thing as coloured light, but only electro-magnetic radiation of different wavelengths. Colour is a matter of perception, a result of the effect of light on the eye and brain. Newton had an inkling of this, commenting that 'the rays ... are not coloured'. It is astonishing that we perceive such major (and uneven) changes in hue for rather small changes in wavelength – as if the sea were to switch from green to red as the wind drops and the waves lengthen.

Only in the past two centuries has it really been appreciated to what extent colour itself, as opposed to measurable features of materials such as light absorption, is a contingent phenomenon. The many tricks that our visual system plays when 'colours' are presented in different contexts attest to this.

Everyone who has spent early years mixing paints with the child's engaging blend of instinct and empiricism is astonished when they first see that mixing red and green light produces not brown light but yellow. A little more knowledge and a little more thought only make the puzzle more profound. Yellow light has a wavelength of around 580 nanometres (a nanometre is a millionth of a millimetre), while the wavelengths of red and green light are typically about 620 and 520 nanometres. Do the latter two, then, somehow combine to create electromagnetic radiation with a different wavelength? Not at all. The 'yellowness' is not intrinsic to the light signal, but arises in our perception of it. Clearly Newton was right – the rays do *not* have to be 'coloured' yellow for us to experience this hue.

But we are taught that yellow is a primary colour, which cannot be made by mixing others. Were we misled, then? How many fundamental colours, after all, will suffice to mix all the others, and which are they? The question of 'irreducible' primary colours is one that has long preoccupied colour theorists in both the arts and the sciences, and it underpins one's entire conceptual and semantic landscape of colour. Newton's experiments on light seemed, if anything, to make this issue less clear than ever.

Mapping colour space

The idea that colours, like chemical substances, have elementary components from which they are comprised goes back to antiquity. For the Greeks there were just two vast primary kingdoms in Colour Space, and they did not exactly correspond to 'colours' at all but to light and dark. Blue was dark with a little light added, red was light and dark in equal measure, and so forth.

It was not until the seventeenth century that the three modern primaries – red, yellow and blue – became established. In 1601 an Italian professor of medicine named Guido Antonio Scarmiglioni proposed that there were five 'simple' colours from which all others were presumed to be constituted: white, yellow, blue, red and black. Robert Boyle, the chemist who is commonly credited for the modern concept of a chemical element, echoed this quintet with more authority in 1664, claiming that with these five 'the skillful Painter can produce what kind of Colour he pleases, and a great many more than we have yet names for'.

But how do these relate to the 'irreducible' colours of Newton's rainbow? White sunlight is clearly not just composed of the three primaries, but contains also green, orange and (if we acknowledge the arbitrariness of Newton's final two subdivisions) purple light. Yet these three are the *secondary* colours, each of which can be mixed by the painter from two primaries. In the rainbow, green falls tidily between yellow and blue, and orange between yellow and red. But purple, the mixture of red and blue, lies (in the guise of violet) beyond blue, at the opposite end to red. The obvious invitation is to unite the spectrum in a loop: a *colour wheel* (Plate 2.1). In his *Opticks* (1704), this is just what Newton did, marrying up red against violet via a colour not 'of the prismatick Colours, but a purple inclining to red and violet'.

In terms of physics, the colour wheel is a wholly artificial device, since the light that it denotes increases in frequency from red to violet before leaping across a discontinuity back to red. But the wheel organizes colour space into a pleasingly symmetrical pattern in which primaries and secondaries alternate with their mixing relationships clearly defined. This is not, however, quite how Newton saw it: he awarded no particular prominence to the hues we now regard as primary, and his wheel was a seven-spoked affair of unequal slices (Figure 2.3). Subsequent colour theorists tended to emphasize the symmetry (Figure 2.4).

Even if there was not total agreement over the number of subdivisions, the colour wheel became iconic within the colour theories of the nineteenth and early twentieth centuries, and few artists were unfamiliar with this emblematic representation of the territory they negotiated. One of the most impressive colour wheels was that published by the French theorist and chemist Michel-Eugène Chevreul in his book *Des couleurs et de leurs applications aux arts industriels* (1864). Here the smooth gradations from one colour to the next (Plate 2.1) stretched the contemporary colour-printing technology to its limits, and the printer, M. Digeon, won an award for the work from the French Société d'Encouragement pour l'Industrie Nationale. It was well deserved: the original wheel looks as stunning as ever today.

The colour wheel provides an organizing principle for artists,

Figure 2.3
Isaac Newton's colour wheel divides the spectral colours according to
their proportions in the rainbow.

but it does not help us resolve the apparent discrepancies between
the primary colours in pigment mixtures and those in mixtures of
light. In the former case, yellow is primary and green secondary; in
the latter case, the reverse is true. In addition, red, yellow and blue
paints mix to black (or nearly so), whereas Newton claimed that
the entire rainbow of hues mixes to white. Goethe and his acolytes
were quick to seize on this apparent inconsistency in Newton's
theory. Any fool could see that no mixture of pigments gave one
pure white, nor anything remotely like it.

James Clerk Maxwell dispelled the confusion – among scientists,
at least – by showing in 1855 that three kinds of coloured light
suffice to generate almost any colour: orange-red, blue-violet and
green. (This triad is usually denoted simply as red, blue and green.)

Mixing light, Maxwell explained, is not the same as mixing
pigments. By blending light rays of different wavelengths, one is
synthesizing colour by the addition of various components, which
together stimulate the retina in the eye to create a particular colour
sensation. This is called *additive* mixing. Instead of using light rays,
one can achieve additive mixing by rapidly alternating the separate

Figure 2.4

Many systems for organizing colours in the nineteenth century, such as
Auguste Laugel's colour star from *L'Optique et les arts* (1869) (*a*), tended
to favour symmetrical arrangements in order to emphasize the primary
and secondary relationships and the juxtaposition of complementary
colours. George Field's colour wheels from *Chromatography* (1835) (*b*)
and Charles Blanc's colour star from *Grammaire des arts du dessin* (1867)
(*c*) find space for tertiary colours too.

colours in the visual field. Maxwell's initial experiments, assisted
by the Scottish colour theorist and interior decorator D. R. Hay,
employed spinning discs painted with the three additive primary
colours. The discs were made from interlocking and overlapping
segments that allowed Maxwell to vary the proportions until they
mixed to an achromatic silvery grey. In 1860 Maxwell devised an
instrument that enabled him to synthesize a wide range of colours
directly from light by mixing rays of three different wavelengths
('red', 'blue' and 'green') in various ratios.

A blend of pigments, on the other hand, *subtracts* wavelengths
from white light. That is to say, the pigments themselves are not the
sources of the light that triggers a colour sensation, but are media
that act on a separate source of illumination. A red pigment plucks
out the blue and green rays, and much of the yellows; only red light
is reflected. A yellow pigment might take out the reds, blues, and
much of the greens. So a mixture of red and yellow reflects only
those rays in the narrow range where the absorption of both materials
is not too strong – in the orange part of the spectrum. Each time a
pigment is added to a blend, another chunk of the spectrum is
subtracted from the reflected light. As a result, the colour gets duller
and murkier. Each time a light ray is added to a mixture, on the
other hand, more photons are injected into the resulting ray, and
the combined light beam gets brighter.[8] Thus making colours by
mixing pigments is called *subtractive* mixing.

Subtractive mixing inevitably penalizes the luminosity of the
pigments, since more of the illumination is absorbed by the mixture.
For example, most red and yellow pigments inevitably absorb a little
orange light. So the orange that results from their mixture isn't very
brilliant – some of the orange light is lost from the white light that
illuminates the image. In contrast, a genuine orange pigment absorbs
virtually no light in the 'orange' part of the spectrum and so doesn't
suffer from this defect. This is why a genuine orange pigment may
be more vibrant than a mixture of red and yellow. The nineteenth-
century colour technologist George Field explains this in his book
Chromatography, at the same time alluding to the chemical hazards
of mixing (the possibility that the pigments might react with one
another; see Chapter 11):

Now, the more pigments are mixed, the more they are deteriorated in colour, attenuated, and chemically set at variance. Original pigments, that is, such as are not made up of two or more colours, are purer in hue and generally more durable than those compounded . . . Cadmium orange, for instance, which is *naturally* an orange pigment and not composed of red and yellow, is superior to many mixtures of these colours in a chemical sense, and to all such mixtures in an artistic sense.[9]

So the ancient taboo on mixing (see page 19) was still strong in the nineteenth century; until this time, there was not a single good, pure orange pigment available to artists, nor violet either.

Called-for colours

The six-part colour wheel captures another set of colour relationships that is of vital significance for the artist. Each primary sits opposite the secondary composed of the other two primaries: red against green, blue against orange, yellow against violet. You could say that each of these pairs contains everything, colourwise, that the other does not. They are complements of one another, like the positive and negative prints of a photographic image. (The analogy here is exact, in fact.)

Goethe recognized that strong hues tend to generate an impression of their complementary colour in the surrounding field, like a contrasting halo. The same effect arises in the 'after-image' produced when one stares at a colour for long moments and then looks away. Goethe relates how, in an inn lit by a setting sun, he saw an after-image of a fair-skinned girl in a red dress as a dark-faced figure robed in 'beautiful sea-green'. He called these opposites 'called-for' colours as though each one demands its complement.

The observation was not wholly original: among those who had previously remarked on the phenomenon of after-images in the eighteenth century were the French naturalist Comte de Buffon, the colour theorist Moses Harris, and the scientists Joseph Priestley and Benjamin Thompson (Count Rumford). But Goethe appreciated that this sensation of complementaries is a product of the visual system, and has nothing to do with the light reaching the eye at that moment. 'Every decided colour does a certain violence to the eye, and forces it to opposition,' he suggested, more or less correctly. It is for the same physiological reason that a colour looks more vivid if juxtaposed with its complementary: the two colours mutually enhance one another, and generate a kind of vibration at their interface. This idea was to become central to the thinking of all colouristically inclined artists in the nineteenth century, particularly the Impressionists.

That certain colour combinations work well was again by no means Goethe's discovery. Such ideas were common currency at least by the fifteenth century, and Leonardo da Vinci's keen eye allowed him to anticipate Goethe's pairings of complementaries:

Of different colours equally perfect, that will appear most excellent which is seen near its direct contrary . . . blue near a yellow, green near red: because each colour is more distinctly seen when opposed to its contrary, than to any other similar to it.[10]

The lens of the mind

Both the additive mixing of red and green light to yellow, and the vibrancy that red and green pigments acquire side by side, are linked to the way that colour sensation is created in the eye. As Goethe rightly intimated, a full scientific understanding of colour has a biological as well as a physical dimension. Maxwell gave his weighty endorsement to this suggestion: 'The science of colour must . . . be regarded as essentially a mental science.'

Newton assumes throughout his *Opticks* that light has a corpuscular nature: this fitted with his view of the Universe as a system of colliding bodies obeying his laws of motion. But the Dutch physicist and astronomer Christiaan Huygens argued in 1678 that light is comprised not of particles but of waves, propagating through an all-pervading ether. At the beginning of the nineteenth century the English scientist Thomas Young educed compelling evidence for Huygens's theory (In the end both Newton and Huygens were right, thanks to the ability of quantum physics to support two interpretations at once.)

Young's interests extended beyond physics to include medicine; and in 1801 he combined the two to propose a theory of colour vision. He assumed that the retina – the part of the eye that light stimulates – contains light sensors that respond to the rays by vibrating in resonance. These vibrations create a signal that is dispatched from the retina along the optic nerve to the brain. But Young deemed it impossible that the infinite gradations of colour across the visible spectrum have a correspondingly infinite number of resonators at every point on the retina. Noting that the three colours then considered to be primaries – red, yellow and blue could be mixed to generate almost any colour, he proposed that three receptors alone were enough to enable the eye to perceive a full range of colours: 'Each sensitive filament of the [optic] nerve may consist of three portions, one for each principal colour.' He imagined that colour blindness arises from the absence of one of the three sets of colour receptors in the eye.

Young's theory was elaborated by the German physicist and physiologist Hermann von Helmholtz, who provided indirect evidence for the existence of three colour receptors. Maxwell's studies of additive mixing of light in the 1860s gave strong support to the proposal that the retina can develop full colour vision with receptors that respond to just the three primaries (albeit the additive primaries: red, blue and green). But direct experimental confirmation of the idea did not arrive for another hundred years.

The light-sensitive entities in the eye – Young's resonators – come in two classes, distinguishable under the microscope because of their different shapes. They sit in the retina at the ends of millions of filaments from the optic nerve, and they are either rod-shaped or cone-shaped (Figure 2.5). There are 120 million rods and 5 million cones in each human retina. Most of the cones are located in a depression of the retina called the *fovea centralis*, which lies at the focal point of the eye's lens. This little pit is devoid of rods, which outnumber cones everywhere else on the retina.

Rods and cones stimulate nerve signals when they are struck by light. The rods absorb light over the entire visible spectrum, but do

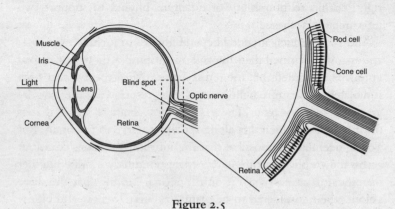

Figure 2.5
The visual system of the human eye, with its photosensitive rod and
cone cells arrayed on the retina.

so most strongly (that is, the chance of the light being absorbed is
greatest) for blue-green light. Absorption of light by a rod triggers
an identical neural response regardless of the wavelength. So rods
do not discriminate between colours, but only between light and
dark. They are extremely sensitive, and are the main light receptors
that we use in very dim illumination such as starlight. This is why
it is hard to identify colours under such conditions. Because their
response is greatest for blue-green light, objects that reflect these
wavelengths (such as leaves) appear brighter than red objects at night.

In bright sunlight, the colour-sensitive cones supply the visual
signal to the brain. Under these conditions, the rod cells are
'bleached' – saturated with light and unable to absorb photons.
Only when the bright light is shut off can the rods relax back to
their initial state, ready to absorb photons and trigger nerve
impulses. This relaxation takes many minutes, which is why we
gain night vision only gradually after leaving a brightly lit building.
If we are outside at dusk, night vision takes over quite smoothly as
the sun's last rays disappear. The differing colour sensitivity of rods
and cones results in a change in the perceived intensity of blue/
green objects relative to red as twilight deepens. This effect was first
clearly identified in 1825 by the Bohemian physiologist

J. E. Purkinje, although artists had already noticed it previously.[11]

Young's hypothesis for colour vision was verified by experiments in the 1960s which measured the absorption properties of single cones and confirmed that they fall into three classes with different colour sensitivity. The blue-light cones are the least sensitive, which is why fully saturated blue looks relatively dark. Blue's late historical arrival as a true colour, as opposed to a kind of black, is thus ultimately for biological reasons.

The overall sensitivity of the eye to the colours of the spectrum is the sum of the responses for all three types of cone, and it rises steadily from red to yellow and then falls off steadily from yellow to violet. So yellow is perceived as the brightest colour. The yellow band in a rainbow stands out not because it is more intense (not, that is, because there are more yellow photons than others) but because the yellow photons generate the biggest optical response from the eye. Curiously, yellow is regarded in many cultures as the least attractive colour, and its metaphorical and symbolic associations are often denigrating. It is traditionally the shade of treachery and cowardice, and clothing designers admit that it is a terribly difficult colour to sell. Yellow is popular in China (it is the emperor's colour, *huang*); but in the West you had better call it gold.

Each 'seen' colour is constructed in the visual system from the combined stimuli from the three types of cone cell. Red light excites mostly the 'red' cones. But a mixture of red and green rays can stimulate red and green cones in the same ratio as does pure yellow light – and so the colour sensations are identical. If blue light is added, we see white. (Although the three types of cone are often linked to Maxwell's primaries of red, green and blue, this is a crude shorthand. Their peak sensitivities are in fact in the yellow, green and violet repectively.)

The rod and cone cells are studded with many thousands of individual light receptors called photopigments. Each of these is a single protein molecule, embedded in the stacked folds of the cell membranes. All photopigments contain a light-absorbing molecular unit called retinal, which has a zigzagging, smeared cloud of electrons very similar to that in the carotenoid pigments of plants. Retinal acts as a kind of switch. There we stand, say, before Yves Klein's blue sculptures, flooding us with reflected blue light. A blue-sensitive photopigment absorbs a photon of blue light, and in response its retinal unit changes shape from kinked to straight. This enables the photopigment to set in train a sequence of molecular events that leads to a change in the electrical impulses in the nerve to which the cone cell is attached. Some region in the visual cortex of the brain stirs into life, and we register 'blue'. Where we go from there is our own business.

Measuring colour

The colour wheel has come a long way since Newton. Its most popular modern incarnation is less pleasing to the eye, but a lot more informative: a colour diagram drawn up by the Commission Internationale de l'Eclairage (CIE) (Plate 2.2), starchily called the CIE chromaticity curve. The 'pure' wavelengths of Newton's spectrum lie on the tongue-shaped periphery, while the colours inside it are the result of various additive mixtures of these rays. Any colour that lies along a line connecting two points on the edge may be mixed from those spectral colours. If the line passes through the white region in the centre, the two peripheral colours may be mixed to white. Thus white light can be created from blue and yellow alone (as it is in monochrome television screens), but not from red and green.

The artificiality of the union of red and violet in the colour wheel is emphasized by the flat base of the tongue – along here the colours are, as Newton confessed, not found in even the finest unweaving of the rainbow's strands.

Yet for all its glory, the CIE diagram doesn't show us all colours. Where is brown? Where is pink? There is clearly a lot more colour space than the mandalas of colour wheels can accommodate.

The defining characteristic of a coloured material is not whether its hue sits closer to the kingdom of red than of blue or whatever, but what its total spectral composition is: how it absorbs and reflects light across the continuum of the visible spectrum. A colour's most discriminating signature is thus a wiggly line that traces the variation in intensity of the reflected light as the wavelength varies.[12] The signature of 'pure' white (though not of sunlight) is a straight line: all wavelengths are reflected fully. Black makes the same mark, but at zero rather than full intensity: every wavelength is negated. What, then, is grey? Along with black and white, grey is sometimes classified as an oxymoronic 'achromatic colour' – we might say that grey has no 'colour' as such, but is more of an intermediary between light and dark. Grey is what we perceive when all wavelengths are absorbed partially, yet more or less equally, from white light. It is, if you will, white light with the volume turned down.

Brown is another difficult one. It sits on the border between a real colour and an achromatic one – a 'dirty' colour akin to grey. Brown is in fact a kind of grey biased towards yellow or orange. A brown surface absorbs all wavelengths to some extent, but orange/ yellow somewhat less than others. Another way of saying this is that brown is a low-brightness yellow or orange, the sensation generated when low-intensity light of these wavelengths impinges on your eye. It is a physiological and linguistic curiosity that, whereas we might classify low-intensity blues, greens and reds still as blues, greens and reds, we feel the need for a new basic colour term (in the sense of Berlin and Kay) for low-intensity yellow.

Brown and grey don't feature on the CIE diagram because it doesn't show the colours produced by brightness variations. To do that requires a whole stack of CIE diagrams, with the white centre getting progressively greyer. As it does so, the orange/yellow part of the diagram gets progressively browner.

This illustrates the fact that colour space – the kind of thing you see in trade paint catalogues – is in fact three-dimensional. The CIE diagram shows just two of the three parameters of colour – two 'dimensions', portrayed on a flat plane. One of these is hue, which is what we usually mean colloquially by 'colour'. Strictly speaking, the hue is the dominant wavelength in the colour, and it is what enables us to characterize a colour as basically red, green or whatever. In this sense, the hue of brown is yellow or orange, while grey has no hue – no dominant wavelength – and so can be regarded as achromatic. In the CIE diagram, the hue varies around the perimeter of the tongue. Purples lie along the sloping bottom side, between violet at the lower left-hand corner and red at the lower right. The diagram brings home rather forcefully the oddity that in English and most other European languages there is still no generally accepted colour term for the hue between yellow and green, or that between green and blue, even though these occupy appreciable parts of the perimeter.

The second parameter of colour on the CIE diagram is saturation, sometimes called the purity or (potentially misleadingly) the intensity. This refers to the extent to which white (or black or grey) is mixed in with a pure hue. Roughly speaking, the saturation of a colour varies along the line between the 'pure' hue on the periphery of the diagram and the pure white spot in the centre. Notice, incidentally, how large the white area is: there is a wide range of whites. True white is defined in the CIE scheme as 'equal energy' white, the white obtained from an equal mixture of the three primaries that lie at the extremities: red light of 770-nanometre wavelength at the lower right corner, violet light of 380 nanometres at the lower left, and green light of 520 nanometres at the topmost point of the upper curve. Sunlight lies slightly to the yellow side of true white.

Omitted from the CIE diagram is the third parameter of colour: brightness, which can be crudely considered as the shade of grey the colour generates in a black-and-white photograph. By the early nineteenth century, colour theorists were already beginning to appreciate that flat colour wheels gave only a partial picture of colour space – a mere slice through the landscape. Some theorists expanded their wheels to include tertiary colours, which are made by mixing the three primaries in different ratios (Figure 2.4*b*). The German Romantic painter and colour theorist Philipp Otto Runge went further, presenting a colour *sphere* in his book *Farben-Kugel* (*Colour Sphere*) (1810) that, roughly speaking, made allowance for variations in brightness of Newton's spectral colours. The fully saturated primary and secondary colours are situated around the equator of the globe-like sphere. Toward one pole, the colours get progressively lighter; towards the other, darker. So one pole is pure white and one fully black.

Yet even this will not suffice, for it does not properly accommodate independent variations in saturation and brightness: grey appears nowhere on the sphere. Its surface is still two-dimensional, whereas real colour space is three-dimensional. In the early 1900s the American artist and teacher Albert Munsell made one of the first attempts to codify all of this space. Munsell hoped that his scheme would allow him to classify colours perceived in nature so that he could reproduce them accurately on canvas in his studio. His first colour scale was published in 1905, and was later expanded in the *Atlas of the Munsell Color System* in 1915 (Plate 2.3). The full Munsell scheme is somewhat like a 3D CIE chart, except that the profile is more like a polychromatic spider than a tongue. As in the CIE chart, hue changes around the perimeter while saturation varies along radial lines towards white at the centre. The brightness varies in the vertical direction, as in our hypothetical stacks of CIE charts, so that the central point runs from pure black through grey to pure white.

Munsell updated his colour notation scheme again in 1929, dividing the colour space into discrete blocks that were intended to progress, in any direction, through equal perceptual steps. Careful psychological tests were conducted by the Optical Society of America to try to ensure that Munsell's colour space was as 'even' as possible.

The Munsell colour scale, in the form of coloured plastic counters or chips, has been used extensively by psychologists and anthropologists conducting research into colour perception. But its value in this arena remains limited by its attempt to impose scientific quantification on concepts of colour that inevitably carry a lot of cultural baggage. John Gage recounts with some glee how Danish anthropologists arrived on a Polynesian island in 1971 ready to test their Munsell chips on the indigenous people, only to receive the deflating response, 'We don't talk much about colour here.' The sociologist M. Sahlins expressed the point very neatly in 1976: 'a semiotic theory of color universals must take for "significance" exactly what colors do mean in human societies. They do not mean Munsell chips.'[13]

By the same token, colour does not mean Newton's rainbow, nor (as the *Oxford English Dictionary* suggests) a material's propensity for light absorption, nor a sensation produced by stimulation of the optic nerve. It is all of these things, but to artists they are mere abstractions. Painters need colour to be embodied in *stuff*, they need to be able to purchase it and get it smeared across their overalls. That is the bottom line, and I would not like to see it obscured (as sometimes it has been) among multi-hued wheels and globes and charts. Painters need paint. Colour is their medium of expression and communication, but to make their dreams visible it needs substance. Let's now see how they got it.

3. The Forge of Vulcan

COLOUR TECHNOLOGY IN ANTIQUITY

Now that even purple clothes our walls, no famous picture is painted. We must believe that when the painter's equipment was less complete, the results were in every respect better.

Pliny, *Natural History* (1st century AD)

I don't suppose you ever thought painting involved so much chemistry and cooking.

Robertson Davies, *What's Bred in the Bone* (1986)

For my part, I cannot believe, that the four capital colours of the Ancients would mix to that surprising perfection we see in the works of Titian and Rubens. And if we have no certain knowledge of *their* methods of Colouring who lived in the last Century, how should we understand theirs who lived Two Thousand years ago?

Thomas Bardwell, *The Practice of Painting* (1756)

The exhibit best remembered from the Great Exhibition of 1851 in London is not any of the fine products of art or commerce on display but the edifice in which they were housed: the Crystal Palace, erected in all its vitreous glory in Hyde Park. Designed by Joseph Paxton and allegedly inspired by the shape of a water-lily, this marvellous glass menagerie was ransacked by fire in 1936 after its reconstruction at the commanding brow of a hill in Sydenham, south-east London.

The daunting task of decorating the building for the Exhibition fell to the Welsh interior decorator Owen Jones. He felt that such splendour could be matched only by an appeal to antiquity, saying:

'If we examine the remains of the architecture of the ancients, we shall find everywhere that in the early periods the prevailing colours used in decoration were the primaries – blue, red and yellow.'[1]

This was largely true. The walls of Pompeii were coloured to a degree that we might now consider gaudy, adorned with brilliant vermilion and polished to a high gloss. The Greeks painted much of their stonework, from pillars to relief work to statues. Figures were depicted on rich grounds of red, yellow, blue and black. As this became evident to archaeologists in the early nineteenth century, Western architects presented brightly coloured reconstructions of how the temples – the pallid stone of their surfaces now laid bare – would have looked in their heyday. Jones was one of those who began to incorporate Classical features, painted in strong primaries, into their own designs.

Yet Jones's scheme for the Crystal Palace was based more on the system of primary colours proposed by one of his contemporaries, the English colour-maker George Field, than on any principles of colour organization upheld by the ancients. He stipulated that the three colours should be distributed in a specific ratio of three parts yellow, five parts red and eight parts blue, proposed by Field as the ideal of harmonious colouring. Other architects baulked at this idea, deemed somewhat indecorous to sober Victorian tastes. As it happened, Jones got his way – but only to a degree, for he was limited by materials. The industrial paints he had to use were by no means as bright as the artists' pigments of the time, and so the Palace was adorned with dirty off-yellow, pale blue, and a heavy brownish-red.[2]

Colour in the art of antiquity is a strange mixture. The early Egyptians devoted more effort and skill to making artists' colours than did any other civilization west of the Nile for several thousand years. The Greeks and Romans showed a taste for interior decoration that would look decidedly bold and modern today, yet many of the fragmentary paintings that remain show a chromatic range scarcely greater than that in some cave art. The Classical Greek painter Apelles was admired by Titian, the prime colourist of the Renaissance, yet – as we saw in Chapter 1 – he reputedly employed just four colours. None the less, the Greeks did not hesitate to use sumptuous gold as a pigment. In comparison with the flat pictograms of Egypt, the scanty remnants of Greek art occasionally show us images painted with a skill and delicacy that puts one in mind of the High Renaissance – but the artistic techniques they used had to be re-invented at the beginning of the fourteenth century. To the Renaissance masters, Classical Greece represented a golden age of art; to us, it is now an almost entirely blank page. What little we do know of the painting methods and materials of that age comes largely from the accounts of Roman writers, which are now the main window on to not only the art of antiquity but also the ancients' ability to rearrange the chemical elements.

The first chemists

Chemistry is unusual among the sciences in being defined at least as much by practicalities as by theoretical understanding – by what it does as well as what it says. It is the science of transforming matter; and this, it must be said, is something that can be achieved as effectively by blind adherence to the recipe book as by informed planning. But placing the line that divides 'true science' from technology between these two poles is merely revisionism – the imposition of modern criteria on the historical world.[3] The fact that the ancient Egyptians were able to conduct chemistry scarcely less refined than that of European chemists at least four millennia later surely forces the issue of why we should choose to regard one but not the other as quantitative, reproducible science.

The blue pigment known as Egyptian frit or Egyptian blue, which has been identified in artefacts dating from around 2500 BC, is not a product of blind chance, a serendipitous outcome of fusing natural materials at random. It is wrought with precision and forethought, a blend of one part lime (calcium oxide) and one part copper oxide with four parts quartz (silica). The raw ingredients are minerals: chalk or limestone, a copper mineral such as malachite, and sand. They are fired in a kiln at temperatures of between 800 and 900 °C. The temperature is crucial, and we must suppose that the Egyptians were able to control the firing conditions with considerable accuracy. The result is an opaque, brittle blue material, which is made into a pigment by grinding it to a powder. It is the oldest synthetic pigment, a Bronze Age blue.

The transformation of raw ingredients to artists' materials in ancient Egypt was a task requiring highly specialized knowledge and practical prowess. How else, for example, could their painters have been supplied with the synthetic pigment lead antimonate? This pale yellow substance has a vexed history of nomenclature – as the medieval *giallolino* or *giallorino* (see page 112) it was never clearly distinguished from several other lead-based yellow pigments, and the seventeenth-century label 'Naples yellow' today signifies a particular hue rather than a chemical composition.[4] We do not know what the Egyptians called it. But they knew how to make it, using reagents that were themselves synthetic: lead oxide or carbonate and antimony oxide, both obtained by chemical transformations of minerals.

This kind of manipulation of nature's materials reveals ancient Egypt as a civilization with a genuine command of chemistry.[5] We might even entertain the notion that such an organized technology – one might reasonably call it an industry – *defines* a civilization. Palaeolithic artists were decorating cave walls at least 30,000 years ago, long before the last Ice Age ended, and they were not wanting in proficiency with the dull earth pigments then available. The cave paintings of Lascaux, Altamira and the Pyrenees display an elegance of line every bit as refined as that in the Egyptian wall paintings several millennia later. But whatever interpretations anthropologists might place on these markings, they do not speak in the same way of the social order and stratified division of labour that we see in Egypt. They are not the product of a culture whose citizens have a trade to offer.

It is of course the injustice of history that the most ancient of scientific innovators, the equals of Newton, Lavoisier and Darwin, predate any means by which their names might be passed down the ages. We can never now erect monuments to the fellow who, around 3500 BC, discovered how to win copper from its ores and thereby to take the immense leap from physical to chemical manufacture of artefacts. Neither is the inventor of bronze from the co-smelting of tin and copper ores accorded due credit, nor even the man or woman who, shortly before the time of Homer in 1000 BC, brought forth iron from its mineral oxide. If the history of science teaches us anything, however, it is that discoveries like this are not made by accident. Good fortune may give one a sporting chance; but as Louis Pasteur remarked, only the perceptive and receptive mind turns it into discovery. Whether we regard these innovations as early science or not is beside the point. To the early artist, making colours was part of the game of art.

Raw earth

Although the birth of chemistry as such had to await the first settlements of the Middle East, the deliberate manipulation of natural materials for the purposes of art came much earlier. Cave painters took their palette from the environment. Red and yellow 'earths' came from the iron oxide haematite crystallized with varying degrees of water; green earths from the aluminosilicate clays celadonite and glauconite; black from charcoal; brown from manganese oxide; and white from chalk and ground bones. At Altamira and Lascaux there is even a violet pigment, made from a manganese mineral. With the exception of greens and violet, these substances are widely available. So we see in the caves of France and Spain an earthy version of the 'classical' spectrum of black, white, red and yellow (Plate 3.1). Surprisingly little seems to be made of the fact that the primordial hues of Berlin and Kay are just those that the earth offers up in abundance.

Yet we should not underestimate the ingenuity with which these unnamed hunter-gatherers made use of nature's hues. It is one thing to smear a charcoal line on a cave wall, quite another to grind haematite systematically into a fine powder with a mortar and pestle, mix it with an organic binding medium such as vegetable oil, and apply it to a surface — a Stone Age oil paint, no less. And who was it who dreamed up the idea of spray-painting the pigment with breath blown through a tube?

This is not all. The Upper Palaeolithic (so-called Middle Magdalenian) artists who created the images in the Niaux caves of the Pyrenees around 12,000 BC, for example, devised new recipes from nature's bounty. No chemical transformations yet, but a physical mixture of pigments with 'extenders': neutral materials that made the precious pigments go further and improved their properties in a paint. Mixed with potassium feldspar, haematite becomes a little darker but sticks better to the rock surface and cracks less readily. Better still was the recipe of the Upper Magdalenians (around 10,500 BC), in which the feldspar extender contained some biotite – a mixture readily obtained from ground granite. The temptation to see Palaeolithic cave art as homogeneous on stylistic grounds is thus challenged by evidence of technical innovation over a millennial timescale that, in palaeontological terms, is positively speedy.

The technologies of colour

The ancient chemist had little more than a single agent of transformation: fire. Heat may stimulate a reaction, and is all one needs to conjure up yellow lead antimonate or blue frit. It will expel gases, turning carbonate minerals like chalk and malachite into oxides by driving out carbon dioxide.

Heat is a pretty blunt tool of transformation, to be sure; but the civilizations of the Nile valley refined it to a degree that commands admiration. Furnaces in Babylonia and Assyria exhibit a range of designs which testifies to considerable experimentation with firing conditions.

Yet it is clear that the technologists of Egypt, Greece and Rome also had some sophisticated chemistry at their fingertips. They made rudimentary use of acids and alkalis – although until the strong 'mineral' acids (sulphuric and nitric) were discovered in the early Middle Ages by the Arabic alchemists, acid treatment could involve nothing stronger than vinegar. That was enough, however, to corrode lead and copper metal into, respectively, white lead (see page 70) and the green pigment verdigris (see page 71). The chemical processes of fermentation (using yeast to make alcohol from sugar), sublimation (heating a solid to a gaseous state), precipitation (extracting a solid from a solution) and filtration (capturing fine solid particles in a suspension) were standard techniques in the ancient world.

But the chemical technology that existed for colour-making in ancient times was not developed specifically for that purpose. The necessary ingredients and skills were fostered by more prosaic crafts, such as glass-making, pottery glazing and soap manufacture. In other words, pigment manufacture in antiquity was an offshoot of a large and thriving chemical industry that transformed raw materials into the substances needed for daily life. We shall see in subsequent chapters that this situation obtains throughout the ages: pigments manufacture has been made both economically viable and techno- logically possible because of its embedding in a much broader landscape of practical science. Art speaks to the spirit but feeds on the mundane.

The manufacture of both glass and soap requires alkalis. In the ancient world these were primarily soda (sodium carbonate) and potash (mostly potassium carbonate). Sodium carbonate occurs naturally as a mineral, called natron in seventeenth-century Europe after the Arabic word for it: *natrun*. But this is hardly a widespread resource, and much of the soda and potash used in the ancient and medieval world came from wood and plant ash. It is extracted by leaching: allowing water to percolate through the ashes, whereupon it dissolves the alkali. Most ash yields potash; but that made from coastal plants contains more soda.

Who first realized that sand and soda will give you glass when heated to melting point? Pliny offers a fine tale for this discovery, which he attributes to the Phoenicians inhabiting the area around the River Belus on the Mediterranean coast, north of Mount Carmel. He says:

There is a story that once a ship belonging to some traders in natron put in there and that they scattered along the shore to prepare a meal. Since, however, no stones suitable for supporting their cauldrons were forthcoming, they rested them on lumps of soda from their cargo. When these became heated and were completely mingled with the sand on the beach, a strange translucent liquid flowed forth in streams; and this, it is said, was the origin of glass.[6]

It is a pretty scenario – but surely apocryphal, since camp fires do not reach the temperatures of around 2,500 °C required to melt sand and soda. Besides, glass was being made over two millennia before Pliny's account – and not in Phoenicia but in Mesopotamia, the land now occupied by Iraq and Syria.

The earliest true glass is found here, and dates from around 2500 BC. The discovery of glass was surely serendipitous, but perhaps not so casual as Pliny would have us believe. It was possibly the offshoot of experiments in another practical craft: the manufacture of coloured pottery glazes.

Blue-glazed soapstone ornaments, imitating the prized blue mineral lapis lazuli, were produced from around 4500 BC in the Middle East by powdering the surface of the stone and heating it in the presence of copper minerals such as azurite or malachite. This blue glassy substance has become known as Egyptian faience (Plate 3.2), although it was produced in Mesopotamia long before it developed into an industry in Egypt. First appearing in the valley of the Tigris and Euphrates, faience was being made in the lower Nile region by 3000 BC, and 1,500 years later trade had spread it throughout all of Europe.

To generate the high temperatures needed for fusing the minerals in faience manufacture, a fire must be fanned or blown. The artefacts were protected from smoke and ash by containment in a lidded vessel or a kiln chamber – pottery kilns in Mesopotamia date back to 4000 BC. It seems highly likely that the developments in kiln technology afforded by the early manufacture of blue-glazed objects led to the discovery of copper smelting from its ore. A love of colour ushered in the Bronze Age.

One can imagine that sand might regularly have mingled and fused with the ashes during the firing of faience – and that, within the cooled furnace, puzzled or delighted artisans would have discovered hard, translucent lumps of coarse glass.

The Mesopotamians found that glass is improved by a dash of lime. A recipe in an ancient cuneiform text reads: 'Take sixty parts sand, a hundred and eighty parts ashes from sea plants, five parts chalk, heat them all together, and you will get glass.'[7] If it was tainted with copper ore from faience manufacture, the glass would turn out blue.

No doubt Egyptian blue frit was another fortuitous offshoot of such experiments, for it shares the same ingredients.

In ancient Egypt glass became a significant technological product around the middle of the third millennium BC. Colour turned it into a material fit to hold the unguents of pharaohs and queens. Cobalt minerals yielded a deeper blue than copper; greens came from iron or copper oxides, yellow and amber from iron oxide, and purple from manganese dioxide. Some metal compounds create opaque colours: yellow from antimony oxide, white from tin oxide. These recipes were used with little change to make the glorious cathedral windows of the Middle Ages.[8]

It is more of a challenge, in fact, to make *uncoloured* glass, for impurities of iron oxides in the natural ingredients impart a greenish or brownish tint. (The Latin word for glass, *vitrium*, stems from the word for a blue-green colour. The Celtic word *glas* also denotes this hue.) Medieval artisans found that the colour could be removed by adding small amounts of manganese dioxide, which became known as 'glass-maker's soap'.

Glass made from sand and soda ash or natron later replaced soapstone as the vehicle for the faience glazing technique in Egypt. Clay objects were also coloured in this way: some of the earliest Egyptian glazes are found on clay beads made by firing them with a mixture of soda and copper minerals.

A true glaze, however, is applied to the surface of the finished artefact, whereas in faience the copper mineral is mixed into the fabric of the item it tints. There is more opportunity to control the thickness and colour of a glaze applied *post hoc*. The earliest pottery glazes were basically thin coats of coloured glass: mixtures of soda and sand, with a little clay to provide adhesion. Many of the pottery glazes on Egyptian earthenware are coloured with the same minerals as those used for glass; we can only speculate about whether the potter or the glass-maker exploited them first.

These 'alkaline glazes' (so-called because of their soda content) were difficult to apply and tended to shrink as they cooled, causing cracking and peeling. From about 1500 BC, glazes throughout the Middle East commonly included lead, which reduces shrinkage. Lead-glazed bricks and tiles were widespread in Mesopotamia from around 1000 BC. The Babylonians made lead glazes simply by grinding the mineral galena (lead sulphide) to a fine dust and painting it on to the pottery clay. When heated, the lead compound melts to produce a smooth, shiny coating. This can be coloured by adding oxides of copper, iron or manganese.

The characteristic red and black ware of the Greek and Roman civilizations is coloured with a clay slip containing red clay and organic matter, or iron oxides. Inspired by a desire to imitate the ceramics of the East, this glazing technique was apparently devised around 1500 BC in Mycenae, and was improved substantially by the Attic Greeks in the sixth century BC. The secret of red and black ware was lost to the West after the fall of Rome around the fourth century AD.

Some 700 years later, the Europeans developed a taste for Moorish 'lustre-ware', sparkling with iridescent glazes containing pure metals or their sulphides. They were made in a complex process that involved copper or silver sulphides, ochre and vinegar, attesting to the formidable prowess of the Arabic chemists. The white pottery ware called *maiolica*, coated with an opaque tin-containing glaze, was also an Eastern innovation. It was introduced to Italy via Majorca, possibly as early as the twelfth century, and gave rise to a major industry in central Italy during the ensuing 400 years.

The other main engine of colour innovation in ancient times was the textiles trade – for coloured garments served the important function of indicating social hierarchy (arguably they still do).

Traditionally, dyes were bound into cloth by mordants – substances that help to attach the colouring agent (usually a natural organic compound) to the fibres of the fabric. Pliny speaks with admiration of the mordanting techniques of the Egyptians:

In Egypt, too, they employ a very remarkable process for the colouring of fabrics. After pressing the material, which is white at first, they saturate it, not with colours, but with mordants that are calculated to absorb colour. This done, the fabrics, still unchanged in appearance, are plunged into a cauldron of boiling dye, and are removed the next moment fully coloured. It is a singular fact, too, that although the dye in the pan is of

NR

BAL Author: **BALL**

BRIGHT EARTH

2008   9780099507130   N : 025793653   U : 025793664

Used In : STANF CHEMENG 12SC

BUY

NEW $36.50

one uniform colour, the material when taken out of it is of various colours, according to the nature of the mordants that have been respectively applied to it: these colours, too, will never wash out.[9]

Pliny does not specify the mordants used here; but they were generally alum (aluminium sulphate).[10] Elsewhere he says that *alumen*, a 'salty earth', is found in many locations from Armenia to Spain. Alum was mined from the beginning of the third millennium BC, and its use for fixing dyestuffs dates at least from the beginning of the second millennium. Its astringent properties made it valued also as a medicine.

Alum production was a large medieval industry. In the thirteenth and fourteenth centuries, most of it came from the Greek islands and the Near East. The capture of Constantinople by the Turks in 1453 cut off this trade and led to an alum shortage, which was later relieved by the discovery of deposits of alunite (a mineral form of potassium alum) in the papal territories in Italy. Mineral forms of alum should ideally be purified before use as a mordant to rid them of the iron salts which are usually present as an impurity, and which damage the dyes. The Arabic alchemists knew this as early as the thirteenth century, when they described a purification process involving treatment with ammonia-containing stale urine.

Dyers benefited from the discovery of caustic soda (sodium hydroxide), first mentioned in Pliny's *Natural History* from the first century AD. Known in medieval times as lye, this is made from soda and quicklime (calcium hydroxide). The latter is the result of heating chalk or limestone (to make lime: calcium oxide) and then 'slaking' it by adding water. Lye, a more potent alkali than soda or potash, aids the extraction of dyes from their natural sources. It is also used to make soap — an invention seemingly not of the 'civilized' Romans but of the 'barbaric' Gauls. Hard soap, made by boiling fats or vegetable oils in caustic soda, seems to have been widely used throughout Europe by AD 800.

And then there were the colours themselves. Among the finest ancient dyes were blue indigo, which is discussed in Chapter 9, and a deep red colourant obtained from a species of insect. In his thunderous warning of the wrath of the Lord to the kingdom of

Judah, the prophet Isaiah informs us of the red-dye technology of the Holy Land in the eighth century BC:

> Though your sins are like scarlet,
> they shall be as white as snow;
> though they are red as crimson,
> they shall be like wool.[11]

Scarlet and crimson are chosen here to evoke the hue of blood, and two millennia later Cennino Cennini acknowledges the dye's 'sanguine colour'. In the Middle Ages it was called kermes, from the Sanskrit word *kirmidja*: 'derived from a worm'. The Hebrew name for it was *tola'at shani*, 'worm scarlet'. The red compound is extracted from a wingless scale insect, *Kermes vermilio*, that dwells on the scarlet oak *Quercus coccifera* in the Near East, Spain, southern France and southern Italy. The dye, principally an organic compound that chemists call kermesic acid, is extracted by crushing the resin-encrusted kermes insects and boiling them in lye.

Kermes is the linguistic root of the English *crimson* and *carmine* and the French *cramoise*. But because an encrustation of kermes insects on a branch resembles a cluster of berries, Greek writers such as Aristotle's pupil Theophrastus (*c.* 300 BC) refer to them as *kokkos*, meaning 'berry'. In Latin this becomes *coccus*, a word found in Pliny's writings on kermes dye.[12] Yet Pliny also uses the term *granum* ('grain'), again alluding to the deceptively vegetative appearance of the insects. 'Grain' thus became one of the perplexing names by which this crimson dye was known in medieval Europe. Chaucer refers to a cloth that is 'dyed in grain', meaning dyed crimson. Because of the strong, lasting nature of this colour, the phrase came simply to mean deeply or permanently dyed. From this comes the English word 'ingrained'. In *Twelfth Night*, Olivia says of her complexion "'Tis ingrain sir! 'twill endure wind and weather' – which is more than can be said for many of the dyes of Shakespeare's time.

The terminology became still more confused in early medieval Europe. In the fourth century, St Jerome calls the kermes dye *baca* ('berry') as well as *granum*. But he is aware that the source is no berry at all but an animal; and so he employs the synonym *vermiculum*, meaning 'little worm'. From this comes the word 'vermilion', a synthetic red pigment made from sulphur and mercury. How a term for an organic dye extracted from an insect became applied to an inorganic pigment made by alchemy is a puzzle that makes sense only within the context of the medieval view of colouration, whereby similarly coloured substances of very different origin might end up with conflated names because hue was deemed to be closely linked to composition.

Recipes for colour

From this cauldron of practically (one might even say domestically) motivated chemistry emerged prescriptions for making pigments that ancient painters could use. Two of the most valuable and revealing windows into these remote crafts were opened in the early nineteenth century when Johann d'Anastasy, the Swedish vice-consul in Alexandria, purchased a collection of ancient papyri written in Greek and probably looted from a tomb. D'Anastasy presented some of the manuscripts to the Swedish Academy of Antiquities in Stockholm; he sold others to the government of the Netherlands, which deposited them at the University of Leiden. They were translated at a leisurely pace, and it was not until 1885 that one of the Leiden manuscripts, designated Papyrus X, was found to contain a number of chemical recipes for making pigments. In 1913 a similar manuscript, written in the same hand, was unearthed from the Stockholm collection (which has since been relocated to Uppsala). They were believed to be the work of an Egyptian artisan in the third century AD, but no doubt represented compilations of information from earlier times.

The Leiden and Stockholm papyri are apparently extracts from a workshop instruction manual. Whoever wrote them evidently wished to be understood by fellow craftspeople. Where the texts are obscure, this is more because the author has taken certain knowledge for granted than because of any deliberate attempt (characteristic of the contemporaneous alchemical literature) at concealment. The Stockholm papyrus contains recipes for dyeing, mordanting and making artificial gemstones. The Leiden papyrus focuses on metallurgy: its 101 recipes tell of methods for gilding, silvering and tinting metals, including such tricks as 'Giving Objects of Copper the Appearance of Gold'.

The documents reveal an impressive amount of chemical skill, a distillation of knowledge accumulated over many centuries. The nineteenth-century French chemist Marcellin Berthelot recognized in the Leiden papyrus a mine of information about the chemistry of antiquity, and he published a French translation of it along with an extensive critical analysis.

Yet to what extent are these recipes informed by real understanding of chemical principles? It is tempting to conclude that they have nothing more to do with science than does the fashioning of stone tools. After all, did not the Assyrians believe that the chemistry of craftsmanship was susceptible to magical and astrological influences?

If one insists on searching these ancient texts for analogues of modern chemical concepts, they will indeed seem ill informed. But the efforts of the ancient proto-chemists to create new colours established some pivotal ideas in the development of chemical theory. The importance of the very idea of transformation cannot be stressed enough. That the substances of the earth are not fixed in composition but are mutable under human influence is a phenomenal realization. The very notion of elements – fundamental constituents of matter – would not have been half so powerful and fecund if it were not believed that they could be interconverted. Without the conviction that base metals can be transmuted to gold, a great deal of practical chemistry would not have been undertaken. In Western natural philosophy the emphasis has long been placed on the immutable in nature: absolute, unchanging principles of geometry, mathematics, physics and astronomy. Even today this bias continues to blinker our perception of the scientific enterprise. Some commentators claim to identify the origins of science in the attempt by Thales of Miletos, around 600 BC, to 'find a fundamental unity in nature' (in the words of biologist Lewis Wolpert). But Thales realized that any such unity can obtain only through the agency of change and transformation. To the Ionian school of Classical philosophy that Thales founded, 'Everything is in a state of change.' Thales's unifying principle – water – fulfilled its role by virtue of its ability, seemingly unique at that time, to adopt the solid, liquid and gaseous forms of matter.

If the Leiden and Stockholm papyri carry a scientific message, it is this: we can *create*. We can alter the shape, form and appearance of matter. And in doing so, we can add to the beauty of the world.

Colours of the gods

The author of these papyri spoke for generations before him, as well as for many that followed. His Egypt was not the same as that of the First Dynasty (*c.* 3100 BC), but it had a comparable technology of colour. The early Egyptian civilization was considered by its citizens to be the work of the great Creator, the god Ptah of Memphis. Just as Ptah brought order to the elemental chaos of a primeval world of water, so the Egyptian priest-kings regarded art and craft as a rationalization of everyday life. The High Priest of Ptah was denoted the Greatest of Craftsmen, and the craftsman's skill was highly esteemed.

One of the most striking aspects of Egyptian painting is its mundanity, in the literal sense. It is, to the good fortune of anthropologists, a documentary art. Here are people going about their daily duties: fishing, washing, building, hunting, taking offerings to the Pharaoh (Plate 3.3). The overall impression is of a calm, orderly society. The world of the Egyptians did not necessarily conform to this harmonious image; rather, the artist depicted an ideal, a wish that chaos should yield to order and reason. And art was an instrumental means to this end, since it was invested with a magical power to transform the world. The completion of a work of art was accompanied by a ritual through which it acquired this divine influence.

The social importance of Egyptian art was reflected in the culture's systematic accumulation of bright pigments. Most of these were simply ground-up natural minerals: the copper ores malachite (green) and azurite (blue), the arsenic sulphides orpiment (yellow) and realgar (orange), along with the dull earth colours such as the ochres (iron oxide), soot black and lime white. The Egyptians occasionally made greens by mixing blue and yellow pigments – blue frit and yellow ochre, for example. Natural copper silicate offered another variety of green; the Greeks called this mineral *chrysocolla* – 'gold glue' – and used it as an adhesive for gold leaf.

For painting on papyrus, these pigments were generally mixed with a water-soluble gum, creating a primitive version of water-colours. Size – a kind of glue made from boiled animal skins – and egg white were also used as binding agents. Thus Egyptian painting technique was basically what we would call a tempera method (see page 101).

But the Egyptians knew that nature's palette can be made more vivid by chemical 'art'. In addition to blue frit and lead antimonate, a few discoveries deserve special mention: the manufacture of white and red lead and the creation of lake pigments from organic dyes.

Enduring white

Lead may have been liberated from its ores as early as the third millennium BC; there is extensive evidence of lead smelting in Anatolia from around 2300 BC. The manufacture of white lead from the metal is remarkable partly for its methodical and protracted character and partly for its longevity: much the same process described by Theophrastus, Pliny and Vitruvius, and most probably employed centuries earlier in Egypt, was still in use in the nineteenth century. It is likely that this method was also practised in China from around 300 BC.

White lead is basic lead carbonate (see page 34). It is made via an intermediate substance, the salt lead acetate, which is formed when acetic acid reacts with lead metal. Acetic acid is a primary constituent of vinegar, and was in no short supply in the viticultural society of Egypt.

This is how the transformation was achieved. Lead strips were placed in clay pots that had a separate compartment for vinegar. Stacks of these pots were left in a sealed shed with animal dung. The vinegar fumes convert lead to its acetate, while carbon dioxide gas from fermentation of the dung combines with water to generate carbonic acid. This acid advances the transformation from lead acetate to lead carbonate. It really amounts to nothing more than the corrosion of the metal by acids. But lead is an inert metal, sluggish to react – and the white pigment could take a month or more to mature.

The blue-green pigment verdigris (copper acetate) was made in a similar process, by corroding copper metal with vinegar fumes. Theophrastus provides the earliest known account of the method. Having described the manufacture of lead white (which he calls *psimythion*), he says: 'Also in a manner somewhat resembling this, verdigris [*ios*] is made, for copper is placed over lees [dregs] of wine, and the rust which it acquires by this means is taken off for use.'[13]

Pliny repeats this description, calling the pigment *aerugo* or 'copper rust'. He says that *aerugo* can also be scraped from natural copper ore, indicating that he drew no distinction between verdigris proper (the acetate salt) and the naturally occurring copper carbonates of similar appearance.

From white lead one could make red lead, called *minium* in medieval manuscripts. In a tenth-century text describing the Roman arts of colour-making, the monk Heraclius describes how the transformation is effected by heat. Vitruvius asserts that the process was discovered by the accidental exposure of white lead to fire, which seems entirely likely. Pliny calls red lead 'false sandarach' – true sandarach being the rare orange-red realgar. The abundant use of minium in the small, exquisite scenes of medieval manuscript illumination gives us the word 'miniature', from the Latin *miniare*, 'to colour with minium'. The contemporary connotation of a miniature as a small-scale work is thus quite unconnected with the Latin *minimus*, 'smallest'.

Red lead is used lavishly in Oriental art. Its manufacture is described in a Chinese manuscript from the fifth century BC, and it was known during the Han Dynasty (second century BC to second century AD) under the name 'lead cinnabar' (*ch'ien tan*) – cinnabar being a different red mineral. Red lead features particularly prominently in Indian and Persian 'miniatures' from the fifteenth to the nineteenth century, which are finely detailed but by no means tiny.

It is hard to imagine a history of art that lacked white lead, for the early alternatives – chalk and ground bone – cannot provide the ivory opacity that any artist needs. Not until the nineteenth century was white lead superseded by newer synthetic products; before this, it was the only white pigment on the European palette for easel painting in oils. How else but with this chemically manufactured substance could the bright highlights of Renaissance chiaroscuro have been achieved? Where else could the Dutch Masters of the Baroque era have found a white to stand up to their deep blacks? And as an added bonus, the ubiquity of this pigment lets us see the prevarications of the Old Masters. Lead absorbs X-rays strongly, and so X-rays reveal the white underpainting of a work's planning stages (see page 290).

Lake colours

Cinnabar and red lead have an orange tint, and red ochre is dull. The dyers of ancient Egypt enjoyed the richer, darker hue of kermes – but with occasional exceptions such as indigo, dyes are too translucent to serve as paints on wood, stone or plaster. The Egyptians knew of a solution to this shortcoming, although we cannot tell if they invented it. The water-soluble crimson dye is affixed to an inorganic, colourless 'carrier' powder, generating a relatively opaque solid material called a lake pigment.

'Lake' is now a generic label for any dye-based pigment, but once it pertained to red alone. In the Middle Ages red lake was made not just from the gummy secretion of the kermes insect (which became known as carmine lake) but from a related resin called *lac*, *lak* or *lack*. This encrusts the twiggy branches of trees indigenous to India and South-East Asia, and is exuded by the scale insect *Laccifer lacca*. The modern lacquer shellac is a processed form of lac resin. Lac was imported to Europe in large quantities from the early thirteenth century, and as a result it became a blanket term for all red dye-based pigments – including those already in circulation, such as carmine.

Making a carmine lake pigment from kermes dye involved a *tour de force* of early chemistry. Medieval recipes are remarkably detailed, and there is no reason to suppose that the procedures of the ancient Egyptians were substantially different. A common method involved the roundabout route of first dyeing cloth or silk in the raw dye extracted from the crushed insects, and then boiling the clippings in lye to redissolve the dye. The dye was then extracted from hot alkaline solution by adding alum, which precipitates fine-grained alumina (hydrated aluminium oxide) when the solution is cooled. The dye is absorbed on to the surfaces of the alumina particles, which dry to a dark red powder.

Thus the lake pigment was often a by-product of the dyer's trade, manufactured from the offcuts and shearings. Cennino warns against this kind of second-hand product, however, saying that 'It does not last at all . . . and quickly loses its colour.'

The Egyptians also made a deep red dye from the root of the madder plant, of which more is said in Chapter 9. To judge from Heraclius's text in the tenth century, the art of making madder lake was well known to the Romans.

The four colours of Greece

Egyptian chemical art was of a robustly practical variety. But the ancient Greek philosophers were more comfortable with theorizing than with experimenting. It is for this reason that the chemistry of Classical Greece is relatively barren, almost oxymoronic – most of the Greeks' practical knowledge was imported from the East, and was conducted by craftsmen who held a lowly position in society. It is here that we find the origins of the prejudice against manual skills that pervaded medieval thought, influencing the views of Renaissance artists and persisting even today in the division between 'pure' and 'applied' science, or between science and technology.

How else but through a distaste for experiment can we explain the curious ideas about colour mixing advanced in the writings of Plato and Aristotle, which a craftsman could have dispelled in an instant? Democritus, the 'father of atoms', maintained resolutely that pale green (*chloron*) could be mixed from red and white. Plato defended his assertion that leek green (*prasinon*) could be made from 'flame colour' (*purron*, presumably an orange) and black (*melas*) with the lofty disclaimer that 'He . . . who should attempt to verify all this by experiment would forget the difference of the human and divine nature.'

Although not wholly averse to experiment, Aristotle too preferred doctrine, which is why his text *On Colours* is scarcely a painter's handbook.[14] He stresses that the true study of colour was to be conducted not 'by blending pigments as painters do', but by comparing reflected rays – in effect, by removing the physical substance (as Newton later would do so brilliantly).

From where did these scholars get their seemingly strange beliefs about colour-mixing relationships? To understand a culture's preconceptions about colour use, we must look to its colour theory and terminology. The Greek light–dark scale described in Chapter 1 reveals why, for example, Plato believed that red could be shifted towards green by adding a little 'light' (white).

It is hard to say to what extent the Greek dislike of pigment mixing was motivated by theoretical prejudice and to what extent practical experience – the loss of brilliance (see page 44) – played a part. Either way, it accentuated the painter's dependence on materials. There are plenty of hues in nature for which no pure pigment was available to the ancient artists, not the least of which was a convincing flesh tone for portraiture. Theophrastus states that a kind of red ochre called *miltos* (from Miletos) was found in many shades, some of which approached the rosiness of flesh. But most flesh tints, as well as other graduated shades, in the art of the ancient world were achieved by cross-hatching of tones rather than mixing pigments.

Because so little Greek painted art survives, we are forced to make deductions about the Greeks' use of colour from ancient writings – and these largely from the writers of the Roman Empire such as Plutarch, Vitruvius and Pliny who, unlike the Classical Greeks, wrote about art for its own sake. The belief, prevalent until the mid-Victorian era, that Greek sculpture was left in chalky whiteness rather than being coloured, is probably the most famous example of modern misconceptions about Classical art derived from a misguided aesthetic bias (the supposed 'purity' of white). To the Greeks there was nothing sacred about plain stone that required it to be preserved from an enlivening lick of paint. Nor were they subtle about it: beards were deep blue (a kind of black, remember) and, if we can judge from Roman statues and relief works, gods often had bright red faces.

There is ample reason to suppose that most if not all the pigments known to the Egyptians were available to the Greek painters as well. Yet both Pliny and Cicero insist that four-colour painting (see page 14) was a strong tradition during the heyday of Classical Greek art, around the fourth century BC. The age-induced discolouration of many of the pigments in surviving Greek and Roman art has no doubt encouraged a sombre palette; but there is more to it than that. Pliny names several renowned four colour artists from this period: the pre-eminent Apelles, along with Aetion, Melanthius and Nicomachos. Cicero's list has a slightly longer reach, including the early-fifth-century painter Polygnotos as well as Zeuxis and Timanthes from the early fourth century. The tradition of limiting the palette seems to have begun in the mid-fifth century BC, when Empedocles was refining the idea of the four elements and Democritus was postulating atoms.

Nietzsche proposed rather contentiously that the Greek painters avoided blue and green because they 'dehumanize nature more than any other colour'. But the real reason is probably more practical than metaphysical. During the fifth century BC the Greek artists began to paint three-dimensionally, using a chiaroscuro ('highlight and shadow') technique to depict depth. This development might have motivated the four-colour technique as a means of bringing colour under control while artists worked out how to manage light and dark. As Renaissance artists were to discover, the larger the palette, the more difficult it is to achieve harmony of hue and tone so that no one colour stands out jarringly from the others. By restricting the range of hues, and moreover by rendering them in low-keyed earth pigments rather than bright ones, it becomes easier to master a three-dimensional world of light and shadow.

Once this system was in place, it may have metamorphosed from a technical necessity into an aesthetic principle. Pliny makes no bones about his preference for 'austere' over 'florid' colours. That Rome inherited the tradition can be seen, for instance, in the four-colour 'Alexander' mosaic in the House of the Faun at Pompeii (which is in fact a copy of a painting by Philoxenos of Eritrea, a pupil of Nicomachos) (Plate 3.4).

Yet pure, bright colours were not shunned in the decorative arts. They were used by the Greeks to adorn buildings, as evident in the reds and yellows at Olynthus, dating from the fifth to fourth century BC. Egyptian blue frit has been found in wall paintings at Knossos in Crete dating from before 2100 BC, on buildings from the Mycenaean period of ancient Greece (around 1400 BC), and on artefacts throughout the waxing and waning of Greek civilization. Theophrastus says that an artificial blue pigment was imported from Egypt, suggesting that the Greeks did not know how (or did not bother) to make it. The Etruscans used Egyptian blue in the sixth century BC, as did the Romans who succeeded them. It is found not only on the walls of Pompeii but also unused in the city's colour shops, as well as in the tombs of Roman painters. There was ample justification for Owen Jones's choice of the antique palette, in spite of the formal absence of blue from Pliny's list of colours.

Chemistry ignited when West met East in the crucible of Hellenistic Alexandria, bringing the logical world-view of Classical Greece into contact with the Eastern penchant for practical experimentation. By the same token, the use of colour in Western art became more inventive and more gorgeous when Alexander's empire found new aesthetics and new materials in the East.

The bright red mineral cinnabar (mercury sulphide), for example, was used as a pigment in China long before it appeared in the West. Even the Egyptians may have been ignorant of it, and evidence of it in Greek art before Theophrastus' time is rare. Indigo was imported from India: the Greeks called it _indikon_, and Vitruvius tells how the Romans used it as an artist's pigment in the first century BC.

The Indian 'blood of dragons and of elephants' that Pliny disparages is a red resin extracted from Asian plants: according to one account it came from the fruit of the rattan palm _Calamus draco_, although art historian Daniel Thompson attributes it to the sap of the shrub *Pterocarpus draco*. Dragons, the legendary source, have left their mark in either case. In medieval times the colourant was known as dragonsblood, and was still believed to be literally that. Pliny is the first to mention the myth; later it became luridly embellished, as Jean Corbichon indicates in his translation of Bartholomew Anglicus's thirteenth-century *De proprietatibus rerum* (*On the Properties of Things*):

According to Avicenna [an Arabic alchemist], the dragon wraps his tail around the legs of the elephant, and the elephant lets himself sink upon the dragon, and the blood of the dragon turns the ground red; and all the ground that the blood touches becomes cinnabar, and Avicenna calls this dragonsblood.[15]

But perhaps more significant than an infusion of new 'florid' pigments was the brightly hued artistic aesthetic of Persia and India, contrasting with the austerity of the Greeks. It was this influence that led to the gorgeous riches of Byzantine art, later to inspire the Europeans towards bolder use of colour when it was brought west in the Crusades.

The Hellenistic culture had a more relaxed attitude to colour mixing, based on empiricism rather than misconceived dogma. Alexander of Aphrodisias in the third century AD explained how (contrary to Aristotle's belief) green could be made from yellow and blue, and violet from blue and red. But, he said, these 'artificial' (mixed) colours are no match for the corresponding pure hues seen in nature. And indeed they are not – for mixing requires good primaries if it is to avoid a loss of brilliance. Limitations of materials were restricting the artist's capabilities.

Wax works

The Classical artist sat at no easel, held no palette board, and did not create a work simply by applying a brush to a surface. For painting on wooden panels, Greek and Roman artists used the technique of wax encaustic (from the Greek *enkaustikos*, 'to burn in'). Beeswax was heated over coals and mixed with pigments (and sometimes with resins), and the molten mixture was applied to the surface with a hot spatula. Finally, the colours were burned into the wood with hot irons held close to the paint surface.

This method is surprisingly robust, and attempts have been made to revive it in later times – notably by the German J. H. Müntz in the eighteenth century through his book *Encaustic: Or Count Caylus's Method of Painting in the Manner of the Ancients* (1760). The German art academic Max Doerner recounts how one Herr Fernbach touted an elaborate and spurious recipe for the 'Pompeiian' encaustic technique in 1845 that involved 'wax, oil of turpentine, Venice turpentine, amber varnish, and India rubber'.

None the less, says Doerner, paintings in wax encaustic may be 'durable beyond a doubt'. The wax does not discolour, and creates a hard, strongly coloured finish. It is stable enough in the hot, dry Mediterranean climate, but it translates less well to the dampness of northern Europe. Apelles reputedly invented a dark protective varnish that, says Pliny, softened the tones of his paintings and made them look even more naturalistic.

Wax encaustic does not work well for murals, however – Pliny calls it 'alien to that application', and no instances of its use have been found on interior or exterior walls at Pompeii. (All the same, wax colours are seen on stonework such as Trajan's column in Rome, and a wax layer was often applied to painted walls for protection.) Wall paintings were generally produced by brushing the pigment, mixed with a little water and gum, on to wet, 'fresh' plaster: the technique is now known by its Italian name, *fresco*. The plaster for wall murals was typically made from sand and lime. The lime binds the sand grains as it dries, and is then slowly transformed in air to chalky calcium carbonate. The pigment is applied as a wash over the penultimate layer of wet plaster, and a final thin layer of plaster is applied over the top. The pigment becomes dispersed and fixed in the plaster as it dries. This method tends to produce colours with a slightly chalky appearance.

The fresco technique used at Pompeii, which Vitruvius describes, is very elaborate. Six coats of plaster were applied: the first three with increasingly finer grades of sand, the final three with ground marble instead to give a hard, glossy finish. The dried wall was then polished to a mirror-like smoothness. This laborious process paid off: many of the Pompeiian murals have lasted extremely well (Plate 3.5). But others were done more quickly and cheaply, using pigments mixed in glue (distemper: see page 102) and applied to the dry plaster walls (*a secco*, as the Italians would say). Colours applied this way can be rubbed away simply with a wet finger, and will not last long when exposed to sun and air. The twentieth-century Swiss artist Arnold Böcklin once attended an excavation of some frescos at the Forum in Rome in which the colours, as fresh as if recently painted when the fragments were first exhumed, rapidly faded once out in the open. Sometimes the past is too fragile to bear our gaze.

4. Secret Recipes

ALCHEMY'S ARTISTIC LEGACY

For although men normally accord highest rank to, and guard with
the greatest care, every precious thing that has been sought after
with much sweat and acquired at extreme expense, yet if now and
then similar or better things turn up or are found for nothing, they
are guarded with similar or even greater vigilance.

Theophilus, *De diversis artibus* (*c.* 1122)

Simple substances, vegetable, mineral and viscous. Leave to simmer
in the crucible of the well-born artisan's heart, stir well and serve
flaming.

Georges Duthuit, *The Fauvist Painters* (1950)

If we are to judge from Ben Jonson's play *The Alchemist*, first staged
at London's Globe Theatre in 1610, the art of alchemy was not
highly esteemed in Shakespeare's England. Subtle, the title role, is
an unabashed 'coz'ner at large', a con-man who bedazzles the
credulous with mystical prattle while cheating them of their money.
Although there is never any doubt that Subtle is a bogus alchemist,
it is possible that Jonson wished to cast similar aspersions on those
who claimed to be authentic practitioners. The mockery is all the
more pointed because Jonson was no ignorant outsider constructing
straw men. It has been asserted that his knowledge of alchemy 'was
greater than that of any other major English literary figure, with the
possible exceptions of Chaucer and Donne'. When Subtle speaks
in impenetrable alchemical language, he is by and large using the
same terms as practising alchemists, and with the correct sense. It is
likely that he is modelled after Simon Forman, a contemporaneous
pseudo-alchemist who was several times imprisoned for deception

but managed to make a lucrative living selling love potions, charms and 'many strange and uncouth things' to the gullible society ladies of London.

Chaucer shared Jonson's scepticism. The Canon in his *Canterbury Tales* (c. 1387) is an archetypal 'puffer', one who laboured in vain in a smoky laboratory to make the Philosopher's Stone that transforms base metals to gold. As such, he is a shabby, bedraggled sight: 'His over cote is not worthe a myte . . . it is al filthy and to-tore.' As his assistant tells in the *Canon's Yeoman's Tale*, others of the same profession are no better than Subtle: one of the Yeoman's former employers swindled an avaricious priest with a fraudulent demonstration of the transmutation of base metals to silver.

This popular image of alchemists as charlatans and mountebanks has left chemistry eager to evade association with its predecessor. But in recent times alchemy has begun to shed its tarnished reputation, as scholarly studies have fleshed out a more faithful picture of its goals, its practitioners and its legacy. Without a doubt there were many rogues and tricksters who claimed alchemical allegiance; and there were also the ignorant puffers for whom greed rather than curiosity was the prime motivation. But for most true and knowledgeable 'adepts' of the esoteric art, wealth was not the objective. Theirs was an inquiry into the nature of the world, in which the properties of matter and its transformations were inseparable from the attributes of Man and his spiritual life.

Until the seventeenth century, it was perfectly common for educated people to have some knowledge of alchemy. The great thirteenth-century scholars Albertus Magnus and Roger Bacon were familiar not only with alchemical tradition and literature but also with its practical methods; Bacon's experimental skill enabled him to improve the recipe for gunpowder. Martin Luther confessed that 'The art of alchemy . . . appeals to me very much . . . on account of its allegories and secret meanings, which are quite beautiful.' Luther's contemporary Paracelsus, the Swiss physician often regarded as the father of chemotherapeutic medicine, was one of the most influential alchemists of the sixteenth century. Isaac Newton possibly spent more time on his alchemical experiments than on the physical theories that transformed eighteenth-century science; but by his day such interests were regarded as somewhat disreputable, and he took great pains to conceal them.

Several artists too were alchemically literate. The woodcut illustrator Hans Weiditz of the Augsburg school, a contemporary of Albrecht Dürer and Lucas Cranach, has left us one of the most arresting visions of the alchemist at work in a picture dating from 1520 (Figure 4.1). Dürer himself filled his copperplate engraving *Melancolia* (1514) with alchemical symbolism; this features also in works by Cranach, Grünewald and Jan van Eyck. Its influence was not confined to the North: the Italian artists Giorgione, Campagnola and Parmigianino also appear to have woven alchemical allegories into their pictures.

Alchemy's principal influence on art is not, however, as a source of cryptic symbolism. For its origins lie not in the metaphysics but in the practical crafts of ancient times. Alchemy is, at root, an art of transformation. It provided a theoretical framework that enabled experimenters to make some sense of the changes that the agencies of fire, water, air, vapours and time wrought on materials. Since, as

Figure 4.1

An alchemist at work in his laboratory, from a woodcut by Hans Weiditz in 1520. The bellows, used for raising the temperature of the furnace fires, are a reminder of why alchemists were often disparaged as 'puffers'.

we have seen already, these changes were often accompanied by an alteration in colour, it can come as no surprise that practical alchemy became the means by which artificial colours were provided to artists. Cennino Cennini, ever a practical man, refers time and again in *Il Libro dell'Arte* to the preparation of pigments by alchemy, and there is no reason to suppose that he considered he was doing other than telling his readers that their materials could be manufactured industrially.

But just as 'chemist' today can denote an academic scientist or a high-street drug dispenser, so 'alchemist' meant many things. The medieval artists bought their materials from apothecaries and pharmacists – tradespeople who may have manufactured pigments personally. They were a distinct bunch from the 'chrysopoeian adepti', those who sought the esoteric secrets that enabled the transmutation of lead into gold, or who wrestled with the philosophical and religious aspects of the art. In his seminal work *The Sceptical Chymist* (1665), the chemist Robert Boyle makes it clear that there is a line to be drawn between the practical 'laborants' – Chaucer's puffers, whose brains, says Boyle, were 'troubled with the smoak of their own furnaces' – and the theory-oriented 'adepti'. Charlatans and fools populate the former group, Boyle asserts, while the latter are serious-minded fellows.

At least, that is what Boyle would like us to believe – since he aspired to be an adept himself.[1] But the distinction was surely more akin to that often drawn today between graphic and fine art, or technology and science: the laborants might harbour a desire to attain the status of adepts; the adepts look upon the laborants as vulgar recipe-followers. The two may not share common cause, but they draw from the same intellectual well. In alchemy, colour is the crucial link between theory and practice. It was the key to the chrysopoeian art, and one can hardly imagine that the discoveries made in these endeavours would not have filtered down to the prosaic level of pigment manufacture. It is no coincidence that artists and alchemists were using the same materials.

And we must remember that magic was as real to the ordinary folk of the Middle Ages as it was to the alchemical adepts. Magic was woven into the fabric of Western culture, and for long centuries the threads would have parted without it. It was blended with religious belief, to the occasional discomfort of the Church. Painting too was primarily a religious affair: at the same time a mundane craft and a devotional activity that could be invested with a spiritual power akin to that of the art of ancient Egypt. Small wonder, then, that the colours of the painter could surpass their own materiality and take on an almost divine significance. When the sixteenth-century Venetian writer Paolo Pino called the composition of colours on canvas 'the true alchemy of painting', we must bear in mind that he is not using the word 'alchemy' in the glib and debased manner that is popular today. He means to imply a genuine correspondence whereby, as art historian Martin Kemp writes, the materials 'mysteriously transcend the nature of their individual parts'.

The Great Work

Take the vitriol of Venus . . . and add thereto the elements water and air. Resolve, and set to putrefy for a month according to the instructions . . . Separate and you will soon see two colours, namely white and red. The red is above the white. The red tincture of vitriol is so powerful that it reddens all white bodies, and whitens all red ones, which is wonderful. Work upon this tincture by means of a retort, and you will perceive a blackness issue forth. Treat it again by means of the retort, repeating the operation until it comes out whitish . . . Rectify until you find the true, clear Green Lion . . .[2]

Never before or since the Middle Ages was colour so central to chemistry. We can recognize through their colour changes the transformations, albeit half-obscured by the alchemists' secretive terminology, that these proto-chemists were conducting in their elaborate alembics and pelicans. For all its mythical resonance, vitriol of Venus is nothing other than the blue copper sulphate, familiar from many a school laboratory.

Colour underpins the alchemical belief in transmutation. A substance's colour was deemed an outward manifestation of its inner properties. Lacking much information beyond this superficial characteristic, alchemists had every reason to suppose that a metal with the appearance of gold was none other than gold itself. Thus we risk mistaking genuine conviction for improbity. The scientist and historian Joseph Needham has pointed out that the distinction between counterfeiting and transmuting gold is a cultural one – it depends on what you think you are doing. In the chemistry handbooks of antiquity, fraud tends to be explicit: a recipe in the Leiden papyrus (see page 67) for faking gold from copper comments reassuringly on the difficulty of detection, while another for faking silver warns of the possibility that silversmiths might notice the difference.

The language of dyeing and colouring suffuses the alchemical literature. Stones and metals may be 'dyed' as readily as textiles. The Philosopher's Stone itself is commonly called the Tincture.

It has been suggested that this wondrous red substance, also called the 'Red King', was none other than vermilion, the medieval painter's finest red pigment. Vermilion is a synthetic form of mercury sulphide; as we saw earlier, the natural form (the mineral cinnabar) served as a pigment from antiquity. According to the tradition of the influential eighth-century Arabic alchemist Jabir ibn Hayyan (known in the West as Geber), sulphur and mercury (medieval writers call it 'quicksilver') are the elementary 'principles' from which all metals are formed. In Jabir's scheme, base metals like lead differ from gold only in their relative proportions of the two principles, and so they can be elevated to gold simply by adjusting the mixture. Albertus Magnus wrote that 'we may say that in the constitution of metals Sulphur is like the substance of the male semen and Quicksilver like the menstrual fluid that is coagulated into the substance of the embryo'.[3] These two principles were brought into perfect balance in gold, whose yellow tint was attributed to the presence of sulphur. Thus vermilion apparently contains the two ingredients necessary to effect transmutation of all metals.

But we must be careful. The sulphur and mercury of vermilion are not at all the same as Jabir's Sulphur and Quicksilver. These principles are 'subtle', intangible substances, of which earthly sulphur and mercury are but corrupt shadows. Thus it is highly doubtful that vermilion was ever truly regarded as the Tincture, especially since it was relatively easy to manufacture. Some recipes for the Philosopher's Stone, in fact, use cinnabar as the mere starting material.

Vermilion – a marriage of fundamental substances – was none the less of indisputable interest to alchemists, and knowledge of its synthesis was derived from their writings. The process may have been invented in China, and around AD 300 the Hellenistic alchemist Zosimus of Panopolis hints that he knows of it. But the first clear description occurs in the eighth- or early-ninth-century manuscript *Compositiones ad tingenda* (*Recipes for Colouring*). The works attributed to Jabir also mention how mercury and sulphur unite to form a red substance, and the ninth-century text *Mappae clavicula* (*Little Key to Painting*) includes two recipes for making it.

All this cannot but have been to the advantage of painters, who considered synthetic mercury sulphide superior to cinnabar. Cennino says that the pigment 'is made by alchemy, prepared in a retort [a closed vessel]'. But he cares little for the symbolic resonances of this process, and declines to relate the technical details with the dismissive comment that it would be 'too tedious'. Buy it ready-made, he advises – but in an unbroken lump, for unscrupulous apothecarists were known to dilute the precious substance with red lead or brick dust.

The Benedictine monk Theophilus (Roger of Helmarshausen) is more expansive in his technical handbook *De diversis artibus* (*On Divers Arts*) (*c.* 1122), describing a dramatic alchemical synthesis in which sulphur and mercury are placed in a sealed pot and buried in 'blazing coals'. 'You hear a crashing noise inside,' he says, 'as the mercury unites with the blazing sulphur.' Perhaps Theophilus is more entranced by the mystery: the manufacture of vermilion was still novel in Europe in the twelfth century, whereas it was commonplace in Cennino's lifetime.

Daniel Thompson regards the synthesis of vermilion as the central technological innovation of medieval painting:

No other scientific invention has had so great and lasting an effect upon painting practice as the invention of this colour ... If the Middle Ages had not had this brilliant red, they could hardly have developed the standards of colouring which they upheld; and there would have been less use for the inventions of other brilliant colours which come on the scene in and after the twelfth century.[4]

It was certainly the medieval prince of reds. It is used sparingly in early medieval manuscripts; until at least the eleventh century it remained as costly to cover the page with vermilion as with gold. But by the early fifteenth century it is employed with abandon (Plate 4.1), and during the Renaissance it is ubiquitous.

The pigment in these pictures was produced by the direct synthesis of the elements, as Theophilus relates – the so-called dry process. This generally produced a lump of solid red vermilion. 'If you grind it every day for twenty years,' said Cennino, 'the colour would still become finer and more handsome.'

The dry-process synthesis was later modified in Holland, which became the principal centre of vermilion manufacture in Europe in the seventeenth century. In the Dutch method, mercury and sulphur combine to form a black form of mercury sulphide, sometimes called the *Aethiops mineralis*, with a slightly different crystal structure from the red form. The black material is then pulverized and sublimated by strong heating, whereupon it is converted to red vermilion.

In 1687 a German chemist named Gottfried Schulz found that the ethiops mineral can be converted to red vermilion by heating it in a solution of ammonium or potassium sulphide. This 'wet' process is less laborious and less costly than the Dutch method, and also produces a finer powder with uniform grain size and an orange-red colour, as compared with the bluish red of the dry-process product. Most vermilion in the West today is made using the wet process.

Making the Tincture

There is good reason to argue that red is the primary hue of both medieval chemistry and art. Alchemy accords red a special significance. It is the 'colour' of gold (which was more beautiful when more ruddy) and it signifies the culmination of the Great Work: the creation of the Philosopher's Stone. 'Red is last in the work of Alkimy,' said the fifteenth-century alchemist Norton of Bristol.

The preparation of this fabled substance is described in several surviving medieval texts. In general these recipes say that a particular sequence of colour changes indicates the successful progress of the Work. Before ending in red, the transformations were commonly supposed to generate the other three principal colours of the Classical world: black, white and yellow, in that order.

The American chemist Arthur Hopkins, attempting in 1934 to unravel the actual chemical transformations that alchemists were conducting, regards the critical colour sequence as black–white–yellow–purple – a progression reported by Zosimos. According to Hopkins, the alchemist began his work with a black alloy of lead, tin, copper and iron: the *tetrasoma*, or four-membered body. Adding arsenic or mercury formed a white surface coating. Yellowing was achieved by adding gold or 'sulphur water' (a solution of hydrogen sulphide). The final step of *iosis* generated a purple colour that Hopkins regards as a violet-bronze gold-containing alloy.

Some modern scholars of alchemy have asserted that *iosis* denotes the formation of a red rather than a purple substance. But to the medieval scholar this would have been a meaningless distinction, since purple was generally deemed a kind of red. The medieval red pigment sinoper, for instance, was equivalently known as porphyry, the Greek word for purple. And it seems likely that an adept of the Middle Ages would have perceived a symbolic significance in the association of the chrysopoeian sequence with the colour quartet of antiquity. Thus the appearance of *either* a bright red *or* a deep purple colour in the retort would have been considered a sign of success. It is no wonder that one adept might have been experimenting on a quite different set of compounds from another.

Both arsenic and lead form simple compounds that can be interconverted between red, yellow, white and black materials – some of which were used by artists. For the alchemical adept, an attraction of arsenic – not then recognized as an independent element – is that it was commonly confused with sulphur. Yellow arsenic sulphide – orpiment – was often regarded as a variant of pure sulphur. It is found naturally in mineral form, but artists preferred a synthetic version. Cennino considers this synthesis a task best left to the alchemists – for orpiment is 'really poisonous', and the painter should 'beware of soiling your mouth with it'. As for realgar, the orange form of arsenic sulphide, 'there is no keeping company with it . . . Look out for yourself.'

We can conjecture that lead held a similar attraction to alchemists, but for the drawback that its compounds are harder to purify using heat alone. It too can be interconverted between black (metallic lead and lead dioxide), white (white lead), yellow (massicot: lead monoxide) and red (red lead: lead tetroxide) forms by chemical transformations involving heat (see page 34). Red lead shares the orange tint of vermilion or cinnabar, and there was much scope for confusion of the two. Georgius Agricola calls red lead *minium* in his *De re metallica* (1556); but to Pliny *minium* denotes cinnabar, and red lead is merely *minium secondarium*. The distinction may have been further blurred by the common practice of adulterating ground vermilion with the cheaper lead pigment.

Red lead was also conflated with realgar (Pliny's 'sandarach').And Cennino creates more confusion by speaking of a red pigment called cinabrese, apparently not related to cinnabar but to sinoper, the red ochre preferred by the classically-minded Pliny. Daniel Thompson says, 'The confusion of medieval terminology in regard to red colours is immense. *Minium* and *miltos* and *cinabrum* and *sinopis* and *sandaracca* are a complicated tangle' – into which we can weave also the problem of vermilion and *vermiculum* mentioned previously (page 67). There is no reason to suppose that chrysopoeian alchemists had these distinctions any clearer in their minds than did the pharmacists and apothecaries who made and supplied artists' colours, or the scholars who wrote about them.

Close inspection of the recipes given for pigment manufacture reveals an influence of not only the practical but also the theoretical side of alchemy. The ratio of sulphur to mercury recommended for the synthesis of vermilion by several sources, including Theophilus and Albertus Magnus, does not accord with their actual proportions in the compound. The substance contains a little over six times more mercury, by weight, than sulphur; yet medieval recipes specify a ratio of typically 2:1. The practical alchemists were certainly skilled enough to spot an error of this magnitude, which would be evident from a residue of unreacted sulphur in their flasks – yet apparently they persisted with the 'wrong' quantities. This can be rationalized, however, if one assumes that equal amounts of sulphur and mercury were considered necessary to give a perfect 'balance' in chrysopoeian terms. This corresponds to a 2:1 ratio according to the relative weights posited by the Aristotelian system of elements, which underpins all of medieval alchemy. Thus the recipes may be knowingly erroneous to fulfil theoretical criteria. Whether Theophilus and other writers of handbooks knew of these considerations, or simply perpetuated an error picked up from alchemical sources, is not clear.

Art conservator Spike Bucklow has suggested that some of the other pigment recipes recorded by Theophilus and Cennino can also be interpreted in terms of alchemical theory. Theophilus tells how to make a colour called Spanish gold (the name immediately speaks of a Moorish, and thus alchemical, origin). Amongst the sound practical advice in his manual, Theophilus' prescription here seems to suffer an outbreak of pure magical thinking: 'There is also a gold named Spanish gold, which is compounded from red copper, basilisk powder, human blood, and vinegar. The heathen, whose skill in this art is commendable, create basilisks for themselves in this way . . .'[5] He goes on to explain how these fabulous creatures emerge from hen's eggs hatched by toads fed on bread. 'When the eggs are hatched, male chickens emerge just like chickens born of hens, and after seven days serpent tails grow on them.' The blood, meanwhile, must come from a red-haired man, and must be dried and ground. Of course, there is nothing particularly outlandish in a twelfth-century belief in basilisks, but Bucklow suggests that this can be seen as an allegory for the preparation of an alchemical elixir from a red 'sulphur' (the blood) and a white 'mercury' (the basilisk ash). Certainly, the reference to the pigment as 'a gold' suggests that the author saw no reason to distinguish it from the metal itself.

Bucklow also posits alchemical influences in some of the recipes for yellow pigments, such as mosaic gold (see page 111) and lead-tin yellow (see page 113). Their ingredients can be interpreted as allegorical sulphurs and mercuries combined with a third 'principle', salt. This triumvirate was popularized by Paracelsus, but its origin is probably older.

Alchemical theory and pigment manufacture intersect even in the works of Robert Boyle. In his *Origine of Formes and Qualities* (1666) Boyle describes the extraction of a blue tincture from copper metal, leaving a residue of a white metal 'exactly comparable to silver'. The idea of tinging (or in this case, bleaching) metals was clearly alive and well in the seventeenth century.[6]

Reading nature's secrets

There is a striking contrast between the writings of the alchemists, wreathed in arcane terminology and symbolism designed to exclude the non-initiate, and the ingenuous recipe lists of Theophilus and Cennino, who talk about some of the same chemical transformations in plain terms and in the same breath as they describe how to make engraving tools, church organs, distempered walls and body casts. Nevertheless, many of the craftsman's manuals from which much current knowledge of ancient and medieval pigment manufacture derives, such as the Leiden and Stockholm papyri, stem directly from the alchemical tradition.

Technical handbooks ambivalently called Books of Secrets were widespread in the early Middle Ages. These works were bizarre anthologies, collating medical and culinary recipes, practical tips on crafts such as gilding and stained-glass-making, amalgamated with magical formulae, parlour tricks and practical jokes. They came from a long tradition of encyclopedic compilations, which can be traced back as far as the Assyrian civilization and embraces the synoptic works of Roman writers such as Pliny's *Natural History*. These were regarded in their time as short cuts to the vast learning of the ancient world.

In Hellenistic Egypt, steeped in alchemy, these collections meta-morphosed into a more cryptic format. Pliny's *Natural History* purports simply to describe nature, whereas the alchemical or 'Hermetic' compilations of Egypt take a different attitude to the natural world. Scientific truths known to the ancients cannot, they say, be accessed by rational inquiry or from literary inscriptions, but only by divine revelation. This lends a decidedly ambiguous flavour to the Leiden and Stockholm papyri. At face value they are plain lists of recipes. Yet they seem to be descended from an alchemical treatise of the first century AD called *Physica et mystica*, by Bolos of Mendes. The author of the papyri was probably an alchemist, but the works have lost the mystical dimension of *Physica et mystica*, in which this mysterious declaration is appended to all the recipes: 'One nature delights in another nature; one nature triumphs over another nature; one nature dominates another nature.'

In the technical craft manuals of the early Middle Ages this alchemical or esoteric theoretical component has atrophied, and what is left is a strange mixture indeed. The recipes persist, copied with uneven fidelity from older texts; but their utility as guides for the craftsman is highly questionable. Poorly transcribed, 'born of drudgery, not inspiration' as engineer and historian Cyril Stanley Smith puts it, they had become confused and all but useless as 'how to' instruction booklets. It is clear from the misconceptions they perpetuate that the authors had little practical experience in the arts: they are monks working as copyists, perhaps with no interest at all in the material. These books of rote prescriptions hold a distorted mirror to the learning and technology of ancient times, and they show scant evidence of having been subjected to the wear and tear of a workshop environment.

So what purpose did they serve? Probably an esoteric one. No longer explicitly magical, the books were nevertheless apparently regarded as 'keys' to the lost wisdom of the Classical world. To the early medieval monk, this knowledge bordered on the sacred. The word of Aristotle (or whatever version of it found its way to medieval eyes) had an almost divine authority, and dissent was akin to heresy. One of the works in which this knowledge was brought together is the *Mappae clavicula*, which originates from ninth-century southern Italy. Only fragments of this work survive, some of them later transcriptions. 'Key' is to be understood here not in the sense of a step-by-step set of instructions, for all that the work is full of recipes for making pigments, coloured glass and so forth. Rather, the key unlocks ancient insights. Or such, at least, was the hope of the monks who would have kept the text in the library and referred to it with reverence: 'For just as access to locked houses is impossible without a key . . . so also, without this commentary, all that appears in the sacred writings will give the reader a feeling of exclusion and darkness.'[7]

These works were rather repetitive and derivative: recipes from the *Mappae clavicula* can be found in scores of later manuscripts, and can themselves be identified in a slightly earlier manuscript, the *Compositiones ad tingenda* of the eighth or early ninth century – which is itself linked to Alexandrian alchemical works. The implication that these works were 'keys' is particularly explicit in *De coloribus et artibus Romanorum* (*On the Colours and Arts of the Romans*), a tenth-century work by the Italian monk Heraclius. He says:

Who is now able to show us what these artificers, powerful by their immense intellect, discovered for themselves? He who, by his powerful virtue, holds the keys of the mind, divides the pious hearts of men among various arts.[8]

These manuscripts are clearly from the secretive tradition, circumscribed with warnings not to let this arcane lore fall into vulgar hands. The author of the *Mappae clavicula* swears that he will hand on his learning to no one except his son, 'when he has first judged his character and decided whether he can have a pious and just feeling about these things and can keep them secure'.

But despite their lack of inspiration, the compilations provide valuable insights into the chemistry of the Middle Ages. The *Compositiones*, for example, introduces the term 'vitriol' for iron sulphate, later to become associated with acids. A twelfth-century version of the *Mappae clavicula* includes a recipe for distilling alcohol, a 'water' that burned.

As the arts and crafts became increasingly secular in the Middle Ages, and the profession of painting was transferred from monks to lay tradesmen, little more than lip-service was paid to the need for secrecy in transmitting the 'secrets of nature'. Indeed, the Books of Secrets became a genre in which the very suggestion of forbidden knowledge was used as a marketing strategy. Writers could make a living by recycling these putative arcana in a popularized manner. The German translation of Pseudo-Albertus's *Secreta mulierum* (*The Secrets of Women*) by Walther Hermann Ryff notched up thirty editions and was a best-seller in sixteenth-century Germany. The advent of printing turned such efforts into the popular science of its day, spawning the German *Kunstbüchlein* ('skills booklets') which became extremely widespread in the sixteenth and seventeenth centuries.

Some of the *Kunstbüchlein* drew heavily on the *Secreti* (1555) of Alessio Piemontese, who was possibly a pseudonymous character invented by the Italian writer Girolamo Ruscelli (1500–*c.* 1566), complete with an exotic personal history to lend colour to his work. These 'secrets' are mundane fare: medical treatments for burns, bites, sores, fevers and warts, recipes for domestic items such as perfumes, body powders and soaps. (In the sixteenth century the physician Cornelius Agrippa recounted a proverb: 'Every alchemist is either a physician or a soap-maker'.) But scattered through the *Secreti* are technical procedures for the craftsman, including a recipe for ultramarine and descriptions of the methods of Italian artists. Translations of the *Secreti* may have been a primary source of information on these matters for northern European painters and craftsmen.

From monk to guildsman

Against this chequered history of the transmission of technical know-how in the arts and crafts, Theophilus's book stands out for its unusual directness and clarity. It is no random collection of snippets from ancient books, but presents systematically the techniques of the practising artist. Indeed, unlike the authors of most of the recipe collections, Theophilus was a practising artist: his formulations bear the stamp of experience. And there is no call for secrecy, but instead an entreaty towards openness: 'Let [the artisan] not hide his gifts in the purse of envy, nor conceal them in the storeroom of a selfish heart but . . . let him simply and with a cheerful mind dispense to those who seek.'[9] To Theophilus, art was a devotional activity, the aim of which was to glorify God. To this extent he exemplifies the painter of the twelfth century: a monk, whose work is exclusively religious, and who is accomplished in a variety of arts and crafts including manuscript illumination and metalwork. All of these, including painting, were conducted as anonymous activities – opportunities for pious meditation rather than for self-advancement. Even secular works in the early Middle Ages are usually unsigned. And the largest body of religious art from this time consists of illuminated manuscripts, the painstaking and often gorgeous work of innumerable nameless monks.

Little is said in Theophilus's book about design and composition. The emphasis is all on techniques and materials, strengthening the impression that much monastic painting was formulaic. The monk did not need guidelines for how to compose a scene – he'd merely copy another. Moreover, his choice of style and materials reflects a view of the world in which icons and images are not simply symbols of devotion but are invested with the power to intervene in everyday life. Several illuminations depict painters being rescued from misfortune as they work on images of the Virgin Mary. In one such, from the thirteenth-century *Las Cantigas* of King Alphonso the Wise of Castile, a devil causes a painter's scaffolding to collapse, but he is saved from falling by adhering to the picture of the Virgin on which he is working (Figure 4.2). Don't be misled by the resemblance to an amusing cartoon strip; scenes like this show that a well-made icon or picture was considered to possess real religious efficacy. The use of precious materials by artists, such as gold and ultramarine, does not simply imply a wish to show piety by lavishing expense but reveals the hope that the supernatural potency of the work will thereby be enhanced.

But between the eleventh and the fourteenth century, the practice of painting was transferred from the monastery to the towns, where it was conducted by lay professionals who considered themselves tradespeople with skills for hire. Inevitably, this had consequences both for working practices and for the art that was produced. Even

Figure 4.2

A painter working on an image of the Virgin Mary is saved from a fall
when a devil demolishes his scaffolding. The power of the image itself
confers protection.

if the distinction between monastic and lay craftsmen is on occasion over-emphasized – secular painters were sometimes employed by monasteries only to stay on and become monks – none the less artists were increasingly members of a profession: the 'peynturs' as they were known in England. They followed a trade like any other. Like the woodworker, the potter, the baker and the weaver, the painter offered his technical proficiency for a fee. He was by no means above asking the baker for use of his ovens to make charcoal, employed as a black pigment. Nor would the artist sneer at the cook, with whom he had many skills in common. Cennino assumes that the artist knows what he means by the instruction that plaster should be made as if preparing batter.

One of the consequences of this transition from monk to artisan was increasing specialization. Painters were just that, and not to be confused with illuminators, dyers or workers in wood and metal. Such distinctions were rigidly enforced by the guilds that developed to safeguard the employment of tradespeople against competition and economic uncertainty, and heaven forbid that a painter should be called in to illuminate a book page. There were even fine distinctions drawn among painters. In fifteenth-century Spain, one could find specialists in altarpiece painting, fabric painting and interior decorating. Concomitant with these divisions was a hier-archy of trades in which status tended to reflect the value of the materials. Goldsmiths were the most prestigious and powerful artisans, painters more humble, and woodworkers still more so. Guild restrictions prohibited the use of the most valuable pigments, such as ultramarine, for vulgar purposes such as the painting of playing cards, carts or 'parrot perches'. Thus these valuable pigments played a role in establishing the social standing of painters: it was in their interests to use fine materials.

Yet the art of painting was still regarded as a mechanical process. There was good and bad, to be sure, but the task of the painter was to meet the specifications of a contract, not to give free rein to artistic inspiration. It was the employer – the patron – who called the shots. Initially the patrons of lay painters, when not ecclesiastical, tended to be royal or aristocratic, and the painter could find him-self affiliated to a court. But as a prosperous middle class emerged during the late Middle Ages, the base of patronage broadened and artists could find commissions among the mercantile echelons of society.

Patrons were not noted for their originality of taste. Often they might request a painting imitating another that had taken their fancy. The artist might find room for personal flair in executing his designated subject, but under such a system conservatism was the order of the day. Such was the dominance of the patron in determining the subject matter of an image that *patron* in medieval terminology is a synonym for 'design'.

It was the patron, moreover, who would typically specify the materials to be used, generally insisting on the most lavish and opulent – whilst demanding that the painter kept his fees reasonable. A patron might even determine the supplier from which the artist bought materials – either by written agreement in the contract or by designating a price for the finest pigments, which ensured the artist did not seek them at lower cost from an inferior source. Assessors could be called in to verify that the painter had followed the contractual obligations concerning pigments.

Yet many patrons were not averse to economy, and the painters' guilds would often have to insist on their members' right to be permitted good, pure materials in the face of attempts to get a job done on the cheap.

Membership of a guild was attained by apprenticeship. Aspiring painters would serve a training period of typically between four and eight years in a workshop, beginning as all apprentices do with the most menial of tasks, such as grinding pigments and making glue. Pigment grinding was a particularly arduous and time-consuming job, and painters might need to allow several days for this alone in their scheduling for a commission (Plate 4.2). To qualify as a 'master painter' ready to accept contracts, an apprentice would present a 'master piece' to the guild for approval. Strange, then, that this term has come to refer to an artist's most accomplished piece of work rather than his or her first attempt to gain recognition.

A workshop undertook a commission as a group, much as a band of builders or thatchers would (and still does) perform a job collectively. The master or *magister* was responsible for the overall execution of the work, but the application of paint to surface was as much, if not more, the responsibility of his apprentices. Thus the signatures that appear on later medieval art are simply trade stamps, denoting the name of the workshop's master. This traditional training accorded little value to personal talent or inspiration: a person became a painter simply by dint of hard work, dedication and adherence to the master's demands. 'Skill', or what Theophilus calls *ingenium*, was the product of diligence.

Cennino's *Il Libro dell'Arte* was written within this later social context. The book was, he said, 'for the use and good profit of anyone who wants to enter the profession', not for the greater glory of God. To Cennino, the inspiration that drives one to become an artist is not divine, despite his invocation of 'High Almighty God, the Father, Son and Holy Ghost'. No, it is simply a delight in the creation of art – though the financial motive is not to be sneered at either:

There are those who pursue it, because of poverty and domestic need, for profit and enthusiasm for the profession too; but above all these are to be extolled the ones who enter the profession through a sense of enthusiasm and exaltation.[10]

This Humanistic spirit looks ahead to the Renaissance. Yet although Cennino's book is a late-fourteenth-century work, his outlook is still rooted in the Middle Ages, and his methods and attitudes show continuity with the medieval practices depicted by Theophilus almost three centuries earlier.

Work in progress

The tradesman's approach to art is reflected in the products of the medieval artist. These were typically functional and decorative: altarpieces, wall murals and book pages rather than works to be hung in a gallery. It is a testament to the human instinct for creativity that unmistakably great art could be generated 'on the job', as it were.

The main surface for medieval painting was parchment: the skins of calves, goats, sheep and deer, dried, stretched and scraped to a delicate smoothness – and no stranger to chemical treatment. Alkalis were applied to draw out the oils by converting them to soluble soap-like salts. Alum was used to make the material harder. Parchment might be dyed before use. In the most sumptuous works, whole pages were coloured a glorious purple using 'whelk red', a variant of the famous purple of Tyre, all the better to contrast with yellow gold leaf.

But most of the large-scale paintings of the Middle Ages that are still in existence are rendered on wood, carved and ornamented and often joined into two or more hinged panels in a polyptych. The wood was coated first with size and then with several layers of gesso, a kind of plaster-like undercoat that gave it a smooth surface. Gesso was composed of chalk, gypsum (calcium sulphate) or alabaster, bound with glue or gelatine so that the paste set hard. Thin gesso (*gesso sottile*) was used over areas of delicate carving that should not be obscured, and thick gesso (*gesso grosso*) for flat areas.

The preparation and application of gesso was a tedious affair, and therefore fit for apprentices. But it was nevertheless an essential and important part of the process, and Cennino provides very detailed instructions for how to conduct it. The chemistry is not by any means trivial. Ordinary plaster of Paris is made by heating gypsum or alabaster to drive off some of the water bound up in the mineral structure. Adding water to the powdered mineral lets it recrystallize and solidify; but if this recrystallization takes place in a size such as gelatine or glue, it happens more slowly and the crystals are welded together more robustly – with the result that the solid is harder.

Wall painting on plaster was also practised very widely in the Middle Ages, in churches as well as in private halls and palaces. Fresco painting on wet plaster produced robust results so long as the wall did not become exposed to moisture; but it required the painter to work fast, while the plaster was still damp. Curiously, some painters maintained that only natural mineral pigments were stable enough to use in fresco – a largely false distinction that might nevertheless have severely constrained the palette of fresco painters who heeded advice such as that of the Italian G. B. Armenini in 1587:

artificial pigments never do well in fresco, nor can any art make them last long without changing . . . you may leave to foolish painters those secrets of theirs, which no one envies them, of using vermilions and fine lakes; because . . . in the long run, their pictures become ugly daubs.[11]

Cennino himself proudly traced the provenance of his fresco technique to the Florentine artist Giotto di Bondone (c. 1266–1337), via Giotto's godson Taddeo Gaddi and Taddeo's son Agnolo, Cennino's teacher. The blue heavens in Giotto's frescos in the Arena Chapel in Padua (c. 1305) (Plate 4.3) are as glorious today as they were when visitors in the fourteenth century were promised a reduction of one year and forty days off their stay in Purgatory.

Giotto was also a master of *secco* wall painting, exemplified by his work in the Peruzzi Chapel in Florence. This technique, like panel painting, required a binding medium or tempera for the pigment. The tempera (from the Latin *temperare*, to mix) holds the pigment particles in place. In Italy, until the fifteenth century the principal binding medium for pictures painted on panels was egg yolk. Pigment mixed with yolk and a little water forms a fluid paste that dries to an opaque, smooth and durable finish. Egg yolk is a natural emulsion: a dispersion of oily droplets in water. The medieval painter might add a variety of substances to egg tempera to modify its behaviour. Vinegar, for instance, acted partly as a preservative (its acidity deters certain bacteria) and partly to offset excessive oiliness (which made the paint hard to work with). Fig-tree sap, soap, honey and sugar are variously mentioned in recipes through the ages, but Max Doerner, one of the twentieth-century authorities on old painting techniques, dismisses such adulteration: 'There is no end to tempera recipes. Their number is incredibly large. Most of them are not only useless but definitely harmful.'

Egg tempera is relatively quick-drying, and so the artist must work swiftly, especially when blending colours. Dry, aged egg tempera paint is virtually waterproof and, if skilfully prepared, discolours less rapidly than oil paints. Some of the colours in medieval tempera panels are more vivid today than those in Renaissance oils. On the other hand, the paint lacks the flexibility of oils and so has a tendency to crack if the wooden panel swells or shrinks owing to changes in temperature or humidity.

Cennino offers several prescriptions for egg tempera, and the rediscovery and translation of his book in the nineteenth century revitalized interest in the method. He recommends egg yolk not as an all-purpose binder but only for specific pigments, since the compatibility depends in part on how the yolk affects the pigment's optical properties. Cennino cautions that some pigments, such as blues and certain mixed greens, should be used only with size – basically a kind of gelatine and glue, made by boiling up trimmings or scrapings of animal-skin parchment or of rabbit skin. In distinction from egg tempera, paints in which pigments are suspended in size are commonly called 'distempers'.

Egg white was used as a binder for illuminated manuscripts under the name *glair*. It was liquefied by being whipped and left to stand, or squeezed in and out of a sponge. The eleventh-century manuscript *De clarea* (*On Brightness*) warns against the perils of insufficient whipping: 'when mixed with the colour it makes that colour string like a thread, and the colour is utterly ruined'.

The origin of oil painting is a complex and contentious matter, and I shall deal with it in the next chapter. It will suffice here to say that while the techniques of oil painting became pre-eminent throughout Europe during the fifteenth and sixteenth centuries – the period of the High Renaissance – there is clear evidence of its use at much earlier times, especially in northern Europe. But oil paints were long considered an inferior medium, fit only for mundane interior decoration: Theophilus describes the use of linseed oil as a binder for paint used to 'redden doors'.

Medieval colours

The red pigments that Theophilus mentions in this passage are minium and cinnabar – inherited from antiquity, like most other medieval pigments. Yet there were new discoveries too, and alchemy played a major role both in colour innovation and in providing a systematic technology for manufacturing.

Blues near and far

The most illustrious of these new pigments was the rich blue ultramarine. It is made by a laborious process (which I shall discuss in more detail in Chapter 10) from the blue mineral lapis lazuli. This semi-precious stone was widely used for decorative purposes from the beginnings of Egyptian civilization, but there is no indication that it was used as a pigment in antiquity. It seems likely that the process by which the blue pigment is extracted was an alchemical invention.

Lapis lazuli is found primarily in the East. The principal deposits throughout the Middle Ages were in Afghanistan, where a crude kind of ultramarine has been identified in wall paintings dating from the sixth and seventh centuries. Its use in the West did not become widespread until the fourteenth century. The name reflects the pigment's status as a long-distance import: in 1464 the Italian A. A. Filarete wrote in *Trattato dell'Architettura* (*A Treatise on Architecture*) that 'Fine blue is derived from a stone and comes from across the seas and so is called ultramarine.' This, in conjunction with the difficult process of extraction, meant that the pigment was very expensive and highly prized.

A less costly (but by no means cheap) blue was the mineral azurite, a form of 'basic' copper carbonate (see page 34). Its sources were closer to home for the Western artist: there were deposits in eastern France, Hungary, Germany and Spain. The Romans used it: to Pliny the mineral was called *lapis armenius*, reflecting its Armenian source. Azurite was often called German azure ('azure of Almayne') in medieval England; the Germans themselves referred to it as *Bergblau*, 'mountain blue'. Albrecht Dürer, like most of his compatriots, relied mostly on local azurite for his best blues, as celebrated in a poem of 1552 by Kaspar Scheit:

> After a few days they
> Crossed the river Saar.

Close to this place is sited a blue-coloured mountain
Where the colour for Dürer's panels
Was taken before he died.[12]

In the Middle Ages, a colour denoted 'azure' – from the medieval Latin *lazurium*, itself derived from the Persian *lajoard*, 'blue' – could refer equally to azurite or to a generalized blue: such are the ambiguities when a colour term attaches itself to (or stems from) a material. The potential for confusion of azurite with lapis lazuli is obvious: although the two were nominally distinguished as citramarine azure and ultramarine azure and are chemically quite different, they have a similar appearance. To tell them apart, the careful apothecarist or paint-maker would heat a small sample of the mineral fragments until they were red-hot: azurite turns black on cooling, whereas lapis lazuli does not. This test is mentioned in many medieval compilations; indeed, Heraclius even suggests it as a means to prepare a black colour for painting vases, although it is hard to credit that many craftsmen would have been prepared to squander the valuable azurite in this way. All the same, the painter had to be constantly vigilant to avoid deception or simple misunderstanding: it has been suggested that Dürer sometimes painted with azurite that he believed to be ultramarine. The complexity of the matter is very evident in the fifteenth-century Bolognese manuscript *Segreti Per Colori* (*Secrets of Colours*), which contains page upon page of diverse recipes for preparing 'various kinds of natural azures', with little explicit reference to the distinction between their mineral sources.

When very finely ground, azurite develops a pale sky-blue hue with a hint of green – very suitable for skies, but inferior to the purple richness of ultramarine. A darker tone requires coarser grinding, which made the pigment hard to apply and somewhat translucent. Glue-like size, rather than egg tempera, was then needed to hold the large particles securely, and several coats were required to produce a saturated, opaque colour. The result could be very beautiful, with each of the coarse grains sparkling like a tiny jewel. Azurite was specified in many medieval contracts, and it was the ultimate height of luxury to use ultramarine instead.

In *Saints Peter and Dorothy* (c. 1505–10), painted by the Master of St Bartholomew, the artist has used two different grades of azurite to obtain different colours. St Peter's robe is a strong, deep blue, rendered in highest-grade azurite that would have cost the Master dearly (Plate 4.4). But a cheaper grade is used for the greenish cuffs, where the lighter shade results from the smaller size of the pigment particles (see page 32).

Other sources of blue for the medieval artist were dyestuffs: woad and indigo. They have a greenish or blackish tone that is not particularly attractive, although the colour is pleasant enough when lightened with white. The preparation of a kind of lake pigment from indigo is described in a twelfth-century manuscript: ground white marble, 'put . . . into hot dung for a day and a night', is mixed with the foam from a cauldron 'in which clothes are dyed the colour of indigo'. 'When it is dry . . . it acquires a good azure colour,' says the author, adding that white lead can be used as the carrier material too. Cennino describes 'a sort of sky blue resembling azurite' which can be made by mixing 'Baghdad indigo' with white lead or lime white.

Crossing the rainbow

To these traditional blue dyes, the Middle Ages added another: turnsole or folium, an extract from the plant medieval scholars call *morella* and which has been identified with *Crozophora tinctoria*, native to southern France and called *maurelle* in Provence. The Latin name *folium* may derive from the practice of keeping the colourant in the form of cloths saturated with the stuff ('clothlets'), which would be placed between the pages (*folia*) of books. Turnsole is from *torna-ad-solem*, 'turn to the sun', a characteristic of the plant from which the dye originates.

To extract the folium colourant, the seed capsules were gathered and gently squeezed. The cloths were repeatedly dipped in the juice and dried until they were thoroughly permeated with it. Moistening a small piece of the cloth with water or glair would release the dried colour. Its transparent finish was particularly desirable for manuscript illumination.

The fresh juice of *morella* is not blue, however, but red. Theophilus tells us that in fact there are 'three kinds of folium, one red, another purple, and a third blue'. How is it so versatile? Turnsole is a representative of a broad class of vegetable extracts that change colour depending on the acidity of the solution: red in acid, purple when neutral, blue in alkali. Litmus, an extract of a Scandinavian lichen, is another, and so is the juice of red cabbage. Such substances are still employed in chemistry today as 'indicators' that signify the pH (acidity) of a solution by their colour changes.

Robert Boyle was one of the first to investigate these changes from a chemical perspective. In his *Experimental History of Colours* (1664) he lists turnsole amongst a whole range of extracts from berries, fruits and flowers that share the same property. Boyle reveals that knowledge of the colour change stems from the arts, and he makes the first suggestion that it might be used to measure acidity. A hundred years later this was developed into the chemical technique of analysis known as titration.

Theophilus describes how to prepare purple and blue folium from the acidic red plant juice using alkalis: lime and potash. The reversible nature of the colour changes does not appear to have been noticed – perhaps because rather strong acids would have been needed to achieve it, whereas the only acids known until the fourteenth century were weak organic ones such as vinegar and fruit juices. All the same, the blue form of turnsole had a natural tendency to veer towards purple over time, owing to the slight acidity of moisture in the air.

Folium was one of the very few purple colourants known to medieval artists, and 'turnsole violet' was highly regarded in four-teenth-century Italy. Some painters made use of the purple dye extracted from the lichen called archil or orchil (*Roccella tinctoria*). And in the early Middle Ages the purplish 'whelk red' extracted from shellfish native to the coasts of England and France was used for dyeing parchment. It was no doubt as laborious to extract as the Tyrian purple of antiquity, and was little used after the eighth century: folium gave a better colour for less effort. Most purples in medieval panel painting were, however, made by mixing a blue such as azurite with a red lake. Painters seem to have preferred the purplish-reds offered by crimson lake over the delicate violet colour of organic extracts.

Red woods

Vermilion went unchallenged as the painter's best red pigment until the twentieth century. But medieval painters made extensive use of red lake pigments manufactured from dyestuffs. Kermes crimson lake was widespread, and lac lakes were common in fifteenth century Florence. Another red dye was extracted from the root of the brazil tree *Caesalpinia braziliensis*, which was imported to medieval Europe from Ceylon via Alexandria. After the discovery of the New World, the dye was obtained from the species of brazil native to Jamaica and South America (*Caesalpinia crista*), which eventually gave its name to a nation.

The red dye was extracted by soaking and boiling the powdered wood in lye or alum. The lake pigment was made by adding alum to a lye solution or vice versa, precipitating dye-coated alumina particles. Adding white substances such as chalk, white lead, marble dust or powdered eggshell during the process gave the pigment a rosy pink colour; in England brazil lake was known as roset.

Some historians believe that brazil provided the foremost red lake of the Middle Ages; it was certainly cheaper than the insect-derived kermes lake. Daniel Thompson claims that 'the amount of brazil wood colour used in the Middle Ages both for painting and for dyeing was colossal'. Yet there is not a single case of a positive identification of this pigment in a medieval painting, so one must treat such assertions with caution. Until relatively recently the dyes in early lake pigments were hard to identify chemically, and much of what we know about their use relies on supposition. Whereas recipe books such as the *Mappae clavicula* indicate that red dyes such as kermes were well known, their conversion to lake pigments is a difficult, complex process that was probably not perfected until the Renaissance. Furthermore, brazil was known to be very fugitive (prone to fade) when exposed to light, for which reason it was sometimes banned by dyers' guilds. Panel painters might well have avoided it for the same reason.

In the late Middle Ages two other red dyestuffs – madder from northern Europe and cochineal from Poland – began to appear. The madder dye is a root extract of the madder plant *Rubia tinctorum*, which was cultivated in Europe at least since the thirteenth century. Madder lake is more permanent than brazil lake, but also more difficult to make. It features prominently in the palettes of artists from the seventeenth to the nineteenth century, but it is hard to find in the Middle Ages. Heraclius describes a recipe for madder lake in the tenth century, but it seems unlikely that it was widely used for panel painting until much later. There is madder in Dieric Bouts's *The Virgin and Child with Saints Peter and Paul* (c. 1460), and the extensive madder fields of Zeeland made its use more common among the fifteenth-century Netherlandish painters than their contemporaries elsewhere.

If you wanted the crimson lake made from cochineal, you often needed a heavy purse. To harvest the cochineal insects from the perennial knawel plant of eastern Europe, the plant had to be dug up and the resinous crust of insects picked off by hand; the plant was then replaced in the soil. There was just a two-week window for harvesting, traditionally after the feast of St John on 24 June. If the crop failed, prices soared. In early-fifteenth-century Florence, cochineal sold for twice the price of kermes.

There seems to be something about red pigments that attracts linguistic confusion. We saw earlier how the *sinopis* of Pliny, a sombre red ochre from Sinope on the Black Sea, begat the medieval colour term *sinople*, which could stand for either red or green. In medieval England and France another pigment that bore the Latin name *sinopis* was a complex red lake, composed of 'mader and greyne . . . and brasil and lak'. This substance, sometimes called cynopre or cynople in English, became popular in the fourteenth and fifteenth centuries. Yet when Cennino speaks of a 'sinoper' he is referring to a mineral, saying that it is 'a natural colour' also known as porphyry. Moreover, 'the handsomest and lightest sinoper obtainable' he calls cinabrese, promoting further confusion with cinnabar. We might be best advised to draw a veil over these ambiguities and to conclude simply that medieval technologists found both reasons and technical means for preparing complicated red lakes, among which the distinctions, even if they were clear at the time, are lost to us now.

Gilt complex

The one colour the alchemists could not conjure up for painters was that which they laboured hardest to devise. Struck by slanting rays of the sun, gold set the medieval altarpiece ablaze with light. In Byzantine churches like the sixth-century San Vitale in Ravenna, golden mosaic tiles create a dome shimmering with holy radiance. Whatever the cost of ultramarine or vermilion, gold has ancient associations that make its value transcendental.

Gold is the substance of royalty; so what could be more pious than to offer it up to God in sacred art? And unlike silver and other metals, it was seemingly immune to the passing years – it did not tarnish and lose its splendour.

The use of gold in medieval art shows us more clearly than anything else how the nature of materials took precedence over any concern for realism. Until at least the fourteenth century, holy figures on altar panels are framed not by nature's skies or foliage, nor by draperies or masonry, but by a golden field that permits neither depth nor shadow.

In later ages this metallic sheen was pushed back on to the gilded frame that held the canvas; but for the medieval artist gold was a colour in its own right. It was applied to the gessoed panels in the form of thin sheets: gold leaf. There was no need to visit the apothecary to procure this colour, for it was to be found in the purse of every wealthy person. The craftsmen of the Middle Ages, unrestricted by laws protecting currency, made their gold leaf by hammering and hammering at golden coins, transforming them to sheets so thin as to feel almost weightless.

This task was carried out by professional goldbeaters who, even into the twentieth century, measured the weight of gold leaf by the ducat, the gold coinage of medieval Italy. The thickness of the foil was determined by the number of leaves (each about 8.5 centimetres square) beaten from a single ducat. Cennino specifies which thickness is best for various uses:

Let me tell you that for the gold which is laid on flats [panels] they ought not to get more than a hundred leaves out of a ducat, whereas they do get a hundred and forty-five; because the gold for the flat wants to be rather dull. If you want to be sure of the gold, when you buy it, get it from someone who is a good goldbeater; and examine the gold; and if you find it rippling and mat, like goat parchment, then consider it good. On mouldings or foliage ornaments you will make out better with thinner gold; but for the delicate ornaments of the embellishment with mordants it ought to be very thin gold, and cobweb-like.[13]

The slightest film of moisture will bind these delicate sheets to just about any surface. Glair, gum, honey and plant juices were all used to stick gold leaf on to manuscript parchment. They were called 'water mordants' – water-soluble substances that mordanted ('bit' or fixed) gold. Because dampness loosens water mordants, a varnish was generally needed to secure the gold on panels. Alternatively the panel painter might use oil-based mordants, generally mixed with a little coloured pigment.

Mordanted gold leaf conforms to all the irregularities of the underlying surface, causing it to scatter light. This produces a rather flat, opaque yellow appearance. Only if the surface is smoothed down (burnished) by rubbing with a hard object does it regain the reflective lustre of the metal. A rounded stone or a tooth was often used for this purpose: once the gold leaf has dried fast, says Heraclius, 'let him make it very brilliant with the tooth of a savage bear'. Burnishing literally means 'making brown', as it darkens the gold in the shadows, while making the highlights more reflective. 'The gold then becomes almost dark from its own brilliance,' says Cennino.

It seems likely that many of the gold 'fields' (*fondo d'oro*) of medieval panel paintings were rubbed to a shining, mirror-like smoothness before the other elements of the scene were added on top. They usually look unburnished now (Plate 4.5) because of cracking in the underpainting, or because of other irregularities or contaminants picked up over the course of time. The burnished gold lettering on manuscripts has often fared better.

But some gold backgrounds were intentionally left unburnished, fixing the scene within a shimmering, luminous light. Gold is here representing light itself, and it was still used during the Renaissance to suggest an other-worldly illumination. It is the colour of haloes, of highlights on the robes of saints. Cennino recommends a sprinkling of gold mixed with green paint for 'making a tree to look like one of the trees of Paradise'. Botticelli laces his goddess's hair with gold in *The Birth of Venus* (c. 1485), and scatters it among the leaves of the trees behind her.

Not all of this gold was laid down as leaf; it was also used as a powdered pigment. But since gold is a soft and ductile metal, not a brittle mineral, the pressure of grinding with a pestle and mortar does more to weld gold particles together than to break them into still finer fragments. Heraclius recommends that gold be ground in wine, and Theophilus gives a detailed description of a mill for grinding gold leaf in water. But this must have been a frustrating affair. So medieval craftsmen had to delve into alchemical metallurgy to develop methods of hardening gold for grinding.

The alchemical conviction that metals were but blends of the same basic ingredients was bolstered by the observation that gold can be blended with fluid mercury. This amalgam is a waxy paste; wrapped in cloth and squeezed to remove excess mercury, it becomes hard and brittle, suitable for grinding. Heating vaporizes the mercury to leave a gold powder, provided that care is taken not to let the heat fuse the gold grains. An alternative technique was to beat gold to very thin leaf and then to grind it with honey or salt, which helps to prevent the welding together of the gold particles. Both these methods are mentioned in the *Mappae clavicula*.

Painting in gold – chrysography – could create some stunning effects, few more so than that in Jacopo Bellini's *The Virgin and Child with (?)Leonello d'Este* (c. 1440). Here the Virgin's robe is given highlights using a fine peppering of gold dots, creating a fine, silky and quite numinous quality in the cloth.

No wonder medieval artists seem to have cared little for true yellow pigments – they were pale substitutes for the magnificence of gold. One of their principal uses was to tint white metals such as silver and tin so that they resembled the regal metal. A yellow pigment called mosaic gold (*oro musivo* in medieval Latin, or *aurum musaicum*) was seemingly used in parchment gilding as a 'fake gold'. It is a form of tin sulphide, and Cennino provides a recipe for it that ranks among his most complex – although even this may be an oversimplification of the process: 'Take sal ammoniac, tin, sulphur, quicksilver, in equal parts; except less of the quicksilver. Put these ingredients into a flask of iron, copper, or glass. Melt it all on the fire, and it is done.'[14] Whether this substance truly offered a convincing imitation of gold is doubtful, and the association may have been as much a construct of alchemical theory as a description of appearance. Thompson says of a sample of the pigment in a medieval manuscript in Florence, 'It is only fair to add that mosaic gold is so little golden that it might easily be mistaken, in a casual inspection, for orpiment, or even ochre.'

Orpiment was another suggestive stand-in for gold, particularly in its sparkling mineral form. Its very name recalls this connection: *auripigmentum*, 'colour of gold'. The ancients fostered the distinctly alchemical idea that the superficial resemblance had deeper roots: that orpiment contained gold itself. Pliny says that the Roman emperor Caligula extracted gold from the natural mineral form of orpiment. Wary of its deadly nature – Pliny calls it *arrhenicum*, from which the word arsenic is derived – the Romans used slave labour to mine it from the earth. In Cennino's day, the painter used synthetic orpiment from the alchemist's laboratory; his seemingly unlikely claim of its 'handsome yellow more closely resembling gold than any other colour' has a certain chrysopoeian ring to it.

The yellow lead antimonate pigment of the Egyptians was probably the pigment Cennino calls *giallorino*. Much debate has arisen from his claim that it was 'produced artificially, though not by alchemy'. Some have supposed that Cennino was referring to a natural, volcanic, lead-containing yellow mineral found on the slopes of Vesuvius, near Naples; 'artificial' would then refer to a chemical transformation wrought by geological, rather than human, agency. In her seminal study of historical pigments (1849), Mary Merrifield claims that one kind of 'Naples yellow' was indeed a natural mineral associated with this region, and that another was synthetic lead antimonate.

But exactly how these relate to the term *giallorino* is hard for us now to discern. Medieval painters also used yellow pigments made from lead and tin oxides according to various recipes, now termed lead-tin yellows. No doubt painters often confused these with lead antimonate, although by at least the fifteenth-century alchemists could certainly tell their tin from their antimony. Merrifield says that massicot (yellow lead oxide) also went under the name of *giallorino*, and it is probably wisest for us to regard this as a blanket term denoting any yellow pigment containing lead.

To complicate matters further, a synthetic yellow pigment containing lead, tin *and* antimony has been identified in seventeenth-century Italian paintings by Poussin and others. It seems that by this time pigment manufacturers knew how to impose some control on the manufacturing process and thus on the hues obtained. The Englishman Richard Symonds, who journeyed to Rome between 1649 and 1651 (where he met Poussin), reported that 'there is 3 or 4 sorts of giallo lino some redder, some yellower'.

Cennino is more explicit that alchemy supplies the yellow lake he calls arzica, which is made from the weld plant *Reseda luteola*. Sometimes called 'dyer's herb', weld was cultivated for its yellow dye even into the twentieth century; it was particularly valued for dyeing silk. Yellow lake made from weld could be brilliant and fairly opaque, and provided a good (and harmless) substitute for orpiment. But Cennino is not enthusiastic about it, saying that arzica is 'little used' and has 'a very thin colour . . . [that] fades in the open'.

More significant for the medieval manuscript illuminator was the yellow lake made from the saffron plant *Crocus sativus* and from other crocuses. Mixed with glair, saffron produced a strong, pure transparent yellow; combined with azurite, it offered a vibrant green. Cennino says that a blend of saffron and verdigris produces 'the most perfect grass colour imaginable'.

Georgius Agricola records that verdigris 'was first brought to Germany from Spain', from which we might again deduce that it was a product of Arabic alchemy. Even Theophilus four centuries earlier calls it *viride hispanicum*; in modern German verdigris is still called *Grünspan*. An artificial copper-containing green listed in Grünewald's estate inventory after his death in 1528 is denoted simply *alchemy grun*. But the medieval *vert de Grèce* implies a Greek

origin; the *Mappae clavicula* refers to it as *viride grecum*. The ancient
Greeks certainly used it, and were not the first to do so.

Verdigris was a popular but unpredictable pigment. The organic
acids used to make it have in some cases attacked the parchment or
paper on which they are painted, cutting out neat holes as if nibbled
by green-loving insects. And some pigments are prone to deteriorate
if set close to verdigris. These defects motivated the development
of alternative greens by the fourteenth century, chief among them
two organic colours called sap green and iris green.

The first is derived from the juice of buckthorn berries, which
is thick enough to be used without any binder. With the addition
of some gum it makes an excellent water-colour, and is still in use
in this form (though the 'sap green' sold as an oil colour in the early
twentieth century was in fact a synthetic lake compound). Iris green,
made from the juice of iris flowers, was mixed with water, and
possibly a thickener like alum, and used for manuscript illumination.
These greens, like folium and weld, are the colours of the meadow,
not the mine, and directly accessible to the diligent monk, as
Heraclius observes:

He who wishes to convert flowers into the various colours which, for the
purpose of writing, the page of the book demands, must wander over
the cornfields early in the morning, and then he will find various flowers
fresh sprung up.[15]

These natural juices were well suited to adorn the monk's bright
page, but were not robust enough for the altarpiece.

In spite of its reliance on the distorted records and techniques of
ancient technology, the Middle Ages was thus a period of considerable innovation in colour production. At the same time, the changing social structure moved painting to a new milieu: from a
craft concerned with adornment in a religious context to a trade
performed by guildsmen for mercantile or noble patrons, who drew
on a wider range of subject matter. This change reflected a broader
transformation of society in which mystery and magic – a world
pervaded by spiritual forces, a world in which icons had real power
– gave way to commerce, to the primacy of trade over religion, to

a practical outlook. To some degree the same process overtook alchemy itself, which kept the trappings of its mystical roots but was, to a craftsman like Cennino, simply a means of manufacturing. These trends reached their logical conclusion in the centuries that followed, as the forces of rationality began to challenge the authority of the Church and as painters transformed their practice into a wholly secular discipline: not a holy craft but a scholarly and intellectualized 'liberal' art.

5. Masters of Light and Shadow

THE GLORY OF THE RENAISSANCE

Painting is a combination of light and shadow in close mixture with the diverse qualities of all the simple and complex colours.

Leonardo da Vinci

I should like, as far as possible, all the genera and species of colours to appear in painting with a certain grace and amenity.

Leon Battista Alberti, *Della Pittura* (1435)

Did art reach its peak in the Renaissance? Aspiring to resurrect the ideals of Classical times, the painting of the fifteenth and sixteenth centuries nevertheless shares none of that period's reputed chromatic austerity. Instead, it bears witness to a delight in the riches of raw, lustrous colour that was not to be revisited until twentieth-century painters made colour art's subject.

It is through their use of colour that we can distinguish the Renaissance artists' varied interpretations of this 'rebirth'. Stripped of the theological certainties of the Middle Ages, with its formulaic approach to painting known as the International Style, artists were compelled to find new ways of organizing the steadily expanding range of colours at their disposal. No longer was it sufficient to present flat fields of expensive pigments as a devotional offering to God; the new watchword was truth to nature. For the first time in the history of Western art, painters strove to depict the world as it truly appears to the eye.

The practical and theoretical chemistry of the fifteenth and sixteenth centuries was not significantly different from that of five centuries earlier. Advances were incremental and evolutionary, reflecting none of the revolutionary transformations in the arts and humanities. Yes, new pigments duly left their impression on painting – but there was nothing in this pivotal period of art history to parallel the technical innovations in colour chemistry of the nineteenth century, when art gained a wholly new set of clothes. None the less, we do not have to look far to discover how issues of pigment availability and usage left a profound mark on the works that this high point in Western art has bequeathed to us.

The Humanist ideal

Italian artists of the fifteenth century perceived that a revival of the noble principles of their Classical forebears had been gathering pace ever since the time of Giotto di Bondone, the founder of the Florentine school of painting. Giotto's innovation seems retrospectively almost trivial, but it overturned the medieval artistic orthodoxy. He attempted to show objects in relief, with shadows and highlights picked out by an identifiable source of illumination.

This emergence of light and shade as features of the painter's landscape is one of the distinguishing aspects of Renaissance art. For the first time, people and things cast shadows. The consequence is plain to see: it is as if, with Giotto, the artist's imagined world suddenly leaps to life.

Needless to say, there is more to the Renaissance than the introduction of a technique for painting three-dimensionally. Giotto's approach is a symptom of a profound change in philosophical outlook that affected all areas of learning in the West. The reason medieval artists did not represent figures and scenes as they 'really' appeared is not because they lacked the ability or perceptiveness to do so, but because such a goal was irrelevant to them. Painting was a way of telling a story without words. What mattered was that each of the important characters could be clearly identified in the scene, in positions and at a scale that suited their status, and in colours that encoded symbolic meanings and redounded to the splendour of the Lord.

Giotto rejects this schematic, narrative kind of illustrative art in favour of what we might naively call realism. The observer is not reading the image as if reading a book, but is present in the scene, a witness to the action. Nothing illustrates this better than the way Giotto was prepared to paint figures with their backs to us, faces concealed – for example, in *The Betrayal of Christ* (*c.* 1305) (Plate 5.1) and *The Mourning of Christ* (*c.* 1306). We see people in this attitude all the time, but to the medieval painter it is meaningless to include a figure without a face, which then becomes a mere blob of colour. Equally shocking is the way in which Jesus, in *The Betrayal of Christ*, is all but hidden by the enveloping cloak of Judas, painted in the characteristic yellow of the traitor's clothing. Only the face of Christ remains visible, whereas a medieval artist would have deemed it essential to reveal the Son of God in all his glory.

Within such images lies all that is inherent in the Humanistic outlook of the Renaissance. Real human experience is emphasized in preference to the eternal, transcendent verities of theology. Religious scenes contain people who look life-like, not cartoon-like; and they appear as they might have been seen in the instant. One can say that Giotto's naturalism makes *time* a component of painting – the image is no longer an immutable symbol but becomes fixed at a moment in real, passing time.

The ramifications for the painter were tremendous. In nature, the appearance of a scene depends on the ambient lighting, which changes over time: gloomy and overcast, or bleached in the harsh Mediterranean sun, or softened by the glow of evening. This offered the artist new possibilities for creating dramatic atmospheres, but it also demanded that he have a thorough understanding of natural lighting effects. And an insistence on truth to nature freed the artist from the stylized conventions of medieval composition, since nature offers infinite variety of form and colour. But at the same time, naturalism raised a new challenge, for there is no law that imposes on nature the kind of harmonious arrangement of colours and objects that the artist requires for a pleasing composition.

As well as acquiring the dimension of time, the Renaissance artist gained the ability to locate objects precisely in space. The advent of linear perspective, pioneered by the Florentine architect Filippo Brunelleschi (1377–1446), was the essential accompaniment to the introduction of light and shade in allowing the artist to conjure a world from the flat plane of the panel or wall. Brunelleschi deduced the mathematical laws that enabled artists to determine how size diminishes with distance, and his discoveries were enthusiastically assimilated by the Florentine painter Masaccio (1401–28).

Underlying these innovations was an acknowledgement that, in order to depict the world in a naturalistic way, the artist needed to study nature carefully and systematically – which is to say, scientifically. To draw the human form faithfully, the painter needed to have a good grounding in anatomy. The artist's skill derived not from rote learning of stylized conventions in a workshop apprenticeship, but from rational apprehension of nature's laws and principles.

This appeal to reason is explicit in the writings of Leon Battista Alberti, to whom we owe a great deal of our knowledge of artistic attitudes at the height of the Italian Renaissance. Of Genoese birth, Alberti lived and worked in Florence and, for a time, in the Papal Court. His texts demonstrate just how thoroughly he and his contemporaries, in Florence in particular, dispensed with the theological preoccupations of the Middle Ages. In his influential book *Della Pittura*, Alberti says:

The function of the painter is to draw with lines and paint in colours on a surface any given bodies in such a way that, at a fixed distance and with a certain, determined position of the centric ray, what you see represented appears to be in relief and just like those bodies.[1]

This, he claims, may be achieved by the application of rational principles such as perspective. But he stresses that first and foremost the painter must strive for beauty. Recognizing that not all of nature is beautiful, he insists that the artist should select and combine only its most lovely and pleasing aspects. But there is nothing subjective in this procedure. Beauty, to Alberti, is not in the eye of the beholder but is instead an almost quantifiable property, 'a kind of harmony and concord of all the parts to form a whole which is constructed according to a fixed number, and a certain relation and order, as symmetry, the highest and most perfect law of nature, demands'. Thus beauty is an absolute property on which all well-informed observers could agree.

This emphasis on harmony of proportion is characteristic of the Florentine outlook. To these artists, the most elevated element of painting was skilful rendering of form: the ability to draw well. Colour, they said, is secondary. Alberti does attach importance to harmony of colour (see page 20), but he allows colours no intrinsic beauty of their own, nor their physical substance any inherent merit. He lambasts those who waste their time using gold and rich colours while paying scant heed to their proper deployment.

This division of the artist's craft into line or drawing (*disegno*) and colour (*colore*), and the debate about their relative importance, became a major theme in Renaissance art. The quarrel was to continue until the late seventeenth century; in the French academies the two sides were represented by the Poussinistes and Rubenistes, advocates of the styles exemplified by the sober Poussin and the florid Rubens. But the discussion eventually came to turn on the merits of formal planning versus spontaneous composition, as opposed to those of drawing and colouring.

It is generally said that in Florence Alberti's outlook prevailed – *disegno* being most prized – while in opulent Venice there was more stress on the use of rich colour. But one should not overlook the fact that the greatest masters of Florence – Leonardo, Michelangelo, Raphael – all gave much thought to the problem of colour.

Controlling colour

Why a problem? Because the constraints imposed on the painter both by convention and by limitations in materials meant that there was a discontinuity between his desire to paint nature faithfully and his ways and means of capturing her colours. Although pigments such as vermilion and, for a time, ultramarine became gradually less prohibitively expensive and therefore less revered in unadulterated form, the taboo against mixing pigments remained strong. Until oil-painting methods made mixing both more acceptable and more feasible (as we will see), this meant that the Renaissance painter possessed a range of colours scarcely broader than that of the medieval artist, while facing a new need for accuracy in their use.

So there were in fact two problems. First, nature has more hues than the artist. Second, the strident vermilion, gold and ultramarine colour-fields of the Middle Ages are unacceptable to the artist whose audience no longer prizes the pigments for their own sake, and whose objective is colour harmony rather than an ostentatious show of wealth.

One of the difficulties of harmonious composition is that the variations in brightness (see page 52) of colours create imbalance. White and yellow look bright, fully saturated blue and purple dark. This means that yellow-robed figures leap out of a crowd, while those dressed in blue draw the eye far less. This is bad enough as it is, particularly when the painter has little option but to use every colour for crowd scenes to achieve all the variety of which his limited, unmixed palette is capable. How much worse, though, if blue is to be reserved for Christ, and yellow for Judas!

The situation is not helped by the shading scheme recommended by Cennino, who derived it from Giotto. He tells us that the pigment is to be used in full saturation for the deepest folds, and progressively lightened with white lead as one works towards the highlights (Plate 5.2). This permits the deepest folds of a robe to be no darker than the fully saturated hue (which, for yellow, is not particularly dark).

Alberti advocated instead that black be added for the shadows. The unmixed, full-saturation colour then appears in the midtones. This allows for a greater dynamic range (a greater contrast between light and dark) and a better representation of relief, as well as going some way towards equalizing differences in brightness. But it can also make the colours look somehow 'dirty': the works of Antonio Pollaiuolo (*c.* 1432–98), for instance, suffer in this respect.

A question of style

Not surprisingly, no unique solution to these difficulties emerged. Instead, we can discern several different methods for organizing colour in the works of the Italian Old Masters. It seems unlikely, however, that their practitioners applied these schemes in a systematic and prescriptive manner; nor did the use of one imply the exclusion of the others. The late fifteenth century was after all a time of stylistic experiment – for style, not technical skill, was becoming the painter's most marketable attribute. Moreover, in the use of colour more than in just about any other aspect of art, dogmatic systems have never succeeded in making intuition dispensable.

Leonardo da Vinci was perhaps the supreme naturalist among the Florentine painters – and consequently he was one of the most methodical. The attentiveness with which he observed the shapes, forms and patterns of nature is attested by his extraordinary note-books (although there is little consistency in the conclusions that he drew from them). Like Alberti, Leonardo believed that the creation and judgement of art is a rational process. But he had little interest in trying to improve on nature, as Alberti recommended, by appropriate selection of its best features. He showed nature as it is, whether beautiful or ugly; indeed, he felt that ugliness could be useful as a foil to make beauty shine all the more brightly. In contrast, Alberti's insistence that figures should conform to a single ideal of harmony leads to the stilted uniformity of the six archers of Pollaiuolo's *The Martyrdom of St Sebastian* (1475), or the sterile blandness of the women in Pietro Perugino's *The Virgin Appearing to St Bernard* (c. 1490).

Leonardo studied colour carefully. The idea that objects have an intrinsic colour, independent of the lighting conditions, reflections and so forth, has been a persistent fallacy in Western art; but Leonardo's astute observations gave him an inkling of its essential falsity. Describing an experiment in the mixing of coloured lights, he even teeters on the brink of establishing the long-confused distinction between additive and subtractive mixing (see pages 42–4). But it was an experiment he never performed. Had he done so, he would have been astonished to find blue and yellow lights combining not to a 'most beautiful green', as he claimed, but to white.

Leonardo's main contribution to the use of colour during the Renaissance was the way that he created tonal unity with desaturated, neutral colours of a very restricted range of lightness. In the interests of a unified whole, he sacrificed brilliant colour and used muted greens, blues and earth colours whose midtones – used for those surfaces neither in highlight nor shadow – have a similar brightness. This allowed for a more even depiction of relief, but its effect can scarcely be called joyful. Leonardo felt that strong contrasts in tone confused the eye and should be avoided, and he recommended the use of subdued lighting: 'When you want to make a portrait, do it in dull weather, or as evening falls.' To such methods and principles the Mona Lisa (*La Gioconda, c.* 1502) owes much of her mystery and ambiguity of expression.

The few surviving paintings of Leonardo are made all the more sombre by his technique of *sfumato* – literally, smokiness. Away from their point of focus, the pictures blend into murky shadows where colour is leached away until a dark monochrome is all that remains. This use of graduated shadow enables the artist to direct the eye wherever he wants it to go, by bathing those places in a subdued, hazy light (Plate 5.3). To achieve this low-keyed tonal unity, Leonardo laid his pigments over an underpaint ('ground') of neutral grey or brown.

Allied to the *sfumato* method and easily confused with it is the technique of chiaroscuro, with which Leonardo is sometimes also improperly credited. Literally 'light and shade', this style depicts shadows that are more black than smoky, with abrupt and dramatic transitions from light to shade. There is less tonal restriction than in Leonardo's *sfumato*, and colours in the midtones appear with more or less full intensity. The result can be very striking, as testified by the paintings of Correggio (*c.* 1489–1534) and Caravaggio (1573–1610). Caravaggio's figures are spotlighted in the midst of impenetrable darkness, and as a result the colours are often bleached and subdued in the glare. In *The Burial of Christ* (1604) the pallid flesh and white drapery of the dramatically lit figures are moderated only by earthy reds. In *The Calling of St Matthew* (1599–1600), the rich red velvet of several of the figures' sleeves glows all the more lucidly amid the sober, earthy hues caught in the slanting light of a high window. These works keep colour under such strict constraint that the question of how to organize it scarcely arises.

Sfumato and chiaroscuro together constitute the so-called 'dark manner' of the Renaissance. In contrast, lively, bold colours characterize the style called *unione*, associated with Raphael's early works. Raphael Santi (1483–1520) has a lovely manner with colour, and his skill in drawing puts paid to the idea that artists of his time had to choose between *disegno* and *colore*. His genius was to find a way of working with brilliant hues that nevertheless sit together in harmonious balance. Raphael avoids hard contrasts: the ultramarine blue of the Virgin's robe in *Madonna Alba* (1511) is softened with lead white, and the bright red against aquamarine blue in *The Madonna del Granduca* (c. 1505) (Plate 5.4) is harmonized by the deep shadows and the golden glow of the flesh tones. Raphael's facility with these colours seems almost magical, and his contemporaries thought so too. Certainly, the Florentine writer and artist Giorgio Vasari, who vouched that 'unity in painting is produced when a variety of different colours is harmonized together', made his adoration plain enough: 'One can claim without fear of contradiction that artists as outstandingly gifted as Raphael are not simply men but, if it be allowed to say so, mortal gods.'[2]

If anyone was more worthy of deification in Vasari's eyes than Raphael, it was Michelangelo:

What a happy age we live in! And how fortunate are our craftsmen, who have been given light and vision by Michelangelo and whose difficulties have been smoothed away by this marvellous and incomparable artist! You artists should thank heaven for what has happened and strive to imitate Michelangelo in everything you do.[3]

Michelangelo (1475–1564) worked primarily with the fresco technique, in which he was much more of a colourist than has sometimes been supposed. The modern cleaning of his ceiling mural in the Sistine Chapel revealed bright colours that shocked those accustomed to its subdued tonalities. But he took a bold and unusual path towards colour harmony. *Unione* seeks with strong colour what *sfumato* attempts more sombrely: an elimination of tonal contrast. The trick called *cangiantismo*, to which Michelangelo was much given, instead balances different colour values by shifting hues rather than tones. An object that begins as one colour in the highlights might become another in the shadows. This is an artificial use of colour (unless being employed to depict 'shot' fabrics like silk, which truly look like this). But it is 'clever' and eye-catching:

just the thing to appeal to the late-sixteenth-century Mannerist painters such as Francesco Salviati and Vasari himself. Even they, however, acceded to a decorum that prohibited such flashiness from being lavished on revered figures such as the Virgin.

Michelangelo used *cangiantismo* to suggest an other-worldliness in some of his images – something that ran against the grain of the Humanist aspiration towards an objective, scientific truth. To Michelangelo, however, nothing was of greater importance than beauty. Yet this is not Alberti's rational beauty, but something altogether incommensurable. Michaelangelo had little time for the scientifically inclined theorists: 'all the reasonings of geometry and arithmetic, and all the proofs of perspective were of no use to a man without the eye'. In this respect he anticipates the Mannerists, who elevated intuitive judgement and questions of 'taste' above reason in art.

Oil change

There is a rather gratifying irony in the way that the art of the Italian High Renaissance owes its greatest debt to a technical innovation imported from the North, source of the 'Gothic' styles that to the Italians represented all that was barbaric and uncouth about the Middle Ages. Even the patriotic Vasari, for whom the Florentine painters were surpassed by no one, tells how oil painting was brought to his homeland from the Netherlands, where, he informs us, it was invented by 'John of Bruges in Flanders'. This John is the Flemish painter Jan van Eyck (c. 1390–1441).

The double twist is that Vasari actually attributes much more to van Eyck than is due. Van Eyck was certainly not the first to use oil as a binding medium for pigments; even Italians were doing so before Antonello da Messina learnt van Eyck's methods and brought them back south in the 1470s (which is how Vasari tells it). But it was indeed van Eyck who discovered how to release the true potential of the new medium.

The oils used as a pigment binder are so-called drying oils – primarily linseed, nut and poppy oils – which form a water-resistant, elastic film as they dry. The oil must be refined carefully to acquire satisfactory drying properties; sometimes drying agents (siccatives) such as metal salts can help. In any event, drying was slow in comparison with egg tempera: it took hours or even days, rather than minutes. This was regarded in the Middle Ages as a distinct inconvenience.

The preparation of nut and poppy oils is described by Dioscorides and Pliny, but they make no mention of their use as paint media. The first written record of this application is by the Roman Aetius in the late fifth century, and a recipe for an oil varnish (in which a drying oil is mixed with natural resins) is listed in an eighth-century document known as the Lucca manuscript. The clearest indication that oil painting of a kind was practised well before van Eyck's time appears in Theophilus' *De diversis artibus*. Having described the preparation of linseed oil, he says:

Grind some minium or cinnabar with this oil on a stone without water, spread it with a brush on the doors or panels that you want to redden and dry them in the sun ... All the kinds of pigments can be ground with this same oil and laid on woodwork, but only on things that can be dried in the sun, because, whenever you have laid on one pigment, you cannot lay a second over it until the first has dried out. This process is an excessively long and tedious one in the case of figures.[4]

Max Doerner points out that Theophilus (and presumably those who followed his recipes) made his problems worse by using a standard olive-oil press to squeeze out the linseed oil from flax seed. Olive oil is a so-called non-drying oil, which means just what it says; even minor contamination from an imperfectly cleaned press would have had serious consequences. 'No wonder the linseed oil would not dry!' Doerner thunders.

The transparency of oil paints also recommended them for tinting metals: thin coats of red (glazes) were applied to gold to make it look more lustrous (the redder the better), and a yellow glaze on tin was used as a cheap imitation of gold itself.

It appears that van Eyck's contribution was to rescue oil paint from its unappealing reputation. He realized that the glazing process has tremendous value for the artist, who, by judicious technique and patience, can obtain deep, rich and stable colours that egg tempera alone can never match. He developed glazing from a craftsman's decorative technique into a method suitable for the finest of paintings.

Van Eyck's technique was to glaze oils over a tempera ground, combining the quick drying of the latter with the rich lustre and blending possibilities of the former. Thus it would be wrong to imagine painters abruptly ditching their tempera methods for the new approach: the two coexisted for a long time, and are well suited to such a marriage. A mixture of tempera and oils is very common in fifteenth-century art; one of the earliest examples is Cosimo Tura's gorgeous *Allegorical Figure* (c. 1459–63) (Plate 11.2).

A glaze acts as a kind of colour filter: a red lake glaze over a blue ground transforms it to rich purple. By carefully building up layers of oil glazes, van Eyck produced saturated, jewel-like colours that look as sensuous today as they must have done at the time. It is hard to imagine his *Virgin of the Canon van der Paele* (1436) ever being any richer than it is now; and the fabulous chromaticity of his *Arnolfini Marriage* (1434) (Plate 5.5) makes it one of the most admired works in the Western canon.

Whether these techniques were devised solely by van Eyck is unclear. But they were widely practised by the Flemish painters of the fifteenth century, some of whom – such as Rogier van der Weyden (1400?–64) – took their knowledge south during visits to Venice. The Italians were already experimenting with oils in the early fifteenth century; by the century's end oil paint had become their predominant medium.

Oil paints have other advantages that enhanced their popularity. In oil, each pigment particle is 'insulated' by a layer of the fluid. So pigments that react chemically with one another in tempera might be stably combined in oil. The painter could then be less fearful about making up complex pigment mixtures on the palette. And the slow-drying nature of the paint is a benefit to the naturalistic painter, offering the opportunity for blending tones and blurring outlines on the canvas. This was particularly felicitous for the painterly depiction of skin tones: Willem de Kooning once said,

'Flesh was the reason why oil painting was invented.' Thus the sharp contours characteristic of tempera work gave way to new styles, as oils encouraged the painter to engage physically with his materials. Towards the end of his life, Titian was described by one contemporary commentator as painting 'more with his fingers than with his brushes'.

Vasari, writing in 1550, had no doubts about the virtues of painting in oils:

A most beautiful invention and a great convenience to the art of Painting was the discovery of colouring in oil . . . This manner of painting kindles the pigments and nothing else is needed save diligence and devotion, because the oil in itself softens and sweetens the colours and renders them more delicate and more easily blended than do the other mediums. While the work is wet the colours readily mix and unite one with the other; in short, by this method the artists impart wonderful grace and vivacity and vigour to their figures.[5]

But changing the medium invariably changes the paintbox. Oils, like any binding medium, do not carry raw pigment without modifying its appearance. As the refractive index of oils differs from that of egg yolk, pigments are not necessarily the same colour in both (see page 38). Ultramarine in oil is blacker than in egg tempera; the rich blueness is recaptured by mixing it with a little lead white. In the face of this insult to its purity, ultramarine could scarcely retain its medieval mystique. Similarly, vermilion – the red jewel of the Middle Ages – appears less vibrant in oil, and red lakes were awarded greater favour. The low refractive index of green malachite leaves it fairly transparent in oil, and its use declined. Verdigris suffers similarly in oils, and was commonly mixed with lead white or lead-tin yellow to restore opacity. An alternative green called copper resinate, a copper salt of organic acids found in wood resins, became popular around the middle of the fifteenth century. These consequences of using oil media were known, in northern Europe at least, as early as the late fourteenth century: a manuscript from this time called the *Liber diversarum artium* (*Book of Divers Arts*) warns how, in oil, 'azure' (ultramarine or azurite) darkens, indigo does not dry, and vermilion must be used with red lead. Such adulteration of the once precious red would have horrified medieval artists.

The allure of the new

The introduction of copper resinate is just one indication that the chemical technologists of the fifteenth century were still searching for new colours. The pigment was made from verdigris, typically by combining it with turpentine resin extracted from pine trees. A Florentine author named Birelli describes a recipe in 1601:

Take one pound of fine white turpentine resin, three ounces of mastic . . . and half an ounce of new wax. Put everything together in a small newly glazed pot, and boil the aforesaid things on a moderate fire of charcoal . . . Then add to these things an ounce of verdigris and put it in little by little, mixing it all the time in the jar with a little stick so that it is well incorporated.[6]

Formulations like these give a possibly misleading impression that copper resinate was a well-characterized pigment whose preparation was methodical and deliberate. The truth is murkier. Some of what now passes for 'copper resinate' may instead be the result of adding a little resin-based varnish to verdigris mixed as an oil paint. It was common practice for painters to blend resins with their paints to achieve a smoother, harder finish. Van Eyck probably did so; the legend of his 'invention' of oil painting has it that it stemmed from his brother Hubert's experiments to find a varnish made from boiled, thickened oil that would dry in the shade to avoid the cracking caused by sunlight.

Copper resinate is therefore something of a modern umbrella term for a variety of mixtures of green copper salts with resins; it is not a solitary pigment with the unambiguous status of ultramarine or red lead. Yet in one form or another, this new green was used enthusiastically throughout the late fifteenth and sixteenth centuries, notably by Giovanni Bellini, Raphael, Gerard David, Tintoretto and Paolo Veronese. But its disappearance soon thereafter may indicate that its Achilles' heel had already become apparent: copper resinate (at least in some formulations) darkens rapidly to brown (see page 299).

One can imagine that the Humanistic concern to match colours to nature placed a greater demand on greens than on any other colour. Artists overcame their habitual reluctance about mixing to create a wide range of greens from blues and yellows; even precious ultramarine was deployed to this end. We can feel sure that these painters, seeking novelty in place of traditional formulas, were more hungry than ever for new colourants.

Renaissance blues

Their appetite was certainly keen for new blues. Ultramarine was still distressingly expensive in the late fifteenth century, and azurite was hardly cheap. The patron or client who wanted a brilliant blue but could afford neither of these had another choice – a synthetic 'copper blue', essentially an artificial approximation to azurite (basic copper carbonate). Poorly understood in terms of composition, such pigments are obscured by another lexicological thicket. Manufacturers producing much the same substance by different means might award them different names. And as pigments ceased to be anchored in their substance of origin and became instead generic labels or even abstract colour terms, the same name might end up attached to different substances. Small wonder that artists did not always know what they were using.

To the English artist of the seventeenth century, for example, natural azurite might go by the name of blue bice, or simply bice. In the fourteenth century, *bys* was merely an adjective meaning 'dark'; 'azure bys' was a dark blue. But by the fifteenth century *bys* or *byse* was a true colour term for blue, by which means it attached itself to the most common blue pigment: azurite. In the seventeenth century, it seems to have had no other meaning. Yet by the eighteenth century we find it applied to a substance, without a specific colour connotation: 'bice' was a generic name for a copper-based pigment (generally a carbonate), and could refer to a green as well as to a blue material. By and by, the word has come to designate an

PLATE 1.1 Anish Kapoor's *As If to Celebrate, I Discovered a Mountain Blooming with Red Flowers* (1981) is covered with raw pigment that encroaches on to the surrounding floor, creating an intensity of colour hard to match with regular paints.

PLATE 1.2 In Kandinsky's *Yellow Accompaniment* (1924) the relation to musical scores is clear.

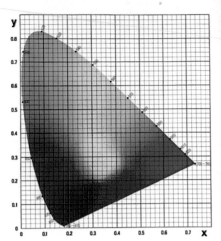

PLATE 2.1 The colour wheel devised by Michel-Eugène Chevreul in 1864 has smooth gradations that taxed colour-printing technology to its limits.

PLATE 2.2 The CIE chromaticity diagram is a modern colour wheel, re-shaped to permit a scientifically precise measurement of colour. The spectral colours appear on the tongue-shaped rim; the straight lower edge links violet to red with non-spectral hues.

PLATE 2.3 A page from Albert Munsell's colour atlas, which attempts to map out all of colour space in discrete patches separated by perceptually equal steps.

PLATE 3.1 Cave art from Altamira, Spain, dating from *c.* 15000 BC.

PLATE 3.3 The riches of Egyptian colouring, including prominent use of Egyptian blue, are evident in this wall painting, probably from the tomb of Nebamun (18th dynasty, *c.* 1350 BC).

PLATE 3.2 The ancient technology for making blue-glazed stone known as Egyptian faience may have stimulated the production of glass and the smelting of copper, as well as the synthesis of the Egyptian blue pigment. This is a *shabti* figure from the tomb of Sety I (19th dynasty, *c.* 1290 BC).

PLATE 3.4 The 'Alexander' mosaic from the House of the Faun, Pompeii (before AD 79). This mosaic is a reproduction of a four-colour painting by the Greek artist Philoxenos from the 4th century BC.

PLATE 3.5 This wall painting from the Villa of Mysteries, Pompeii (*c.* 50 BC) shows that Roman artists were not averse to bright colour.

PLATE 4.1 In the altarpiece *Saints Jerome and John the Baptist* (*c.* 1423–8), attributed to Masaccio and Masolino, Saint Jerome is robed in the distinctive bright orange-red of vermilion.

PLATE 4.2 The medieval artist at work: the female painter Thamar, with an assistant grinding colours behind her.

PLATE 4.4 St Peter's robe in the altarpiece *Saints Peter and Dorothy* (*c.*1505–10) by the Master of Saint Bartholomew is painted in two different grades of azurite: the finest is used for the deep-blue robes, whereas a lighter, greener grade with smaller particles is used for the cuffs.

PLATE 4.3 The Arena Chapel in Padua, with murals painted by Giotto around 1305.

PLATE 4.5   Altarpieces of the late Middle Ages, such as *The Ascension of St John the Evangelist* (*c.* 1410–20) by Giovanni del Ponte, are glorified with gold leaf. The gold grounds on which the figures are displayed were often burnished to a high polish, but their reflective gloss has been tempered by time.

PLATE 5.1   In Giotto's *The Betrayal of Christ* (*c.* 1305), some of the figures have their backs turned – an almost unthinkable prospect in stylized medieval art.

PLATE 5.2   The shading method recommended by Cennino is employed in Nardo di Cione's *St John the Baptist with St John the Evangelist(?) and St James* (*c.* 1365). Fully saturated pigments are used in the folds of the robes, and are progressively lightened with white towards the highlights.

PLATE 5.3   Leonardo da Vinci's *The Virgin of the Rocks*
(*c.* 1508) illustrates his *sfumato* method of shading and
his sombre palette, as well as his use of highlight to
direct the eye.

PLATE 5.4   Raphael's *The Madonna
del Granduca* (*c.* 1505) is robed in an
exquisitely matched red and aquamarine.

PLATE 5.5 Jan van Eyck's *The Portrait of Giovanni Arnolfini and His Wife (The Arnolfini Marriage)* (1434) displays the rich, jewel-like colours characteristic of the oil paintings of the Northern Renaissance.

PLATE 5.6 Carlo Crivelli's *Annunciation, with St Emidius* (1486) uses non-naturalistic gold to signify other-worldliness in a scene otherwise typical of the Renaissance.

artificial copper blue, and it is in this context that one generally encounters it in the modern literature.

Rosamond Harley, in her masterful survey of artists' pigments from 1600 to 1835, draws a distinction between blue bice and the pigment known as blue verditer, which is unambiguously a synthetic copper pigment. But blue verditer already verges on being an oxymoron, since it is not difficult to recognize the term's origin from the old French *verd de terre*, a 'green earth' if you please. From this we must infer that the first verditer synthesized was indeed green, and that the blue variant followed subsequently.

Both green and blue verditer have the same chemical constituents, which are also those of natural azurite: copper, carbonate and hydroxide ions. But even small variations in the ratio of carbonate to hydroxide ions alter the colour imparted by the copper ions: with less carbonate, the substance is greenish. In azurite, there is as much hydroxide as carbonate; in green verditer there is twice as much, just as in the copper mineral malachite.

Artificial copper pigments of this ilk were sometimes called 'refiner's verditer', a reflection of their origin in silver refining. Native silver is often alloyed with copper. To remove it, the copper metal is converted to copper nitrate, which dissolves in water. The seventeenth-century Swiss physician Sir Theodore Turquet de Mayerne claims that, about a 100 years previously, silver miners had cast a copper nitrate solution on to chalk (calcium carbonate), which at once turned green.

Yet this serendipitous process was also fickle and hard to control: sometimes it yielded the green pigment, sometimes the blue. When Robert Boyle investigated the manufacture of blue verditer in the seventeenth century, he commented on this unreliability. In 1662 Boyle's contemporary Christopher Merret described the situation as follows:

Tis a strange and great mystery to see how small and undiscernable a nicety . . . makes the one and the other colour, as is daily discovered by the refiners in making their Verditers, who sometimes with the same materials and quantities of them for their Aqua-fortis [nitric acid], and with the same Copper Plates, and Whiting [chalk] make a very fair Blew

Verditer, otherwise a fairer or more dirty-green. Whereof they can assign no reason, nor can they hit on a certain rule to make constantly their Verditer of a fair Blew, to their great disprofit, the Blew being of manifold greater value than the Green.[7]

Such puzzles must have posed an irresistible challenge and stimulus to the chemist, although it was not until the late eighteenth century that a Frenchman named Pelletier was able to manufacture the two colours reproducibly. Whether the product is blue or green depends on the temperature at which it is made, and so it seems that the vagaries of the weather may explain the refiners' perplexity.

By the seventeenth century, blue verditer was no mere by-product but an industrial concern in its own right. In France it was known as *cendres bleus*: blue ashes, hazarding confusion with the low-grade pigment called ultramarine ashes. To make matters worse, some English manufacturers in the eighteenth century took it upon themselves to anglicize this name, selling it as 'Sanders blue'. For a time this pigment was sold (or at least bought) under the belief that it was a different pigment from blue verditer – or blue bice as it might then have been called. It was with some dismay that the chemist Robert Dossie, author of the influential treatise *The Handmaid to the Arts* (1758), discovered that his Sanders blue and his blue verditer were one and the same.

The process of verditer manufacture may lie at the root of late-medieval recipes for making a mysterious blue substance purportedly from silver. Before the technique for making ultramarine was perfected, this 'silver-blue' was reputedly the best of all blue pigments. The recipes vary, but typically involve exposing silver to the vapours of vinegar or ammonia. We might suppose that alloyed copper metal in the silver reacts to form blue copper salts; but the mystery resides in the common specification that the silver must be very pure, free from copper contamination (and medieval silversmiths were quite capable of achieving this). The fact that the recipes are often said to originate from the 'Saracens' tells us of their alchemical origin, so perhaps buried in here is some confusion of metals in which one is assumed to be transformed to another.

Although Cennino makes no mention of artificial blue copper

pigments, they seem to have been widely used from at least the sixteenth century. Their relative cheapness commended them to interior decorators. By the seventeenth century refiner's blue verditer was a standard material for house paint, both as a distemper and as an oil paint. Blue verditer can be found on the walls of many stately homes of England, such as the Great Drawing Room of Bowood House in Wiltshire: it was one of the earliest 'commercial' pigments.

Dossie had more reason to decry the careless naming of commercial colours than perhaps he realized. Had he purchased blue bice, he might have found it to be not a copper-based pigment at all but something quite different: the blue cobalt-containing glass called smalt.

Smalt has obscure origins. Tradition attributes its invention to a Bohemian glassmaker named Christoph Schürer, some time between 1540 and 1560. But its appearance in Dieric Bouts's *The Entombment* (c. 1455) belies this, and it has been accredited instead to Italian glass-makers of the fourteenth century. (Giovanni Bellini's use of smalt in the late fifteenth century has been attributed to his interest in glass-making technology.) Another possibility is that it was not a European invention at all but originated in the Near East. Cobalt ores were, after all, used by the ancient Egyptians for colouring glass, and by the Persians for making blue enamels and glazes.

Cobalt occurs naturally in several minerals, notably the ore smaltite – a mixture of cobalt and nickel arsenides. When exposed to air, this forms a brilliant blue fibrous crystal known to miners as 'cobalt bloom'. It is a dangerous flower, for the arsenic compounds in the mineral dust are toxic and corrosive. Cobalt ore is abundant in Saxony, and the silver miners there were warned in Georgius Agricola's treatise *De re metallica* (1556) to beware of 'a certain kind of *cadmia* [cobalt/zinc ore] which eats away the feet of the workmen when they have become wet, and similarly their hands, and injures their lungs and eyes'. In the German translation of Agricola's treatise this devilish stuff is called *kobelt*, the name given to the gnomes and goblins thought to haunt the mines and torment the miners. The scholar Johann Mathesius warned in 1562 that, 'Whether or not the Devil and his hellish crew gave their name to *cobelt*, nevertheless *cobelt* is a poisonous and injurious metal even if it contains silver.'[8]

Smalt was a pigment widely used by the middle of the sixteenth century, by which time it was being manufactured on a large scale, most notably in the Netherlands. The method was probably much the same as that described in the seventeenth century by one J. Kunckel, the manager of a glassworks. The ore is roasted, he says, expelling noxious arsenic-containing vapours. The residue is cobalt oxide, which is then pulverized and heated with quartz (sand) and potash to create a molten glass. This is plunged into water, whereupon it cracks into fragments that may be ground to make the pigment. To retain its strong, deep blue colour, smalt must not be ground too finely; its consequent gritty texture makes it a difficult material to paint with.

The best grade of smalt had a purplish cast, commending it as a substitute for ultramarine. But this lustre is sadly diminished when mixed with oil – smalt fares better in water-colours or frescos. It appears, for example, in a fresco in the Fondaco dei Tedeschi in Venice (*c.* 1508) on which both Giorgione and Titian worked. But the Venetian painters were not shy of using smalt in oils: Titian employs it in *Madonna and Child in an Evening Landscape* (*c.* 1560), and it is found in many works of Tintoretto, including *The Crucifixion* (*c.* 1560) and the paintings of the Gonzaga Cycle (*c.* 1579). Paolo Veronese and El Greco used the pigment, as did van Dyck (*A Woman and Child* (1620/21)), Rubens (*Descent from the Cross* (1611–14)) and Rembrandt (*Belshazzar's Feast* (1636–8)). Smalt is common in works of the eighteenth century, and was still being manufactured in the 1950s.

The cost of colour

The Renaissance painter, having secured his commission from a wealthy patron, was not short of choice for materials. The nature of the commission dictated whether it was to be painted in fresco, on gessoed wood panel or, increasingly during the sixteenth century, on primed canvas (Botticelli's *The Birth of Venus* (*c.* 1485) is one of the earliest large-scale works on cloth). But which pigments did he select for his reds, his sky blues, his foliage and flesh tones?

The patron had a great deal to say about that. In 1434 the Flemish painter Saladijn de Stoevere, for example, was instructed that his Virgin in the altarpiece for the Franciscan church in Ghent was to have a robe of gold cloth lined with fine 'azure' (ultramarine or azurite) and glazed with *sinopere* (crimson lake). Azurite was specified in the contract between Nicaise Barat of Tournai and the church of St Peter at Antoing in 1446. The patrons knew what they were doing; left to their own devices, the artists would be inclined to economize, using smalt or indigo instead of the expensive blues. Dieric Bouts's *The Last Supper* (1464–8) contains no ultramarine, only azurite, perhaps because there were no stipulations about materials in the contract. 'What niggardliness wouldn't be forgiven,' says Alexander Theroux of the use of ultramarine during the Renaissance, 'in places where its application could be avoided?'

Sometimes the contractor would accede to such compromises to keep costs down: the sculptor Otmaer van Ommen was told that his work for the church of St Martin in Ypres in 1593 might be painted in either smalt or a cheaper variety of copper blue. In such cases the patron might entreat the artist to use his skill to make a cheaper pigment resemble a finer one.

The craftsmen's guilds enforced such standards as they could. Their regulations forbade members from substituting poorer materials for good ones: the Florentine painters were prohibited by statutes of 1315–16 from using azurite in place of ultramarine, and Sienese regulations of 1355 prevented red earth or red lead from being substituted for fine vermilion. The guilds might also have to argue their members' cause in the face of penny-pinching employers. But the painters were at the mercy of inflation: around 1497 Filippino Lippi was forced to take legal action against the heirs of Filippo Strozzi of Florence, who commissioned him to adorn the chapel of the church of Santa Maria Novella, when Lippi ran out of money owing to rising pigment prices while the work was in progress.

Good red lakes were expensive in the fifteenth and early sixteenth centuries, since their manufacture was still quite new and required specialized skills. Thus it was not unusual for these colours to be specified in contracts, as in Saladijn's. That lakes had displaced alchemical vermilion as the most princely red is evident from the common practice in northern European art of using the latter as mere underpainting for the former.

The patrons did not much care about the yellows, greens or blacks, which were all relatively cheap: and so artists tended to use lead-tin yellow over the more attractive but more expensive orpiment. Lucas Cranach is the only German artist of this period known to have used orpiment – and one can suppose that this was not unrelated to the fact that he himself owned a pharmacy, and so had ready access to more exotic materials.

One of the clearest indicators of the decline in the medieval role of pigments as a display of conspicuous consumption is the use of gold. Gilding is clearly non-naturalistic: gold leaf laid on a flat surface does not look like a three-dimensional golden object. Alberti warns that its appearance changes depending on how the light is reflected: 'when done in gold on a flat panel, many surfaces that should have been presented as light and gleaming, appear dark to the viewer, while others that should have been darker, probably look brighter'.[9] He therefore exhorts the painter to render golden surfaces such as brocade using pigments and skill, not the metal itself – for 'there is more admiration and praise for the painter who imitates the rays of gold with colours'.

It is fascinating to follow the demise of gilding throughout the fifteenth century. A curious transitional piece between the medieval gold grounds and the later more naturalistic use of gold is *The Conversion of St Hubert*, painted in the second half of the fifteenth century by the Workshop of the Master of the Life of the Virgin in Cologne. Here we find a gold 'sky' juxtaposed with an attempt at a naturalistic landscape (although the painter shares none of Leonardo's attentiveness to nature and seems to have learned aerial perspective – the blueing of distant hills – from a book). In *Madonna with Four Saints* (1446) by the Venetian Antonio Vivarini in collaboration with Giovanni D'Allemagna, gold is used for the Madonna's halo and some of the brocade in the robes, but yellow pigments are used for the throne and panelled walls – so adroitly that the eye is almost fooled. Already the artist's skill is taking precedence over the value of the materials. The Magi are still awarded red-glazed gilt crowns in Vincenzo Foppa's *The Adoration of the Kings* (c. 1510–15?), but the rest follows the Renaissance style. And Carlo Crivelli's astonishing *Annunciation, with St Emidius* (1486) (Plate 5.6) presents us with immaculate, almost pedantic perspective and rich, varied use of colour – yet the beam from heaven striking the brow of the Virgin is gold leaf. Here the non-naturalistic character of the gilding serves to remind us that the heavenly ray is outside of nature. It is like a parting shot from the Middle Ages, before human experience displaced divine authority as the artist's guide and mentor.

As the materials lost their symbolic virtues, the painter's colouristic decisions became purely financial. The price lists of pharmacies – the main suppliers of artists' pigments in the early sixteenth century – give a good indication of why certain colours were preferred over others. In 1471 Neri di Bicci paid two and a half times as much per ounce for good azurite in Florence as for a good green (*verde azurro*, probably malachite), a good red lake and a fine yellow lake (*arzicha*). Giallolino (here called *giallo tedesco*, probably lead-tin yellow) was one-tenth the price of azurite, and white lead was a mere hundredth of the cost. Ultramarine, meanwhile, was ten times more expensive than azurite. So the price differential was vastly greater than that a painter would encounter today – no doubt with a proportionate influence on the choice of colours.

And the artist had to be prepared to travel for his materials. Although many large towns had a local supplier, the finest pigments were often to be found only in major commercial cities. Florence drew artists from far and wide: Guillaume de Marcillat, a French painter, ordered even lowly smalt and earth pigments from that city for his frescos at Arezzo. Lippi's contract for the Strozzi chapel implies that even Florence may not have been able to meet his needs: it mentions that he might need to travel to Venice, presumably to obtain pigments. German and French painters would journey to Cologne; the Flemish artists flocked to Antwerp and Bruges.

These trips were no mean undertakings, as the very need to specify them contractually implies. So the painter would have to plan carefully – he could perhaps sell off excess stock to his colleagues, but running short was another matter. And he was at the mercy of geography, for the availability and quality of different colours varied from region to region.

No wonder, then, that painters treasured their materials so highly, and took such care in their preparation and application. While both activities were often conducted by apprentices in their master's workshop, exacting standards were enforced. Like any other master painter of his time, Dürer did not apply every brush-stroke to all the works attributed to him; but when he did, the colours on his palette had been ground by his own hand, and mixed with oils that he had purified personally. To protect the finished work, he trusted only his own hand-made varnish, fearing (possibly with justification) that those made by others would discolour:

After a year or two or three I intend to varnish them with a new varnish which is not known to others, so that a hundred years will be added to their life. I will not allow anybody else to varnish them, because all other varnishes are yellow, and they would spoil my panels.[10]

The care and attention that Dürer lavished on his paintings is apparent in a letter he wrote to Jakob Heller in 1508 describing his labours on an altarpiece. 'I have it in mind to underpaint some four, five, or six times,' he said (and this is just the undercoat). A year later he adds 'I have used the very best colours I could get, especially good ultramarine . . . and since I had prepared enough, I added two more coats at the end so that it would last longer.' We can see that these artists were, as far as they knew how, painting for all eternity.

City of colour

If we want to appreciate the extent to which colour use in the Renaissance became embroiled with vulgar commerce and lucre, we can look into the heady cauldron where exotic pigments from the East first arrived *en route* to western Europe: Venice. The island port was trading with the Arabic world as early as the ninth century; Martin da Canal said in his *Cronique des Vénitiens* (1267–75) that 'Merchandise passes through this noble city as water flows through fountains.' From the Aegean Islands came sugar and wine, from the Far East spices, porcelain and pearls. Northern Europe supplied minerals, metal and woollen cloth, while Egypt and Asia Minor were sources of gems, dyes, perfumes, ceramics, pigments, alum and rich textiles.

Venice was also the principal conduit for Byzantine art brought west from Constantinople following the Crusades of the thirteenth and fourteenth centuries, in which the Venetian navy participated. This was an art resplendent in dazzling jewelwork, which used rich colour to convey an impression of light and space. It was these qualities, not the mathematical perspective of Brunelleschi, that came to preoccupy the Venetian artists. Although they certainly used perspective, they clung to an ideal of space as something felt and seen, not calculated through geometry.

It seems likely that the climate of the city itself also played a part in determining the Venetian style. The steamy atmosphere creates subtle shifts of light, the waterways cast strong reflections, and forms are rendered hazy in contrast to the hard brightness of Tuscany and central Italy. The Byzantine-style mosaics that make the Venetian basilica of San Marco so resplendent educated the city's painters in shimmering optical effects.

The Venetian painters took great delight in experimenting with the new colours that entered the port. Titian used an unusually large range of pigments, including orpiment and the only 'true' orange of the Renaissance, realgar, available in Venice from around 1490. The reputation of Venice as the best source of fine pigments is evident in the travel concession in Filippino Lippi's contract for the Strozzi chapel; Cosimo Tura came to Venice from Ferrara in 1469 to procure materials for his work on the Belriguardo chapel.

The Venetians adopted canvas as the main support for their works from around the 1440s – earlier than the rest of Italy, no doubt encouraged by the presence of a burgeoning shipbuilding industry that produced the fabric for sails. This preference may have been abetted by the tendency of the humid, saline air of the lagoon to attack frescos more avidly than in central Italy. The coarse texture of the canvas favoured imprecise outlines over the crispness that the Florentines executed in panel works. The Venetian artist Tintoretto

(Jacopo Robusti, 1518–94) experimented with the possibilities that this texture offered, abandoning the thick gesso coats usually used to smooth the canvas so as to exploit the grainy weave for effects that, in large works, gained in strength from a greater viewing distance. Titian used the grain to develop something like optical mixing (see page 211), letting undercolours show through in the gaps where a brush-stroke had passed over the textured surface. There was none of the invisibility of effort that Vasari so exalted; Titian, like the artists of China and Japan, left the energy of his brush-strokes evident, which is why his paintings are bursting with vitality.

Ever since Giovanni Bellini (c. 1431–1516) introduced the techniques of oil painting into Venice in the 1470s, the Venetian painters used them to create bold and luminous colours – the elements of a poetic visual language that spoke of drama, passion, heightened sensibilities. Theirs was a sensual art, a counterpoint to the rational ways of Florence.[11]

Vasari tells us that all three of the great Venetian painters of the High Renaissance – Giorgione (c. 1478–1510), Titian (c. 1490–1576) and Sebastiano del Piombo (c. 1485–1547) – were trained in Bellini's studio, where they would have learnt his style of creating rich and complex colour gradations by many-layered glazing. Titian's use of this approach is extreme – some of his works have complex layered paint structures that are almost impossible to interpret. 'Glazes, thirty or forty!', he is said to have exclaimed. This is surely an exaggeration, but not by so much: an analysis of the black cloak of Bishop Averoldi in Titian's *Resurrection* (1519–22) has revealed nine distinct layers between the gesso and the varnish, incorporating lead white, vermilion, lamp black, azurite and some kind of violet lake.[12]

Colour as composition

Titian uses colour as a constructive medium: not for decorative or symbolic purposes but as the very means of artistic expression. His pictures are composed and unified with colour. Previously, paintings were given coherence by rules that dictated spatial composition –

for example, the Madonna would always be placed centrally. Titian disregarded such strictures – in *Madonna with Saints and Members of the Pesaro Family* (1519–28) the Virgin is seated on the right, while St Peter takes central position and pictorial balance is achieved by counterposing the Virgin with – horror! – a flag. But what a play of bright primaries to satisfy the eye's need for structure! Mary's red gown is matched by the red flag, while her blue robe leads us to the blue of St Peter's garments, stunningly contrasted with a yellow robe.

The strong local colours in this and other early works of Titian are clear descendants of the 'chromatic painting' of the fifteenth century, with their isolated bright primaries, their Albertian contrasts of reds and greens, blues and yellows. Titian's ability to reconcile these strident hues seems miraculous.

The complexity of the paint surface in Venetian art is not solely a consequence of efforts to achieve new shades. Many of these works were extensively altered while being created – an indication that the Venetians did not always carefully plan and draw their designs first as a Florentine artist would have done, but composed as they painted. Giorgione was one of the first to work in this way. An X-ray of his famous and enigmatic painting *The Tempest* (c. 1508) reveals a woman dipping her feet in the water, painted out beneath the soldier on the left. This earlier composition would, needless to say, have radically changed the whole mood of the picture, indicating that Giorgione had no fixed idea in mind when he began it. Titian sometimes painted his background in full before laying the foreground figures on top. A fresh white ground beneath the outline of the figures ensured that the colours retained their luminosity.

This is how Titian's most famous work, *Bacchus and Ariadne* (1523) (Plate 5.7), was put together. The commissioning patron, Alfonso d'Este of Ferrara, sent Titian texts from Catullus and Ovid to inform the artist of the mythological context. The picture shows Ariadne watching the ship of her lover Theseus depart, when the god Bacchus arrives and leaps from his chariot to claim her for his own. Ariadne is turning away virtuously – but Bacchus's conquest is ultimately successful.

This painting includes almost every pigment known to the early sixteenth century. The greens are malachite, green earth, verdigris and 'copper resinate'. Ultramarine is used profligately – not only in Ariadne's robe but also in the remarkable sky, the distant hills, and even in the shadows of some of the flesh tones. Ariadne's scarf is vermilion, its strong opacity here needed to contrast with the blue robe; and Titian has given it added brilliance by glazing a thin layer of coarse-ground, darker pigment over a thick layer that is more finely ground. Such touches make it clear that the painter knew how to extract the best from his materials. The orange robe of the cymbal player in Bacchus's entourage is unusually vivid, for Titian has here taken advantage of Venice's access to realgar.[13]

The picture blazes with bold, differentiated colour; yet Titian breaks the 'rules' of Alberti's colour contrasts, placing the blue robe adjacent to the blue sea and sky, and warm orange and tan tones next to one another. He relies on materials to distinguish the robe from the sea – ultramarine for the first, greenish azurite for the second.

The dominating blue sleeve in Titian's *Portrait of a Man* (*c.* 1512) (Plate 5.8) shows how far painting had moved on from the stark colour fields of the thirteenth century. The 'blue' shifts constantly in tone and hue, and in fact much of it is nearer to grey; yet the overall impression of a higher-keyed tone comes largely from the stronger blues on the shoulder. One is reminded of the remark sometimes attributed to Titian, that the painter should use Venetian red (an earth colour) but make it look like vermilion.

In Titian's later works these subtle modulations are used to produce a *continuity* of colour, a harmonious overall tonality in a style known as 'tonal painting'. This is what we see in *The Annunciation* (1559–62), *Tarquin and Lucretia* (1568–71), *Danae* (1553–4), in the *Venus* (1538) painted for the Duke of Urbino, and in the extraordinary, almost Impressionistic *Death of Actaeon* (1559–*c.* 1562), which looks poised to bring us straight into the nineteenth century. The sharply delineated and contrasting colours of the late Middle Ages have been discarded, and a central colouristic theme runs through the whole composition. In *Danae* this theme is the rosy magenta-pink of the goddess's body and its shadows, which deepens harmoniously to magenta in the draperies or to violet at the fringes of the fiery clouds. There are blues, greens and greys in this picture, but they are not allowed to disrupt the unity of the scene.

The tonal painting of the Venetians shares something in common with Leonardo's use of colour to unite elements rather than to set them apart – but without sacrificing high-keyed colour. It was a style adopted, in their own distinctive ways, by Titian's successors Tintoretto and Paolo Veronese.

Titian delighted and awed the Venetians with his dramatic new styles. Legend has it that the Emperor Charles V stooped to pick up a brush that the Master dropped as he worked in his studio, a gesture of supplication the gravity of which it is hard for us to appreciate fully today. For centuries afterwards, painters must have felt that they were working in Titian's shadow. How can one possibly supersede such genius?

6. Old Gold

THE REVIVAL OF AN AUSTERE PALETTE

Begin by painting your shadows lightly. Guard against bringing
white into them; it is the poison of a picture, except in the lights.
Once white has dulled the transparency and golden warmth of your
shadows, your colour is no longer luminous, but mat and grey.

Attributed to Rubens

Dark is the basic tone of his paintings, and darkness occupies a large
area in them . . . but how full of life is such darkness! Beginning
with the most glowing middle tones of brown and yellow, they
are gradually deepened through glazes and accents and made so
unutterably rich in values!

Max Doerner, *The Materials of the Artist* (1949), on Rembrandt

Titian has been dead some sixty years, and here is Anthony van
Dyck (1599–1641), the Dutch 'picture-drawer' to Charles I of
England, painting his royal patron's portrait on horseback (Plate
6.1). The setting – distant hills and sky to the left, forest to the right,
the terrain gently sloping to follow the central figure's gaze – is,
minus the sea, just like the spot where Bacchus surprises Ariadne.
But there the comparison stops. Where Titian's sky blazed, van
Dyck's is low-keyed and greyish. Titian's greens are those of spring-
time; the summer has passed in van Dyck's sombre woodland. Skin
glows warm in Titian's image, and his draperies are vivid. Charles
and his horse are cool-fleshed; even the royal saddle-cloth is muted.

What has happened to the palette, that it should have become so
sober and restrained? Van Dyck had access to all the colours that
Titian used (though some more readily than others). Yet on the
palette depicted by Rembrandt's pupil Aert de Gelder in his *Self-*

portrait as Zeuxis (1685) only red shows up as a bright primary in the transition from white, through ochre, to brown and black – and the picture reflects as much. There is little ultramarine in the sky above van Dyck's Charles I: it is mostly greyish-blue smalt and white. The saddle-cloth is fringed with indigo and white; the foliage and foreground are glazed with ochres, browns and black.

It would be unfair to attribute all of the picture's drabness to van Dyck: the varnish has darkened, some of the lake pigments have faded, and the smalt sky is probably discoloured. But the artist clearly had no desire to emulate the riches of Renaissance art. Van Dyck did occasionally paint images in bright colours, but his portraits from the court of the English king speak of a new aesthetic that was wary of chromatic brilliance.

The Baroque period represents a strange episode in the story of the creation and use of colour in art. The painters of the late sixteenth and the seventeenth centuries did not value novelty so much as sobriety and control in their colour choices. By the dawn of the seventeenth century the advocacy of Giorgio Vasari and the scholars of the Italian academies had largely secured the superiority of *disegno* over *colore*. The influence of this idea soon spread to France, and a muted palette and dark chiaroscuro became the predominant style of European art. When we remember the Frenchmen Nicolas Poussin (1594–1665) and Claude Lorrain (1600–82), or the Dutch portraitists Frans Hals (1580?–1666) and van Dyck, it is not for the exuberance of their colours. Rembrandt, as Doerner rightly says, painted deep shadows and golden light, under which all things turn to warm browns that he made beautiful. But in lesser hands this brownness became the hue of conventionality, of an art made to appease the connoisseurs and conservative patrons rather than to excite the senses.

And so we have for a moment to forgo the dizzy excitement that the previous ages offer to the colour eye, and seek a more subtle savour in the palette of the seventeenth and eighteenth centuries. But the Renaissance did not end with a simple, unanimous capitulation of colour. Rather, it lost its way in the late sixteenth century within a maze of frantic experiment, in which some paths led to gloomy murk while others pointed to lurid, gaudy landscapes. What mattered most was that a painting should capture the eye with drama and novelty. Many strove hard (often far too hard) to impress, their contrived works creating the style of Mannerism. Strangely, this superficially libertarian attitude arose within a social context shaped by the re-emergence of intolerance, authoritarianism and dogma. The Church was fighting back.

The new manner

Luther's Reformation engendered the Counter-Reformation as if pre-empting Newton's law of action and reaction. It was a last attempt by the theocracy to assert dominance before the Enlightenment banished God's Earth for ever from the centre of all creation. The Church, seeing its authority undermined by Humanistic rationalism, rallied and imposed a theological set of values akin to that of the Middle Ages. Classical (that is, pre-Christian) learning, said papal Rome, was all very well; but the ultimate arbiter of all questions of conscience was God (or his representatives on Earth), not science or nature. As judge and gatekeeper of the conscience of Man, the Society of Jesus and the Inquisition offered their services.

The ecclesiastical reactionaries were sophisticated enough to recognize that art is a powerful tool for the propagandist. Pictures – the potential text for a 'Bible of the Illiterate' – speak to the uneducated when words cannot. At the Council of Trent, which began its deliberations on Church policy in 1545, it was decreed that religious art should depict things in a transparent manner, with laborious codification. All angels must have wings, all saints haloes. If their identity is not obvious then they must bear labels, and never mind the demands of realism or aesthetics. Colours became bright again in order to appeal directly to the requisite emotions. Nakedness was frowned upon, even in those cases where there seemed to be biblical justification. Prudery abounded. Michelangelo's naked figures in the *Last Judgement* adorning the Sistine Chapel were much disputed. Pope Paul IV ordered that draperies be painted over exposed loins; more were added at the command of Pius IV. Even so, the fresco barely escaped complete destruction (and El Greco mischievously offered to replace the whole thing with a work 'modest and decent, and no less well painted than the other'). In 1582 the sculptor Bartolommeo Ammanati professed that he would, if he had been able, have destroyed all those images of naked men and women he had carved previously – an attitude that is perhaps unusually extreme among artists but which none the less expresses the spirit of the age.

Those artists who continued to uphold the Humanism of the Renaissance risked censure, and worse. In 1573 Paolo Veronese (*c.* 1528–88) was forced to defend his *Feast in the Home of Levi* before the Inquisition, who demanded to know why the work contained figures not mentioned in the Bible. He confessed ingenuously that they were there to fill up space (there was a lot of it to fill). But still he was commanded to rework the picture. Biblical pedantry was the order of the day.

All this would seem to imply that the Counter-Reformers sought a return to a kind of austere, medieval simplicity. And indeed some of them, such as Popes Paul IV and Pius V, wanted just that. But it became clear towards the end of the sixteenth century that a more vigorous approach was needed to combat the growth of Protestantism. The Jesuits discerned that ecstatic emotion, not dour abstinence, was the better lever on men's hearts. Their anti-intellectual strategy set the tone of the Counter-Reformation from around 1620, but it left its mark on the arts rather earlier.

It is scarcely to be wondered at that Leonardo's insistence on accurate observation and measurement foundered in such a climate. In 1607 the president of the Academy of Drawing in Rome, the architect and painter Federico Zuccaro (*c.* 1543–1609) was prepared to pronounce that

the art of painting does not derive from the mathematical sciences, nor has it any need to resort to them to learn rules or means for its own art, none even in order to reason abstractly about this art: for painting is not the daughter of mathematics but of Nature and of Drawing.[1]

Zuccaro, an influential theorist of his day, stands at a curious juncture. Although he is mystically inclined and opposed to the rational aspects of Humanism, nevertheless he laments the excesses of Mannerism, which he regards as having ushered in a decline in the standards of Italian art. He complains about the caprice, the frenzy, the furious and bizarre invention of the early Mannerists; yet his own works can hardly be considered free from some taint of these showy impulses.

The wild experimentation of Mannerism no doubt received sanction from the anti-rationalism of the Counter-Reformation, but cannot be wholly ascribed to it. By the mid-sixteenth century many Italian academic artists had already come to adopt the courtly stylization characteristic of Mannerism. The value of a work was increasingly seen as a function of the reputation and 'judgement' of the artist, irrespective of his technical abilities. This attitude pervades the writings of Vasari, for whom the last word in good art is good taste. While paying lip-service to the need to imitate nature, Vasari exhorts the painter to excel over her and to develop a cultured eye before a facility with mathematics. In a declaration apt to endorse all manner of arbitrary artistic snobbery, Vasari claims that the highest virtue of an artist – *grazia* or grace – is a natural gift and not to be acquired by any amount of diligence. Such refinement is, he says, exemplified by works that hide any sign of the labour that went into them. Vasari dismisses Titian as too dutiful to nature ('some of whose aspects tend to be less than beautiful'), and upholds Raphael instead as an exponent of graceful colour. He regards 'German' (Gothic) art as particularly abhorrent: barbarous and full of 'confusion and disorder'.

Dispensing with natural rules of proportion and composition, judged and judging only by subjective considerations of taste, and driven almost frantic by the extraordinary outburst of genius that had preceded them, the Mannerists produced some very strange contrivances in an attempt to attract attention. Parmigianino's *Madonna* (*c*. 1532–40) is one of the most notorious of these, surely a contender for the ugliest of all 'great' paintings. The elegant, sterile Virgin has a neck and fingers of almost absurd proportions, while the infant's head is coupled to a body of much more advanced years. Whether or not this ingenuity passed for beauty or grace in the eyes of the Italian courtesans, it certainly seems now to deserve characterization as 'mannered'.

Zuccaro was not alone in asserting that such exaggeration had occasioned a general decadence in art. The only antidote, it seemed, was to study and emulate the techniques of the Renaissance Masters. It was a lament that was to recur in the following two centuries, so that even in the 1790s a (fraudulent) claim of the rediscovery of the 'Venetian secret' – the techniques and materials used by Titian and his contemporaries – was greeted with credulous excitement.

And so painters of the late sixteenth and the early seventeenth century worked in a context constrained by a new religious intolerance yet overheated by pious passion. They were acutely aware of the supreme achievements of their recent forebears, yet the rules with which those works were constructed had vanished. From this confounding maze each individual had to seek his own exit.

In the shadow of the Masters

In Venice, Paolo Veronese was the undoubted heir to Titian's fulsome use of colour. Born, as his name implies, in Verona, he worked in Venice from 1555, and made avid use of every one of the colours the city had to offer: ultramarine, azurite, smalt, indigo, cochineal red lake, vermilion, red lead, lead-tin yellow, orpiment, realgar, copper resinate. Particularly striking in some of his works, such as *Adoration of the Kings* (1573) (Plate 6.2) and *Feast in the Home of Levi*, is a bright green mixed from three pigments applied in two layers. So indelibly did this become a trademark that the eighteenth-century synthetic pigment emerald green (see page 174) was known in France as *vert Paul Véronèse*. Veronese largely abandoned the sophisticated glazing techniques that earlier Venetians had favoured, and instead mixed his colours on the palette. Like Titian, he used complementary contrasts to enhance the vibrancy of his colours, and he never let them be overwhelmed by the heavy chiaroscuro that was becoming popular among his contemporaries. If Veronese was touched by Mannerism, it was of a decidedly Venetian variety, for he employs none of the anatomical distortions characteristic of central Italian art at that time.

Tintoretto was less restrained. True to the fashion of the age, he painted to attract attention – even if that needed to be at the expense of coherence. Works such as *The Miracle of St Mark Freeing the Slave* (1548) and *St George and the Dragon* (*c.* 1560) (Plate 6.3) are full of frenzied melodrama, with colour often working overtime. In *The Annunciation* (1583–7), the over-wrought perspective is tortured mercilessly, while a stream of cherubs tumbles through the window to almost comic effect. Sharp, strong colours were for Tintoretto simply a means to an end, this being to excite and shock the viewer. It is hardly surprising that conservative academics like Vasari saw in Tintoretto's breathless style a lack of proper care over technique. Vasari calls his sketches 'so crude that his pencil strokes show more force than judgement and seem to have been made by chance'.

Several of Tintoretto's works are instantly recognizable by their sombre, heavy tones, in which figures and objects are picked out in almost ghostly, glowing highlights. He sought tonal unity by using dark, reddish-brown grounds – deeper even than those over which Leonardo wrought his *sfumato*. Caravaggio used the same technique to envelop his scenes in velvety shadow. Some of Tintoretto's underpainting deploys mixtures so complex that one is forced to suppose the painter made them simply by scraping his palette. Like Titian, he used just about every pigment he could lay his hands on, blending them in unusual combinations to 'break' the colours.

Unorthodox colour choices were regarded by other Mannerists as a way to make their mark. Michelangelo is sometimes counted, in his later years, as one of these. There can be no question that he cared deeply about colour, but his use of the non-naturalistic *cangiantismo* technique (see page 124) testifies to his lack of concern for rigid realism.

But no one embodies the strange excesses of Mannerism more graphically than the Cretan painter Domenikos Theotokopoulos (1541–1614), whose nationality gained him the nickname El Greco. After studying under Titian in Venice, El Greco moved to Toledo, the Holy City of Spain, where he undertook many commissions for the Church. How even in the fractious and unrestrained artistic climate of the late sixteenth century his extreme non-naturalistic colouring, coupled with alarming distortions of anatomy, could have won any critical approval remains something of a mystery. What did the painter's contemporaries make of these pallid figures robed in blue, madder and honey-brown, writhing in a world of ghastly light? El Greco's landscapes – notably his remarkable paintings of Toledo – would not look out of place beside Cézanne's hillsides. Indeed, it was not until twentieth-century styles had retutored the eye that his works were 'rediscovered' after being long regarded as incomprehensible. It is telling that the Orphists Robert and Sonia Delaunay, who in the 1910s experimented with abstraction in bright colours, considered El Greco a predecessor.

Autumn's colours

Another response to the problem of how to advance the tremendous colouristic invention of the Renaissance was to sidestep it, by subjugating colour to extreme light and shadow. For Cennino and Alberti, chiaroscuro meant lightening or darkening the tone of pure, bright pigments by adding black or white. But the late Renaissance and the ensuing Baroque period became an era of deep shadows, of brooding blacks placed in dramatic counterpoint to fulvous highlights. Correggio, Caravaggio and Rembrandt were the thaumaturgists of black and brown.

Can it be coincidental that amidst this golden glow and heavy gloom emerged several new yellow, ochre and brown pigments? Never before the seventeenth century was the artist so well equipped to cover the canvas with lustrous highlight, modulating through ruddy shades to a pitchy murk.

Browns are surely the least glamorous of all pigments. They have enjoyed scant attention from artificers, since they can be dug from the ground in a wide range of hues. Among the ochres (iron oxides) that have been employed since time beyond record, those from the Tuscan city of Sienna gained special respect during the Renaissance. Raw sienna is a yellowish pigment; roasted to become burnt sienna, it takes on a warm brownish-red shade.

For the sombre palette there is nothing to match the profundity of umber. Darker than sienna pigments owing to a liberal proportion of manganese in the iron oxide, umber found its way into European painting around the end of the fifteenth century. Some writers have assumed the name to be of geographical derivation (like sienna): from Umbria in Italy. But umber seems more likely to stem from the Latin *ombra*, shadow. European umber was, after all, imported mostly from Turkey rather than Italy; and the rich red-brown of roasted (burnt) umber was highly valued for rendering deep but translucent shadows. The Englishman Edward Norgate wrote in the 1620s that burnt umber is 'a Collour greasy and foule, and harde to worke withall if yow grinde him as he is bought, yett of very greate use for Shadowes and hayres etc.'[2]

If painters are awarded the colours they deserve, we shall know what to expect in the works of Anthony van Dyck. The pigment Cassel earth, which became known in England as Vandyke brown from around 1790, is of a singular brown drabness. It is an 'earth' only in so far as it is taken from the ground; this is no mineral, but an organic material derived from peat or lignite. The earliest sources of the pigment were close to the German cities of Cologne and Cassel; in the seventeenth century alternative names included Cologne earth or corruptions thereof: earth of Cullen, Colens earth. At that time it was often listed as a kind of black, and Norgate praises its qualities for the kind of compositions that were becoming increasingly fashionable: it is, he says, 'very good to close upp the last and deepest touches in the Shaddowe places of pictures by the life, and likewise very usefull in Landscape'. The transparency of the pigment in oil makes its gloom spacious, and van Dyck employed it as a sobering glaze.

In nineteenth-century Belgium, Vandyke brown went under the name Rubens brown, for van Dyck acquired his habits from his teacher, the greatest Master of Antwerp. Max Doerner claims that Rubens used Cassel earth 'mixed with gold ochre as a warm transparent brown which held up well, particularly in resin varnish'. It is not an easy pigment to identify unambiguously, but has been reported in works by Rubens and Rembrandt, and possibly by Velázquez. Thomas Gainsborough (1727–88) made much use of 'Cologne earth' – like his rival Joshua Reynolds (1723–92), his debt to van Dyck extended to a shared taste in pigments.

Van Dyck and the English school that succeeded him also took their browns from an unappealing tarry substance called asphaltum or bitumen. It is hard to credit that this unpromising stuff, a residue from the distillation of crude oil, would ever have been accorded much value except in an age obsessed with brown. Rembrandt was a skilful enough craftsman to use it without mishap in his reddish-brown glazes; but in the hands of an immoderate experimenter like Reynolds it was disastrous. It does not dry properly at all, and thick films tend to run. Moreover, as the surface layer congeals, it shrinks and wrinkles, causing any material painted over the top to crack and curl. The French painters of the early nineteenth century, in thrall to a version of chiaroscuro that demanded deep, translucent shadows, seized on bitumen's seductive warmth of tone, only to discover its insidious effects too late. Théodore Géricault employed it to his cost in *Raft of the Medusa* (1819), and even the Realist Gustave Courbet made ill-advised use of it. In the 1920s, Max Doerner cautioned sternly that 'Its use is advised against in every technique.'

Van Dyck was fond of glazing his shadows with a similar dark, tarry pigment called bistre – it features, for example, in his portrait *Lord John Stuart and his Brother, Lord Bernard Stuart* (1638–9). This was made from the soot of burnt beechwood or birch bark. It was not a new material, having been used in manuscript illuminations since at least the fourteenth century; but one needed skill and knowledge to make much of it in oils.

How aptly this name now suggests a meaty brown sauce, like the 'brown gravy' that the Impressionists despised in early nineteenth-century academic art, and which seeps through the canvases of Reynolds, Gainsborough and Constable. Nothing reflects the stodgy conservatism of this era better than the words of the artist and connoisseur Sir George Beaumont, patron of Constable: 'A good picture, like a good fiddle, should be brown.'

(In fairness to Constable, we should remember that he protested by placing a violin against grass to show how nature was not really so sombre. Many of Constable's works, austere to modern eyes attuned to twentieth-century colour, were considered daringly bright in their time, to the extent that a member of the Royal Academy is said to have called one of them a 'nasty green thing'.

Constable pushed against the injunction to tone down one's colours
so as supposedly to match the contrasts of nature; but he did not
push hard enough to look 'modern' today.)

At least these murky materials were relatively cheap. The same
can be said of the red ochres and earths that colonize much of van
Dyck's canvases. Yet colour manufacturers of the Baroque period
discovered how to make their own versions of these natural pigments, and thereby to gain control over their hues. Iron, the martial
metal of the alchemists, gave birth to the Mars pigments: synthetic
iron oxides that ranged in colour from yellow through red to brown
and even a kind of chocolate purple ('Mars violet').

Quite how this innovation came about is not clear. The reaction
– the oxidation of iron in air – is simple enough, and we know
that medieval alchemists conducted it and called the ochre-tinted
product *crocus martis*, a literal Latin rendition of 'Mars yellow'. Yet
there seems to be no mention of this artificial substance as an artist's
pigment until Sir Theodore de Mayerne, Hugenot refugee and
physician in the court of Charles I, supplies a recipe in an early-
seventeenth-century document. Although he too calls it *crocus martis*,
or even 'saffron', he makes it quite clear that the product is red. In
fact de Mayerne quotes no fewer than three recipes, all merely
different ways of making the oxide: by heating iron filings, or
dissolving them in *aqua regia* (a mixture of hydrochloric and nitric
acids) and roasting the resulting iron salt, or heating iron sulphate
('martial vitriol') directly.

Later methods of manufacturing Mars red allowed the colour of
the product to be tailored to order. The real impetus for the
production of Mars compounds came, however, in the eighteenth
century, when sulphuric acid became an important commercial
item – especially as a bleach for the textile industry. Iron oxide is a
by-product of the manufacturing process and so, like many other
synthetic pigments before and after, enjoyed economic viability by
riding on the back of a larger concern within the blossoming
chemical industry.

There was no longer much call for the stark orange-tinted tones
of vermilion, which served now mainly as an opaque underpaint
for red lake glazes. Rembrandt seldom used vermilion, anchoring

his red lakes instead with red ochre. It became common for artists of the seventeenth century to adjust their reds by mixing several different lakes – the range was broadened by the colonization of the New World. From Central America came a new kind of cochineal, along with abundant brazilwood and the related species fernambuco and peachwood. The New World cochineal caught on: by the nineteenth century, this and madder were the pre-eminent dyestuffs in red lakes. The new wood-based dyes, on the other hand, acquired a reputation for impermanence that was even worse than that of Old World brazil. In 1553 the writer William Cholmeley described brazil as 'disceytful', a 'fauls colour'.

But it was not just from over the western horizon that alluring new colours were fetched. For this was the age when Europeans began to span the globe in all directions.

Spoils of empire

In 1589 the English explorer Richard Hakluyt served notice of the nascent colonial hubris of Elizabeth's nation. The English, he said, 'in searching the most opposite corners and quarters of the world . . . have excelled all the nations and peoples of the earth'. The East India Company was born as the new century dawned, and the English and Dutch were soon pitched one against the other to bring west the riches of the Orient. Amongst this trade in spices, silks and other exotica were two bright and mysterious yellow pigments.

It is not known precisely when Dutch traders began to import the mysterious golden material called Indian yellow. It appears in some Dutch paintings of the seventeenth century, but does not seem to have found wider use in Europe until the late eighteenth.

The pigment, known in India since about the fifteenth century under the name *purree*, *puri* or *peori*, seems to be of Persian origin. But what was this stuff, sold in hard, dirty-coloured and ill-smelling balls? Speculation abounded, much of it lurid. In the nineteenth century the French colourman J.-F.-L. Mérimée remarked on its smell of urine, but was reluctant to entertain the notion, proposed by others previously, that the substance could really harbour such an ingredient. George Field in England was less circumspect, believing that it was made from the urine of camels; others deemed that the fluid came from snakes.

It was not until 1883 that these rumours were set to rights. The Indian T. N. Mukharji made inquiries in Calcutta after the origin of the yellow balls, and was directed to the village of Mirzapur on the outskirts of the city of Monghyr in north-east Bihar province. Here he discovered that certain cattle-owners – 'milkmen' – created the stuff from the urine of cows fed exclusively on a diet of mango leaves. The yellow solid precipitated from the liquid when it was heated. Pressed into lumps and dried, it was then shipped to Calcutta and Patna for sale. It seems that the entire output of the pigment from India to Europe came from this village.

Given no other source of nutrition for fear that it would diminish the output of the colourant, the mango-fed cows were in a very poor state of health – to the disgust of Monghyr's regular dairy farmers, who called the milkmen 'cow-destroyers'. The discovery of the pigment's source helped to accelerate its demise: the practices of the milkmen were denounced as inhumane and laws were passed to prohibit them. By 1890 the legislation in Bengal to prevent cruelty to animals had become sufficiently stringent to make the manufacture of Indian yellow illegal, and it had all but disappeared by 1908.

Urine is, however, just an incidental component of the pigment. The colourant is a calcium or magnesium salt of an organic acid released by the mango. Despite the unpromising appearance of the raw balls, the ground pigment is rather lovely, giving a deep golden yellow. Its properties are better suited to use as a water-colour than as an oil pigment.

More or less coincident with the introduction of Indian yellow to Europe was that of another organic yellow pigment, called gamboge. Apparently taking its name from Camboja, the old form of Cambodia, gamboge was imported by the British East India Company from around 1615. It has been identified in works from the Far East dating back to the eighth century. The hard, mineral-like raw material is the solidified resin of trees of the *Garcinia* family native to South-East Asia. The gum is extracted from incisions in the tree bark, and once hardened it can be ground to a bright yellow powder. But like many organic colourants it fades rapidly in bright light.

Gamboge again fares best as a water-colour pigment, but it does appear in some works in oils – notably those by early Flemish painters, who were best placed to benefit from the Dutch trade in India. Rembrandt used it, attracted perhaps by the golden hue that it acquires in oil. Gamboge is also an ingredient of the eighteenth-century water-colour called Hooker's green, in which it is mixed with Prussian blue (see page 273) or indigo. Among its curious distinctions is the use of its fine, dancing particles by French physicist Jean Perrin to demonstrate Brownian motion in 1908, providing evidence of the existence of atoms. Its importation to the West was doubtless boosted by the fact that druggists also sold it as a pharmaceutical.

Another organic yellow common in northern European painting in the seventeenth century offers us a further glimpse of the mercurial propensities of colour terms. 'Pink' was a pigment of diverse provenance – recipes identify it as an extract of weld, broom, or unripe buckthorn berries – but often of an indisputably *yellow* hue. Pinks were in fact defined in terms of neither their ingredients nor their colour – for there were also green pinks, brown pinks and rose pinks. It appears that the noun refers instead, like 'lake', to the method of synthesis. Pinks were comprised of an organic colourant carried on an inorganic powder. The distinction from lakes is subtle, technical, and a testament to the attention given to the chemistry of the production process by seventeenth-century colour-makers. Lakes are generated through a chemical reaction, as hydrated alumina is precipitated from a solution in the presence of a dye. Pinks, meanwhile, result from a purely physical process in which the dye is attached (mordanted) to an inert white substrate, typically chalk, alum or baked and ground eggshell. They are thus a kind of pseudo-lake, distinct from true lakes in that no alkali is used in the making.

A recipe for pink is listed by Edward Norgate in the seventeenth century, and yellow pink was popular throughout that century and the next, particularly mixed with blue to make 'green pink'. Rose pink, prepared from brazilwood, was considered different from the lake pigment derived from the same colourant. Towards the late eighteenth century yellow pink fell into disuse, and although 'brown pink' remained in circulation into the nineteenth century, 'pink' gradually became synonymous with the light red 'rose pink' – until eventually the connotation changed from one of manufacture to one of colour.

Entering the landscape

Despite this apparent profusion of new pigments, artists continued keenly to perceive a paucity throughout the sixteenth to the eighteenth century. The propensity for experimentation with materials increased over this period, indicating that painters were by no means satisfied with those at their disposal.

There was, for instance, a profusion of prescriptions for greens as landscape painting came into vogue. In the early sixteenth century the German artist Albrecht Altdorfer was one of the first in the West to paint landscapes for their own sake, although Leonardo had already advertised their attractions: 'What moves you, man, to abandon your home in town and leave relatives and friends, going to country places over mountains and up valleys, if not the natural beauty of the world . . .?'[3] Could not the painter supply this experience without you leaving your door? Could he not place you amongst that landscape 'where you have had pleasure beside some spring, [where] you can see yourself as a lover, with your beloved, in the flowering meadows, beneath the sweetest shade of trees growing green'?[4]

Some art historians have perceived in such words a longing for a lost Arcadia that made landscape painting so alluring to a people increasingly embroiled in urban commerce. Others point out that landscapes are not depictions but interpretations of nature. Christopher Wood suggests that landscape gave the artist fresh scope for imprinting his authority on a work with unique grandeur of scale. 'Landscape', he says, 'was a hospitable venue for pungent colouristic effects.'[5] The influential seventeenth-century French writer Roger de Piles clearly felt that painters re-created the landscape to suit their own vision – to such an extent that this 'imagined reality' impinged upon the artist's very perception of nature: 'Their eyes see the objects of nature coloured as they are used to painting them.'[6]

If this were so, it places a dramatic responsibility on the greens that artists of that era had at their disposal. They were, by some accounts, quite unsatisfactory. In the 1670s the Dutch painter Samuel van Hoogstraten lamented, 'I wish that we had a green pigment as good as a red or yellow. Green earth is too weak, Spanish green [verdigris] too crude and ashes [green verditer] not sufficiently durable.'[7] The Spanish artist Diego Velázquez (1599–1660) seems to have concurred with these complaints: he never used a pure green pigment in his life, but always mixed them from azurite and yellow ochre or lead-tin yellow.

Painters' manuals were often remarkably specific about how to mix greens for different applications. Henry Peacham's *The Compleat Gentleman* (1622) gives the following advice:

For a deepe and sad Greene, as in the in-most leaves of trees, mingle Indico and Pinke. For a light Greene, Pinke and Masticot [here lead-tin yellow]; for a middle and Grasse-greene, Verdigreace and Pinke.[8]

In *The Practice of Painting and Perspective Made Easy* (1756) (you can begin to see to what manner of audience these books were addressed), Thomas Bardwell suggests greens for landscapes composed of light yellow ochre, green earth, brown pink, Prussian blue, orpiment and white. The use of orpiment underwent something of a revival in the eighteenth century, being especially popular in a mixed green with the new Prussian blue. In Jan van Huysum's *Hollyhocks and Other Flowers in a Vase* (1702–20) the greens contain indigo; by 1736, when he painted *Flowers in a Terracotta Vase*, he had replaced it with Prussian blue. Glazing rather than pigment mixing was sometimes employed: a manual from 1795 describes a 'very lively and beautiful green' obtained by glazing brown pink over blue.

The great French landscape artists Claude Lorrain and Nicolas Poussin used complex mixtures to obtain their variegated greens. One recommended formulation included a green earth, a blue (such as ultramarine), a yellow (lake or ochre), and perhaps a lead white and a black. Such combinations had no pedigree and were often unreliable, exhibiting unpredictable changes over time. The influx of new yellows added to the hazards faced by artists of the seventeenth and eighteenth centuries: many were less stable than the earlier lead-tin yellow and Naples yellow, so the discolouration (of mixed greens in particular) in paintings of these times is often worse than in older works. It is a treacherous business now to discern how these artists chose to represent 'the sweetest shade of trees growing green'.

Northern lights

The great Flemish, Dutch and German artists of the seventeenth century were perhaps better served with materials than those of the Renaissance. The Netherlands had become a major centre for pigment manufacture: lead white, smalt, lead-tin yellow and vermilion flowed from the Dutch factories to brighten the shops of the apothecaries and grocers who sold them. Antwerp was to northern Europe what Venice had been to Italy.

But the traditional fine blues azurite and ultramarine were increasingly difficult to obtain: from the early 1600s, the main mineral sources became either exhausted or inaccessible owing to war. One Northern painter who persisted with ultramarine was Jan Vermeer (1632–75), whose characteristic palette of yellow, blue and pearly white is displayed at its most stunning in his famous painting *The Milkmaid* (c. 1658). These bold, skilfully harmonized blues seem to come from another age, which one cannot quite place as more ancient or more modern. Yet ultramarine cost a princely sum – 45 guilders an ounce in 1626. Charles I's gift of £500 worth of ultramarine to van Dyck and the English painter Anne Carlisle was indeed generosity on a royal scale.

The sparkling, jewel-like colours of Peter Paul Rubens (1577–1640) make him Titian's Baroque heir. Rubens seems reluctant to exclude any hue from the canvas, so that his challenge was that of finding a harmonious arrangement of strong primaries. He was arguably less successful in organizing colour than Titian – some of his works, such as *Allegory on the Blessings of Peace* (c. 1630), verge on the garish, a shortcoming exacerbated by a fleshy choice of subject that, to the modern eye, approaches high camp. But there is no denying the joy with which these works are executed, the brushwork injecting an invigorating energy.

Although German by birth, Rubens was Flemish by descent: his father fled from Antwerp in the wake of Reformation unrest. But the family returned to their home city after the father's death, and it was in Antwerp and its environs that Rubens served his apprenticeship. The magnetism of colour led him inevitably south: in 1600, at the age of twenty-three, he set out for Italy. There, as court painter to the Duke of Mantua, he travelled widely. Visiting Venice at the first opportunity, he studied and copied the works of Titian with relish. The debt is particularly explicit in Rubens's intimate portrait of his second wife, *Helena Fourment as Venus ('Het Pelsken')* (c. 1636–8), inspired by Titian's *Girl in a Fur Wrap* (1535–7).

Both of Rubens's versions of *The Judgement of Paris* (c. 1600 and 1635–7) show a Venetian influence in their use of primaries: bright yellow in the heavenly light and draperies, strong blues in the sky, brilliant reds in the flesh tints and garments. The way that these colours are subtly modulated as they are carried out into the scenery is quintessentially (late) Titianesque. Rubens achieved his pure, glowing colours by applying the pigment on to white grounds, rather than using the muted red-browns or greys typical of the time. Nowhere is this more apparent than in *Samson and Delilah* (c. 1609) (Plate 6.4), where raw colour fills the canvas.[9] Delilah's red dress, which overheats the sexual charge of the scene, is almost unadulterated crimson lake, brightened with touches of vermilion and highlighted with lead white.

The servant's blue jerkin, contrasting with the golden glow of the candle flame and Delilah's hair, contains no blue pigment but is developed from lead white, black, and red lake. The same is true of the purple drapery in the background. It was not unusual for black to stand in for blue; greens were occasionally made by combining yellow and black. This ambiguous attitude to blue harks back to the four-colour palette of the Greek painters. Titian also used the trick in his *Portrait of a Man* (c. 1512) (Plate 5.8), which served as the inspiration for Rembrandt's *Self-Portrait* (1640). Van Dyck evidently learned it from his mentor, for the striking purple of the little girl's dress in his *Portrait of a Woman and Child* (*c.* 1620–1) is concocted from red lake, charcoal and white.

There is a telling lesson in van Dyck's *Charity* (*c.* 1627–8) (Plate 6.5) about how he, and other seventeenth-century Dutch painters, strove to keep their colours under control. The painting is clearly influenced by Titian, and at first glance seems even to share his colouristic enthusiasms. But although van Dyck had ultramarine available for Charity's billowing drapery, he chose to use greyish smalt, or even a plain mixed grey in some places, for the sky. Even the ultramarine drape is underpainted with dark indigo, which tones down its exuberance. The red drapery is constructed from lake pigments painted over vermilion and earth pigments. The lakes have partially discoloured with age, making it hard to judge what effect van Dyck intended; but a careful analysis of the paint composition, and the presence of a brown glaze of Cassel earth in some places, make it clear that he did not seek the rich purple-red we would expect from Titian.

The paintings of Rembrandt van Rijn (1606–69) exude a powerful impression of dark rusty-brown, which persuades us of a certain sincerity and honesty in the artist while at the same time reminding us now of his ruinous, impoverished end. By the 1650s, Rembrandt was using just a half-dozen or so pigments, mostly of dull earthy tones. He was a master at 'breaking' colours – breaking up fields of colour by using complicated pigment mixtures. One contemporary commentator praised Rembrandt's use of these mixtures 'harmoniously to depict nature's true and vivid life', and went on to denounce those who in contrast 'set the hard, raw colours quite bold and hard next to each other, so that they have no relationship with nature'. Clearly we have come a long way from Alberti, who would have been horrified at this deflowering of pigments and little concerned about a colour's 'relationship with nature'.

Surprisingly perhaps, Rembrandt was also an ardent admirer of Titian. More obvious is his debt to Caravaggio, whose heavy chiaroscuro was a prominent feature of the Utrecht school of Dutch painters in the early seventeenth century. Rembrandt adopted this style in his youth, and deployed it thereafter as the main vehicle for creating mood and psychological expression in his work. The sombre, almost despairing tone of his later pictures, painted in times of great financial hardship, certainly have ample precedent in his works from happier times.

Rembrandt's restricted palette excludes several of the brightest pigments available in the seventeenth century. His blacks (charcoal and bone black) and browns (including Cologne earth, as it would then have been called) are supplemented by most of the earth colours: ochres, siennas and umbers. His red lakes were mainly madder and cochineal. Blues, too, he used with restraint: mainly smalt, but sometimes azurite (for example in *Saskia in Arcadian Costume* (1635)). His principal yellow was lead-tin yellow, which was never the brightest of colours. Rembrandt used chalk as an extender, to add translucency to glazes (it is almost transparent in oils) and to give body to his medium. His thick impasto gained some notoriety, evident from Arnold Houbraken's remark in 1718 that a portrait by Rembrandt had colours 'so heavily loaded that you could lift it from the floor by its nose'.

But this limited palette had advantages, for it consisted largely of reliable, stable colours that have aged well. This was no mere good fortune: Rembrandt knew which materials would last, and how to combine them safely. And that is just as well, for his mixtures attain an almost comical level of complexity. Lurking at the threshold of visibility amid his deep shadows are concoctions of truly baroque proportions. In *An Elderly Man as St Paul* (c. 1659), the deep, warm brown of the dimly seen book cover is no mere umber but consists of a semi-glaze of lakes, red and yellow earth and bone black. In *Portrait of Jacob Trip* (c. 1661), a deep orange-brown is mixed from red and yellow lake with smalt. And for *Portrait of Margaretha de Geer* (c. 1661), the incidental dark grey-greenish wall in the background on the left has an unbelievable subtlety of pigmentation lavished on it. The lighter part is made up from a dark brown underpaint of red, orange and yellow earths mixed with bone black and a little lead white, which is then glazed with a mixture of smalt, red ochre and probably a yellow lake. For the deeper shadow, a glaze of bone black with red lake and red ochre is used instead. Yet this wall is hardly distinguishable from black shadow!

One cannot help but wonder whether these elaborate mixtures were systematically blended, or whether Rembrandt was merely making use of the random remnants daubed on his palette. In any event, they bring to mind Monet's determination to mix even the murkiest of shadows from strong, pure colours (see page 206). The consequence is that Rembrandt's colours are often almost indescribable – beyond tertiaries, beyond words. What is the colour of Hendrickje's dress in *Portrait of Hendrickje Stoffels* (*c.* 1654–6) (Plate 6.6), the woman who effectively became Rembrandt's wife after the death of his beloved Saskia? Some might say a pale lilac. Yet once again, there is no blue in here – if there is a violet tint, it comes from the slight blueness of the mixture of lead white and charcoal black, blended with a little red lake.

What better articulation of Rembrandtian colour can we find than the *Self-portrait with Maulstick, Palette and Brushes* (*c.* 1663), painted some six years before his death? Convention focuses on the enormous expressivity of the artist's care-worn face. But what is there on the palette cradled in one arm? Nothing but a bare expanse of ruddy brown, so loosely sketched that the dark coat remains visible beneath. And one can almost believe that no more colour than this, deftly lightened and darkened, was needed to convey all the introspection, frankness and gravity that the portrait reveals.

7. The Prismatic Metals

SYNTHETIC PIGMENTS AND THE DAWN OF COLOUR CHEMISTRY

Chemistry is the art of . . . producing several artificial substances more suitable to the intention of various arts than any natural productions are.

William Cullen, chemist (*c.* 1766)

What land, what Eldorado, what Eden flames with this wild brilliance, these floods of light refracted by milky clouds, flecked with fiery red and slashed with violet, like the precious depths of opal?

Joris Karl Huysmans, 'Turner and Goya' (1889)

There will never be another fifty years in chemistry like those that began in the 1770s, when everything was up for grabs. At the outset, barely any of the real elements were known and scholars still spoke in learned tones of phlogiston, the elusive substance that was supposed to be released when a substance burns. Yet everything was poised on the brink of revolution. (More than one, since so much of the story was staged in France.) By 1820, chemists spoke much the same language as they do today, and chemistry was a profession – potentially a lucrative one. And the list of elements was expanding to proportions none would have dreamed possible a century earlier. In Antoine Lavoisier's seminal *Traité élémentaire de chimie* (1789), the French chemist listed thirty-three elements; between 1790 and 1848, twenty-nine more had been added to the list.

It is no coincidence that this period saw an explosion in the production of new pigments for artists. After centuries of rather little innovation, suddenly painters found themselves spoilt for choice – and increasingly in need of criteria by which to assess the multitude of products that the nascent paint-making industry was asking them to purchase. It was a development that would separate the sheep from the goats: was one to adhere to the traditional, tried-and-tested materials or to experiment with the new? Unsurprisingly, those who chose the latter course tended to be innovators in artistic style too, and ultimately it was to become the very colour on the canvas that would discriminate the conservative from the radical.

Building blocks

The chemist's job was scarcely any simpler when there were but four elements on the ledger, but it was less colourful. Set against the riches of the Periodic Table, in which ninety-two natural elements display their gamut of quirks and idiosyncrasies, the Aristotelian earth, air, fire and water of Classical antiquity seem mundane indeed as the primary components of all creation.

The elements are chemistry's cast of characters, and attempts to dissect matter beyond the atom can never have quite the same appeal as the identification of that illustrious company. For protons and electrons have no hue, no one makes paints by mixing quarks or gluons, and the 'colours' that physicists give them are but flights of fancy. It is by manipulating the elements – altering their ratios, their unions, their electrical charge – that the chemists do their business; and that is how the colour-makers did theirs.

In *The Sceptical Chymist* Robert Boyle challenged the Aristotelian system of elements, suggesting that there might be more than four – perhaps even more than five. What were they? Boyle, perhaps wisely, does not say. But he raises doubts about whether earth, air, fire and water are irreducible and fundamental to all matter. For, he says,

Out of some bodies, four elements cannot be extracted, as Gold, out of which not so much as any *one* of them hath been hitherto. The like may be said of Silver, calcined Talke [talc], and divers other fixed bodies, which to reduce into four heterogeneal substances, is a taske that has hitherto proved too hard for Vulcan [i.e. fire].[1]

It is tempting to attribute too much novelty to Boyle. To some extent Aristotle's quartet had been vulnerable ever since Conrad Gesner showed in 1586 that it was just one of the elemental systems propounded in antiquity. But Boyle's contribution was to take the debate beyond questions of whether one should omit fire or add sulphur and salt (*pace* Paracelsus), by pointing to the need for direct analysis of the substances into which bodies decompose under chemical transformation: 'The surest way is to learne by particular experiments what heterogeneous parts particular bodies do consist of, and by what wayes, either actual or potential fire, they may best and most conveniently be separated . . .'[2] In this manner he defined the primary task of the chemist for at least a century to come. Yet it was not until a hundred years later that the elementary constituents of two of Aristotle's 'elements' – air and water – began to reveal themselves.

Boyle's assistant Robert Hooke was already on the trail with his observation that air contained an inert component which remained after a substance was burnt in a sealed container. But it was not until 1774 that the English scientist and Presbyterian minister Joseph Priestley made the first clear identification of the 'active' component of air, which Lavoisier was to call *oxygène*. To Priestley this was not an element in itself but air robbed of phlogiston. By making oxygen an element that is taken up by burning substances, Lavoisier pointed chemistry in the right direction, and everything else began to fall into place. Its union with hydrogen, produced by the action of acids on certain metals, gave water – an observation made by Henry Cavendish in 1781 and confirmed (one might say appropriated) by Lavoisier over the ensuing two years.

'Chemistry is a French science,' wrote Adolphe Wurtz in 1869, 'it was founded by Lavoisier of immortal fame.'[3] And of considerable cunning, he might have added. Lavoisier consolidated his oxygen theory of combustion, in the face of appreciable opposition (from within England in particular), by renaming and revising the entire scheme of elements. His *Méthode de nomenclature chimique* (1787), written with French chemists Bernard Guyton de Morveau, Claude Louis Berthollet and Antoine François Fourcroy, gave chemistry a new vocabulary and a systematic tabulation of elements that included eighteen metals (some, such as calcium and magnesium, still disguised as compounds, since they were too reactive to be easily separated from oxygen).[4]

The four French chemists established the journal *Annales de chimie* to propagate their system. They were a curious group. The suave Lavoisier was overbearing, marked with the arrogance of one born into privilege. He was quick to take credit and slow to acknowledge the discoveries of others. This combination of bourgeois background and haughtiness made Lavoisier's fate all the more certain when he was arrested by Robespierre's agents after the French Revolution, owing to his activities as a tax collector. Fourcroy pleaded with Robespierre for clemency, but to no avail. Lavoisier was executed in 1794.

Fourcroy, born of a noble family fallen on hard times, was a supporter of the Revolution, and did his bit for *fraternité* by teaching courses on gunpowder manufacture at the Académie des Sciences. Not by any means a brilliant scientist, he owed his modest successes to diligence. Berthollet and Guyton de Morveau were both of wealthy parentage, though the latter quietly dropped the aristocratic prefix during the Revolution: he became a lecturer in chemistry at the Dijon Academy, where he reclaimed his nobility under Napoleon's reign. It was here that Guyton de Morveau found himself engaged in research for the paint industry as the eighteenth century drew to a close.

Lead-free white

Artists were long accustomed to working with hazardous substances, since capricious nature has made them some of the most strongly coloured. Lead is not by any means the worst offender, and there is no indication that the health of bygone artists was disturbed by their minium, massicot or white lead. Yet as the Industrial Revolution increased the scale of manufacture and created a permanent workforce exposed for all their working days to such toxic substances, there was no overlooking the fact that white lead is an inimical material. Even in the seventeenth century Philiberto Vernatti described in the *Transactions* of London's Royal Society the terrible harm suffered by workers in white-lead manufacture:

The Accidents to the Workmen are, Immediate pain in the Stomack, with exceeding Contorsions in the Guts and Costiveness that yields not to Catharticks . . . Next a *Vertigo* or dizziness in the Head with continual great pains in the Brows, Blindness, Stupidity, and Paralytic Affections.[5]

Lead white (as it is now more often known) was made in huge amounts, since it was the only white pigment in wide use and was employed not only in artists' materials but also in domestic paints – posing a danger to house dwellers too. By the end of the eighteenth century, the risk was a matter of serious concern to the public health authorities in France, and an alternative white was demanded.

In the 1780s Guyton de Morveau was approached by the French government to search for a new, safer white pigment. In 1782 he reported that the best candidate was zinc oxide, known as zinc white, which was synthesized at the Dijon Academy by a laboratory demonstrator named Courtois.[6] Not only was zinc white non toxic, but it did not suffer from the darkening that lead white showed in the presence of sulphurous gases, as the lead carbonate is converted to black lead sulphide.

Zinc was on Lavoisier's list of elements: it had been identified as such by the German chemist Andreas Margraaf in 1746.[7] The white oxide was well known to the Greeks, as it is a by-product of brass manufacture. When copper metal is heated with zinc ore, zinc oxide forms a white vapour that condenses in fluffy deposits. Probably for this reason it was known in medieval times as *lana philosophica*, the philosopher's wool, and also as 'flowers of zinc'. The oxide is a mild antiseptic and prevents inflammation; it was recommended as a medicine by Hippocrates in the fourth to third century BC.

Zinc white had a lot going for it, but also some crucial drawbacks. First, cost – Courtois's product was some four times more expensive than lead white. Artists would certainly pay that much more for a superior material, but at the beginning of the nineteenth century zinc white did not look at all superior. Its covering power was not impressive, but worse still, it dried very slowly as an oil pigment. For this reason, its first commercial application was as a water-colour pigment, Chinese white, introduced by the English colour manufacturers Winsor and Newton in 1834.

Courtois tried to improve the drying time by adding zinc sulphate as a drying agent (siccative). But the problem persisted, and despite intense debate (to which Fourcroy and Berthollet contributed) about whether lead white or zinc white was the better pigment, the initial promise of zinc white began to fade.

It was rescued by the crusading efforts of the French colour-maker E. C. Leclaire. In the late 1830s he and a chemist named Barruel identified better siccatives, and in 1845 Leclaire began to manufacture zinc oxide at a plant near Paris. Other French entrepreneurs also braved this risky venture, and by 1849 the status of zinc white was considered secure enough for the French Minister of Public Works to issue a decree cautioning against the use of lead white. By 1909 it was banned from paintwork in all buildings in France. Mass production of zinc white led to a decline in its cost; by 1876 it was marketed at the same price as cheap lead white.

All European manufacturers of zinc white in the mid-nineteenth century made it by oxidizing refined zinc metal in the so-called 'indirect' or French process. But in the 1850s a new method was introduced in the USA. In a story that has all the trademarks of the apocryphal (but which one would like to believe anyway), it was discovered by accident by a worker named Burrows at the Passaic Chemical Company near Newark, New Jersey. The Passaic Company itself did no business in zinc, but the metal was refined in an adjacent plant. On fire duty one night, Burrows found that one of his company's furnaces had a leaking fire flue. He covered the leak with an old fire grate, but for good measure piled on top of it some zinc ore and coal belonging to the company next door, which happened to be lying nearby. Shortly afterwards, he noticed the white fumes of zinc oxide arising from the pile. He had the acuity to mention this later to members of the zinc company named Wetherill and Jones, who then developed the process into a manufacturing method during the 1850s and 1860s. This 'direct' or American process uses the zinc ore itself (sphalerite) as the raw material.[8]

Commercially, zinc white was of immense importance. But artists were hesitant to adopt it. Lead white had served them well for centuries, and its poisonous nature did not pose much of a threat to them – so why change to a newer, untested material? Moreover, zinc white had a cold, flat tone compared with lead white, which did not suit some tastes. So lead white remained the principal white for fine artists throughout the nineteenth century. Even water-colourists deferred – of forty-six English water-colour painters questioned in 1888, only twelve said that they used Chinese white. All the same, zinc white is not hard to find in nineteenth-century art, partly because some paint manufacturers tended to add it to their products as a lightener. It has been found in the works of Cézanne, and van Gogh was particularly fond of it. The Pre-Raphaelite painters used it as a ground for their strong colours in the 1850s.

In his search for a new, non-toxic white, Guyton de Morveau did not confine himself to zinc white. Among the alternatives he tried was the mineral barite: barium sulphate, sometimes called barytes. The mineral was described by Agricola in the sixteenth century, but there is no indication that it was considered as a white pigment. It needed no preparation beyond washing and grinding, and became quickly adopted into the artist's palette as 'permanent white', or 'mineral white' as it was known in England in the 1830s. High-quality deposits of barite are rather rare, however, and in the early nineteenth century barium sulphate was manufactured synthetically as a pigment known as *blanc fixe*.

Permanent white is listed in Bowles's *Art of Painting in Water-Colours* (1783), published only a year after Guyton de Morveau's studies. It serves best as a water-colour, being rather transparent in oils. But barium sulphate was commonly mixed with other white pigments as an extender, and it also served as a base for lake pigments. Because it was relatively cheap it became an important industrial paint, used for airplane camouflage colours in the First World War, and as a component of the US Navy's Battleship Grey from the 1910s.

Zinc smelting was a major industrial process in the early nine-teenth century, and zinc white was not the only incidental benefit for the artist. In 1817 the German Friedrich Stromeyer observed that one of the by-products of the zinc factory at Salzgitter was a yellow-coloured oxide. His subsequent analysis of this material brought to light a new metal, with chemical properties much like those of zinc. The zinc ore was traditionally called calamine or cadmia, and the association of the new element with zinc prompted the name 'cadmium'.

In investigating the chemistry of cadmium, Stromeyer prepared its vivid yellow sulphide ('sulphuret', as he called it). There is no better illustration of how the chemists of the time had become attuned to the importance of pigment manufacture than Stromeyer's comment in 1819:

This sulphuret, from its beauty and the fixity of its colour, as well as from the property which it possesses of uniting well with other colours, and especially with blue, promises to be useful in painting. Some trials made with this view gave the most favourable results.[9]

Stromeyer found that altering the conditions of the synthesis can generate an orange material instead – the hue depends on the size of the pigment grains. Cadmium yellow and cadmium orange are impressive pigments: rich, opaque and immune to fading in sunlight.

But until the 1840s the supply from zinc smelting was not large enough for cadmium yellow to make an impact. There is evidence of its use in oil painting in France and Germany from about 1829, but in 1835 it still does not feature in the lists of any English paint manufacturers. By 1851, however, cadmium yellow was being produced by Winsor and Newton. Yet even in 1870 the English colour chemist George Field commented that 'the metal from which it is prepared being hitherto scarce, it has been as yet little employed as a pigment'; the high cost of cadmium transferred to the pigment, and by that time there were cheaper, equally brilliant alternatives.

Nevertheless, cadmium yellow had its supporters, prominent

among them Claude Monet, who made extensive use of it from at least 1873. It was perhaps Monet's advocacy that encouraged Edouard Manet and Berthe Morisot to make use of the colour in the late 1870s.

Chameleon metals

Deadly green

Barium takes its name from the Greek *barys*, 'heavy' – for it is a dense, ponderous metal. It was identified as an element in 1774, and its discoverer was one of the most accomplished of eighteenth-century element-seekers: the Swedish apothecarist Carl Wilhelm Scheele. In the same studies, Scheele isolated chlorine – although he interpreted it in the convoluted fashion of the time as 'dephlogisticated marine acid' (He was an avowed phlogistonist until his death in 1786 at the age of forty-four.) Scheele isolated oxygen before Priestley, calling it 'fire-air'. And when in 1770 he collected hydrogen from the reaction of acids with iron or zinc, he believed that it might be pure phlogiston itself.

Scheele's experiments on chlorine compounds such as sea salt led him around 1770 to the discovery of a new yellow pigment, lead oxychloride. A chemical manufacturer named James Turner sought an English patent on the colour in 1781, and his subsequent battles against rival manufacturers created an important precedent in English patent law. His struggles clearly left their mark: the pigment came to be marketed as 'Turner's patent yellow', or simply patent yellow – though it did not make much impression on the art of the day.

In the course of investigating the chemical properties of arsenic in 1775, Scheele prepared the green compound copper arsenite. He recognized at once its potential as an artist's pigment, and it was soon being manufactured as 'Scheele's green'. It is not a particularly distinguished colour, however, having a slightly dirty tone. J.M.W. Turner used it around 1805 in an oil sketch of *Guildford from the Banks of the Wey*, and it turns up amongst the throng in Edouard

Manet's *Music in the Tuileries Gardens* (1862); but evidence of its use elsewhere is scanty.

Yet this new green might eventually have found more favour with artists had it not been displaced by a superior, related compound. In 1814 the German paint manufacturer Wilhelm Sattler of Schwein-furt, collaborating with pharmacist Friedrich Russ, chanced upon copper aceto-arsenite, whose brilliant green crystals are made by the reaction of verdigris dissolved in vinegar with white arsenic and sodium carbonate.[10] Known in France not only as *vert de Schweinfurt* but also by attribution to other locations – *vert de Vienne, vert de Brunswick* – it became 'emerald green' to the English.

There had never been a green like it. To nineteenth-century artists searching for strong colouration, such as the Pre-Raphaelites and the Impressionists, it must have seemed the natural choice. It was not widely available until 1822, when the German chemist Justus von Liebig published a report of its composition and synthesis – previously a trade secret guarded jealously by Sattler. Winsor and Newton began selling it as an oil colour in 1832, and its earliest use by Turner, ever eager to try new materials, dates from about the same time.

As it was relatively cheap to make, emerald green also became popular for interior decoration, and both this and Scheele's green were produced on an industrial scale during the mid-nineteenth century. But the arsenic content of these greens brought hazards not just to the manufacturers. Imprinted in thick relief on cheap, patterned wallpaper, these colours produce a toxic dust when brushed. And if exposed to damp, the pigments decompose to release arsine, a deadly gas of arsenic trihydride. In the 1860s *The Times* of London raised the alarm about the dangers of domestic uses of these arsenic-laced greens: 'It was not very uncommon for children who slept in a bedroom thus papered even to die of arsenical poisoning, the true nature of the malady not being dis-covered until it was too late.'[11] Legend has it that Napoleon Bonaparte died of poisoning from the arsenical fumes exuded by the emerald-green paint on the damp walls of his house in exile on St Helena.

The lemon of Siberia

France has rewarded its chemists with greater commemoration than most countries, but one wonders how many Parisians would now identify their rue Vauquelin with the superb analytical chemist who joined the triumvirate of Berthollet, Fourcroy and Guyton de Morveau at the forefront of French chemistry in the 1790s. Working alongside Fourcroy, Nicolas Louis Vauquelin discovered the element beryllium in the mineral beryl, and in 1797 he turned his attention to crocoite, a bright red crystal discovered in the eighteenth century in Siberia.

The French called it *plomb rouge de Sibérie* – Siberian red lead – and it seems to have been first mentioned in the West by the German J. G. Lehrmann in 1762. The mineral becomes deep orange when crushed, but found no use as an artist's pigment.

Vauquelin's investigations revealed a new metal within this mineral, whose compounds tended to be strongly coloured. For this reason, he proposed the name *chrome*, from the Greek for 'colour'; we now know this element as chromium. Crocoite is a natural form of the compound lead chromate; but when Vauquelin subsequently synthesized pure lead chromate, he found it to be a rich yellow. In collaboration with Berthollet, he suggested in 1804 that this substance might serve as a pigment. By 1809, when Vauquelin published his full investigation of the colour chemistry of chromium in the now prestigious *Annales de chimie* (on the editorial board of which he served), 'chrome yellow' was already on the artist's palette. It appears, for example, in Thomas Lawrence's *Portrait of a Gentleman*, painted in 1810.[12]

The exact hue of lead chromate can be adjusted by co-precipitating it from solution with lead sulphate: half and half of each salt gives a primrose yellow, a mixture with 65 per cent lead chromate gives a lemon yellow, and the colour deepens progressively with an increasing proportion of the chromate. Vauquelin found that the colour could also be varied by altering the temperature of the synthesis, which affects the size of the grains. The chemist reports that adding an acid to the solution yields a 'deep lemon yellow', which he tells us is the most highly prized by painters. And if the pigment is precipitated from an alkaline solution, it takes on an orange hue: 'a yellowish-red or sometimes a beautiful deep red'. Predating cadmium orange, chrome orange was the first pure, strong orange pigment that artists had ever encountered (realgar tends towards yellow), and it was soon being deployed to dramatic effect.

But for all their dazzling attractions, chrome pigments had to be affordable if they were ever going to find widespread use. That was never likely while the only source of chromium was in remote Siberia. In 1818 a French dictionary of 'natural history applied to the arts' comments that even Russian artists 'pay quite dearly' for lead chromate. Yet in that same year, deposits of the mineral chromite (iron chromate) were discovered in the Var region of France. Chromite was also found in the British Shetland Islands in 1820. Such was the avidity with which the new pigments were consumed that the Var mines were all but exhausted by 1829. But sources were also discovered in the USA from 1808, and by 1816 chromium ore was being imported across the Atlantic to England for pigment manufacture.

Pure chrome yellows and oranges remained rather expensive during the first half of the nineteenth century. But because the tinting strength of the pigment is so strong, it can be mixed with appreciable quantities of extenders such as barium sulphate. This encouraged the use of the yellow in commercial paints. Its appearance on the coaches of Europe pre-empted the canary-yellow taxi cabs of the USA.

Vauquelin's 1809 paper also mentions '*un vert extremement beau*' prepared by roasting an extract of crocoite. This is chromium oxide, which, because of its excellent stability, soon became valued as a ceramic glaze. 'On account of the beautiful emerald colour which it communicates', Vauquelin enthused, the pigment 'will furnish painters in enamel with the means of enriching their pictures, and of improving their art'. The truth is, however, that pure chromium oxide is a rather dull pigment and it did not gain much popularity with painters.[13]

But in 1838 the Parisian colourman Pannetier developed a recipe for turning chromium oxide into a deep, cool and slightly transparent green which became known as *vert émeraude* in France (not to be confused with the English emerald green, copper aceto-arsenite). In England this pigment was called viridian. The Impressionists adored it, and it is Cézanne's definitive green.

Viridian is simply hydrated chromic oxide: there are some water molecules in the crystal lattice. But that makes all the difference, tuning the chromium ions to a much more attractive hue than in the pure oxide. Pannetier guarded his recipe closely and charged dearly for the pigment. In 1859, however, the French chemist C. E. Guignet devised another method for making it, and viridian soon found a wide and receptive market. It eclipsed the poisonous emerald green for printing, domestic and industrial uses almost at once.

There is potential for confusion of viridian with so-called chrome green, a mixture of Prussian blue and chrome yellow that was marketed commercially in the nineteenth century. The identity of this mixed colour is further obscured by the peculiar practice of calling it cinnabar green or zinnober green. The mixtures range from strident green to olive, and because they were cheap they commended themselves to mass use. As an artist's pigment chrome green has significant drawbacks – it discolours under strong light or in acidic or alkaline conditions – but nevertheless it features in some nineteenth-century works.

Vauquelin's investigations of chromium's prismatic chemistry brought to light other new pigments, leading to a baffling profusion of chromate-based yellows. A pigment sold as 'lemon yellow' could have one of many different compositions: not only lead chromate or some admixture with lead sulphate, but alternatively chromates of the so-called alkaline earth metals barium and strontium (or more rarely, calcium). Barium chromate, described by Vauquelin in 1809, was also oddly called *outremer jaune* (yellow ultramarine). It is less opaque than lead chromate but is more stable – the tendency of chrome yellow to turn brown was much lamented later in the century. Vauquelin also made zinc chromate, which was sold as the artist's colour zinc yellow from the 1850s. Because of its rust-preventing properties, it was widely used on military equipment during the Second World War.

The cobalt rainbow

But then there was the question of blue. For painters of the late eighteenth century there was still no material that compared with the intransigently expensive ultramarine. So seriously did the Napoleonic administration take this deficiency that the Minister of the Interior, Jean-Antoine Chaptal, commissioned the distinguished chemist Louis-Jacques Thénard to devise a synthetic substitute for ultramarine.[14]

Thénard climbed high from humble beginnings. First taken on by Vauquelin as a bottle-washer and scullery boy, he was later promoted to the role of laboratory assistant. With Vauquelin's patronage, Thénard became a demonstrator at the Ecole Polytechnique in Paris, where his experiments on Scheele's chlorine secured his reputation as a skilled analytical chemist. Thénard and his colleague Joseph Gay-Lussac concluded (tentatively, since Lavoisier had claimed otherwise) that this substance, then known as oxymuriatic acid, might in fact be an element. And so it was, as Humphry Davy in London soon asserted more strongly. Davy named it for its pale leek-green colour, the *chloros* that the Greeks had once upheld as a primary.

In contemplating Chaptal's challenge, Thénard was aware that the potters of Sèvres made use of cobalt-containing salts in their blue glazes. He wondered whether these materials might also furnish a fine blue for artists. Cobalt is, after all, the colouring agent in the medieval pigment smalt, a kind of blue glass. In the early eighteenth century the Swedish chemist Georg Brandt analysed smalt and identified cobalt, already named for its ore, as the element responsible for the colour.

In 1802 Thénard synthesized a blue solid by mixing cobalt salts with alumina. Thénard's blue (cobalt aluminate) had a purer tint than azurite, Prussian blue or indigo, and was taken up immediately as a pigment. The method of synthesis was later simplified so that natural cobalt ore could serve as the starting material. The pigment entered into the artist's repertoire as cobalt blue.

It was expensive but popular none the less – the only serious competition came from the synthetic version of ultramarine manufactured from the 1850s (see page 276). Yet there was more to be had from cobalt, whose chameleon-like propensities rival those of chromium. Another cobalt blue, a mixture of cobalt and tin oxides (cobalt stannate), became available in the 1860s as a water-colour marketed by Rowney in England. By the 1870s it was sold as an oil colour: cerulean blue in England, *bleu céleste* in France. Bearing a greenish tinge, it was somewhat comparable to azurite. Cerulean blue acquired a reputation for impermanence by the 1890s, but the Neo-Impressionist Paul Signac was one of those sufficiently enamoured of it that he was prepared to take the risk.

In the mid-nineteenth century, three more cobalt colours appeared on the market. Cobalt green had a composition similar to cobalt blue but with some or all of the alumina replaced with zinc oxide. It had in fact been discovered before cobalt blue, by a Swedish chemist named Sven Rinmann in 1780; but only when zinc oxide became readily available was the manufacture of cobalt green viable. In 1901 the chemist and amateur painter Arthur Church praised it as 'chemically and artistically perfect' – a bright colour with excellent stability. But it did not have particularly good opacity; and like all cobalt pigments, it remained expensive. The same defects hindered cobalt violet, which was manufactured in France from 1859.

The most complex of the cobalt colours was a yellow that painters knew as aureolin, and chemists as potassium cobaltonitrite. It was synthesized in 1831 by the German N. W. Fischer, yet was not sold as a pigment until its independent rediscovery in the early 1850s by the Frenchman E. Saint-Evre in Paris. It was first marketed in 1861, but found general use only as a water-colour – Winsor and Newton launched their 'primrose aureolin' water-colour in 1889. For oil painters there were better, less expensive yellow pigments readily available.

Colour on trial

How was the artist to cope with this sudden expansion of the palette? The new colours looked enticingly brilliant, and many painters fell under their spell at once. But the art academicians advised caution, pointing out that the durability of the new colours was largely unknown. Never before had there been a greater need for rigorous testing of materials. This was a job for the specialist – that is, for the chemist. In 1891 the French painter Jean-Georges Vibert recommended a carefully selected list of pigments that the artist could count on to 'preserve their brilliance and freshness'. Among them were zinc white, cadmium yellow, strontium chromate yellow, cobalt blue, chromium oxide green (not viridian but the non-hydrated, opaque version), cobalt green, cobalt violet and manganese violet, discovered in 1868.

Such counsel drew on the studies of a new breed of colour technologists: men who were chemically adept, familiar with the latest colour theories of scientists such as Chevreul, Helmholtz and Maxwell, and intimately connected to the world of fine art. They were a bridge between science and art, and of an ilk that all but vanished when the century turned.

In France, Chaptal, ever concerned that artists should benefit from French eminence in chemistry, commissioned the chemist J.-F.-L. Mérimée at the Ecole Polytechnique to seek out new coloured materials. Having also trained as a painter, Mérimée had analysed the techniques of the Flemish Old Masters. He felt that artists had better understand these traditional methods if they were to avoid the deterioration evident in some contemporary works:

The paintings of Hubert and Jan van Eyck . . . whose colours, after three centuries, amaze us by their brilliance, were not painted in the same way as those which we can see perceptibly altered after only a few years.[15]

This was to be a recurring lament in the ensuing decades. But Mérimée's search for new pigments was not especially fruitful, although they did lead him to a new form of madder lake, *carmin de garance*, which became popular in France.

'A Rembrandt born in India'

The blazing works of John Mallord William Turner (1775–1851) break through the brown crust of early-nineteenth-century convention. At times his use of *colore* seems intent on dispensing with *disegno* altogether, and even admirers such as John Ruskin sometimes professed bafflement at this new, luminous way of painting. 'Pictures of nothing, and very like', was how harsher critics saw it.

Turner was a respected member of the Royal Academy from the end of the eighteenth century until his death in 1851, although his social awkwardness did not endear him to his contemporaries. Even in 1795 the young painter gave some inkling of his programme with *Fisherman at Sea*, a work dominated by the colouristic effects of light seeping through auburn and violet storm clouds. The atmosphere dominates Turner's works, in which pale suns struggle to penetrate all manner of mists, fogs, clouds and tempests. *Sun Rising through Vapour* (c. 1807) was said by one critic to be a potentially generic title for most of Turner's paintings.

These atmospheric confections needed rich, vibrant colour, not the subdued earth colours preferred by Constable. And as Turner's suns and vapours came increasingly to crowd out and veil his landscapes, his oeuvre seemed 'to tremble on the verge of some new discovery in colour', according to an encyclopedia in 1823. For some critics it was all too much. As Turner used colour in ever less naturalistic ways in his attempts to capture the subjective quality of hazy sunlight, one newspaper entreated in 1826 that 'We . . . wish Mr Turner to turn back to Nature and worship her as the goddess of his idolatry, instead of his "yellow bronze" which haunts him.' When Turner exhibited his Classical seascape *Ulysses Deriding Polyphemus* (1829) (Plate 7.1), a glowing mélange of primary reds and yellows, mauves and fire-orange, the *Morning Herald* commented that

This is a picture in which truth, nature and feeling are sacrificed to melodramatic effect . . . In fact, it may be taken as a specimen of colouring run mad – positive vermilion – positive indigo; and all the most glaring tints of green, yellow and purple contend for mastery.

Turner's hues were exotic, Oriental – as if 'done by a Rembrandt born in India', according to Joris Karl Huysmans, at that time a prominent art critic.

Such vivid colour was unfamiliar and disconcerting. The Victorians preferred, in the words of art historian Eric Shane, 'verisimilitude to painterliness, saccharine colouring to the brilliant hues [of] Turner': Reynolds and Gainsborough, in other words, who created no doubts about what you were supposed to be seeing. And yet truth of a kind was precisely what Turner and the Impressionists sought rather than shunned: not the 'truth' of academic convention, which was a mere idealization and formalization of nature, but the truth of the impression that it leaves in the observer's mind. As for the 'brilliant hues', there can be no doubt where these came from, and why they shocked – for until the early nineteenth century, no one had seen such greens, yellows and violets as now radiated from the works of the innovators.

Turner seized on the new pigments almost as fast as the chemists could dispense them. Cobalt blue, emerald green, viridian, orange vermilion, barium chromate, chrome yellow, orange and scarlet, as well as new yellow and red lakes – he put each novel material to use within a few years of its introduction. To do so was certainly to risk disaster: a contemporary engraver, J. Burnet, remarked that Turner *dared* to use these new pigments when other artists did not. One unfortunate consequence is that, by the end of the nineteenth century, the poor stability of some of the new pigments left several of Turner's works in sorry repair.

We can catch a glimpse of Turner's avid appropriation of the new synthetic pigments in a tale of his habitual behaviour at the Royal Academy on 'varnishing days', when members brought pictures to be hung for varnishing. They were allowed a few days for final retouching before the protective coat was applied. But in the 1830s Turner took to bringing canvases bearing dull, unremarkable compositions. Once they were displayed next to those of his rivals (for this is how Turner regarded them), he began most of the real work *in situ*:

Turner went about from one to another of them on the varnishing days, piling on . . . all the brightest pigments he could lay his hands on, chromes, emerald green, vermilion, etc., until they literally blazed with light and colour . . . Artists used to dread having their pictures hung next to his, saying that it was as bad as being hung beside an open window.[16]

What an explicit confession by Turner's contemporaries that their more conservative painting styles did not, after all, come close to capturing the glow of real daylight!

It was not solely by means of new pigments that Turner achieved these dazzling effects. He also knew how to make good use of contrast to enhance brilliance, as Constable found to his cost. On one occasion, an otherwise drab greyish seascape made a daub of red lead, added *in situ*, all the more bold, outshining the vermilion and red lake in Constable's adjacent picture. 'He has been here and fired a gun,' said Constable bitterly.

The colour professional

To acquire the new pigments so rapidly, Turner needed a reliable source. He purchased his colours from several London-based suppliers, including J. Sherborne, James Newman, and Winsor and Newton. But his primary source was the leading English colourmaker of the nineteenth century, George Field, with whom Turner forged an acquaintance around the beginning of the century. There can be little doubt that, without this collaboration with so adept a chemist, Turner would have been hard pushed to achieve his brilliant effects with lesser materials. And no doubt we have Field to thank, by dint of his thorough testing of colours, for the fact that Turner's paintings are not now still more discoloured than they are.[17]

The paradox of Field's career as a colour manufacturer is that he had a rather poor grasp of colour theory. He did not believe Newton's ideas; maintaining that 'it is not possible to compose white by any mixture of colours whatever', he never appreciated the distinction between additive and subtractive mixing. He was primarily a technologist, and by all accounts had little contact with leading scientists – despite his claims to have studied chemistry under Humphry Davy and Michael Faraday. Yet Field's treatise on colour and pigments, *Chromatography* (1835), was highly influential among painters looking for guidance on materials. (Ruskin warned students, however, to ignore the book's remarks on 'principles or harmonies of colour'.) The most prominent artists of the day, among them Constable and Thomas Lawrence, came to Field for their colours.

Field began his business by making madder lake in London, later expanding this enterprise into a colour-making factory near Bristol in 1808. He made attempts to cultivate the madder plant, which was much in demand for the dyeing industry. In 1755 the Society for the Encouragement of the Arts offered a premium for successful cultivation of madder in England to reduce dependence on Dutch imports – an unreliable source in times of war with other European nations. Field developed a press for extracting the dye, and improved the preparation of madder lakes, including brown, pink and purple varieties as well as the rich red madder carmine.

An adherent of the primary trinity of red, yellow and blue (which he linked to theological considerations), Field regarded it as important to identify and manufacture the pigments corresponding to these pure hues. These, he maintained, were lemon yellow (or at an earlier point, Indian yellow), red madder and ultramarine. Yet for all that he was contributing to Turner's fireworks, Field's own tastes were far more conservative. He preferred low-keyed landscapes that used tertiary colours: 'The chaste eye receives greater satisfaction from the harmony of the tertiaries in which the three primitives [primaries] are more intimately combined.' To this end, Field strove also to develop pure pigments for the tertiary colours, cleaving to the old (and not unjustified) belief that 'the Artist should use his colours as pure and unmixt as possible'.

The pigments that Field manufactured were held in high regard by many British artists. Most treasured was his 'orange vermilion', a version of the traditional synthetic mercury sulphide that he developed after studying the colours made by the eighteenth-century German painter Anton Raphael Mengs. Field himself claimed that his colour gave 'purer and more delicate warm carnation tints than any known pigment, much resembling those of Titian and Rubens'. It was popular from the 1830s onwards, and was sold by the colour merchant Charles Roberson and later by Winsor and

Newton. But Field did not reveal how it was made, and the Pre-Raphaelite William Holman Hunt said after Field's death that 'I believe he carried his secret to the grave.' All the same, said Hunt, 'the tint is still always sold with his name as its best recommendation' – even if it did not always live up to that promise (see page 303).

Field's tests of the permanence of new pigments were some of the most exacting of his time. His *Chromatography* contains countless hand-painted samples, whose state of repair today is sometimes a sharp reminder of the hazards that the nineteenth-century artist faced. Iodine scarlet, for instance, was a superficially attractive pigment based on the eponymous element discovered by Bernard Courtois in 1811–12 and named by Humphry Davy in 1814. In that same year, Vauquelin studied the deep red compound of iodine and mercury, and it was introduced shortly thereafter as a pigment. Field's tests left him unenthusiastic about the 'treacherous' new colour: 'Nothing certainly can approach it as a colour for scarlet geraniums, but its beauty is almost as fleeting as the flowers.' He seems to have warned Turner away from this alluring red – it appears in the artist's studio materials, but he almost never used it in oils.[18] It soon became obsolete; and from the patchy, bleached smear in Field's book we can see why.

Field's relationship with Turner was prone to fluctuations, which is hardly surprising given their very different tastes in colour. During the 1820s the two were close, even geographically: Turner in Twickenham, Field in Isleworth, west of London. But in the second edition of Field's *Chromatics; Or the Analogy, Harmony and Philosophy of Colours* (1845) the colour-maker took Turner to task for

the beautiful error of applying the prism to his eye while painting, instead of representing objects as they naturally appear through the diffused solar spectrum of broad light and shade, by which error he converts the scene into a fool's paradise, seen through artifice, but not by the natural eye.[19]

There is no need to ask now, of course, which we would prefer: 'objects as they naturally appear', or Turner's 'fool's paradise' (an old term for the prism). The painter himself was airily dismissive: 'You have not told us too much,' he said to Field.

The romance of colour

Turner's prismatic vision is nowhere more evident than in *Light and Colour (Goethe's Theory) – The Morning After the Deluge* (*c.* 1843), an almost abstract composition in which murky, barely visible figures occupy a colour field ablaze with primaries. As the title indicates, this picture was painted after the artist had read Sir Charles Eastlake's English translation of Johann Wolfgang von Goethe's *Theory of Colours* (1810).

Perhaps it is for providing some relief from the sluggish current of brown gravy – some reawakening of the possibilities of prismatic colour – that we should mostly be grateful to Goethe. The poet's scientific works seem guided as much by subjective dogma as by methodical investigation, and the intemperate attacks on Newton's 'veritable fortress of learning' in Goethe's *Contribution to Optics* (1791) and the subsequent *Theory of Colours* are as reactionary as they are mistaken. Goethe reasserts, for example, the Aristotelian idea that colour results from a mixture of light and dark. Lacking knowledge of the distinction between additive and subtractive mixing, he raises the old objection that white light could not possibly be compounded of all the colours of the rainbow (as Newton asserted) because the corresponding pigment mixture gives almost the precise opposite. Yet he could not bring himself to check Newton's *experimentum crucis* by repeating it, advising all and sundry instead to 'avoid the darkened chamber, where they show you twisted light'.

To Goethe, light and dark could be equated with the only two 'pure' colours: yellow and blue. Red, he said, is not 'an individual colour, but . . . a property which can attach itself to blue and yellow'. Thus red arises in some manner by an 'overlaying of [blue and yellow] particles'. This, he supposed, was distinct from the result when the two colours were 'mixed, but not united' – in that case, green was produced. In a manner frequently symptomatic of confused pseudo-scientific thinking, Goethe seeks to make such dualities the basis for a whole set of polar opposites: blue is 'cold' and 'male', yellow 'warm' and 'female' and so forth. One of the unhappy legacies of his philosophy is this tendency towards extremely polarized ontologies, later adopted without reservation by the Theosophist and Anthroposophist movements.

Yet out of Goethe's blend of practical experiment and fantastical thinking emerge some useful concepts. His theory of colour focused much-needed attention on the psychological, as opposed to purely physical, aspects of colour. And his stress on polarities helped to establish the idea of complementary colours that was to be so central to much of the theory and practice of colour use by nineteenth-century artists.

Romanticism was the avant-garde of the early nineteenth century, and Goethe's philosophy spoke to its imaginative spirit. In Germany Goethe corresponded with the Romantic artist Philipp Otto Runge (1777–1810) on colour theory. In England Romanticism found expression in the bright, primary colours of paintings by the Pre-Raphaelite Brotherhood and by William Blake (1757–1827).

The impassioned fantasies of the Pre-Raphaelites John Everett Millais (1829–96), William Holman Hunt (1827–1910) and Dante Gabriel Rossetti (1828–82) demanded vibrant colour; and their use of it incited almost as much uproar in the British art world of the 1850s as the Impressionists were to ignite in France two decades later. Their refusal to mute nature's bright tones to conform with the strictures of good taste led *The Times* in 1851 to denounce their 'singular devotion to the minute accidents . . . seeking out every excess of sharpness and deformity'. For their part, the Pre-Raphaelites derided the murky chiaroscuro of the Royal Academy and dubbed its head, Joshua Reynolds, 'Sir Sloshua Slosh'. Holman Hunt inveighed against the way that the Old Masters in the National Gallery had been allowed, through the agencies of time and thick varnishes, to become 'as brown as grandmother's tea tray'.

To obtain the best from their pigments, the Pre-Raphaelites copied the habits of Rubens and the Venetian Old Masters by glazing thin coats of barely mixed colours over opaque white grounds to ensure maximum luminosity. Their colour merchant Roberson provided them with canvases primed with bright grounds of zinc white. Millais's *Ophelia* (1851–2) is filled with new materials: cobalt blue, chromium oxide, zinc yellow, chrome yellow and the richest madder lake. The bright greens here are mixed from Prussian blue and chrome yellow. The Pre-Raphaelites tried all manner of mixtures of the new yellows and blues to capture verdant nature: barium and strontium chromates with Prussian blue, synthetic ultramarine or cobalt blue. The results, said detractors, were 'unripe enough to cause indigestion'.

Holman Hunt had a deep interest in materials and technique, and corresponded with Field about the permanence of pigments. He strove to use them unmixed as far as possible, just as the colour-maker recommended. In *The Awakening Conscience* (1853), Hunt employs strong yellows – chrome and, strontium yellow – as well as cobalt blue, emerald green and, notably, a relatively new pure orange, Mars orange. Vivid reds and purples stand out in his *Valentine Rescuing Sylvia from Proteus* (1850–51) (Plate 7.2), where even the earth glows with the fiery hues of autumn, dappled with a shimmering light that prefigures the revolution in painting about to unfold on the other side of the English Channel.

8. The Reign of Light

When you go out to paint, try to forget what objects you have
before you, a tree, a house, a field or whatever. Merely think here is
a little square of blue, here an oblong of pink, here a streak of yellow,
and paint it just as it looks to you, the exact colour and shape, until
it gives your own naive impression of the scene before you.

Claude Monet

Soil three quarters of a canvas with black and white, rub the rest
with yellow, distribute haphazardly some red and blue spots, and
you'll obtain an *impression* of spring in front of which the adepts will
be carried away by ecstasy. The famous *Salon des Refusés*, which one
cannot recall without laughing . . . was a Louvre compared to the
exhibition on the boulevard des Capucines.

E. Cardon, critic at the first Impressionist exhibition (1874)

Among the inventions of the nineteenth century – aspirin, plastics,
the laws of thermodynamics – is that of the artist as lone, misunder-
stood genius. By the 1800s painting was no longer a trade but a
profession, an academic subject bound by rules and agreed standards
of practice and taste. It was respectable, earnest – and moribund.
The scene was ripe for a new personification of the artist: rebel and
outsider, the archetypes of modern mankind.

There was nothing new about neglected artists living and dying
in poverty – that was Rembrandt's fate, after all. But in the nineteenth
century we see the emergence of painters whose priorities were
neither commercial nor academic. It is true that the Impressionists
might indulge in a more popular style and technique for a picture
that they hoped to sell (and some of those works we admire today

may never have been intended for exhibition); but this group, and those that followed, had no time for the prescriptions of the art establishment, nor for the conservative instincts of the public or the critics. What rules they applied were to be of their own devising.

This is scarcely surprising when one considers the stifling atmosphere of the Fine Arts academies at the beginning of the century, epitomized by the Ecole des Beaux-Arts in Paris. Here students learned next to nothing about colour; rarely if ever would they be allowed to apply raw paint to canvas. Rather, the emphasis was on drawing, on line and form, light and shade – a triumph of *disegno* over *colore* that was secured in the French Academy of the seventeenth century. Painting itself had to be practised outside the Ecole – the student would enrol with one of the many private studios (*ateliers*), which operated more in the manner of an art school than of a workshop where one served an apprenticeship.

And even when the student was considered to have mastered drawing sufficiently to be allowed to hold a paintbrush, the first assignment was to copy the pictures of the Old Masters in the Louvre, or those provided by the master of the studio. All of this would be done in a context that suppressed innovation and invention: the artist's hand was supposed to remain invisible in the finished work. The style differed little from that of the High Renaissance in many respects, not least in the choice of 'appropriate' subjects such as scenes from Classical mythology. It was a training for staid professionals, who could then make a living by selling their safe and unremarkable products to the wealthy middle classes.

The market-place had its own rigidly imposed conventions. Just about the only way for young artists in Paris to exhibit their work to a wide public was through the exhibition organized every year by the French Academy, called the Salon. Selection for the Salon was conducted by jury, and most of the jurors were academics with traditional tastes. They expected the exhibits to display the smooth, glossy finish of prevailing fashion. Radical new styles stood little chance of being included. And the Salon itself was indeed a market-place: walls packed from floor to ceiling with works, with no concern for setting and little more for visibility. Yet it was this or nothing.

Small wonder, then, that the Impressionists – Pissarro, Monet, Renoir, Manet and Degas most prominent among them – caused outrage and sensation, when they were not simply the objects of ridicule. Their works were considered sketchy, unfinished, undisciplined, and they depicted highly indecorous subject matter: real people, for goodness' sake, going about their everyday business!

Impressionism was a movement motivated by the ineluctability of artistic integrity and by the artist's need to search rather than slavishly to follow. But the images it produced, steeped in brilliance of colour, could never have been made without the right materials. It is not abstract intellectual thinking alone that provokes revolutions in art, nor are they fuelled merely by reaction against tired convention. Rather, it is when there is a confluence of such forces with new possibilities in the artist's materials that exciting things happen. And so it was: after a half-century of some of the most dramatic innovations in pigment manufacture that visual art had ever seen, the stage was set for the plot to take a new direction. Art has never looked back.

Paths towards the light

No revolution begins without warning shots, though often they pass unheard. The Impressionists were not the first French artists to challenge the conservatism of the French Academy: Eugène Delacroix (1798–1863) threw down the gauntlet in the 1830s with sweeping brush-strokes and bold colouration (Plate 8.1) that proved too heady for the Salon. But by 1855, when the young Camille Pissarro (1830–1903) came to Paris to see the grand World Fair, Delacroix had become almost an establishment figure. Nevertheless, no one better personified this establishment than Delacroix's arch-rival, the rigid, bigoted and haughty figure of Jean-Auguste-Dominique Ingres (1780–1867).

A simplistic dualism labels Ingres as the Classical counterpart to the Romantic Delacroix: a conservative painter who championed line over colour in the age-old debate, who represented reason in the face of Delacroix's passion. The truth is more complex. Yes, Ingres was firmly rooted in the past ('he is completely ignorant of all the poets of recent times', said Theodore Chassériau, a former pupil who defected to Delacroix); but he was a highly eclectic artist who could draw on Oriental themes and colours as readily as on seventeenth-century subjects and styles or the historical and mythological topics of Greek and Roman art. In Ingres's hands, even hackneyed scenes could become works of genius when from lesser artists they elicited nothing but sterile emulation.

Perhaps Baudelaire's judgement is the most apt: Ingres, he said, was despotic, 'a man full of stubbornness, endowed with highly special capacities, but determined to deny the utilities of those capacities which he does not possess'. Obsessive about line, Ingres condemned works – such as those of Delacroix – in which objects were not precisely delineated. He insisted that a 'noble contour' could atone for any other deficiencies – of colour, for example. Ingres's own works exemplify the smooth textures, free from visible brush-strokes, expected by the French academics.

And yet there is ample common ground with Delacroix, if only the two could have brought themselves to acknowledge it. Both were supreme colourists, even if Ingres considered this of minor importance. His *Odalisque with a Slave* (1839–40) glories in rich reds, greens and orange. And Delacroix, progressive though he was in many respects, shared Ingres's conviction that there was a hierarchy of subject matter for the painter: works based on grandiose, Classical themes from history, myth and religion were inherently superior to landscapes, still lifes and the depiction of everyday life (disparagingly called genre painting). In their 'grand' works, both artists show not real people but idealized, allegorical figures. Ingres would have been furious to discover that his 'Classical' works command scant notice today, whereas his portraits, often painted for purely commercial reasons, are (rightly) regarded as some of the most stunning psychological studies of the age.

But it was colour that divided Delacroix and Ingres more than anything else. One can't fail to notice what delight Delacroix found in colour. He felt that his contemporaries were largely ignorant of how to use it:

The elements of colour theory have neither been analysed nor taught in our schools of art, because in France it is considered superfluous to study the laws of colour, according to the saying 'Draughtsmen may be made, but colourists are born.'[1]

He lambasted the academic school of Jacques Louis David (1748–1825), under whom Ingres trained, for its dull tones and avoidance of rich pigments, in which he perceived an almost Classical attitude to the formation of colour. These painters imagined, he said,

that they could produce the tones Rubens got with frank and vivid colours such as bright green, ultramarine, etc., by means of black and white to make blue, black and yellow to make green, red ochre and black to make violet, and so on. They also used earths, such as umber, Cassel, and ochres, etc. . . . if the picture be placed near a richly coloured work such as a Titian or a Rubens, it appears what it really is: earthy, dull, and lifeless.[2]

For his part, Delacroix constructed elaborate palettes of up to twenty-three pigments, encompassing nearly all of those available at the time. He considered colour to be not a localized property, intrinsic to the object, but 'essentially an interplay of reflections'. Because Ingres took no account of these reflections – of the effect of light falling from an object on to its surroundings and vice versa – Delacroix complained that Ingres's work depicted 'crude, isolated, cold' things. The tale is told of how Delacroix, seeking to give emphasis to a yellow drapery, decided to go to the Louvre to see how Rubens would manage it. The cabs in Paris were at that time painted canary yellow, and Delacroix noticed that the cab standing in wait for him cast a violet shadow in the sunlight. This was the knowledge he sought; he paid the cabman and returned to work.

Here, then, is where Delacroix antecedes Impressionism: he wished to capture the play of light. But there was no mistaking the official position in 1855: it was Ingres and his imitators who took the medals at the World Fair, and who garnered the favour of the viewing public. Delacroix was repeatedly denied membership of the French Academy, of which Ingres was an influential member. Their enmity became legendary, the subject of newspaper caricatures.

Delacroix would later be lionized by the Impressionists. But another undeniable influence was Turner, who towards the end of his life had also come to abandon many Classical ideals and to search for artistic integrity in a reign of light. To see Turner's works progress, as they do in a single room of the Tate Gallery, from the Claudian Neo-Classicism of his early landscapes to the dream-like swirl of bright primaries of his later paintings is to see the path of contemporary art prefigured in a single man's life-work. Pissarro and Monet saw some of these pictures in London in the 1870s, and they clearly left their mark. Turner's gouache sketch of Rouen cathedral (c. 1832) is clearly a forerunner of Monet's several studies of the great building painted in 1892–4. Monet was later reserved in his praise, however, admitting in 1918 that 'Over the years I have liked Turner a great deal' – only to add, 'But now I like him far less.'

Out of doors

In the 1860s the German physicist and physiologist Hermann von Helmholtz suggested that it was futile for the artist to attempt to re-create the effects of light and colour seen in the real world, for the available pigments were too limited – they necessitated an altered scale of brightness, a toning down of hues which introduced a certain brownness. This meant that, despite their pretense at naturalism, traditional artists were simply applying conventions for representing the play of light that bore only a schematic resemblance to the image that the artist saw. In consequence, said Helmholtz,

It is not the colours of the objects, but the impression which they have given, or would give, which is to be imitated, so as to produce as distinct and vivid a conception as possible of these objects.[3]

And this – as good a description as any of what it was the Impressionists were attempting – is something that cannot be achieved in the studio by reconstructing a scene from sketches, imperfect memory and idealized forms. Rather, it requires that the painter work in the midst of his subject, translating his visual impressions directly to canvas. He (with apologies to Berthe Morisot and Mary Cassatt) has to get out more.

Among the myths that have come to surround the Impressionists is that they were the first painters to work outside. Of course they were not; Turner, for one, had fitted out a boat so that he might paint *en plein air*, as it came to be known. And one can hardly imagine that William Holman Hunt could have deduced by pondering in a studio how to capture so brilliantly the prismatic shadows of the late-afternoon sun in his *Our English Coasts* (later *Strayed Sheep*) (1852) (Plate 8.2). The blues, reds and yellows in the sheep's fleeces and the striking violet of the grass combine to create a natural glow of quite unprecedented persuasiveness – enough to convince John Ruskin that, whatever Helmholtz had asserted, Hunt had found a way to translate between sunlight and pigments:

It showed us, for the first time in the history of art, the absolutely faithful balances of colour and shade by which actual sunshine might be transposed into a key in which the harmonies possible in material pigments should yet produce the same impression upon the mind which were caused by the light itself.[4]

It is striking how both Ruskin and Helmholtz invoke the word 'impression' – a reminder that the style of the Impressionists was not uniquely dictated by their intentions.

The image of the Impressionist out in the middle of nature with portable easel and parasol is an enduring one, however, encouraged by the Impressionists' own depictions of this activity (both Renoir and John Singer Sargent painted Monet at work outside) and by their endorsement of the myth. Monet claimed in 1880 that 'I have never had a studio, and I don't understand how someone could shut himself up in a room' – although his own works bear testimony to later retouching in the studio.

For the conservatives of the French Academy, open-air painting was regarded as a practice suited only to making sketches from which an original would be reconstructed indoors. The immediacy and naturalism of the sketch would be scrupulously erased in the process. The traditional chiaroscuro technique of the academics demanded that the pale tones of a sunlit scene be darkened in their 'historical landscapes' to create a highly stylized rendition of light and shadow. This convention was challenged in the mid-nineteenth century by 'Realist' painters such as Camille Corot (1796–1875) and Gustave Courbet (1819–77). Rather than darkening the tones of his outdoor scenes, Corot added white to the colours to enhance the luminosity and capture a true record of the visual sensation. 'Never lose the first impression which has moved you,' he said, in what might as well have been a slogan for the young radicals like his pupil Pissarro.

For the Impressionists it was absolutely essential to convey on to the canvas at first hand these impressions of exterior light and shade. This sometimes put them to extraordinary trouble. Monet would dart between several works at once, braving rain, wind, snow and tides, trying to seize the precious moments when in each case the natural illumination returned to its desired state. Morisot lamented the young hordes that would gather around her as she pitched easel outside.

Only this close observation of natural lighting could have revealed to the Impressionists the subtleties in the colours that shimmer across surfaces and lurk in shadows. Writing in Provence, Paul Cézanne said, 'The sunlight here is so intense that it seems to me that objects are silhouetted not only in black and white, but also in blue, red, brown and violet.' For these painters, nature was alive with a dance of glorious hues that could hardly be mimicked by mixing traditional materials. They needed a wider rainbow. The French poet Jules Laforgue commented in 1883 that

[i]n a landscape flooded with light ... the Impressionist sees light as bathing everything not with a dead whiteness, but rather with a thousand vibrant struggling colours of rich prismatic decomposition ... The Impressionist sees and renders nature as it is – that is, wholly in the vibration of colour.[5]

How did these painters set out to capture the 'vibration of colour'? No doubt intuition and empiricism played a prominent part; but the Impressionists also drew heavily on scientific principles, at least in so far as they could grasp them and translate them into painterly terms. Of greatest significance was the concept of contrast in complementary colours, developed in the early nineteenth century by the chemist Michel-Eugène Chevreul.

The science of contrast

Chromatic dualisms abound in Goethe's *Theory of Colours* (1810); but it was Chevreul the chemist, not Goethe the would-be physicist, who did more to instruct artists in the rational use of complementary colours. In 1824 Chevreul was made director of the Gobelins dyeworks in Paris and was asked to improve the apparent dullness of the dyes used there.[6] But he found that there was no cause for complaint in the dyestuffs; rather, it was the way the dyed threads were being woven that destroyed their brilliance. Complementary or near-complementary hues were being placed side by side, and the result was that, when viewed from a distance, the colours could not be distinguished but instead merged on the retina to produce a kind of greyness. This is a form of additive mixing, akin to that generated by James Clerk Maxwell with his spinning discs (see page 44). Isaac Newton had observed something of the sort in experiments on the mixing of dry pigments. He reports how a mixture of yellow orpiment, bright purple, light green and blue blended to give an impression of brilliant whiteness at a distance of several paces.

Chevreul's observations led him to experiment with the effect of placing complementaries next to one another, and he found that, for a viewing distance less than that required to generate optical mixing, the juxtaposition actually enhanced the strength of both colours: 'In the case where the eye sees at the same time two contiguous colours, they will appear as dissimilar as possible, both in their optical composition and in the height of their tone.'[7]

That the perception of a colour is influenced by its surroundings had been long known to painters in an empirical way; but Chevreul systematized this view with the (increasingly respected) stamp of scientific authority. His findings were published in 1828 and were rapidly disseminated among art theorists. And when Chevreul expanded and generalized his work in *De la loi du contraste simultané des couleurs* (*On the Law of Simultaneous Contrast of Colours*) (1839), it became an essential manual for painters.[8]

Chevreul illustrated the relationships between colours with one of the most complex colour wheels ever devised, subdivided into seventy-four segments and with twenty degrees of tonal variation between white and black: the beginnings of a rigorous mapping of three-dimensional colour space. These colour scales were depicted in his *Des couleurs et de leurs applications aux arts industrielles* (1864), a technical manual aimed primarily at paint and dye manufacturers.

Delacroix professed a dislike of scientists ('always waiting for someone more able than themselves to open the door a finger's breadth for them'); but any artist interested in colour could ill afford to ignore this fundamental aspect of colour perception. He drew on Chevreul's insights by using adjacent complementaries in his designs for several interiors, and their influence can be detected (though not as clearly as some have suggested) in *Algerian Women in Their Apartment* (1834) (Plate 8.1), considered by the young Renoir to be 'the most beautiful painting in the world'. But Delacroix's reputation as a 'scientific' colourist is questionable, and owes more to the vigorous promotion of this notion by his friend, the art critic Charles Blanc, than to the evidence of his works. Moreover, contrasting complementaries feature also in *Odalisque with a Slave* by Ingres, who places the brilliant red of the drapery against the pale greens of the floor and furnishings – a composition that Delacroix predictably disparaged.

It was not until the 1860s that Chevreul's laws of contrasting complementaries became well known through translations of his book. Charles Blanc's espousal of these ideas in *Grammaire des arts du dessin* (1867) was also to become a standard manual in France, and exerted a formative influence on the Neo-Impressionist Paul Signac. But by the 1860s, many painters drew instead on the colour-mixing studies of Hermann von Helmholtz, whose seminal paper on the subject in 1852 was quickly translated from German into French.[9] Helmholtz promoted much the same contrasting pairs as

Chevreul, and he argued that it was only through the use of colour
contrasts that the artist could hope to mimic the effects of natural
light with pigments that fell short of nature's true radiance: 'If,
therefore, with the pigments at his command, the artist wishes to
produce the impression which objects give, as strikingly as possible,
he must paint the contrasts which they produce.'[10]

What painters particularly valued in Helmholtz's writings was
that, from experiments with spinning discs, he translated Chevreulean complementaries into mixtures of the specific pigments
available to artists. This approach was carried further in *Modern
Chromatics* (1879) by Ogden Rood, an American physicist at Col-
umbia University. An amateur (water-colour) painter with a knowledge of chemistry, Rood was concerned to root colour theory in
materials. His colour-wheel-like diagrams of contrasts augmented
the bare hues of 'blue', 'green' and so forth with pigments such as
ultramarine, emerald green, vermilion and gamboge (Figure 8.1).
Rood's book became a standard text for the Impressionists, yet its

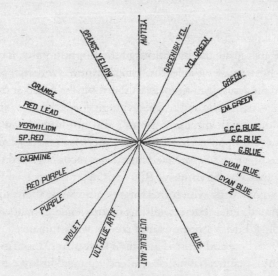

Figure 8.1

In his *Modern Chromatics* (1879), Ogden Rood showed colour contrasts
in terms of real artists' pigments, as determined by experiments with
coloured spinning discs.

author's artistic traditionalism meant that he loathed their works. On seeing them exhibited, he is said to have exclaimed, 'If that is all I have done for art, I wish I had never written that book!'

Claude Monet (1840–1926) gives us some of his most Chevreulean colour contrasts in works depicting water, where the play of sunlight is at its most luminous. In his *Regatta at Argenteuil* (1872) (Plate 8.3) the blue water is embellished with strong orange; the red-roofed house sits amongst green foliage; and violet figures and shadows stand against the creamy yellow sails. Monet was explicit about his intentions – in 1888 he echoed Helmholtz when he said, 'Colour owes its brightness to force of contrast rather than to its inherent qualities . . . primary colours look brightest when they are brought into contrast with their complementaries.' When Monet employs the same bold juxtaposition of orange and blue in *Impression: Setting Sun (Fog)* (1872), the sun's disc seems almost to leap off the canvas.

Light into matter

Once we appreciate the intentions of the Impressionists, it becomes obvious how indispensable the brilliant new synthetic pigments were to their goals. Jean-Georges Vibert, who worked at the Ecole des Beaux-Arts in the 1890s, called them *éclatistes* ('dazzlers') who worked 'only with intense colours'; and no doubt he was right. Vibert was not opposed to the novel materials in themselves; as we saw in the previous chapter, he praised and recommended some for their 'brilliance and freshness'. But what upset the art establishment was the vigour with which the Impressionists put them to use: in unadulterated, energetic strokes, their opulence enhanced by the surrounding hues. 'Never paint except with the three primary colours [red, blue and yellow] and their derivatives,' Pissarro advised his student Cézanne, having purportedly purged his own palette of black, burnt sienna and the ochre pigments.[11]

Vibert was right, moreover, to be concerned about the stability of these unproven pigments. The Impressionists were not always heedful of the dangers, and sometimes paid the price. In severing with the formal methods of the past, they were also abandoning the technical training that enabled painters better to understand their materials. They accepted the bright new paints with great enthusiasm but with little discernment, generally relying on their suppliers or manufacturers for an assessment of quality. Deficiencies did not go unnoticed – Monet complained in the 1880s about the inadequacies of his materials – but the painters lacked the will or the ability to do much more than register dissatisfaction with their suppliers

Who were these dealers in the raw substances of art? By the mid nineteenth century, the provision of artists' materials had become a regular trade with its own well-defined distribution channels. In the seventeenth and eighteenth centuries pigments, as commercial merchandise, tended to be categorized either with imported spices or with drugs (since some artists' materials also had pharmaceutical uses), and so they were sold by grocers who dealt also in foods and medications – recalling how in ancient Greece pigments were called *pharmakon*. In the mid-eighteenth century the grocers (*épiciers*) of France began to specialize, some becoming primarily dealers in art supplies: *marchands de couleurs*.

But as paint manufacture became increasingly a matter of chemical synthesis rather than simple grinding of solid pigment, it was transformed into an industry, and most retailers did little more than package the ready-made paints from manufacturers. Some of the cheaper colours – lead white, zinc white, chrome yellow, Prussian blue and synthetic ultramarine – were manufactured and sold on a huge scale for interior decorating.

The boom in amateur painting in the eighteenth century, stimulated by the development of convenient water-colour cakes, created a lucrative market for colour-makers who specialized in supplying the finest-quality materials for artists. Among them were the Reeves brothers, William and Thomas, who established their firm in London in 1766. An award in 1781 from the Royal Society of Arts conferred on the company the right to claim royal patronage, which it was not hesitant to mention in its advertisements. Yet business in London in the eighteenth century held alarming perils, as the *Morning Herald* recorded in October 1790:

Yesterday an overdrove ox ran into the shop of Mr Reeves, Colourman
to her Majesty, Holborn Bridge; broke the windows of the shop and
knocked down near the whole of the colours and stock; he was at last
secured and taken to the slaughter house. He tossed two women in
Holborn and bruised them in so dreadful a manner that they were
conveyed to an hospital without hope of recovery.[12]

By the early nineteeth century, London was replete with com-
peting suppliers of artists' materials. One of these was the firm of
William Winsor and Henry Charles Newton, established in 1832.
Winsor and Newton's colours were highly regarded by English
painters, including Turner. It was incumbent on such businesses to
possess some scientific training: Winsor was a chemist, Newton an
artist.

From the 1740s pigments were crushed between mechanized
stone rollers in horse-powered 'paint mills'. By the 1820s the mill
wheels were driven by steam. But hand-grinding benefited from
the grinder's skill and judgement, and initially the mechanically
ground products were rather poor. It was not until 1836 that the
Parisian colour merchant Blot first began to use them for the 'fine
colours' demanded by artists.

Another major innovation in paint supplies was the collapsible
metal tube, invented in 1841 by an American portrait painter named
John Rand. The tin tubes replaced the parcels of pig's bladder in
which oil paints had previously been stored, and made paints far
less liable to dry out in their packaging. This was particularly
significant for the Impressionists' predilection for painting out of
doors; Renoir remarked that 'Without paints in tubes, there would
have been no Cézanne, no Monet, no Sisley or Pissarro, nothing of
what the journalists were later to call Impressionism.' No Renoir
either, one presumes.

This commercialization of artists' supplies contributed to the
distancing of the painter from his or her materials – the beginnings
of that impersonal, unloving attitude to the primary substance of
paint that was ultimately to impel artists of the twentieth century
to take up household emulsions. J.-F.-L. Mérimeé complained in

1830 that painters were no longer able to distinguish good materials from bad.

And there certainly were bad materials around. To paint merchants, the bottom line was profit, and they often cared little for the quality or long-term stability of their colours. These people, said Mérimée, 'had a stronger feeling towards their own immediate profit, than any regard to the preservation of pictures'. They used binding media that gave the paints a long shelf-life, but at the cost of creating poor drying properties on the canvas. Because the pigment was the most expensive component of the paint, the colour-makers would be inclined to minimize the amounts used. But as all oils turn slightly yellow as they dry, paints with a high oil-to-pigment ratio discolour more markedly. And to keep the paint stiff while lowering the pigment content, some manufacturers added wax – which produced a sticky material that was liable to crack. Some retailers adulterated their pigments with extenders – inert materials such as chalk or gypsum that merely made the coloured stuff go further. There were even cases of deliberate falsification: one pigment being passed off as another more expensive variety, or surreptitiously mixed with it. The ambiguous relation of some paint names to the pigments they contained only heightened the temptation for duplicity.

As a protection against such practices, many artists strove to establish a good relationship with a particular colour merchant, relying on them to provide quality control. Pissarro and Cézanne, and later van Gogh, used Julien Tanguy, who ran a small shop in the rue Clauzel in Montmartre from 1874. The Danish painter Johan Rohde described it as a 'paltry little shop, poorer than the most miserable second-hand dealer's in Adelgade [in Copenhagen] . . . There were stacks of pictures – no doubt payment for materials – and very valuable things among them' – which drew many visitors to the shop. The wild van Gogh was befriended by Tanguy when he came to Paris in 1886, and he twice painted the merchant's portrait, despite complaining on several occasions about his wares. Tanguy ground his own colours, and one of the advantages for the artist of such a supplier was that he could provide materials to order:

van Gogh, for instance, made specific requests for coarsely ground pigments.

Among the Impressionists, only Edgar Degas (1834–1917) showed much curiosity about what was actually in his colours. His notebooks contain many chemical recipes and technical notes, and he conducted his own experiments on materials – albeit idiosyncratically and barely informed by chemical theory. Concerned about the discolouration that had occurred in some of Manet's paintings, Degas sought for ways to protect his own works from the ravages of time. His abiding interest in the theoretical aspects of colour, meanwhile, is attested by a tribute from Huysmans: 'No other painter since Delacroix, whom he has studied at length and who is his true master, has understood as M. Degas does the marriage and adultery of colours.'

The Impressionist technique

One of the Impressionists' numerous bludgeon-witted critics suggested that they might have achieved their results by loading a gun with bright colours and firing it at the canvas. After a catastrophic auction in 1874, another brayed that, 'We had good fun with the purple landscapes, red flowers, black rivers, yellow and green women, and blue children.' What were these colours that provoked such ire, disguised as wit?

There is, needless to say, no unique 'Impressionist palette'. But the works of the group's main figures draw on a fairly consistent colour range that is biased heavily towards the new materials (Plate 8.4), and it is these that tend to contribute the most striking effects in Impressionism's radiant repertoire. Of the twenty principal pigments identified in Impressionist pictures, twelve were the new synthetics: lemon yellow (barium chromate), chrome yellow, cadmium yellow, chrome orange, Scheele's green, emerald green, viridian, chrome green, cerulean blue, cobalt blue, artificial ultramarine and zinc white.

Like Monet, Pierre Auguste Renoir (1841–1919) heightened the tones of his river scenes with adjacent complementaries. *Boating on the Seine* (1879–80) (Plate 8.5) has a strident orange skiff set against the deep blue water, while the red shadows of the prow complement a patch of green foliage in the foreground, and pale buildings cast yellow highlights amid the purples of their shadowy reflection. The pigments in this picture (in addition to lead white) are limited to just seven, with all but the reds being 'modern' synthetics: cobalt blue, viridian, chrome yellow, 'lemon yellow' (strontium chromate), chrome orange (basic lead chromate), vermilion and red lake. They are applied almost unmixed, and the impact of the new pure orange is never more apparent, used in thick, pure strokes for the boat's outline. The river is portrayed in pure cobalt blue, with only white added in places and with a glaze of red lake to produce the purple shadows. This is Impressionism straight from the tube.

Monet too made much use of unmixed colours, exemplified by his *Lavacourt under Snow* (c. 1879) (Plate 8.6). Here is a very different kind of atmospheric lighting: cold and brumal, veiled in the shadows of a low sun. Yet the hues are anything but subdued – the snow glistens with a harsh blueness, fashioned from pure cobalt blue in its brightest places. Ultramarine and red lake are added to lend the snow field greyish or mauve tints. Cobalt blue, red lake and viridian can all be found in pure form among the cottages. There are dull tones here, and in the trees and the pale yellowish sky – olive, khaki, red-brown – but they are not ochres or earths: they are mixed from bright hues: cobalt blue, viridian, cadmium yellow, vermilion. With viridian, emerald green, synthetic ultramarine, red lake and lead white, these make up the entirety of the palette; even in this winter landscape Monet avoids black.

This painting demonstrates with great clarity the Impressionists' attitude to white, the conventional 'colour' of snow. Renoir once told a student that

White does not exist in nature. You admit that you have a sky above that snow. Your sky is blue. That blue must show up in the snow. In the morning there is green and yellow in the sky . . . in the evening, red and yellow would have to appear in the snow.[13]

Wallace Stevens echoes the description in his *Sea Surface Full of Clouds*:

> In the morning in the blue snow
> The catholic sun, its majesty,
> Pinks and pinks the ice-hard melanchole.

One might say that the Impressionistic white is always utterly shattered into its spectral fragments. There is a sense in which all the Impressionists painted in white; for their works are typically spectrally inclusive, leaving out no primary or secondary, just as Pissarro's *Palette with a Landscape* implicitly confesses. Thus it has been said that a Monet painting, like the colour wheels used by Maxwell to study additive mixing, would blur to a silvery grey if spun.[14]

The other side of the coin is black. Shadows – the complementary counterpart to light, if you will – play a central part in the Impressionistic style. But to these painters, shadows were not dark but infused with colour. 'Shadows are not black; no shadow is black,' said Renoir. 'It always has a colour. Nature knows only colours . . . White and black are not colours.' Van Gogh concurred: 'Absolute black does not really exist.'

How, then, was Claude Monet to tackle the gloomy, sooty interior of *La Gare Saint-Lazare*, of which he painted no fewer than four versions in 1877? Here is *plein-air* painting with a modern, industrial flavour: we look out of the station's canopy through billows of smoke and steam emitted by the idling locomotives. Yet the greys, browns and indeed the blacks in the darkest work of the series are constructed without earth pigments and almost entirely from complex mixtures of the new bright artificial colours: cobalt blue, cerulean blue, synthetic ultramarine, emerald green, viridian, chrome yellow, again the older red of vermilion – and a strong crimson lake that is probably based on a modern synthetic dye. The white is lead white, and Monet does make some sparing use of ivory black. But on the whole the dark, blackish hues of the roof, trains and passengers are a result of a fantastic mixture of all the pigments bar yellow and white. In places this 'dark' is tinged with green, elsewhere with purple. It represents an extraordinary demonstration of the Impressionist conviction, taken almost to philosophical extremes, that even the murkiest of shadows are full of colour.

The browns too, which could have been managed with earth pigments, are here painstakingly constructed from intricate blends, such as vermilion mixed with cobalt and cerulean blue along with both greens, the red lake and the chrome yellow. In contrast to *Lavacourt under Snow,* unmixed pigments are almost absent.

The other views of the station interior in this series are somewhat brighter: one rich in greens, another in blues, mauves and yellows. But they all contain complicated pigment mixtures, bearing witness to Monet's determination to construct his scenes from vibrant materials.

If there is no black in nature, do shadows have any particular colour? If so, then to the Impressionists it was surely violet, the complementary colour to the yellow of sunlight.[15] The abundance of purple in Impressionist paintings was the subject of much derision: they were accused of 'violettomania', and even the more thoughtful Huysmans regarded them for a time as afflicted with 'indigomania', as if it were a genuine collective disease, a species of colour blindness. Yet there was nothing outstandingly new in this identification of purple shadow. Goethe comments on one occasion that 'During the day, owing to the yellowish hue of the snow, shadows tending to violet had already been observable.' And in 1856 Delacroix, describing a boy climbing up a fountain in bright sunlight, spoke of the 'dull orange in the lights, very lively violet tones for the parts emerging from shadow'.

But Monet went further, proclaiming, 'I have finally discovered the true colour of the atmosphere. It's violet. Fresh air is violet. Three years from now everyone will work in violet.'[16]

Despite this predisposition for violets and mauves, the Impressionists tended to achieve them by mixing (generally cobalt blue or ultramarine glazed with red lake) rather than by taking advantage of the cobalt and manganese violet pigments that became available in the 1850s and 1860s. These new pigments had only a modest tinting strength, but gave a stronger hue than could be attained by mixtures. Monet favoured them more than most; Renoir, on the other hand, retained the lake/cobalt blue mixture for the pervasive mauves and purples in *At the Theatre* (1876–7) and *The Umbrellas* (1880–81).

The Refusés

No innovator can expect an easy ride; but it is a wonder that the Impressionists found the strength of will to pursue their course in the face of the scorn, ridicule and vitriol that was heaped upon them at every step in the 1860s and 1870s. At first they were virtually invisible to the art-viewing public – their works would simply be rejected time and again from the all-important Salon. This was a kiss of death as far as sales were concerned; there are even stories of purchasers demanding a refund if the picture they had bought was subsequently rejected by the jury. The adjudication process remained firmly in the hands of the implacable establishment, even after various reforms of the selection procedure for the jurors in the late 1860s.

Amongst the early group who were to become labelled as Impressionists, Edouard Manet (1832–83) was almost alone in winning the occasional (if grudging) favour of the Salon. Manet, perhaps the least radical of the group, had at least one influential supporter in the person of the ageing Delacroix, who by 1857 was no longer regarded as a danger to art and was finally elected a member of the Academy. Manet did not, in fact, consider himself to be a revolutionary at all, and throughout his life his craving for public and academic acceptance created an uneasy relationship with his companions, particularly the uncompromising Edgar Degas. In many respects Manet considered himself to be following the trail blazed by Gustave Courbet, who achieved prominence and some notoriety in the 1850s as a Realist painter. Courbet's works, painted directly from nature, captured a spontaneity and sincerity that owed nothing to the calculated grace and poise of the French academic artists. When some of his most prized works were rejected by the jurors of the 1855 World Fair, Courbet took the dramatic step of constructing his own exhibition near to the official building – and incurred much wrath and mockery from critics as a result. Realism was considered dangerous, and at the opening of the 1857 Salon the French Minister of State entreated artists to remain 'faithful to the traditions of their illustrious masters' and to 'the high and pure regions of the beautiful and traditional paths'.

Claude Monet and Auguste Renoir also admired and imitated Courbet, although he remained wary of the homage from these young men whose version of Realism went beyond the pale. Realism informs Manet's *Déjeuner sur l'Herbe* (1863) and Monet's *Women in the Garden* (1866), both rejected by the jury. Surprisingly, Manet's nude study *Olympia* (1863) was accepted by the Salon of 1865, though it caused blusters of outrage for daring to portray a real person ('a puny model stretched out on a sheet') instead of the idealized figurines of Classical tradition. It was this, as much as the novel use of colour and bold execution, that drew antagonism. These young Realists had the vulgarity to show people as they were – often, in fact, one another or their partners. Manet professed to hate using professional models.

The Salon jury of 1863 was particularly severe, rejecting two-thirds of the paintings submitted. This excluded much more than the small band of Realist innovators, and caused such uproar that the Emperor Napoleon III was forced to intervene, decreeing that the refused works should be exhibited separately in another part of the Palais d'Industrie. But this 'Salon des Refusés' was a disaster. Stigmatized by its origins, it became simply a spectacle for the public to jeer at, and the jury decided it was 'inconsistent with the dignity of art' and should not be repeated.

Yet once established, the idea obviously became a stick with which many a disgruntled artist could beat the Salon, and in 1873 a second Salon des Refusés was held, providing a showcase for the soon-to-be Impressionist group but again meeting ridicule from the press and public. By 1874 the group had had enough, and Renoir, Monet, Degas, Pissarro, Sisley, Morisot, Cézanne and others decided to hold their own exhibition. Manet, revealing his more conservative instincts, abstained from taking part because he felt that only through the Salon itself could one achieve proper recognition.

Monet took a very casual attitude towards naming his works, and when pressed to declare titles before the 1874 exhibition he suggested that they simply be prefixed with 'Impression' – hence *Impression: Setting Sun (Fog)* (1872), one of the archetypal Impressionist works. The term was taken up by a sarcastic critic of the exhibition, who dubbed the entire group 'the Impressionists'. They were not at all unhappy with the label, and soon began to use it themselves.

The break-away exhibition was, if anything, more disastrous than the Salon des Refusés, and the entire group was savaged for rejecting 'good artistic manners, devotion to form, and respect for the masters'. In 1876 they held a second group exhibition, to much the same response. Their bright and unfamiliar colours offended the sensibilities of the critics: 'Try to make M. Pissarro understand that trees are not violet, that the sky is not the colour of fresh butter,' said one, while Renoir's 'green and violet spots' in flesh tones 'denote the state of complete putrefaction of a corpse'. Needless to say, all except Manet (and occasionally Renoir) found no commercial success, and Monet in particular was frequently in desperate straits, forced to write begging letters to benefactors to avoid being turned out on the street.

Points of colour

But as with so many revolutionary changes, slowly hostility gave way to indifference and then to a gradual incorporation into the mainstream. By the 1880s the tide of opinion was turning, aided in part by a few critics (such as Huysmans; but most other supporters were outside of France) who had some inkling of what the group was trying to achieve. In 1884 the group of 'independent' artists that had arisen out of the original Impressionist circle established the Groupe (later the Société) des Artistes Indépendants, a formalized foundation for their mutual support.

It was through this group that Paul Signac (1863–1935) became aware of the work of Georges Seurat (1859–91), who exhibited *Bathers at Asnieres* (1883–4) at the first group exhibition. This intense and haunting work, painted 'in great flat strokes, brushed one over the other', struck a chord with Signac, who recognized in it an 'understanding of the laws of contrast, the methodical separation of elements – light, shade, and local colour, and the interaction of colours – as well as their proper balance and proportion', giving the canvas 'its perfect harmony'.

Signac had deduced Seurat's programme correctly. It was, said

PLATE 5.7 Titian's *Bacchus and Ariadne* (1523) is a chart of nearly every pigment known at the time.

PLATE 5.8 Titian's *Portrait of a Man* (*c.* 1512) is alternatively known as 'Man with a Blue Sleeve' – but this is a real, constantly shifting blue, not the monochrome drapery of the Middle Ages. The identity of the sitter is not known with certainty.

PLATE 6.1 Van Dyck's *Equestrian Portrait of Charles I* (*c.* 1637–8) typifies the muted tonality of the Baroque palette.

PLATE 6.2   The bright green favoured by Paolo Veronese is evident here in his *Adoration of the Kings* (1573).

PLATE 6.3   While Tintoretto's use of strong colour is recognizably Venetian, the result is often passionate melodrama, as in *St George and the Dragon* (c. 1560).

PLATE 6.4   There is no mistaking the sexual association of red in Rubens's *Samson and Delilah* (c. 1609).

PLATE 6.5 Don't be misled by the Venetian influences in van Dyck's *Charity* (*c.* 1627–8); he seems, on close examination, to have carefully toned down the strength of his pigments.

PLATE 6.6 Rembrandt's *Portrait of Hendrickje Stoffels* (*c.* 1654–6) contains such complex mixed colours that we struggle for words to characterize them.

PLATE 7.1 Turner's *Ulysses Deriding Polyphemus* (1829) was the object of some derision when it first appeared: 'colouring run mad', said one critic.

PLATE 7.2 The reds, oranges, purples and greens of William Holman Hunt's *Valentine Rescuing Sylvia from Proteus* (1850–51) belong emphatically to the new era of colour chemistry.

PLATE 8.1 Eugène Delacroix's *Algerian Women in Their Apartment* (1834) typifies his lively style – 'unfinished', by the prevailing standards of the French Academy – as well as his love of the bold colours that were to be found in the East.

PLATE 8.2 John Ruskin claimed that William Holman Hunt's *Our English Coasts* (later *Strayed Sheep*) (1852) was the first painting truly to capture the play of sunlight across the landscape. Notice how rich in colour are the 'white' fleeces of the sheep.

PLATE 8.3 Claude Monet's *Regatta at Argenteuil* (1872) is a study in pairing of complementary colours: blue against orange, red against green, yellow against violet.

PLATE 8.4 The materials typically used in Impressionist paintings. From top left to bottom right: zinc white, lead white, 'lemon yellow' (barium chromate), chrome yellow (lead chromate), cadmium yellow, Naples yellow (lead antimonate), yellow ochre, chrome orange (basic lead chromate), vermilion, red ochre, natural madder lake, crimson (cochineal) lake, Scheele's green (copper arsenite), emerald green (copper acetoarsenite), viridian (hydrated chromic oxide), 'chrome green' (Prussian blue/chrome yellow), cerulean blue (cobalt stannate), cobalt blue (cobalt aluminate), artificial ultramarine, ivory black (bone black).

PLATE 8.5 In Auguste Renoir's *Boating on the Seine* (1879–80), cobalt blue and chrome orange play against one another in a dazzling display of complementaries.

PLATE 8.6 Monet's *Lavacourt under Snow* (c. 1879) is a winterscape in cobalt blue, endorsing the Impressionist tenet that 'white does not exist in nature'.

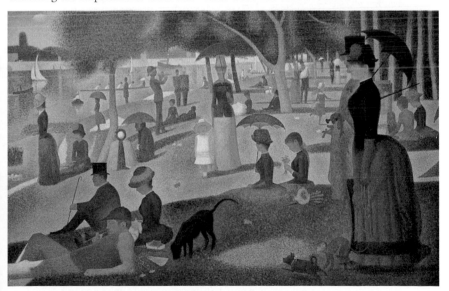

PLATE 8.7 Georges Seurat's *Sunday Afternoon on the Island of La Grande Jatte* (1884–5) is the definitive Neo-Impressionist work. The colours are mixed not by blending of pigments but by the close juxtaposition of tiny dots in complementary hues, which were meant to set up a 'vibration' in the eye of the viewer.

PLATE 8.8   Paul Cézanne's *Hillside in Provence* (*c.* 1885) shows his love of viridian, and his technique of painting in colour patches or *taches*.

PLATE 8.9   Paul Sérusier's *The Talisman* (1888) was an impulsive sketch that inspired the Nabi group to use brilliant colour.

PLATE 8.10   Of *The Night Café* (1888), Vincent van Gogh said, 'the picture is one of the ugliest I have done.' But intentionally so, for 'I have tried to express the terrible passions of humanity by means of red and green.'

Seurat, 'the purity of the spectral element [that was] the keystone of the technique . . . ever since I have been holding a brush, I have been searching on this basis for a formula of optical painting'. Seurat's quixotic (as it turned out) quest for pure luminosity in colour led him to the most systematic of attempts to achieve a truly scientific approach to colouration in art; and it was this that made his work not really Impressionistic at all. Despite the superficial similarities, Seurat's style was something quite new, and it captivated Signac.

Georges Seurat's training was supremely traditional in many respects. At the Ecole des Beaux-Arts he initially idolized Ingres, though he was also attracted to Delacroix. Perhaps via his interest in the latter, he encountered the colour theories of Chevreul and their exposition by Charles Blanc, which inspired him to limit his palette to just the additive and subtractive primaries: red, yellow, blue and green, which he mixed only with white. Much has been written on how Seurat tried to apply these theoretical ideas to the creation of colour on canvas, and much of it is misleading. There has been a tendency to ascribe to him complete mastery of the optical physics of his day, whereas in fact it seems that his understanding was sketchy and imperfect. These limitations doomed his chances of a wholly successful realization of his intentions, but so too did the shortcomings of his materials.

Seurat was aware that subtractive mixing – blending – of pigments inevitably degraded their brightness, and so undermined efforts to portray the luminous glow of sunlight on surfaces. Instead he resolved to achieve his mixtures optically: by placing side by side small dots of complementary colours, he hoped they would mix optically on the retina to achieve greater luminosity than a mix of pigments. This effect was clearly described in Ogden Rood's *Modern Chromatics*:

different colours are placed side by side by lines or dots, and then viewed at such a distance that the blending is more or less accomplished by the eye of the beholder. Under these circumstances the tints mix on the retina, and produce new colours, which are identical with those that are obtained by the method of revolving disks.[17]

This was just what Newton observed in his experiments with coloured powders, and what Chevreul deduced from his studies of woven threads. John Ruskin described much the same phenomenon in his *Elements of Drawing* (1857), in which he spoke of the blending of colours by painting one with a dry brush over canvas and placing dabs of another 'cunningly into the interstices' so as to produce 'minute grains of interlaced colour'.[18] But most attractive to Seurat was the fact that, at the viewing distance just before that where two complementary colours blend, the eye hovers on the verge of seeing two colours become one, and the paint surface seems to flicker as if luminous. This, Seurat believed, was how the artist could truly paint with light, capturing for instance the glow of sunlight on grass. He called himself an *impressioniste–luministe*, and he referred to his method of painting in closely spaced dots as *peinture optique*. It later became known as pointillism.

But it is not clear that Seurat had read Rood when he painted *Bathers*,[19] and the work evolved as his understanding of optical mixing deepened. The picture was painted initially not with the pointillist technique but in a kind of precursory style where short brush-strokes were interwoven in a criss-crossed manner. Seurat reworked it in 1887 in a more emphatic pointillist style – but only in some places, suggesting that he saw no particular need for uniformity in applying his ideas.

A number of factors are crucial to attainment of 'clean' optical mixing. First, the dots must be sufficiently small. Yet Seurat does not seem to have been too concerned about this question of scale in relation to the distance of the viewer. In his masterpiece *Sunday Afternoon on the Island of La Grande Jatte* (1884–5) (Plate 8.7), the size of the dotted brush-strokes varies considerably; sometimes the edges of objects are strengthened by making the dots smaller there.

Moreover, the effects achieved by optical mixing depend very much on the colours used to create them. As Thomas Young found when trying to re-create white from spinning discs of the three 'primaries', spectrally impure primaries will create grey rather than white. With this in mind, one might have anticipated that Seurat would have worried about the nature of his pigments, rather than taking it for granted that the blues, yellows, reds and greens with which nineteenth-century chemistry provided him were adequate for the task. Yet he appears to have been content to use a fairly typical Impressionist palette without qualms or further investigation: cadmium yellow, perhaps chrome orange, vermilion, cobalt violet, artificial ultramarine, cerulean or cobalt blue, viridian or emerald green, and chrome green.

Rood's quantitative, pigment-specific prescriptions for optical mixing should have been very useful to Seurat and his followers, except that Rood used several older pigments in his experiments: gamboge, Indian yellow, red lead, carmine lake, Prussian blue. But it is not clear that Seurat or Signac accorded much importance to the critical spectral differences between these 'primary' pigments and those on their own palettes. Might it have been otherwise if the artists had been less removed from their materials?

Yet this is not the only gap in understanding that let Seurat down. The critic Félix Fénéon, who provided a detailed (if somewhat misconceived) analysis of Seurat's work in 1886,[20] listed the following distinctions that the artist made among the contributions to perceived colour:

1. **Local colour:** the colour of the object under white light
2. **Directly reflected light:** the portion of the illumination that is reflected unaltered from the surface
3. **Indirectly reflected light:** 'the feeble portion of coloured light which penetrates below the surface and which is reflected after modification by partial absorption'
4. **Colour reflections projected by neighbouring objects**
5. **Ambient complementary colours**

This is a more thorough systematization of Signac's list. But it contains some curious ideas. Seurat was still in thrall to the notion of 'local colour', which Monet and Renoir had rejected. Local colour was a very traditional concept to artists, and may have been given weight in Seurat's mind by Rood's comment that what artists call local colour is the colour of an object in white light. But this colour has meaning *only* under white-light illumination, and is not some inherent property of the object that manifests itself come what may. In other words, Rood is saying that the colour that we perceive is primarily that of the directly reflected light, which becomes 'local colour' only if the illumination is pure white light. So Seurat's first and second items above are really the same thing, under different lighting conditions.

Seurat seems to have equated 'directly reflected light' with pure sunlight – which necessitated that he attribute some colour to sunlight itself. He concluded that it is basically orange ('solar orange'), which was suggested by both Blanc and Delacroix; and this led him to include dots of orange amongst his green grass.

Fénéon's commentary provides a clearer summary of what Seurat hoped to achieve than anything the artist himself wrote:

One has . . . not a mixture of coloured pigments but a mixture of coloured light . . . It is known that the luminosity of optical mixture is always much greater than that of pigmentary mixture, as the numerous equations for luminosity established by Rood show.[21]

But the consequence of Seurat's incomplete understanding was that his dots of paired complementaries tend to create an impression not of luminosity but of greyness – recalling, ironically, Chevreul's problem with the Gobelin tapestries. As a result, his pointillist works seem covered over with a pearly sheen – not the intended effect, but surely nevertheless a reason for the dreamy sensation that the paintings evoke. For Signac, however, this greyness was a failure of strict pointillism:

Pointillage . . . simply makes the surface of the paintings more lively but it does not guarantee luminosity, intensity of colour or harmony. The complementary colours which are allies and enhance each other when juxtaposed, are enemies and destroy each other if mixed, even optically. A red and a green if juxtaposed enliven each other; but red dots and green dots make an aggregate which is grey and colourless.[22]

Seurat's early death in 1891, at the age of thirty-one, curtailed his search for a 'scientific' approach to colour. None the less, when Pissarro first saw the effects of the technique in 1885, he was greatly excited by what he perceived in its possibilities, and for a time he was a convert. He confessed that he sought

a modern synthesis of methods based on science, that is, based on the theory of colours developed by Chevreul, on the experiments of Maxwell and the measurements of O. N. Rood; to substitute optical mixture for the mixture of pigments, which means to decompose tones into their constituent elements, because optical mixture stirs up luminosities more intense than those created by mixed pigments.[23]

In this regard Pissarro revealed himself as the most supremely open-minded and inquisitive of the 'old' Impressionists – unlike his former peers, many of whom (such as Monet) despised the point-illist innovation. Pissarro regarded the older group as 'romantic Impressionists', as distinct from the 'scientific Impressionists' Signac, Seurat and himself. In 1886 Fénéon coined a new label for them: Neo-Impressionists. Yet when they contributed to the last Impressionist group exhibition in 1886, they were confined to a separate room, dominated by *La Grande Jatte*. Pissarro's former pupil, the acerbic Paul Gauguin, was especially vociferous in his disdain for the new group, calling them 'little green chemists who pile up tiny dots'. And by 1888 Pissarro had lost patience with the laborious process through which pointillist works had to be constructed, so inimical to his fresh and immediate approach. In a letter to his younger associates that is a model of delicacy, he explained that he was abandoning their bold but ultimately narrow methods.

Towards abstraction

Possibly no one amongst the early Impressionist group was subjected to more scorn than Paul Cézanne (1839–1906); and it is probably no coincidence that he was both the most radical and, in the long term, the most influential of the group. Cézanne founded no school;

instead, one might say that he founded the entire twentieth-century concept of colour as the constructive principle of art. Gradually his approach – breaking up a flat field of colour into a mosaic of prismatic facets – took him further from the Impressionists, further from the subjective and fleeting in art and closer to capturing the unchanging aspects of a scene. He began to use blocks of colour in an architectural sense to build the fundamental structure of what he saw, the 'motif' – an objective reality, without the intervention of mind or emotions. He exhibited with the Impressionists for the last time in 1877, and by 1904 he was voicing an opinion that placed him at an opposite pole: 'Light does not exist for the painter.'

Cézanne's palette displays a wide variety: from strong, bright tones to subdued, earthy colours. He was influenced by the writings of Chevreul and Charles Blanc on complementaries, but embodies them more in the form of colour relationships than simple juxtapositions. For Cézanne, modulation was the watchword: his use of high-toned pigments was modulated by more subtle hues, welding the patches of colour into a coherent whole that achieves a pearly warmth rather than the bold, shimmering contrasts of the Impressionists. His use of the new synthetic pigments was restricted and cautious, partly because he was careful to avoid fugitive colours but also because, somewhat surprisingly, he retained a traditional streak to his technique. Of the newest pigments, only viridian features prominently in Cézanne's work; and the only pigment of poor stability that he used seems to have been chrome yellow.

This mix of old and new materials is found in Cézanne's *Hillside in Provence* (c. 1885) (Plate 8.8), a typical example of the artist's work in the 1880s. There are splashes of brightness, but the overwhelming impression is of strong greens among subdued earths. For the former, both emerald green and viridian are used, while the orange and brown rocks are composed of yellow and ochre earths mixed with vermilion. The foreground is lent a yellowish-green tinge by a glaze of yellow lake. There is black pigment in the shadows, in itself a sign of the rift with the Impressionists. The occasional Chevreulean contrasts are depicted in muted tones. One can deduce from this composition that Cézanne did not regard the new pigments with quite the same sense of opportunity as his fellow

Impressionists. Although he was one of the foremost colourists of the modern age, his agenda was less a product of technology.

Paul Gauguin (1848–1903) also became increasingly isolated from the Impressionist group in the 1880s, both geographically and stylistically. He grew tired of the Impressionists' tendency to represent nature so literally, to retain 'the shackles of representation' (already an indication of how far attitudes had changed since the 1860s!). In a comment that anticipates the entire era of modernism, he implored, 'Don't copy too much from nature; art is an abstraction.' His own style, which he called 'Synthetism', veered towards a purely imaginative or symbolic use of colour. 'Since colour is itself enigmatic in the sensations which it gives us,' he wrote, '. . . we cannot logically employ it except enigmatically' Yet to a deeply imaginative artist such as Wassily Kandinsky, this impulse towards abstraction was suggested even by the 'old' Impressionists. When the young Kandinsky saw Monet's *Haystacks* series exhibited in Moscow in 1895, he saw the future of pure colour as the basis for an abstract art: it showed him 'the object . . . discredited as an indispensable element of the picture'.

In 1891, Gauguin left France for Tahiti, drawn by a taste for exoticism that was quite alien to the urbane Impressionists. There he hoped to live 'on ecstasy, calmness, and art', and aside from brief visits to France he remained in the tropics until his death in the Marquesas Islands in 1903. His palette stayed rich but matured in subtlety of tonality. Not for him the stark contrasts of complementaries, nor did he eschew earth pigments: he found burnt ochre indispensable for depicting the olive-skinned Tahitians.

He used most of the modern colours – cobalt blue, emerald green, viridian, cadmium yellow, chrome yellow, cobalt violet, and a mixture of cobalt blue and barium sulphate called 'Charron blue' – but seldom applied them straight from the tube. Prussian blue and ultramarine were the only colours Gauguin commonly used unmixed – as a substitute for black, which he largely avoided. But in remote Tahiti he suffered the frustrations of poor access to materials. In a letter of 1902 to the picture dealer Ambrose Vollard, who supplied him with materials, he voices his predicament:

I have opened your box. Canvas and glue – perfect. Japanese paper – perfect. But the colours!!! . . . What do you expect me to do with 6 tubes of white and terre verte, which I seldom use? I have only one small tube of carmine lake left. So you must send me immediately: 20 tubes of white, 4 large tubes of carmine lake . . .[24]

. . . and so forth through the modern palette. In place of canvas, Gauguin often used unprimed hessian and sackcloth – not just for economy, but because he seems to have enjoyed its rough texture.

Gauguin's Synthetism, which he described as 'artistic unity, harmonious composition, internal unity of conception, the understanding and the coherence of forms and colours', informed the group of French painters who called themselves the Nabis: Maurice Denis, Edouard Vuillard, Paul Serusier, Ker Xavier Roussel, Pierre Bonnard and others. Impelled by an expressive use of colour, the Nabis crystallized around a single small work painted by Sérusier on the lid of a cigar box, dubbed *The Talisman* (Plate 8.9). Sérusier created this chromatic landscape under the guidance of Gauguin at Bois-d'Amour, near Pont-Aven in France. The advice of the older man reputedly ran along these lines:

Gauguin: 'How do you see the colour of that tree?'
Serusier: 'Yellow.'
'Well, use your very best yellow. How do you see the colour of the earth?'
'Red.'
'Then use your very best red.'[25]

The Nabi group, a kind of spiritual cousin to the Fauves (see page 346), was short-lived – exhausted by 1900. But Gauguin's influence reached far wider and lasted far longer.

Vincent van Gogh (1853–90) was another of the iconoclasts who emerged from the Impressionist movement to pave the way to a new kind of painting as the *fin de siècle* approached. Born in Holland, van Gogh went to Paris in 1886 to live with his brother Theo, who had described to him the new style created by the Impressionists. Van Gogh became interested in effects of simultaneous contrast and of complementaries by studying the works of Delacroix; but his palette was initially rather subdued. On seeing the bold, raw colours employed by the Impressionists, his art was transformed. Yet he would later claim that his work was 'fertilized by the ideas of Delacroix rather than by [the Impressionists]', and he took the same path as Gauguin in making very free, associative use of colour: 'instead of trying to reproduce exactly what I have before my eyes, I use colour more arbitrarily so as to express myself forcibly'.

And there can be scarcely any more forcible expression of colour in all of Western art than in paintings like van Gogh's *The Night Café* (1888) (Plate 8.10), a pure nightmare of red and green complementaries bathed in an acidic yellow light. 'I have tried to express the terrible passions of humanity by means of red and green,' he told Theo. 'Everywhere there is a clash and contrast of the most disparate reds and greens.' Could any but the nineteenth-century greens, yellows and oranges stand up to these 'blood-red' walls? Indeed, this picture tells us just how much red is under challenge, for it alone had not been substantially renewed by the end of the nineteenth century.

Like Cézanne, van Gogh fostered no followers. But his anguished scream of colour and his whirling energy gave a vocabulary to the Norwegian Edvard Munch (1863–1944) and to German Expressionism. If Henri Matisse made colour the substance of pleasure and well-being, and Gauguin revealed it as a mysterious, metaphysical medium, van Gogh showed colour as terror and despair. Munch's remark apropos of *The Scream* (1893) that 'I . . . painted the clouds like real blood. The colours were screaming' echoes van Gogh's sanguine comment on *The Night Café* – 'a place', he explained, 'where one can ruin one's self, go mad, or commit a crime'.

Van Gogh's café is created from paint piled on thickly, which is all too easy to read as the product of wild, frantic, unfettered strokes of the brush and palette knife. But van Gogh reveals another motivation in one of his letters to his brother:

All the colours that the Impressionists have brought into fashion are unstable, so there is all the more reason not to be afraid to lay them on too crudely – time will tone them down only too much.

Indeed, his orders for materials reveal a penchant for some of the most fugitive colours on the market (see pages 257 and 284), and clearly van Gogh was neither ignorant of this nor too crazed to care. Rather, one almost has the impression that his primary concern was not for longevity but simply to get these garish visions out of his head.

It was a head that, by all appearances, burned with sickly yellow, the 'citron yellow' of his café's lamps, the sulphur yellow he perceived in Arles. In *The Sower* (1888) it is the yellow of the sun's baleful glow, an orb that offers no warmth or comfort but looms like a sickly, incandescent moon.

Yet colours of all sorts struck van Gogh with unusual intensity. '*Colour expresses something by itself*,' he insisted, 'one cannot do without this, one must use it; that which is beautiful, really beautiful – is also correct.' His every vision was seen in the pure hues a painter might use:

The deep blue sky was flecked with clouds of a blue deeper than the fundamental blue of intense cobalt, and others of a clearer blue, like the blue whiteness of the Milky Way . . . The sea was very deep ultramarine – the shore a sort of violet and faint russet as I saw it, and on the dunes . . . some bushes of Prussian blue.[26]

All this makes it tempting to suppose that van Gogh worked from instinct alone. Yet his treatment of colour, for all its apparent pathology, was methodical. His letters to his brother Theo, and the instructions they contain for purchasing paints, show that the painter worked hard to get the colour combinations right. He had a strong interest in colour theory, and was aware of Chevreul's laws of simultaneous contrast. To van Gogh, black and white were colours too, and complementary in just the same way as red and green, or blue and orange. This was an idea promoted by the psychologist Ewald Hering in the 1870s.

And van Gogh makes clear how essential the new materials were in allowing him to transfer his inspiration on to canvas:

I have got new ideas and I have new means of expressing what I want, because better brushes will help me, and I am crazy about those two colours, carmine[27] and cobalt. Cobalt is a divine colour, and there is nothing so beautiful for putting atmosphere around things. Carmine is the red of wine, and it is warm and lively like wine. The same with emerald-green. It is bad economy not to use these colours, the same with cadmium.[28]

Yet the 'terrible passions of humanity' were certainly at play in Vincent van Gogh's inner world. When the kindly Pissarro first met him in Paris, he decided that the Dutchman 'would either go mad or leave the Impressionists far behind'. In the end van Gogh did both: he never truly recovered from his breakdown in 1888 (during which he attacked Paul Gauguin), and despite Pissarro's efforts to find a good doctor for the unbalanced young man, he committed suicide at Auvers-sur-Oise, France, in 1890. 'He rests', wrote Theo to his wife, 'in a sunny spot amidst the cornfields.'

9. A Passion for Purple

DYES AND THE INDUSTRIALIZATION OF COLOUR

Who has not heard how Tyrian shells
Enclosed the blue, that dye of dyes,
Whereof one drop worked miracles,
And coloured like Astarte's eyes
Raw silk the merchant sells?

Robert Browning

Alchemists of old spent their days and nights searching for gold, and
never found the magic Proteus, though they chased him through all
gases and all metals. If they had, indeed, we doubt much if the discovery
had been as useful as this of Perkins's [*sic*] purple ... A discovery that benefits trade is better for a man than finding a gold mine.

All the Year Round (September 1859)

'Purple is the magisterium,' says essayist Alexander Theroux, and
who can doubt it, when the most precious of ancient dyestuffs, the
purple of Tyre, was worth more than gold itself? In the third century
AD a pound of purple-dyed wool cost around three times the yearly
wage of a baker.

The tremendous worth of the ancient purple, and its association
with royalty and high office, have become the stuff of legend. It is
no coincidence that, when the first synthetic mauve dye appeared
on the market in the mid-nineteenth century, it was sold under the
canny (and wholly inaccurate) name of Tyrian purple.

Yet it is hard now to know to what hue these legends attach
themselves. 'Purple' is a fluid chromatic concept in antiquity, and
the ancient dye ranged in colour from bluish to a deep red, depending
on how it was prepared and fixed in the cloth.

The Greek word generally associated with purple is *porphyra*, which is rendered in Latin as *purpura*. But throughout the ancient and medieval world, *purpura* could equally mean a shade of dark red or crimson; and indeed purple is steeped in associations with blood. 'The Tyrian colour', says Pliny, 'is most appreciated when it is the colour of clotted blood, dark by reflected and brilliant by transmitted light.' In the third century AD the Roman jurist Ulpian defined as *purpura* all red materials other than those coloured by *coccus* or carmine dyes.

The story of dyestuffs is shot through with this sanguine colour, whether crimson, scarlet or the blue-biased lustre of a true purple. There is nothing of the violet about these dyes, nothing pale or greyish or retiring. No, the most prized dyes have been bold, strident colours; one might reasonably call them martial colours in the days when dazzling visibility was more desired than camouflaged obscurity. Nature provides these deep reds more abundantly than any other colour of comparable brilliance and saturation, and the best of them have long commanded princely sums.

It is remarkable that the era of modern dyes began – by chance rather than design – with a purple to rival the most celebrated of ancient dyes. The influence of the nineteenth century's multiparous chemistry on dye colours is even more dramatic and more emphatic than its impact on pigment manufacture, and its consequences reach further afield. Synthetic dyes were soon thereafter to appear on artists' canvases, but it was their encroachment into the fashions of the city streets that spawned an immense global industry. In this chapter we shall see colour's impact on chemistry as clearly as we shall see the converse.

Dyed in the wool

Pliny has no doubts about the virtues of the true purple attributed to the Phoenician city of Tyre:

that precious colour which gleams with the hue of a dark rose . . . This is the purple for which the Roman *fasces* and axes clear a way. It is the badge

of noble youth; it distinguishes the senator from the knight; it is called in
to appease the gods. It brightens every garment, and shares with gold the
glory of the triumph. For these reasons we must pardon the mad desire
for purple . . .[1]

The Phoenicians ventured forth from Crete around 1600 BC.
According to one story, the exodus was instigated by their love of
dyeing, for which purpose they made use of ammonia from stale
urine; this unsavoury business left the Phoenician dyers shunned by
polite society. In Athens, dye shops were relegated to the city's outer
limits for this reason, even though their purples were revered.

The manufacture of Tyrian purple was known in Asia Minor
from the fifteenth century BC. The Greeks learned the art from the
Phoenicians; garments dyed with Tyrian purple are mentioned in
Homer's *Iliad* and Virgil's *Aeneid*. The dye is extracted from two
species of shellfish native to the Mediterranean Sea, known in Latin
as the *buccinum* (*Thais haemastroma*) and the *purpura* (*Murex brandaris*).
According to George Field, Greek legend has it that Tyrian purple
was discovered by Hercules, who, seeing the purple-stained mouth
of his dog, attributed it to the shellfish the dog had just eaten. Others
say the dog's master was the Phoenician god Melkarth.

The colourants are produced in a gland called the 'flower' or
'bloom' near the head of the mollusc, which contains a clear fluid.
This liquid was extracted either by breaking open the shells or by
squeezing them in a press. On exposure to sunlight and air, the fluid
becomes transformed from a whitish colour to pale yellow, green,
blue and finally purple. It is hard to imagine that the alchemical
significance of this sequence (see page 88) would not have excited
great interest.

Aristotle describes the extraction process in his *Historia Animalium*:

The 'bloom' of the animal is situated between the quasi-liver and the
neck, and the co-attachment of these is an intimate one. In colour it looks
like a white membrane, and this is what people extract; and if it be
removed and squeezed it stains your hands with the colour of the bloom
. . . Small specimens they break in pieces, shells and all, for it is no easy

matter to extract the organ; but in dealing with the larger ones they first strip off the shell and then abstract the bloom.[2]

Each shellfish yielded just a drop of the dye, which was why the stuff was so fiendishly precious, and why a significant proportion of the Phoenician population was employed in its manufacture. One ounce of the dye required the sacrifice of around 250,000 shellfish. The shell piles of the Phoenicians still litter the eastern shore of the Mediterranean.

The shade most prized from these extracts was produced by mixing the fluids from the two species. The tincture of *Murex* alone is brightly coloured, whereas the hue that the Romans desired was tinged with blackness. Pliny describes the process in his *Natural History*:

The buccine [*buccinum*] dye is considered unsuitable for use by itself, for it does not give a fast colour, but it is perfectly fixed by the pelagian [*purpura*], and it lends to the black hue of the latter that severity and crimson-like sheen which is in fashion. The Tyrian colour is obtained by first steeping the wool in a raw and unheated vat of pelagian extract and then transferring it to one of buccine.[3]

This glorious colour was reserved in Republican Rome strictly for those of high rank. A purple and gold robe could be worn only by triumphant generals, while generals in the field were entitled to a robe of plain purple. Senators, consuls and praetors were permitted broad bands of purple at the edges of their togas, and knights and others of comparable rank wore narrower bands. But in Imperial Rome the strictures were more severe: by the fourth century AD, only the emperor himself might don 'the true purple', and there were heavy penalties for any who owned cloth coloured with this 'royal' dye – or even with cheaper imitations. (The Stockholm papyrus (see page 67) contains three recipes for imitation purple dyes.) Under Valentinian II, Theodosius and Arcadius, the manufacture of Tyrian purple outside the Imperial dye works was punishable by death.

These royal associations valorized the colour even when

dissociated from the dye. Mosaic stones of an inorganic purple material are used for the robes of the Emperor Justinian I in the sixth-century church of San Vitale in Ravenna; those of the Empress Theodora in the same mosaic are of purple edged with gold. The Byzantine emperors were by this time regarded as Christ's represen-tatives on Earth, and so it was natural to transfer the royal colour to Christ himself: the San Vitale mosaics show Jesus in a purple gown. The use of red, crimson and purplish ultramarine for Christ's robes in later centuries gained validity from the link with the Tyrian hue.

But the centuries-old method of preparing purple was lost to the Western world when Constantinople fell to the Turks in 1453. Despite the accounts of the Classical scholars, it remained a mystery for centuries thereafter, until a French zoologist named Félix Henri de Lacaze-Duthiers rediscovered it in 1856 – an auspicious year for purple, as it turned out. The Frenchman saw a Mediterranean fisherman mark his shirt with a yellow design using a *Thais* shellfish; the design subsequently turned purple-red in the sun. It was not until 1909, however, that the Austrian chemist P. Friedlander deduced the full chemical nature of the colourant molecule – and discovered that it was almost identical to blue indigo.

Chemical cousins

Who would suspect that a pea plant native to India should have anything to do with shellfish in the Mediterranean? Yet the organic compound responsible for the Imperial *purpura* differs from the blue extract of the *Indigofera* plant only to the extent of having a couple of bromine atoms where hydrogens sit in indigo. Why shellfish should produce such a close variant (chemists would say *derivative*) of a complex substance found in a plant is not at all clear.

The Roman writer Vitruvius refers to indigo in the first century AD, the first mention of the dye in the West. Pliny says that it is second in value only to Tyrian purple, and hints at the kinship of its rich, dark hue with that of the imperial colour:

Indigo [*indicum*] . . . comes from India, where it attaches itself as mud to the foam of the reeds. When it separates in this manner, it is black; on dilution, however, it yields a beautiful blue-to-purple colour. A second kind of indigo floats on the vats in the purple dye houses, which is the foam of purple.[4]

This 'second kind' may be the result of light-induced degradation of the Tyrian purple itself to indigo by loss of bromine. Indigo seems to have been employed by the Romans not as a dye but only as a pigment for paints – it was used on the parade shields of the Roman army. Unlike most natural organic dyes, it can be used in pure, powdered form as a pigment rather than having to be made up as a lake.

Using indigo as a dye requires some chemical subtlety, since it does not take well on wool. It must first be treated with a so-called reducing agent, which transforms it to a colourless, soluble form called indigo white or 'leuco indigo'. One can only speculate at what gave ancient dyers the confidence to persevere with this unpromising stuff, which is taken up by wool fibres only in the colourless form – but is then transformed back to the rich blue on exposure to air. 'Think of the existential agony of the protochemist here,' says chemist Roald Hoffmann, 'to have gained the colored dye with so much labor, then to be forced to watch its color disappear, hoping, hoping that it will come back.'

In spite of these complications, indigo dyeing seems to be very ancient. Its presence is suspected on a robe from Thebes dated at around 3000 BC; it provides the edging stripes on Egyptian mummy bandages from about 2400 BC; and is thought to have been used in India from at least 2000 BC. The Israelites used a blue dye that seems to have been a mixture of indigo and its bromine-seasoned cousin dibromoindigo – that is, Tyrian purple. The Hebrew God instructed Moses that his people should wear garments bearing fringes of which one strand was dyed a blue colour called *tekhelet*. This dye was prepared from the rock snail *Trunculariopsis trunculus*. The male of this species secretes indigo itself, the female releases dibromo-indigo. But the secret of making *tekhelet* was lost to the Jewish tradition in the eighth century AD, and the strands of the prayer shawls of orthodox Jews have remained uncoloured ever since. Hoffmann raises the interesting question of whether authenticity should now be judged according to chemical composition or to means of preparation. It was a question that preoccupied many dyers when other natural dyes were synthesized in the nineteenth century.

The indigo molecule is also the blue colourant in the dye called woad, an extract of the plant *Isatis tinctoria* which is widespread in Europe and Asia. Woad was widely used as a dye in northern Europe until ousted by imports of indigo from India beginning in the seventeenth century. Famously, it was the substance with which the Celts decorated themselves to face the Roman legions, as Julius Caesar recorded: 'All Britons dye themselves with woad which makes them blue, in order that in battle their appearance be more terrible.'[5]

Despite the chemical identity of the colourant, woad was regarded as a different dye from indigo. Pliny calls it *glastum*, derived from the Celtic word *glas*, connoting blue. Like indigo, the woad dye is extracted from its source plant by fermentation. A recipe in the Stockholm papyrus specifies that the plant be soaked in urine under the heat of the sun and trampled daily for three days. Anyone who believes that natural dyeing is a gentle and benign process will be shocked to discover how destructive and unpleasant woad dyeing was apt to be. The fermentation releases large quantities of ammonia, perhaps one of the earliest examples of noxious 'industrial' emissions. And the woad plant, a highly nutrient-hungry species, depletes the soil in which it grows. In consequence, woad cultivators were inclined to be mobile, leaving exhausted, infertile wasteland in their wake. Laws were passed in medieval Europe to curb this devastation.

The art of indigo dyeing was brought very deliberately to the West: by the sixteenth century, the superiority of the tinting skills of the Persians and Asians was widely acknowledged. The English explorer Richard Hakluyt commented, with characteristic chauvinism, that

For that England hath the best wool, and cloth of the world, and for that the cloths of the Realme have no good vent if good dying not be added: therefore it is much to be wished, that the dying of forren Countreies were seene, to the end that the arte of dying may be brought into the Realme in greatest excellencie.[6]

To this end he dispatched the master dyer Morgan Hubblethorne to Persia, telling him, 'You must have great care to have knowledge of the materials of all the Countreies that you shall passe through, that may be used in dying, be they hearbes, weedes, barkes, gummes, earths, or what els soever.'[7]

In due course, indigo began to find its way westwards, and there followed a struggle between the importers and the home-grown woad cultivators. The truth was that indigo, while identical in terms of the colouring agent, made the better dye. Yet whether through inexperience in its handling or pure malicious rumour, word got about that it was not to be trusted: it was denounced as 'pernicious, deceitful, eating and corrosive' in seventeenth-century Germany. The dyers of Nuremberg had to swear an oath even at the end of the eighteenth century that they would not use it – though by then this was largely a formality, since it had already eclipsed woad throughout Europe.

Scarlet fever

While ultramarine blue was the most prized pigment for medieval painters, the finest cloth was dyed deep red. This would explain some of the colour symbolism in paintings of the late Middle Ages that appears unrelated to the value of the pigments themselves. In Sassetta's *St Francis Renouncing his Heritage* (1437), the act of renunciation is shown as a casting aside of a precious red robe. And the glorious crimson-red folds of the Madonna in *The Virgin with Chancellor Rolin* (*c.* 1437) by Jan van Eyck (Plate 9.1) contrast with the ultramarine garb of earlier medieval paintings while, by virtue of the purplish tint, securing an association with the most valued dye of antiquity.

Scarlet or crimson cloth was generally dyed in the insect extract kermes, the colourant of carmine lake pigment. A dyers' manual from Florence in the fifteenth century describes this rich red as 'the first and the highest and the most important colour that we have'. Yet there was ambiguity as to whether it was the quality of the cloth or of the colour that determined the fabric's value, to the extent that the two could become indistinguishable. While scarlet is today

a near-synonym of crimson, in the eleventh century it referred
to a type of cloth of unspecified hue. The scarlet of early medieval
Germany was a particularly fine woollen cloth, which might be
dyed almost any colour from black to blue to green. Yet inevitably
the valuable textiles tended to attract the valuable dyes – why
squander one by not colouring it with the other? So good scarlet
cloth was most often dyed with kermes. By the fourteenth century
'scarlet' denoted the dye; soon thereafter it became a colour word.

For purplish dyes the same transition happened in reverse. In
tenth-century Spain *purpura* had come to denote a silk fabric, and
for several centuries subsequently a 'purple' cloth could be pretty
much any colour. This shows how intimately ideas about colour
and its uses were linked to the materials that embodied them. As
we see in the case of indigo – the extract of both a snail and a pea
plant – even naming colours for materials has limited validity
so long as the underlying chemical composition of the coloured
substance stays mysterious. In the nineteenth century this question
of identity in the manufacture and use of dyes was to be picked
apart as never before. Even the distinction between natural and
artificial was to vanish, and in its place came a scheme in which
colourants were defined solely by the cryptograms of the chemist.

A public taste for colour

In Imperial Rome, one could control the application of and demand
for a colour by royal decree. By the mid-nineteenth century there
was a new determinant of colour use in the textiles industry: fashion.
Once the burgeoning Industrial Revolution created a prosperous
middle class, the process began of persuading Europe's populace
(the women in particular) of the supreme importance that adhered
to the correct choice of attire. Just as today, the fabric manufacturers
flattered their consumers with the conceit that they were the
engineers and not the victims of fickle fashion. Scottish dyer John
Pullar enthused to the colour chemist William Perkin in 1857
about the prospect of winning over 'that *all-powerful* class of the
Community – the Ladies' to Perkin's new dye. 'If they once take a

mania for it and you can supply the demand,' he assured the young man, 'your fame and fortune are secure.'

It was no exaggeration. The textiles industry – especially cotton manufacturing – was the most significant single sector of the Industrial Revolution. It was largely responsible for Britain's industrial supremacy before 1850, and its travails played a central role in the country's subsequent economic decline. Based in the northern towns of Manchester and Glasgow, the British textiles industry depended on the production of cotton garments and on cheap calico printing. Advances in spinning technology have often been stressed as a major factor behind industrialization, but calico printing may in fact have been the dominant aspect of the cotton industry. Woollen and silk products went to a more refined (though still highly lucrative) market – the industrial eminence of Lyon in France relied on its silk factories. Mulhouse and Rouen were the other main centres of French textiles. But it was in Paris, of course, that new dyes stood or fell before the merciless gaze of the doyens of *haute couture*. In the early part of the century Britain and France possessed the most powerful textiles industries in Europe; Germany, Holland and Switzerland were in the second rank.

Dyeing was a firmly established, guild-regulated trade by the late Middle Ages. But its path divided in the seventeenth century. The application of coloured patterns to textiles, which became fashionable at this time, posed a considerable challenge to the dyer, who could not then simply soak the entire cloth in the dye. Woad and indigo were patterned on textiles using 'resists' – pastes and waxes that masked the blank areas and were subsequently removed. This kind of 'blue printing' seems to have been practised in Europe from around the 1620s. The alternative was block printing, which was applied in Spain and Italy from at least the thirteenth century. Around 1500, book printers began to use engraved copper plates in place of wood blocks, and the textile printers soon followed suit. Because block-printing of textiles was carried out with oil paints and inks rather than dyes, and because the prints were often hand-finished by brush, the practice was typically seen as a branch of the painting and printing trade rather than that of the dyers.

This division was reinforced when new methods of textile

patterning were introduced to Europe from India in the 1670s. The Indians developed recipes for making colourfast patterns resistant to washing or fading in sunlight. This involved the use of mordants: fixing agents that enable the dye to adhere to the threads of the fabric and to hold fast when washed. The mordant forges a link between the compounds in the fabric's threads and those in the dye. Early dyers typically found the right mordant by trial and error – there was no obvious rhyme or reason for why one substance worked while another did not. Many mordants were metal-containing salts, but certain organic substances such as albumin (a blood extract) or casein from milk were also effective.

The importance of mordants was recognized in Europe before the introduction of Indian patterning methods; but the Indian dyers perfected techniques for combining mordanting with multicolour patterning. The printed textiles imported from India, called chintz in England after their Hindi name *chint*, were typically dyed with madder red. When the European dyers started to use the Indian techniques, a split developed between the 'blue printers', who worked with indigo, and the chintz-makers, who worked with madder. Blue printers sometimes found themselves in uneasy relation to the dyers' guilds, who considered that they alone were authorized to apply indigo to fabrics. The red chintz-makers, allied to ink and oil-paint printers, encountered less complaint from this quarter.

A career in colour

The extraction of dyes from their natural sources and their fixation into textiles increasingly required chemical expertise. Throughout the late eighteenth century, dye manufacturers became increasingly aware of the benefits of seeking advice from professional chemists, for example on such matters as the development of new mordants. That chemical art could serve the textile industry was highlighted in 1766 by the Scottish chemist William Cullen:

Does the mason want a cement? Does the dyer want the means of tinging a cloth of a particular colour? Or does the bleacher want the means of discharging all colours? It is the chemical philosopher who must supply these.[8]

Of course, Theophilus could have said much the same of alchemy in the twelfth century. But what was so special to Cullen's time and the century that followed was the appearance both of the means to conduct sophisticated modifications of nature's organic and inorganic substances, and of theoretical understanding of what the practical chemist was doing.

All the major dye companies of the early nineteenth century came to employ professional colourists: people versed simultaneously in chemical theory, the applied chemistry of colour-making, and the practices of the textile trade. We can trace their origin not to the dyers of the early eighteenth century but rather to the guilds of painters, draughtsmen, designers and printers. It was still by no means obvious in the early 1700s that the chemist had a large role to play in the dyer's trade. True enough, the Royal Society in London had in 1664 appointed a commission (which included Robert Boyle) to investigate methods of colourfast printing on fabrics. And early-eighteenth-century chemists such as Georg Ernst Stahl and Pierre-Joseph Macquer had asserted that dyeing could not be practised without a good knowledge of chemistry. But the idea that dyeing could be competitively conducted along the lines of a medieval craft, by the rote-like handing down of traditional wisdom, was not seriously challenged until certain technological innovations appeared towards the middle of the century.

The foremost of these novelties was the introduction in the 1730s of the 'English blue' process, called 'pencil blue' in England. This enabled indigo to be printed directly on to cloth from metal plates. Previously, areas that were to be left plain had to be masked off, since the traditional mordanting methods of indigo dyeing were not compatible with printing techniques. This problem was overcome in the English blue process by the expedient of adding orpiment to the vats. In 1764 this approach was combined with mechanical innovations to enable English blue printing using blocks instead of plates. A chemical training was a prerequisite for managing the complex mixture of dyes and mordants in this process.

In addition, direct metal-plate printing of red madder dye became possible from 1752, when Francis Nixon in Ireland devised a thickener for the mordant so that it would stay on the plates. These innovations made multi-colour textile printing possible, and soon four-colour (red-blue-yellow-green) printing became standard throughout Europe.

The importance of chemistry was further highlighted by the development of bleaches. In the early eighteenth century textiles were bleached with sulphuric acid, which was scarcely beneficial to the fabric. The French chemist Claude-Louis Berthollet showed in the 1780s that chlorine, discovered by Carl Scheele, exhibited bleaching power without the corrosive consequences of the acid.

Dye manufacturers tended to find their chemists among the ranks of the painters' guilds – for the association of chintz printing with this guild, rather than that of the dyer, had established a pool of colour professionals familiar with the demands not only of artists but of textiles manufacture and printing. These individuals were to secure the link between professional chemistry and the technology of colour.

Writing around 1766, the Basel-based calico printer Jean Ryhiner claimed that a good colourist should possess a sound knowledge of chemistry, of the composition of colours and of the specific practicalities of textile printing. (He went on to claim, apparently hinting at the indispensability of his own position as factory manager, that such people did not yet exist.) Ryhiner also identified a separate category of colourist – itinerant 'Arcanists' who sold their secrets of colour manufacture and application from factory to factory. So the medieval idea of arcana – tightly guarded, exotic secrets – was clearly alive and well. Such people were, said Ryhiner, a danger to the industry; but they were not destined to survive for long in the new industrial age. By the late eighteenth century most colourists were employed by a single firm for many years. And in the mid-nineteenth century the profession of colourist in a textiles printing works was seen as one of the most important career options for the training chemist.

Black magic

One of the first progeny of the tentative union between chemistry and the dyeing trade was a yellow dye called picric acid. This organic compound, discovered in the late eighteenth century, could be made by treating phenol with nitric acid. It was manufactured as a dye from the 1840s, after a method was found of making phenol from coal tar, a by-product of the coal-gas works that provided the fuel for gas lighting. Making picric acid from this unappealing viscous black residue was truly a case of drawing 'gold' from baser stuff.

As gas lighting gained in popularity during the 1830s, there was much interest in finding ways to turn its tarry residue into something useful. It was to this very practical issue that the German chemist August Wilhelm Hofmann turned his attention in the 1840s. Having studied coal tar under Justus von Liebig at Giessen in the late 1830s, Hofmann came to London in 1845 as the first director of the Royal College of Chemistry.

Here Hofmann and his students discovered that distillation of coal tar would yield up all manner of different hydrocarbons, including benzene, xylene, toluene, napththalene and anthracene. All these compounds were strong-smelling ('aromatic') and had a curiously high carbon-to-hydrogen ratio relative to the paraffin compounds such as methane, ethane, propane and butane, found in crude oil. Hofmann's pupil Charles Mansfield devised procedures for separating these pungent compounds from the black mess, and in 1848 he took out a patent on the process – a sign that the commercial possibilities were not unappreciated.

Phenol (also known as carbolic acid) is an acerbic substance with disinfectant properties. It was first developed as a commercial coal-tar product in 1847 by the chemist and industrialist Frederick Crace Calvert in England. From the 1850s, phenol was used in soap, in sewage treatment and as a disinfectant in hospitals. Benzene and the closely related compounds toluene and xylene found application as solvents, for example in the newly invented dry-cleaning process. Clearly, there was a market for coal-tar products.

Picric acid's bright yellow crystals provided the first indication that the aromatic substances in coal tar were the potential raw materials of strikingly coloured compounds. Silk readily imbibes the saffron hue of picric acid, and in 1845 the Lyon silk dyers Guinon, Marnas and Co. began to use the dye. Four years later they were manufacturing it on an industrial scale, and in 1851 the company's yellow silk was proudly displayed at the Great Exhibition in London.

In the mid-nineteenth century, Britain and France were the great dyestuffs centres of Europe, and an innovation in one country would inevitably be copied by the rival nation. Crace Calvert began making picric acid in 1849, while in 1855 the company of Louis Raffard established a factory devoted to its synthesis near Lyon. A means of applying picric acid to wool was discovered at the Guinon factory in the same year. Yet the dye had serious drawbacks, and was destined for a short career. For one thing, it was not easy to attach it securely to cotton fibres, preventing its application to calico printing – where the real fortunes resided. But its fate was ultimately sealed by its poor light-fastness. By 1863 it had fallen from grace, although variants were manufactured for many years thereafter.

The purple years

Another short-lived synthetic dyestuff of the mid-nineteenth century was a purple dye called murexide, which was synthesized from uric acid extracted from Peruvian guano. Huge deposits of these solidified bird droppings, rich in urea and uric acid, were quarried and exported to Europe from 1835. In Britain murexide was also sold as 'Roman purple' in an attempt to exploit associations with the fabulous dye of antiquity. Indeed it was even asserted in the 1850s (quite falsely) that murexide was chemically identical to Tyrian purple – whose secret was rediscovered, to the excitement of Paris but to no commercial benefit, towards the end of that decade.

Perhaps the marketing trick worked, for the fashion-conscious of the mid-century developed a taste for purple. An alternative to this synthetic colour was the so-called French purple, a rich, relatively colour-fast natural extract of certain European lichens. Related to the turnsole of medieval dyers, and also to the litmus extract used as an indicator of acidity, this substance could vary in hue from blue to red depending on the fixing agent. But it was the strong purple form that was most in demand, and in 1853 the dyer James Napier commented, 'Could this colour be obtained of a permanent character, and fixed upon cotton, its value would be inestimable.' It could be applied to silk and wool without mordants, and the discovery in the late 1850s of a suitable mordanting process for cotton led to much enthusiasm for French purple. It was also known as 'mauve' in France (after the word for mallow), and by 1857 this word was a colour term in England rather than an identifier of a dyestuff. Mauve became the colour of high fashion; the late 1850s and early 1860s constituted the 'Mauve Decade'. The glorious swathe of purple fabric that dominates Arthur Hughes's *April Love* (1856) (Plate 9.2) offers a paean to the colour.

Frederick Crace Calvert narrowly missed the opportunity to make a decisive contribution to the Mauve movement. He was one of the first to see how chemistry, particularly when applied to coal-tar products, might open up a new world of synthetic dyestuffs, and in 1854 he experimented on another coal-tar extract: aniline. That this compound might be intimately connected with agents of colouration was implied by its appearance as an extraction product of indigo. The name itself is derived from *anil*, the Portuguese word for indigo, which in turn comes from the Arabic *an-nil*, an adaptation of the Sanskrit *nila*, meaning dark blue.

Crace Calvert reported that when aniline was treated with oxidizing agents, which introduced oxygen-containing chemical groups into the compound, it yielded purple and red dyes which could be fixed on to suitably mordanted silk, wool and cotton. A dyer and chemist named Alexander Harvey in Glasgow obtained similar results when he oxidized aniline using bleaching powder. But as rich crimson dyes were already available from the extract of the madder plant, these synthetic alternatives were not developed further.

At that time there was probably no chemist in the world who knew more about aniline than August Wilhelm Hofmann. During the 1840s he elucidated its close relationship to phenol and to the 'parent' compound from which both are derived: the hydrocarbon benzene. In the 1850s Hofmann began to suspect that coal-tar compounds might supply suitable precursors for the chemical synthesis of quinine, the principal anti-malarial drug. Malaria was still rife in Europe in those days, and there was great demand for quinine. The substance, first isolated chemically in 1820, was extracted from the bark of the South American cinchona tree. It was expensive to produce and to import, so a method of synthesizing it from abundant raw materials such as coal-tar extracts would be of tremendous medical (not to mention commercial) value.

In the mid-1850s Hofmann set one of his young students, William Henry Perkin, on the quest for synthetic quinine. The son of a London builder, Perkin showed a talent for chemistry in his teens under the tutelage of Thomas Hall at the City of London School. Hall, a former student of Hofmann, arranged for Perkin to enter the Royal College of Chemistry in 1853, when the lad was just fifteen years old. Hofmann set him the task of making aniline analogues of aromatic coal-tar hydrocarbons, and Perkin set up his own personal laboratory in his parents' home. This was not a new situation to the Perkin family. William's grandfather Thomas Perkin conducted experiments in the cellar of his house at Black Thornton in Yorkshire, gaining a local reputation as an alchemist.

So it was in a garden shed at his home in Shadwell, East London, that Perkin attempted in 1856 to make synthetic quinine. His starting material was a compound called allyltoluidine, derived from coal-tar toluene. Perkin reasoned by little more than atom-counting that two molecules of allyltoluidine might unite with oxygen to generate one molecule of quinine and one of water. In other words, he hoped that oxidation of allyltoluidine might be a means of securing synthetic quinine.

It wasn't. When Perkin treated allyltoluidine with the oxidizing agent potassium dichromate, all he obtained was a reddish-brown sludge. Organic chemists quickly become familiar with this kind of reaction – generally it means that the reagents have combined to give an unintelligible mess that is best flushed down the sink. But Perkin was naive enough to believe the matter was worth investigating further. And this is how the eighteen-year-old young man launched the chemicals industry, experimenting at home like a modern teenager in his bedroom.

Perkin decided to conduct the same reaction using aniline itself as his starting material. This time, oxidation produced a black solid which dissolved in methylated spirit to give a purple solution. Would cloth take up this colour? Perkin coolly explained many years later that 'On experimenting with the colouring matter thus obtained I found it to be a very stable compound dyeing silk a beautiful purple which resisted the light for a long time.' The colour is indeed glorious even today (Plate 9.3).

While striking and unexpected, Perkin's discovery was not of its own accord a breakthrough in dye manufacture. Others before him had found bright reddish colours from coal-tar compounds, and yet nothing had come of it. What made the difference in Perkin's case was that, with his youthful vigour and inexperience, he was not deterred at once by the formidable obstacles to making his discovery commercially useful.

Making a dye from aniline was all very well in the laboratory – but aniline was already an expensive substance, made in two steps from coal-tar benzene. First, benzene is converted to nitrobenzene using nitric acid; then this is 'reduced' to aniline.[9] At that time, multi-step chemical synthesis was unheard of on an industrial scale: according to conventional wisdom, if you couldn't make the product in one pot, it was not worth bothering with.

But before confronting this problem, Perkin needed to know if his dye was any good. He sent samples for testing to the Scottish dyers John Pullar and Sons in Perth, who were impressed by the results – provided, they said, that 'your discovery does not make the goods too expensive'. That was enough to persuade Perkin to apply for a patent, and he travelled to Perth to collaborate directly in attempts to find a suitable mordant for cotton. But the Glasgow calico printers that he visited were underwhelmed, observing that the purple dye was removed by bleach, and fearful of its cost. Perkin's aniline purple seemed destined to be a high-value-added speciality product for silks, not wool or cotton.

At this point, Perkin had several choices. If he had been prone to caution, he might have abandoned the whole idea and resumed his academic studies. Alternatively, he could have sold the rights to Pullar or some other company and left them to wrestle with the dye's commercialization. But instead, he persuaded his father George and his brother Thomas that they should set up a business. In October 1856 he resigned from the Royal College of Chemistry, to Hofmann's dismay, and the Perkin family began to look for a site on which to build a small factory.

Now there was no avoiding the issue of how to scale up the synthesis without making it prohibitively expensive. Perkin identified a relatively cheap way to convert nitrobenzene to aniline; but the large-scale production of nitrobenzene from benzene and nitric acid was hazardous. Iron vessels could not be used since they were corroded by the concentrated acid, and so huge glassware was employed – with the attendant risk of breakage and explosions. Benzene could be bought at a reasonable rate from coal-tar distillers, but in a form so impure that it had to be redistilled before use.

Perhaps it was the craze for purple that saved the Perkins' enterprise, at face value a mad act of faith. In France, the manufacturers of French purple held a virtual monopoly on purple dyes that the Lyon silk dyers wanted to break. The announcement of Perkin's discovery by the Chemical Society of London in March 1857 left it open to plagiarism in continental Europe, where Perkin's patent did not apply. His attempt to secure French patents rights failed, and both French and German colour chemists began experimenting with aniline purple. By late 1858 it was being used by French calico printers, and this placed pressure on the British calico printers to reconsider their own reluctance. Orders increased at the Perkins' factory, now fully operational at Greenford Green, near Harrow.

Perkin continued to confront the technical problems associated with the manufacture and use of the dye. In 1857 he found a mordanting procedure effective for cotton. Later the Perkins were able to replace their glass vessels with iron ones by using less concentrated nitric acid mixed with sulphuric acid. They marketed the dye at first as 'Tyrian purple', but by 1859 it had become known simply as 'mauve' – there was more benefit to be had from an association with Parisian *haute couture* than with antiquity. By May 1857 John Pullar in Perth was able to tell Perkin that 'a rage' had begun for his new colour; and in the next few years it occluded the competitors, murexide and French purple.

The mania for mauve was positively gaudy by today's standards, and conservative commentators frowned on it. The British periodical *Punch* complained that London was afflicted with Mauve Measles. Others were more charitable. Charles Dickens's periodical *All the Year Round* sang Perkin's praises in September 1859 (while failing, however, to spell his name right):

As I look out of my window, the apotheosis of Perkins's purple seems at hand – purple hands wave from open carriages – purple hands shake each other at street doors – purple hands threaten each other from opposite sides of the street; purple striped gowns cram barouches, jam up cabs, throng steamers, fill railway stations: all flying countryward, like so many migrating birds of purple Paradise.[10]

The aniline boom

It seemed unlikely even to the dullest colour chemist that aniline purple was the only rich hue to be had from coal-tar derivatives. Many entrepreneurs set about experimenting with aniline, often armed with little more than determined empiricism. One such was François-Emmanuel Verguin, one-time manager of the picric acid factory of Louis Raffard near Lyon. Verguin seems to have treated aniline with whatever reagents he could find on his shelves, and in late 1858 or early 1859 he struck rich.[11] He mixed aniline with tin chloride, and obtained a deep red substance which he called fuchsine, an invocation of the colour of the fuchsia flower.

Verguin left Raffard in early 1859 and sold his discovery to the rival dye-makers Francisque and Joseph Renard, who began making fuchsine or 'aniline red' in 1859. In the same year, a new procedure for synthesizing the red dye was discovered in England by Edward Chambers Nicholson. Both Nicholson and his business partner George Maule were former students of Hofmann at the Royal College of Chemistry. Together with George Simpson, a London paint-maker, they set up business in Walworth, South London, in 1853 to manufacture fine chemicals. From 1860 the firm of

Simpson, Maule and Nicholson manufactured aniline red under the trade name 'roseine'. But the colour became more popularly known as magenta, named in honour of the Italian town where the French army fought and defeated the Austrians in June 1859.

Hofmann himself discovered in 1863 that treating aniline red with ethyl iodide produced a violet compound. Manufactured under licence by Simpson, Maule and Nicholson from 1864, this 'aniline violet' began to generate stiff competition for Perkin's mauve. And in 1860, French chemists Charles Girard and Georges de Laire discovered by accident that altering the recipe for magenta yielded a new dye, aniline blue.

The aniline dye industry was now in full swing, and new companies abounded in England, France, Germany and Switzerland. Some of these are now the world's major chemicals companies. In Germany, Friedrich Bayer and Company began in 1862 by selling fuchsine and a range of aniline blues and violets. A collaboration of industrial chemists established the aniline dye manufacturers Meister, Lucius and Co. at the town of Höchst, near Frankfurt-am-Main, in 1863. And in 1865 several small German companies merged to form a dye and alkali firm called the Badische Anilin und Soda Fabrik. As Bayer, Hoechst and BASF, these three German companies now dominate the European chemicals market.

Switzerland provided a haven for French industrialists stymied in France by the fact that French patent law applied to the product and not the process. Here in 1859 the silk-dyeing business of Alexandre Clavel in Basel began manufacturing aniline dyes, as did the dye factory of Johann Rudolph Geigy. These two companies – Ciba and Geigy, now merged into one corporation – became the chemical giants of Switzerland.

The influence of theory

A vigorous campaigner for academic chemistry, Hofmann did not miss the opportunity to advertise the success of the new synthetic dye industry as an indication of the value of research in pure chemistry – one of the earliest expositions of the now common refrain that pure research can have valuable technological spin-offs.

Whereas practical men like Perkin and Nicholson applied their chemical prowess to the development of new dyes and better techniques for making and fixing them, Hofmann was determined to develop some understanding of the constitution of these compounds and how this related to their colours. In 1863 he articulated the ambitions that the accelerating understanding of chemical science was fostering:

Chemistry may . . . ultimately teach us systematically to build up colouring molecules, the particular tint of which we may predict with the same certainty with which we at present anticipate the boiling point and other physical properties of the compounds of our theoretical conceptions.[12]

This clear statement is really the fulcrum of my story. Chemical technologists since antiquity were not lacking in interest about *why* the arts that they conducted brought about transformations of colour, nor were they indifferent to the composition of their dyes and pigments. But the main concern was a practical one, and theoretical understanding came *a posteriori*, if it came at all. By Hofmann's time, the chemical climate had shifted. The time was ripe, he thought, for a rational synthesis of colour. Chemists would in future produce colour to order from an understanding of the physical and chemical principles that underlie its manifestation in matter. The chemistry of colour was to be no longer a matter of try-and-see, but an exact science.

Between the late 1860s and the 1880s, Hofmann's dream began to materialize. From empiricism and a makeshift union of academic science and industrial research was to emerge a science-based dye and colour industry that was increasingly guided by theory. This was made possible only by the giant leaps that were taken during these years in fundamental organic chemistry.

The chemistry of dyes is organic, focused on carbon-based compounds. Until the nineteenth century, almost all such substances were extracts of living organisms. The study of these 'natural products' was pioneered by Carl Scheele in the eighteenth century, although it was the arch-analyst Antoine Lavoisier who deduced that the common factor among natural products was carbon. The methods of analytical chemistry available at that time allowed nothing more to be established than the relative proportions of the various elements – generally carbon, hydrogen, oxygen, nitrogen (C, H, O, N) – in these compounds.

This defines the substance's *chemical formula*: a list of the ratios of different elements, written in the chemist's shorthand where subscripts (or, before the late nineteenth century, superscripts) denote the representation of each type of atom. Thus benzene is C_6H_6 – six atoms each of carbon and hydrogen – and quinine is $C_{20}H_{24}N_2O_2$. When Hofmann and Perkin set about synthesizing quinine from coal-tar products, this was all they had to go on. Indeed, it was only their lack of theoretical understanding that prevented them from recognizing how daunting a challenge it truly was.

At that time, however, these formulae were not considered as reflecting the actual constitution of the molecules concerned – they were little more than codifications of the experimental results of elemental analysis. And there was nothing to indicate how the atoms were arranged in space; nor was there even a clear concept of such an 'atomic structure' of molecules, in the sense of a well-defined architectural arrangement of its component atoms. Little was said about how atoms were arranged, because nothing was known. It was rather like writing words by collecting together all the same letters and denoting their multiplicity, so that quinine becomes qui_2n_2e, or a word like 'acceptance' is $a_2e_2c_3ptn$ (or for that matter, $pe_2na_2tc_3$). How to make sense of these formulations, to extract from them their true meaning and form? And harder still, how to reformulate one arrangement into another?

This difficulty was most pronounced in chemistry's organic branch, in which the formulae were commonly complex even though the range of elements was small. The formulae could look similar for compounds that behaved very differently, or they might look different for comparable compounds. And there was such a proliferation, a seemingly endless diversity, of combinations of these elements. Inorganic compounds, in comparison, seemed to be restricted to a rather more limited set of permutations.

So the underlying challenge for organic chemistry in the early nineteenth century was classification, and much of the work until the 1850s was concerned with synoptic schemes – with methods of arranging different organic compounds into groups that showed some commonality of chemical properties. One of the most fruitful ideas in this endeavour was due to the French chemist Auguste Laurent, who proposed in the 1830s that organic compounds contain a 'nucleus' or 'fundamental radical' that determines the group to which it belongs. Compounds should, in other words, be grouped according to their 'nuclei', which are variously embellished with peripheral clusters of atoms.

Uncontentious though it might sound, Laurent's idea was highly controversial because it conflicted with the popular belief of the time that organic molecules, like many inorganic substances, were fundamentally binary, being composed of two oppositely charged 'radicals'. Laurent supposed that the nuclei of organic compounds are basically frameworks of carbon in which the number of carbon atoms provides the basis of classification. This idea of a carbon framework underpins all of organic chemistry today. Within Laurent's scheme, the nucleus of aniline (C_6H_7N) is the group C_6H_5 (today called 'phenyl'), derived from benzene (C_6H_6). Phenol (C_6H_6O) belongs in the same class.

In 1852 the Englishman Edward Frankland formulated a second crucial concept in organic chemistry. He proposed that all atoms of any given element form a specific number of bonds with other atoms – neither more nor fewer. This later became enshrined in the notion of 'chemical valency'. As Frankland put it, 'the combining power of [an] element is always satisfied by the same number of atoms'. This is the central rule of molecule-building.

The German chemist Friedrich August Kekulé revealed the full meaning of valency for the architecture of organic molecules when, in 1857, he showed that the carbon atom is four-valent: it forms four bonds with other atoms. That is why, for instance, the methane molecule (CH_4) contains four hydrogen atoms. By 1858 Kekulé understood that carbon's centrality in life's chemistry stems from its propensity to form chains, offering endless structural variety from the same basic constituents.[13]

But one more concept was needed in organic chemistry before its multitude of substances could be interpreted at the molecular level. Benzene's formula C_6H_6 cannot be rationalized by any chain structure in which all the carbon atoms are attached to four other atoms. The molecule does not seem to contain enough hydrogen to satisfy carbon's four-fold valency. Hofmann showed in the 1850s that many of the coal-tar aromatics, such as toluene, xylene and phenol, were related to benzene, sharing the same hydrogen deficiency.

Kekulé's interest in these aromatic compounds was enhanced by the rich applications they were finding in coal-tar dyes. His solution to the mysterious structure of the aromatic molecules is now the stuff of legend – with all of a legend's ambiguity. How much did the German chemist embroider his retrospective accounts of the breakthrough? How much did he really owe to a dream of a serpent devouring its tail in a closed loop, and how much inspiration did he in fact find in earlier studies of the problem? All we can really be sure of is the published record: in 1865 he proposed that the aromatics have a nucleus, in Laurent's sense, comprised of a ring of six carbon atoms.

Benzene, then, is a hexagonal ring, with hydrogens capping the carbon atoms at each corner.[14] In phenol, one of the hydrogen atoms is replaced by a hydroxy group (OH), while in aniline it is replaced by an amino group (NH_2). With this insight, chemists had a structural basis for their exploration of aniline dyes. The first fruit of this new understanding was both to show that nature's chemistry could be equalled in the laboratory and to initiate the ascendancy of synthetic over natural dyestuffs.

Once that happened, says art historian Manlio Brusatin,

there would be a different way of seeing and perceiving colours because there would be an entirely different way of producing them, with the birth of a modern industry of chemical colours on the horizon, looming over the back room of the old dyeshop with its rare, dyed garments and its antiquated trade in privilege.[15]

Remaking nature's colours

The madder plant *Rubia tinctorum*, source of the crimson red dye used in madder lake pigments, was probably first cultivated in India. Madder growing was widespread in Asia and the Far East in ancient times, and there is evidence of it in Classical Greece. The dyestuff became common in Europe after the Crusades, and fields of madder flourished in medieval France and Italy. Although it seems unlikely that chemical technologists were able to produce good madder-lake pigments before the seventeenth century, the extract was much prized as a dye, giving a strong, permanent red. It was employed primarily in so-called 'Turkey red' dyeing of cotton, a complex operation using metal-based mordants that produced relatively colourfast results.

In 1820 two French chemists, Jean-Jacques Colin and Pierre Robiquet, isolated a red compound from the madder root which they identified as the principal constituent of the dye. They called it alizarine, after the Arabic-derived word for madder used in the eastern Mediterranean region: *alizari*. The root extract also contained a second, related compound which they christened purpurine, responsible (despite the name) for a slight orange tint in the natural dye. The terminal 'e' was later dropped from both compounds. By 1850 a chemical formula had been assigned to alizarin (albeit incorrectly, suggesting an apparent relationship with the coal-tar extract naphthalene), and the search was on for a synthesis that might offer this commercially important dye at a lower cost than the cultivated variety.

Little progress was made until 1868, when German chemists Carl Graebe and Carl Liebermann deduced the correct formula: $C_{14}H_8O_4$. Graebe and Liebermann were working under Adolf Baeyer, one of the finest organic chemists of the age, at the Gewerbe Institut in Berlin. Like the Royal College of Chemistry in London, this establishment placed considerable emphasis on dyes and dyeing, and the two young Germans both came to Baeyer with practical experience of the dye industry.

A fourteen-carbon framework indicated a kinship with anthracene, not naphthalene.[16] In the summer of 1868, the persistent

efforts of Graebe and Liebermann culminated in a three-step synthetic route from anthracene to alizarin. The synthesis was a long
way from being industrially viable, particularly since it required
expensive bromine; but Graebe and Liebermann were able none
the less to sell the rights to the eager Badische dye company, soon
thereafter renamed BASF.

Consider for a moment what this synthesis represents. Mauve
and magenta were synthetic dyes – compounds that did not exist in
nature, and discovered by chance. Alizarin, on the other hand, was
a natural product – a complex organic molecule found in a living
organism – and its construction from readily available raw materials
was a matter of rational planning and deduction.[17] So the creation
of synthetic alizarin – a molecule identical to the natural product,
but made by artificial means – was arguably a more significant step
than the invention of aniline dyes. It showed that organic chemists
were becoming nature's equal, and that the natural dyes that had
been the mainstay of textile colouration since antiquity no longer
needed to be coaxed from many thousands of times their own
weight of animal or vegetable matter. The natural and the artificial
had converged.

But a better scheme than that of Graebe and Liebermann was
needed before synthetic alizarin could be commercialized. It was not
long in coming: the answer was to use sulphuric acid in place of
bromine. Given the enormous market for alizarin and the interest
therefore attached to its synthesis, it is not surprising that this
solution was attained independently by three groups, all in 1869.
Ferdinand Riese, a chemist at Hoechst, was one; and Graebe himself
was another, working in collaboration with BASF's chief chemist,
Heinrich Caro, one of the most creative industrial chemists in
Germany. And in Britain, none other than William Perkin came to
the same conclusion, thereby revitalizing his ailing company at
Greenford Green. BASF and Perkin filed patents just one day apart,
and to avert disputation they agreed to divide up the market between
them: Perkin would sell synthetic alizarin only in Britain, and BASF
only in mainland Europe.

Yet because of the disruptions caused by the Franco-Prussian
War, Perkin was for a short time virtually the sole producer of

synthetic alizarin worldwide. 'In 1870 we produced 40 tons,' he later recalled. 'In 1871, 220 tons; in 1872, 300 tons; and in 1873, 435 tons.' Then in 1873, a rich man at the age of thirty-five, he sold Perkin and Sons to Brooke, Simpson and Spiller, the dye company that was once Simpson, Maule and Nicholson. The increasing competition, and the tribulations of a still hazardous trade, left Perkin of the opinion that 'the prosperity of alizarin [was] past and gone'. He returned to the delights of pure research, and let the passing of time weave him a shy kind of fame.

New horizons

Synthetic alizarin was both brighter and, soon enough, cheaper than the natural version. As dyers and printers came (not without reluctance) to accept this in the 1870s, alizarin became the colour of the decade, rendering aniline dyes obsolete. Madder cultivation too was suddenly redundant, and within ten years it was moribund. In less than a decade, alizarin manufacture in Germany expanded nearly 100-fold: 12,000 tons were produced in 1880. This consolidated the dye industry as one of the major industrial concerns of the age, and Germany dominated the market: by 1878 it produced about 60 per cent of the dyestuffs sold globally.

The synthesis of alizarin provided an indication, if any were still needed, that competitiveness required active support of chemical research by the dye companies. They could no longer make do with colourists prospecting by haphazard trial-and-error; the development of new dyes was now a matter for theoretically knowledgeable chemists. The foundations of modern industrial research can be located in the decade that followed Graebe and Liebermann's triumph.

Academic chemists continued to play a vital role for industry. Frequently, only the acumen of a Hofmann or a Kekulé would suffice to answer difficult questions about chemical structure, now essential knowledge for the practical chemist. It was Hofmann who unravelled the structure of eosin, a bright pink substance made from the coal-tar derivative fluorescein, which was marketed by BASF from 1874. And in 1866 Kekulé clarified the molecular architecture of another tremendously important class of dyes, called azo dyes.

These compounds were discovered in the late 1850s by a German chemist called Peter Griess, who arrived at the Royal College of Chemistry in 1858 to work with Hofmann. His appearance was reportedly outlandish, and scarcely indicative of a soul finely attuned to colour chemistry. The college porter refused to grant entry to this character wearing 'a reddish-brown overcoat surmounting a pair of sea-green unmentionables, a bright red knitted muffler, and a massive top-hat of a size and shape rarely seen in Oxford Street before or since'. The chemist, meanwhile, simply shouted at the porter, in German, 'My name is Griess, and here I stop!' until Hofmann came to relieve the fracas.

The first azo dye was a bright yellow called aniline yellow, made by reacting aniline with nitrous acid. This and other azo dyes were commercialized by Simpson, Maule and Nicholson in 1863. In 1876 the German chemist Otto Witt, working in London, guided dye chemistry into new waters. His careful studies of the relationship between the structures and the colours of azo dyes allowed him to predict successfully the colour of a new orange dye *before* it was synthesized. For the first time, chemical research was shown to be not just a vehicle for *post hoc* understanding that guided synthetic refinements – it could be a predictive tool. Colours could – at least, this was the hope – be manufactured to order.

As they gained in chemical skill, the industrial chemistry laboratories began to diversify. In the 1870s aniline and other aromatics were examined for medicinal use. The analgesic properties of an extract of willow bark had long been known to folk medicine, and in 1860 the German chemist Hermann Kolbe showed that this compound, called salicylic acid, could be synthesized from phenol. A more palatable derivative was marketed by Bayer in 1897 under the trade name aspirin. Hoechst began to move into the pharmaceutical market in the 1880s.

But the concept of chemotherapy – the use of synthetic compounds as drugs – stemmed largely from biological application of coal-tar dyes by the German Paul Ehrlich. In the 1870s Ehrlich used synthetic dyes for staining cells, which made them easier to study under the microscope. He noticed that the dyes adhered to some tissues but not others. (Chromosomes, the gene carriers, owe their

name – 'coloured bodies' – to their tendency to absorb stain.)
Ehrlich hypothesized that similar factors were at play here to those
that determine whether dyes will stick to textile fibres. When he
observed that some dyes killed the micro-organisms that absorbed
them, Ehrlich began to see therapeutic possibilities. He synthesized
dye compounds to test as drugs, and in this way he found in 1909
an arsenic-containing dye that destroyed the spirochete micro-
organism responsible for syphilis. Under the name Salvarsan, this
drug offered the first relief from the deadly disease since the medieval
use of mercury.

By the early twentieth century, several coal-tar dyes had found
their way into pharmaceutical use: Congo red was used to treat
rheumatism and diphtheria; Acridine yellow, Prontosil red and
Gentian violet became anti-bacterial agents; and the fluorescein
dye mercurochrome was applied as a disinfectant. The *Manchester
Guardian* pronounced in 1917 that 'Whatever serves the modern
dyemaker directly serves national health.'

So strongly did the products of coal-tar chemistry impinge on
everyday life that they became celebrated even in the popular press.
Punch was to be found singing their praises:

> There's hardly a thing a man can name
> Of beauty or use in life's small game,
> But you can extract in alembro or jar,
> From the physical basis of black coal tar:
> Oil and ointment, and wax and wine,
> And the lovely colours called aniline:
> You can make anything, from salve to a star
> (If you only know how), from black coal tar.[18]

At no other time has the demand for colour fuelled scientific
advancement more than it did in the final decades of the nineteenth
century. According to historian of technology Anthony Travis,
'Once dye-making evolved into an expanding science-based
activity, the modern chemical industry was born.' Out of bright
purples and lustrous reds, shocking pinks and brilliant yellows,
emerged all that is good and bad in this most mercurial of modern

technologies: cures for devastating diseases, cheap and lightweight materials, mustard gas and Zyklon B, enough explosives to fuel two world wars and more, liquid crystals and ozone holes. The modern age, in other words.

Faded blues

But there was one more challenge to be met before night fell over the nineteenth century and modernism arrived with all its glamour and horrors. Even in the 1880s one of the world's major dyestuffs was still a natural extract. It came out of India, under the colonial auspices of Britain, for whom the indigo industry was the Empire's most lucrative activity in Asia. In 1870 there were 2,800 indigo factories in India. Used in vast quantities for such mass-produced items as military uniforms, as well as being the staple textile colourant in China, the blue dye was a global concern. And the market was commanded by Britain, to the chagrin of the expanding Swiss and German dye manufacturers. A synthesis of indigo would break this dependence.

From 1876 Adolf Baeyer began a collaboration with Heinrich Caro at BASF to make indigo. Baeyer deduced that the compound indole is the 'mother substance' of indigo, in the same sense as anthracene is the 'mother' of alizarin. But anthracene comes ready-made in coal tar, whereas indole has no convenient source. The framework itself must be constructed. This made the synthesis of indigo a challenge of a different order.[19]

Baeyer first succeeded in 1877, using toluene as his starting material – a compound whose high price precluded industrial application. It was not until three years later that he identified a more practical route, by which time Hoechst too was sponsoring him. This and other synthetic strategies were patented over the next few years, but still they were not suitable for commercialization. In part Baeyer was hampered by a lack of knowledge of the molecular structure of his target, which he solved only in 1883. This eminently applied work broke so much new ground in organic chemistry that it won Baeyer the Nobel prize in 1905.

It was not until 1890 that a good method was found for manufacturing indigo on a large scale – and then it was Karl Heumann at the Swiss Federal Polytechnic in Zürich, not Baeyer, who cracked the nut. Heumann devised two synthetic routes to indigo from relatively cheap hydrocarbon compounds. One of these began with naphthalene, which was first converted to phthalic anhydride. The key to making this synthesis of indigo viable was the acceleration of the reaction with a catalyst of mercury sulphate. In one of the many serendipitous accidents through which the dye industry has advanced, this catalyst was discovered when a mercury thermometer broke during the production of phthalic anhydride in Germany, and the mercury metal reacted with the sulphuric acid in the vat.

It is again a reflection of the difficulty of the problem – not to mention the tenacity of the dye companies – that production of synthetic indigo took a further seven years to blossom. Although the cost was at first slightly greater than that of the natural, imported variety, by 1897 BASF was able to manufacture synthetic indigo at the competitive price of 16 marks per kilogram. Over the next seven years the price dropped to less than half of this. One thousand tons of artificial indigo were manufactured in Germany in the first six months of 1900, and indigo cultivation in India began to flounder.

Thus local economies in India based on indigo farming were wholly at the mercy of technological developments taking place in distant Europe. When exports to the West were no longer in demand, the Indian industry was ruthlessly abandoned. This is all the more ironic when one remembers that Europe had learned the skill of fine calico printing from Indian craftsmen. At the same time, it is worth remembering that indigo cultivation was fantastically wasteful of land resources. In October 1900 the managing director of BASF, Heinrich Brunck, proposed that land cultivated for indigo in India should now be turned over to growing food crops – a worthy enough objective, except that its economy was built on the export business.

The implications of synthetic indigo were painfully apparent to Britain. A report in 1899 pronounced that

From a scientific point of view, the production of artificial indigo is undoubtedly a grand achievement, but if it can be produced in large quantities at such a price as to render indigo planting altogether unprofitable it can only be regarded as a national calamity.[20]

In an attempt to stave off such a crisis, the British government decreed that all its military uniforms should be dyed using only natural indigo, not the German synthetic product. But this was grasping at straws: by the beginning of the Great War, over 90 per cent of the European market for natural indigo had vanished, along with a corresponding amount of indigo-growing land in India. The chemical industry had won.

Yet Britain did not begin manufacturing its own indigo until 1916, eventually compelled by the need to dye military uniforms. Even then, it was German technology that provided the means. The dye company Meister and Lucius, augmented by a third partner, Brüning, set up a factory at Ellesmere Port, near Manchester, in 1909 to produce indigo for the British market while evading German patent law. The plant was commandeered during the war and taken over by the enterprising Manchester dye company of Ivan Levinstein.

After the war, Levinstein merged with British Dyes Ltd to form the British Dyestuffs Corporation, which in turn amalgamated with other companies in 1926 to become Imperial Chemical Industries (ICI). In part this consolidation was an attempt to compete with the German giants, who had undergone the same process. In 1916 a group of dye-makers centred around the Hoechst company merged with an extant consortium of Bayer, BASF and the Berlin dye manufacturers Aktiengesellschaft für Anilinfabrikation (Agfa) to become the mighty Interessengemeinschaft Farbenindustrie AG, or IG Farben. It is an amusing yet telling comment on the power that this cartel wielded in the first half of the twentieth century that in his novel *Gravity's Rainbow*, Thomas Pynchon (probably the most chemically literate novelist short of Primo Levi) presents IG Farben as the shadowy superpower orchestrating the course of the Second World War. A fantasy maybe, but not beyond plausibility.

Colourfast at last

It is sobering to realize that most of the major classes of dye now in production – the azo dyes, the 'anthraquinone' dyes related to alizarin, and indigo – were already discovered by the beginning of the twentieth century. Perkin, Hofmann, Baeyer, Caro and their contemporaries did indeed give us a new rainbow: the red of alizarin, the yellows and oranges of azo dyes, the aniline greens and blues, indigo itself, and aniline violets and purples. Aniline dyes have now all but vanished from the market-place; but the azo and anthraquinone dyes can each span the spectrum on their own. Adolf von Bacyer's synthesis of the yellow compound fluorescein in 1871 led to the important family of rhodamine dyes, manufactured by BASF from 1887.

The early azo dyes lacked any affinity for cotton – a major weakness. But in 1884 the German chemist Paul Böttiger created a red azo dye that could be used on cotton without a mordant. This was sold with great success by Agfa as Congo Red, and led to other colourfast azo dyes in yellow, brown and blue.

The blue and green phthalocyanine dyes – the second most important class of dyes after the azo colours – were another accidental discovery. In 1928 a blue substance was noticed during the manufacture of a fine chemical called phthalimide by the Scottish Dyes company (which later merged with ICI). The chemical constitution of this contaminant was elucidated in 1934 by R. Patrick Linstead of Imperial College in London, and was found to be identical to a compound discovered independently by German chemists H. de Diesbach and E. von der Weid in 1927. Christened phthalocyanine by Linstead, it has an affinity with the plant pigment chlorophyll, containing a metal atom embedded in a ring-like organic molecule. A copper-containing phthalocyanine dye called Monastral Fast Blue, with a deep, rich turquoise colour, was developed by ICI between 1935 and 1937. A green version, made by adding chlorine, became an important dye in the 1950s. These colourants are widely used in lake pigments for modern oil paints.

The introduction of synthetic fibres, beginning in the 1920s with cellulose acetate and later extending to polymers such as nylon and polyesters, brought new complications for the dye industry. In contrast to cotton, the fibrous molecules in these synthetic threads are so tightly packed that they are relatively impermeable to dye molecules, with the consequence that traditional dyes do not adhere well. Moreover, the molecular interactions that fix dyes to cotton fibres typically do not operate in the water–repelling synthetic fibres. The commercialization of cellulose acetate was greatly delayed for want of suitable means of dyeing it.

In 1922 the British Dyestuffs Corporation introduced 'ionamine' dyes. These do not dissolve in water but are instead dispersed throughout the liquid as a very fine powder, and will stick to fibres such as cellulose acetate, nylon, polyacrylonitriles and polyesters. In 1923 the BDC and the British Celanese Company simultaneously discovered a new class of anthraquinone dyes that will adhere to acetate fibres.

Cotton, still the most important commercial fabric, has posed a persistent problem for dyers, who have long struggled to find a way of making dyes take to the fibres in a truly colourfast manner. The mordants that fixed aniline dyes such as Perkin's mauve to cotton were adequate for their day, but not for the standards of permanence we would expect today. Even by 1904 the Berlin Aniline Company was still lamenting that 'Absolutely fast dyes do not exist, sunshine and rain finally bleach them all.'

But in 1954 two British chemists, Ian Rattee and William Stephan at ICI, found how to make dyes take permanent root in cotton. The ideal solution is to create a strong chemical bond between the dye molecules and the (cellulose) molecules in the cotton fibres. Rattee and Stephan devised a general method of linking dyes to fibres via a coupling molecule. With the coupler attached, the dyes become 'reactive', capable of forming bonds to cellulose and woollen fibres.

ICI marketed these 'reactive dyes' in 1956 under the trade name Procions. Inevitably, Ciba–Geigy, BASF, Hoechst and Bayer rapidly developed their own versions. For the first time it became possible to manufacture bright, colourfast cotton clothing; within a few years, bold patterns awash with primaries and secondaries became one of the fashion statements of swinging London.

Coal tar on canvas

In view of the venerable history of indigo and madder as artists' colours, one might imagine that the impact of coal-tar dyes and their successors on fine art would have been tremendous. Some painters of the late nineteenth century would have preferred this not to be the case. For Jean-Georges Vibert, aniline dyes were a 'catastrophe for painting', and he called for urgent testing of the new materials. Their loveliness was the very problem: this allure was often a false promise, for the lake pigments made from the new colours tended to discolour or fade rapidly. According to Max Doerner, 'their precipitous and ill-advised introduction into painting was the cause of a great deal of damage'. Vincent van Gogh was one who did not heed the warnings, and a fugitive eosin lake that he favoured has played havoc with some of his works.

When coal-tar colours were first introduced to artists, their deterioration was sometimes so swift – happening in a matter of days – that it did not take long for the new materials to acquire a bad reputation. Thus they do not feature strongly in nineteenth-century art. In the list of pigments recommended as 'reliable for oil painting' in Arthur Laurie's survey of artists' materials from 1960, there is not a single colour based on a synthetic dye aside from 'alizarin lakes'.

This degree of caution was, however, unwarranted. It was certainly wise to be wary of coal-tar colours before the turn of the century, but matters improved somewhat. In 1907 the manufacturers of synthetic colours for artists agreed that their products should be subjected to stability tests over several years before being marketed. Alizarin lake was already acknowledged as a more permanent pigment than natural madder lake, and it was decided that other synthetic colours should be of comparable reliability before they were offered to painters.[21] Doerner's account of subsequent events will not, however, surprise anyone jaded by the realities of the commercial world: 'Unfortunately this agreement was broken by one manufacturer, and the others soon followed to meet competition. Enthusiastic claims and extravagant advertising ensued, to be followed by a return to a more sober consideration of the facts.'[22]

Lemon-yellow coal-tar colours, for instance, which were marketed as brighter, more permanent materials than the existing chrome and cadmium yellows, turned out to be quite the opposite.

But gradually the gold was sifted from the dross. In 1911 the so-called Hansa pigments, related to the azo dyes, were introduced in Germany. Hansa Yellow G proved even more permanent than alizarin lake. Even the wary Doerner advised the use of IG Farben's synthetic Indanthrene yellow, mixed with cadmium yellow, as a substitute for golden Indian yellow, and Indanthrene Brilliant Pink as a trustworthy colour midway between vermilion and light madder lake. IG Farben's Helio Fast Red, he adds, might be risked as a substitute for vermilion, and Indanthrene blue for Prussian blue. If a greenish-blue was desired, phthalocyanine blue lake was regarded by the 1940s as a perfectly safe option.

Confronted with hundreds of synthetic dye-based colours by the mid-twentieth century (Figure 9.1), the artists found that their

Figure 9.1

Coal tar and related organic colours proliferated with dizzying variety by the early twentieth century.

deliberations were not made any easier by the manufacturers' capricious choice of names. Companies had no qualms about naming a new pigment after its classical equivalent, as if deciding that 'Indian yellow', 'vermilion' and 'cobalt blue' designate not a substance but a hue. 'Often the most arbitrary, fantastic names and mixtures are invented,' Doerner complained in 1934, 'which are impossible to check and therefore are better avoided.' But there was, in the end, no avoiding synthetic colours – and increasingly, artists felt little inclination to do so. For many of them, the new materials were not just so many new hues for the palette, but something more profound: representatives of a new age, in which technology reigned supreme.

10. Shades of Midnight

THE PROBLEM OF BLUE

What bliss there is in blueness. I never knew how blue blueness could be.

Vladimir Nabokov, *Laughter in the Dark* (1989)

Blue gives other colours their vibration.

Paul Cézanne

What is blue? Blue is the invisible becoming visible . . . Blue has no dimensions. It 'is' beyond the dimensions of which other colours partake.

Yves Klein

What is it about blue that has lured painters so consistently? Majesty, yes; melancholy, certainly; and mystery too. According to Kandinsky,

The power of profound meaning is found in blue . . . Blue is the typical heavenly colour. The ultimate feeling it creates is one of rest. When it sinks almost to black, it echoes a grief that is hardly human.[1]

Is this grief in the dark sky of the painting that is reputedly van Gogh's last, *Crows Flying over a Cornfield* (1890)? Picasso's Blue Period (1901–4) coincides with his poverty-stricken years in Paris, when the artist was brooding over the suicide of his close friend Carlos Casagemas. Carl Jung suggested that these cool, bleak portraits of sick, hungry, aged and poor beings bathed in a blue glow represent a mythical journey into hell, where 'there reigns the blue of night, of moonlight and of water, the Duat blue of the Egyptian under-world'. *The Absinthe Drinker* (1901) and *Old Woman* (1901), still bearing the influence of Impressionism, are clothed in midnight blues; *The Blue Room* (1901) and *La Vie* (1903) have a subdued, shadowy cast.

But there are exuberant blues too, as Titian's *Bacchus and Ariadne* is among the first paintings to proclaim. The dress of Henri Matisse's *Lady in Blue* (1937) leaves little room in the frame for the accompanying primaries (Clyfford Still's *1953* (1953) leaves even less). In *The Artist and His Model in the Studio at Le Havre* (1929) Raoul Dufy embeds the two figures in a sky-blue room that simply continues the view of sea and sky from the open window. In Matisse's visionary *Blue Nude* (1907), the model herself takes on this shade without yielding her vigour. Her angular figure seems to anticipate the totemic Cubist women of Picasso's *Demoiselles d'Avignon* (1907), who are surrounded in blue like an enfolding sheet.

Kandinsky's affinity for blue took concrete form in 1911 when he and the German painter Franz Marc created an art almanac called *Der Blaue Reiter* (*The Blue Rider*) – named after a painting by Kandinsky from 1903 that features a blue horseman. Marc pursued the theme with dogged literalness in *Blue Horse I* (1911) and *Large Blue Horses* (1911). The name of the almanac became attached to a group of artists centred around Marc and Kandinsky, which included (for a time) Paul Klee and the Parisian Robert Delaunay. Marc was killed in the First World War in 1916; but Kandinsky sustained his passion for blue in *Die Blaue Vier* (the Blue Four), the group he formed in 1924 with Klee, Lyonel Feininger and Alexei von Jawlensky. Klee painted *Battle Scene from 'Sinbad the Sailor'* the previous year, with its Munsell-like tonal patchwork of blue.

I considered briefly whether this book might abandon chronology altogether and instead divide its narrative among the various primary and secondary colours. That might have been fun. But it would have taken an artfulness greater than I possess to avoid constantly retreading the same ground. For even if the technology of any age spawns some colours more readily and more abundantly than others, it generally does so against a backdrop of social, scientific, aesthetic and artistic considerations that apply as much to one colour as to another.

So why nevertheless single out blue for a solo treatment? One can hardly avoid the conclusion, in surveying the history of colour-making, that blue has always been special; this much should be apparent already. It is the most ancient of synthetic pigments and was venerated in the late Middle Ages as emblematic of divine purity. Yet it did not take its place as a primary colour until centuries after red and yellow. And despite the appearance, around 1704, of a blue pigment representing the first of the modern artificial colours, a lack of accessible, high-quality blues was keenly felt by painters until the early nineteenth century.

The fact is that a good blue was hard to find.

The birth of blue

The problem we face in tracing the importance of blue back to antiquity is that, because it was not clearly recognized as a colour in its own right, the oldest colour terms connoting blue are equivocal. Clearly, blue pigments were available to the first civilizations, including azurite, indigo and Egyptian blue frit. Yet there is no sense, in the Classical literature, of the primary nature of blue. It was regarded as a colour related to black – a kind of grey, if you will. In the fifth century BC, the Greek philosopher Democritus wrote that a colour equivalent to indigo (*isatin*) can be mixed from black and pale green (*chloron*, one of Democritus' four 'simple' colours). We can imagine the result of this union and see within it some indication of the casual regard the Greeks had for the integrity of the colour we know as blue.

It would perhaps be more accurate to say that blue, to the Greeks, was a species of darkness. For the word that signifies 'black' in most Greek texts is *melas*, denoting 'dark', the opposite spectral pole to *leucos* or light. In many surviving fragments of Greek painting blue is used as a darkener, and a distinctly bluish-grey can be obtained by mixing some black charcoal pigments with white. (Indeed, we have seen how artists such as Rubens were still making blues this way two millennia later.) It seems that, rather than dulling the senses to blues, this attitude of 'blue as dark' may have heightened the ancients' ability to detect blueness in melancholy hues. The Roman Vitruvius describes a recipe for making a black pigment by burning the dried dregs of wine, and says, 'The use of the finer wines will allow us to imitate not only black but indigo.'

Plato and Aristotle inherited much of Democritus' philosophy (although they did not much approve of his atomism). Aristotle's attitude to blue, and to primaries generally, is rather hard to discern. In *On Sense and Sensible Objects* he identifies deep blue as one of the 'unmixed' intermediate colours between light and dark, while his *Meteorology* lists only red, green and purple as the unmixed colours of the rainbow. The Aristotelian *On Colours* offers only white and golden yellow as primaries – the colours, it is asserted, of the four elements.

All this is not to imply that the ancients had no *perception* of blue as we know it – of the blue of the sky and sea. There are several Greek words that seem to translate as this hue; one is *kuanos*, the origin of our 'cyan'. Yet none of these is equivalent to the English 'blue' as a basic colour term – context-independent, in the sense of the classification of Berlin and Kay. It is as if the Greeks got by with terms like our cyan, ultramarine, indigo, navy, sapphire and azure, without having a word to class them together as a single perceptual concept.

We have seen how, faced with such an uncertain theoretical basis for talking about colour, Classical and medieval authors would anchor a discussion of artists' colours to the material substance of the pigments. In principle this is commendable, since the painter never uses 'blue' but instead indigo, cobalt blue, Prussian blue or whatever. In practice, however, there remains ample scope for confusion. A classic example, bizarre to us today, is the blurring of the distinction between blue and yellow in the Middle Ages (see page 15).

Pliny's account in his *Natural History* of the four-colour palettes of the Greek painters Apelles, Aetion, Melanthius and Nichomachos lists not hues but pigments. Among these is 'Attic yellow' – that is, a yellow pigment from Attica. But the word Pliny used for yellow is a mineral term: *sil*, not the more clear-cut *crocum* or *glaucus*. *Sil* is a kind of yellow ochre. But when, in the sixteenth century, blue emerged as a 'basic' colour, some authors felt that it should surely feature in Pliny's list. The Italian Cesare Cesariano made the improbable claim in 1521 that *sil* was ultramarine. By the later part of that century *sil* had become, in a French encyclopedia of the arts, associated with a shade of violet.

It is perhaps because Pliny states that both the ochre *sil* and the blue mineral *caeruleum* (which is probably azurite) are found in gold and silver mines that the two were initially confused. But the tangle was further ravelled by the use of the term *cerulus* for yellow in the late Middle Ages. Even the Old French *bloi*, from which the English blue and the French *bleu* are derived, could mean either blue or yellow.

The idea that the four-colour Classical palette must have contained blue was established more firmly in the influential *Commentary on Painting* (1585) by Louis de Montjosieu, who said: 'For it is certain that these four colours, white, black, red and blue, are the fewest needed in painting, and from a mixture of which all the others are composed.' This transformation of the four-colour palette was achieved by claiming that, while indeed the mineral *sil* could be one of several colours – sometimes yellow, sometimes violet – the *sil* from Attica was blue. (Even George Field, in 1808, regarded silicates – 'silex' – as the mineral origin of blues.)

It is hardly surprising that the absence of yellow from de Montjosieu's four-colour scheme was in its turn to cause concern. (As far as de Montjosieu himself was concerned, yellow could be made from red and green – an idea derived, it would seem, from Aristotle.) In the mid-seventeenth century the Frenchman Marin Cureau de la Chambre could not bring himself to believe that Apelles managed without yellow, and he concluded that by *sil* Pliny must have meant both blue *and* yellow, since *sil* could apparently be either colour.

Such linguistic juggling reflects the need to reconcile Pliny's authority with the growing desire, by the seventeenth century, to incorporate all of the 'modern' primaries – red, yellow and blue – into the set of basic colours 'of which all the others are composed'. We can locate the entry of blue into these schemes around the late sixteenth century, and it is safe to say that by the seventeenth century there was little argument that blue had to be included. In *Experiments & Considerations Touching Colours* (1664), Robert Boyle asserted this emphatically:

There are but few Simple and Primary Colours (if I may so call them) from whose various compositions all the rest do as it were Result . . . I have not yet found, that to exhibit this strange Variety [a painter] needs employ any more than *White* and *Black*, and *Red*, and *Bleu*, and *Yellow*; these *five*, variously *Compounded*, and (if I may so speak) *Decompounded*, being sufficient to exhibit a Variety and Number of Colours, such, as those that are altogether Strangers to the Painters' Pallets, can hardly imagine.[2]

It was soon to be white and black, the classical origins of all colours, that had to defend an increasingly arbitrary status as primaries. Isaac Newton showed that they were certainly not so in any generative sense. In the nineteenth century Michel-Eugène Chevreul continued to allow that these two, in addition to red, yellow and blue, featured as 'primary' colours in the palettes of the ancients; but Thomas Young's theory of colour vision (see page 47) left no room for them in a scientific dissection of colour.

Across the seas

Blue could in any case have hardly remained a subordinate colour when, during the late Middle Ages, it was manifested in the most celebrated and precious pigment, ultramarine. How could a colour that cost more to procure than the finest red (vermilion) – indeed, more than the medieval analogue of yellow, gold itself – be anything other than a primary? Ultramarine, vermilion and gold were the glories of the medieval palette; and surely a culture that equated value with virtue could not but be inclined to accord the hues of this venerated trinity some privileged status. I think we would not be overstating the case to suggest that it was due to a technical advance in pigment manufacture, as much as to any theoretical considerations, that blue emerged so prominently in the lore of the painter's craft.

Lapis lazuli simply means 'blue stone'. It is a deep, rich, alluring blue (Plate 10.1), but the purity of the colour vanishes on grinding, which is why azurite instead provided the natural blue pigment of the ancient world. The blue stone is actually a mixture of minerals; the colour comes from the dominant component, a mineral called lazurite (not to be confused with azurite).

Ultramarine is unusual among inorganic pigments in that its vibrant colour does not derive from the presence of a transition metal. Lazurite is an aluminosilicate compound, a member of a class of minerals in which the basic framework of the crystal is composed of aluminium, silicon and oxygen atoms. Aluminosilicates are usually colourless, but lazurite is distinguished in possessing sulphur in its make-up too. The sulphur atoms cluster in groups of two and three, and the crystal absorbs red light by shuttling an electron between different sulphur atoms.

The deep blue of lapis lazuli is typically flecked with golden streaks, which add to its attractiveness as a semi-precious gemstone. These are fool's gold – iron pyrite, a compound of iron and sulphur. Calcite (calcium carbonate) and other silicate minerals are generally present too, and they account for the greyness of the powdered stone. Lapis lazuli was nevertheless sometimes used as a pigment prepared by simple grinding. It appears, for example, in Byzantine manuscripts from the sixth to the twelfth century, in wall paintings from the sixth and seventh centuries in Afghanistan, and in eleventh-century Chinese and Indian paintings. But unless the stone consisted of exceptionally pure lazurite, the results were not very grand. Ground lapis lazuli (which we should distinguish from true ultramarine) has not been identified in any Egyptian, Greek or Roman art.

The technique for making ultramarine seems to have been a medieval invention: Arthur Laurie, the Royal Academy's expert on artists' materials in the early twentieth century, suggests that good-quality ultramarine began to appear in Western art only around 1200. Theophilus, writing in the 1120s, makes no mention of it – his azure is azurite.

Lapis lazuli is a rare mineral. Virtually the sole source throughout the Middle Ages was Badakshan, now in Afghanistan. Though poorly accessible at the headwaters of the River Oxus, the quarries seem none the less to have been mined for the precious blue stone since the days of the Mesopotamian civilization. Only much more recently were significant deposits found in Siberia and Chile.

Marco Polo visited these quarries in 1271, and marvelled at them:

Here there is a high mountain, out of which the best and finest blue is mined. There are veins in the earth of stones out of which the blue is made, and mountains whence silver is mined. And the plain is very cold.[3]

We do not know who discovered the method for extracting the princely pigment from the detritus of powdered lapis lazuli. Daniel Thompson suggests that true ultramarine was imported to Europe from the East before the Europeans knew how to make it. Why else, he asks, would they persist in calling it 'ultramarine', when many other raw materials for pigments were also imported? Early descriptions of the extraction process in the Arabic alchemical literature support this idea. One recipe is ascribed to the alchemist Jabir ibn Hayyan, but dates from well after his death in the ninth century and so is one of the many such works that borrow the authority of his name.

The basic challenge is to separate the blue lazurite from the impurities. Most recipes say that ground lapis lazuli should be mixed to a paste with melted wax, oils and resins. This paste, wrapped in cloth, is then kneaded in a solution of lye. The blue particles are washed out and settle at the bottom of the liquid.

The process employed since the late Middle Ages is described carefully by Cennino Cennini, and gives us an indication of the lengths to which the craftsman was prepared to go to obtain this finest of colours:

To begin with, get some lapis lazuli. And if you want to recognize the good stone, choose that which you see is richest in blue colour, because it is all mixed like ashes. That which contains least of this ash colour is the best. But see that it is not the azurite stone, which looks very lovely to the eye, and resembles an enamel. Pound it in a bronze mortar, covered up, so that it may not go off in dust; then put it on your porphyry slab, and work it up without water. Then take a covered sieve such as the druggists use for sifting drugs; and sift it, and pound it over again as you find necessary. And bear in mind that the more finely you work it up, the finer the blue will come out, but not so beautifully violet in colour . . . When you have this powder all ready, get six ounces of pine rosin from the druggists, three ounces of gum mastic, and three ounces of new wax, for each pound of lapis lazuli; put all these things into a new pipkin, and melt them up together. Then take a white linen cloth, and strain these things into a glazed washbasin. Then take a pound of this lapis lazuli powder, and mix it all up thoroughly, and make a plastic of it, all incorporated together. And have some linseed oil, and always keep your hands well greased with this oil, so as to be able to handle the plastic. You must keep this plastic for at least three days and three nights, working it over a little every day; and bear in mind that you may keep it in the plastic for two weeks or a month, or as long as you like. When you want to extract the blue from it, adopt this method. Make two sticks out of a stout rod, neither too thick nor too thin . . . And then have your plastic in the glazed washbasin where you have been keeping it; and put into it about a porringerful of lye, fairly warm; and with these two sticks, one in each hand, turn over and squeeze and knead this plastic, this way and that, just as you work over bread dough with your hand, in just the same way. When you have done this until you see that the lye is saturated with blue, draw it off into a glazed porringer. Then take as much lye again, and put it on to the plastic, and work it over with these sticks as before. When the lye has turned quite blue, put it into another glazed porringer, and put as much lye again on to the plastic, and press it out again in the usual way . . . And go on doing this for several days in the same way, until the plastic will no longer colour the lye; and then throw it away, for it is no longer any good . . . And every day drain off the lye from the porringers, until the blues are dry. Then when they are perfectly dry, do them up in leather, or in bladders, or in purses . . .[4]

It is extraordinary that the method works at all, since it is not perfectly understood even now. Possibly it depends on the surface properties of the mineral grains, the lazurite being wetted most readily by water and so being the first to leave the dough and become suspended in the solution. As Cennino indicates, several successive kneadings in fresh lye are required to extract all the pigment. The largest, most richly coloured particles come out first, while the last 'washings' release colourless impurities as well as the blue particles. This low-grade 'ultramarine ash' was used for creating pale blue oil glazes. 'Bear in mind', says Cennino,

that if you have good lapis lazuli, the blue from the first two yields will be worth eight ducats an ounce. The last two yields are worse than ashes. therefore be prudent in your observation, so as not to spoil the fine blues for the poor ones.[5]

It is inconceivable that the cost and effort involved in making ultramarine would have been tolerated if the result were not so beautiful to gaze upon. Its hue is that which marks the transition from dusk to night, with a purple tint to enhance its majesty Cennino sings its praises rhapsodically: 'Ultramarine blue is a colour illustrious, beautiful, and most perfect, beyond all other colours; one could not say anything about it, or do anything with it, that its quality would not still surpass.'[6]

Symbol and substance

I have already indicated the painterly consequences of the pigment's expense. To use ultramarine was not only to display wealth but – more importantly in the sacred works of the Middle Ages – to confer virtue on the painting. Nowhere is this more apparent than in the ubiquitous blue robe of the Virgin (Plate 10.2). To the monastic painter, the use of such materials conveyed due reverence. But as artists worked increasingly by private contract with a wealthy patron, the use of ultramarine might be stipulated to emphasize the patron's own piety and merit, not to mention his wealth and social standing. Thus for example we find a contract from 1417 commissioning an artist to paint an altarpiece of the Virgin 'with fine colours and especially fine gold, fine ultramarine blue and fine lake'. Similarly, the contract for Andrea del Sarto's *Madonna of the Harpies* (1515) requires the Virgin's robe to be rendered in ultramarine 'of at least five broad florins the ounce'.

There is thus a very worldly reason why the mother of Christ is so typically robed in blue – a convention that persisted long after the Renaissance. Yet historians have often sought to justify the choice of blue on symbolic grounds: blue is the 'heavenly', spiritual colour, connoting humility or whatever (one does not have to look far to find suitable symbolic correlates for any of the primaries). Johannes Itten, the foremost colour theorist of the Bauhaus art school, suggested that 'the retiring nature of blue, its meekness and profound faith, are frequently encountered in paintings of the Annunciation. The Virgin, hearkening inward, wears blue.'[7] Clearly, colour theory risks overlooking the obvious if it does not embrace the substance of colour.

The inception of oil painting, however, presented a challenge to ultramarine's eminence – for in oil it was no longer quite so majestic. To recover the fully saturated blue, artists were forced to add lead white, and thus to corrupt the purity of the material. This technical exigency was no doubt the more acceptable as Humanism eroded the reverence for materials as agents of religious valorization; but it probably contributed to this erosion too. According to art historian Paul Hills, 'Adding white to blue – a seemingly small change – is a telling sign of the turn from medieval to early modern colour.'

Giovanni Bellini was one of the earliest Venetian painters to embrace the oil technique, and in his *Doge Agostino Barbarigo Kneeling before the Virgin and Child* (1488) the mother of Christ is robed in a blue lightened only to the bare minimum with lead white, so that the modelling of the folds is rather shallow. But Bellini's pupil Titian gives us a much paler blue for the Virgin's robe in *Madonna and Child with Saints John the Baptist and Catherine of Alexandria* (c. 1530) (Plate 10.3); by this time, painters had become much less inhibited about mixing ultramarine; and Titian was using painterly skill to suggest the riches of blue silk rather than depending on the primary attributes of his materials. This change in turn freed the artist to create a far wider range of blues, and Hills believes that it helped to flood Renaissance canvases with light:

Only once the long-standing reluctance to mix ultramarine with white was overcome were painters free to discover the value of a whole range of blues in gradations of lightness . . . Blue by the fifteenth century was moving away from its association with starry night, the vault of the heavens, to the cheerful sky of day.[8]

The proclivity for lavish use of ultramarine was confined mostly to Italy, mainly for reasons of commerce: its ports were the conduits through which the pigment came west. Although ultramarine is not uncommon in northern European art, it is used with more restraint: a commentator remarked in 1566 that it was seldom found in Germany. Albrecht Dürer was one of the few German painters to use it, and then not without complaining loudly of its expense in letters to his patron. In 1521 he purchased ultramarine in Antwerp at one hundred times the cost of some earth pigments.

For mural painters, who worked with much larger areas than panel painters, this vast expense virtually prohibited the use of the finest of blues. An exception described by Vasari reveals just how cautiously the precious blue was apportioned. He tells how Perugino was commissioned by the Gesuati friary in Florence to paint a fresco, for which the budget had been stretched to include precious ultramarine. The Gesuati friars were themselves one of the most renowned suppliers of ultramarine in Florence, which is no doubt why they could afford it.

But the prior feared that Perugino might try to substitute some cheaper material, and so he watched over the painter as he worked. Offended by this distrust, Perugino sought revenge. As he dipped his brush into the water-borne pigment, he surreptitiously squeezed the bristles before applying the paint to the wall. In this way, he appeared to be running out of pigment much faster than he really was, since the brush-marks were so faint. And so he kept asking for more pigment to be added to the dish, which gradually accumulated at the bottom. Perugino later recovered this valuable stuff for his own use when the prior was not watching.

Sadly, the story is probably pure invention – but its message is accurate enough. It brings to mind the tale of how, when the Pre-Raphaelites Dante Gabriel Rossetti, William Morris and Edward

Burne-Jones were painting a mural in Oxford University, Rossetti upset an entire pot of natural ultramarine, still even then a hugely expensive pigment. The committee which had to foot the bill was mortified.

The Gesuati prior's anxieties about substitution of a cheaper pigment were in any case misplaced, since for frescos there was no good, convincing alternative to ultramarine. Indigo tends to turn blackish, while smalt had a reputation for being difficult to work with. The usual stand-in, azurite, is useless for fresco, as it turns green when exposed to water: the crystals take up more water, and the copper shifts its hue (see page 131). Azurite can be applied dry (*a secco*) to walls, but this makes it far less durable and liable to flake off. As a result, blue is not much in evidence in medieval and Renaissance frescos. The glorious exception is Giotto's work in the Arena Chapel in Padua (*c.* 1305) (Plate 4.3), where expense seems to have been no constraint. Proust's Marcel in *A la recherche du temps perdu* says of the astonishingly well-preserved murals that 'the entire ceiling . . . and the background of the frescos are so blue that it seems as though the radiant day has crossed the threshold with the human visitor'.

In the late sixteenth century, supplies of azurite became temporarily scarce, and this created a greater demand for ultramarine – which meant that the Italians, through whose ports it came, appropriated most of it. There was something of a crisis outside Italy in the supply of fine blues. Whether this explains why Pieter Brueghel the Elder used neither ultramarine nor azurite but lowly smalt for the Virgin's robe in *The Adoration of the Kings* (1564) is not clear; but almost a century later, the Spaniard Francisco Pacheco wrote that even wealthy painters in Spain were unable to procure ultramarine.

Blue blood

Although things were not always as bad as this, fine blues remained a luxury item for painters for hundreds of years. Compared with reds (vermilion, red lead, madder and carmine lakes) and yellows (Indian yellow, gamboge, Naples yellow, orpiment, lead-tin yellow) the choice of blues was very limited. Smalt and blue verditer were cheap options that approximated azurite, but indigo was for centuries the only alternative with a depth of tone comparable to ultramarine. Yet it is a poor substitute, with a greenish tinge that compares ill with ultramarine's gorgeous purple.

That situation was somewhat alleviated at the beginning of the eighteenth century as the result of a chance discovery by a Berlin colour-maker named Diesbach. It was the kind of happy accident that characterizes so much of the history of artists' colours, and indeed so much of technological innovation in general. I strongly suspect that we would find the same motif accompanying the inception of the older pigments, if the details had not long since joined the book of time's forgotten tales. Diesbach was trying to make one thing and ended up making another, a happy victim of impure reagents. The advance of chemistry has relied heavily on the carelessness of distillers, refiners and manufacturers, and I mean that with no disrespect.

Diesbach was making cochineal red lake, which required iron sulphate and potash. He secured his potash from an alchemist named Johann Konrad Dippel, in whose laboratory Diesbach was labouring. Presumably in an attempt to economize, Diesbach requested that Dippel give him a batch of potash that had been contaminated with animal oil, which was waiting to be thrown away. Diesbach discovered soon enough that it was a false economy, since his red lake turned out extremely pale. Making the best of a bad job, he attempted to concentrate it, whereupon it turned purple before becoming deep blue.

Perplexed and lacking much chemical knowledge, Diesbach turned to Dippel for an explanation. The alchemist deduced that the blue colour came from a reaction between iron sulphate and the contaminated alkali. More than that he was unable to say; but in retrospect we can see that the alkali had reacted with Dippel's oil, prepared from blood, to make potassium ferrocyanide (a compound still known in German as *Blutlaugensalz*). This then combined with iron sulphate to form the compound that chemists call iron ferrocyanide, known more familiarly (even to them) by its pigment name: Prussian blue.

Diesbach made his serendipitous discovery some time between 1704 and 1705, and the blue substance was soon being manufactured in Berlin as an artists' material. It seems to escape mention in the chemical literature until 1710, when an anonymous communication in the *Miscellanea Berolinensis* praises its beauty and advocates it as a colour 'equal to or excelling Ultramarine'.

This report went on to claim that 'it is harmless: nothing here is arsenical; nothing contrary to health, but rather a medicine. Without danger, those things which are made from sugar can be painted with this colour and eaten.' Surprisingly (given its cyanide content), this is largely true: the pigment is not significantly toxic, and is used in cosmetics.

Of the synthetic procedure, the French chemist Jean Hellot remarked in 1762 that 'Nothing is perhaps more peculiar than the process by which one obtains Prussian blue, and it must be owned that, if chance had not taken a hand, a profound theory would be necessary to invent it.' That was undoubtedly true, and the synthesis was a jealously guarded secret until an Englishman, John Woodward, acquired from Germany a description of the process which he promptly published in the *Philosophical Transactions of the Royal Society* in 1724. The method he related was unnecessarily elaborate; so little was known about the product that no one could be sure what was essential and what was not.

By this time the pigment was also being manufactured in Paris by Diesbach's pupil De Pierre, with whom he had shared the secret recipe. (The colour has also borne the name Paris blue for this reason.) The German chemist Georg Ernst Stahl gave a detailed account of the discovery of the blue pigment in 1731, and by 1750 it was widely known throughout Europe. At just a tenth of the price of ultramarine (which cost two guineas per pound in 1770), Prussian blue was a very attractive alternative. It was much used by painters in the late eighteenth century, including Thomas Gainsborough and Antoine Watteau.

Its fullness of hue commended Prussian blue to some colour theorists and technologists as a candidate for 'primary' blue. Jacob Le Blon used it as such in his early attempts at three colour printing (see page 312). Although it is translucent because of its extremely fine particles, Prussian blue has a high tinting strength – a tiny amount added to white will impart a strong blueness. In the USA, where it was known with characteristic American bluntness as 'iron blue', the colour was used from at least 1723 as a house paint, and it also proved amenable as a dye for silk and calico.

Artists and colourmen were more cautious. In 1850 George Field remarked that it was 'by no means equal in purity and brilliancy to those of cobalt and ultramarine, nor [has it] the perfect durability of the latter'. In *Ancient and Modern Colours* (1852), W. Linton called it 'a rich and fascinating pigment to the colourist, but not to be depended upon; and yet difficult to avoid'.

The colour became increasingly less 'difficult to avoid' in the nineteenth century; none the less Prussian blue is not hard to find in works from the eighteenth to the twentieth century. By 1878, Winsor and Newton was selling a range of paints based on the material – not only Prussian blue itself but also Antwerp blue (mixed with white) and two greens in which it was mixed with gamboge. William Hogarth, William Blake and John Constable were among those who used it for mixed greens, and it is found in the blues of Monet, van Gogh (strikingly in *La Mousmé* (1888)) and Picasso, for whom its slightly greyish-green tone better suited his melancholy purpose during the Blue Period than the bright tones of cobalt blue or ultramarine. Though not among the most popular of colours for modern painters, Prussian blue has been employed in dramatic fashion by the British artist and sculptor Anish Kapoor, bound with a resin into a slurry that coats the shapes in *A Wing at the Heart of Things* (1990) (Plate 10.4).

Prussian blue and related ferrocyanide colours are still manufactured in vast quantities today (by a considerably simpler method), being favoured for commercial paints primarily because of their cheapness. The blue was also used as a printing ink until being superseded by aniline dyes.

Synthesizing majesty

Yet for the artist, Prussian blue was still no substitute for ultramarine.

Like indigo, it takes on a greenish tint; and as George Field remarked, it could prove unstable (see page 302). By the dawn of the nineteenth century strong, affordable blues were still desperately sought.

Chemists had by that time become accustomed to the idea that nature's inorganic materials could be re-created by laboratory synthesis. Surely the chemist's art should be able to conjure up artificial ultramarine?

But synthesis required knowledge of the chemical composition, and that was frustratingly elusive. The problem is that the mixture of elements in ultramarine (more properly, in lazurite) is not only complex but variable: the sodium and sulphur (and sometimes calcium) content can differ, and some samples also contain chloride or sulphate ions in the crystal lattice.

In 1806 the French chemists J. B. Désormes and F. Clément published in *Annales de chimie* the first accurate analysis of the composition of ultramarine: a compound, they said, of soda, silica, alumina and sulphur. This led to the subsequent identification of apparently similar blue compounds generated as impurities and by-products of various industrial chemical processes, notably the manufacture of soda. Such substances had in fact been known for some time, albeit with little understanding of their chemistry. In 1787 Goethe commented on the blue deposits found on lime kilns in Italy, and remarked that they were often used locally as substitutes for lapis lazuli in ornamental work. Here, then, was a clue to making the genuine article synthetically.

In 1814 the French chemist M. Tassaert asked Nicolas Vauquelin to analyse a blue material taken from the soda kilns of a glass factory. Vauquelin reported that the substance was similar in composition to the formula Désormes and Clément proposed for ultramarine, and Tassaert suggested to the Société d'Encouragement pour l'Industrie Nationale that chemists might use this insight to develop artificial ultramarine. In 1824 the Société took up the idea by offering a prize of 6,000 francs to anyone who could devise a viable industrial process for its manufacture, provided that the product could be sold at less than 300 francs per kilogram. The bait was not the first of its sort: the Royal College of Arts in England offered a much more modest sum for the same achievement in 1817.

Six thousand francs was enough to attract all manner of charlatans, and the initial entries were nothing more than variants of Prussian blue or of the cobalt blue discovered in 1802 (see page 178). But in February 1828 the Société decided that the colour manufacturer Jean-Baptiste Guimet from Toulouse had met its challenge. Guimet established a workshop in Paris for making ultramarine, and he began selling it at once for 400 francs per pound – about a tenth the cost of the natural pigment. Guimet was awarded the prize.

Yet just one month later the Société received a rival claim from the German chemist Christian Gmelin at the University of Tübingen. Gmelin had independently arrived at a slightly different process for making the pigment – and moreover, he said, he had done so a year earlier, but had not published at that time. Guimet retaliated with an assertion that he had in fact concocted his own process as early as 1826, but had kept it secret until informing the Société.

The matter was disputed for several years. Guimet was in the end apparently able to substantiate his claim to the satisfaction of the French committee (if not to those outside France), and the prize money remained his. As a result, artificial ultramarine retains even today the name 'French ultramarine'.

Although he did not enter the fray, a third industrialist, the German F. A. Köttig, also developed a manufacturing method around the same time as Guimet and Gmelin. He was based at the porcelain works at Meissen, where he manufactured ultramarine during the 1830s. Guimet began industrial-scale production at Fleurieu-sur-Saône in 1830, and there were soon factories making the stuff elsewhere in France and Germany, and then in England, Belgium and the USA.

Both Guimet's and Gmelin's methods were based on the same process, which amounts to little more than throwing all the necessary elements together and cooking them. A mixture of china clay (kaolin, an aluminosilicate), soda (sodium carbonate), charcoal, quartz or sand (silica) and sulphur is heated in a furnace, and the green glassy substance that results ('green ultramarine') is ground and washed to remove soluble impurities. The dry green material is reheated, converting it to a blue substance which is then washed again and ground to yield the pigment. The precise colour of the product can be varied by altering the amounts of the ingredients.

One might imagine that, given the costs associated with natural ultramarine, artists would have welcomed the synthetic product with open arms. The truth is more complex, reflecting perhaps the awe with which ultramarine had long been regarded. Could the product of an industrial furnace really offer something comparable? Nevertheless, the French chemist J.-F.-L. Mérimée reports that Guimet's ultramarine was used by Ingres in *The Apotheosis of Homer* – a painting that is dated 1827, before Guimet had even claimed his prize. This would certainly help to support Guimet's claims of priority, not to mention revealing a progressive streak in the conservative Ingres.

Turner was much inclined to experiment with novel pigments (see page 182), and there is some evidence that he used the synthetic ultramarine as a water-colour in the late 1820s. Yet there is no clear indication that he risked the new material on works in oils, aside from the fact that artificial ultramarine has been found on two of his palettes – one being the last he used before his death in 1851. Indeed, Turner is said to have been deterred from helping himself to some ultramarine on someone else's palette for a work hung for varnishing at the Royal Academy by the cry that it was 'French' – that is to say, synthetic. The artificial pigment suffered, undeservedly, from a poor reputation in England in the first half of the nineteenth century, and Turner was apparently swayed by the prevailing opinion. George Field, whose advice weighed heavily with Turner, continued to make his own ultramarine from lapis lazuli.

Yet the phenomenal difference in cost could scarcely be ignored. Around the beginning of the 1830s, natural ultramarine cost 8 guineas an ounce in England whereas the synthetic version could be had for between one and 25 shillings per pound: a differential of between 100 and 2,500. Moreover, despite the rumours, the synthetic material weathered about as well as the natural one. By the 1870s, artificial ultramarine was the standard blue for painters – even more so than cobalt blue, which was appreciably more expensive. It features prominently in the palettes of the Impressionists, notably Renoir's blue-heavy *The Umbrellas* (c. 1880–5), and was also used in delicate mixtures by Cézanne. The bright blues of van Gogh's *A Wheatfield, with Cypresses* (1889) rely on it.

Twentieth-century blues

There is something poignant in seeing ultramarine, the undisputed queen of pigments in the Middle Ages, relegated to just another off-the-shelf blue in the twentieth century. It is a common trajectory for painting materials: from exotic and illustrious import, with all the mystery of rare spices or incense, to cheap commodity. But maybe this is to take too downbeat a view, for art has certainly benefited from the tremendous broadening of the palette. And that process continued in the twentieth century with the introduction of still more shades of blue.

Two new pigments arrived in 1935: Monastral blue and manganese blue. The first is the English trade name for a lake pigment made from ICI's copper phthalocyanine (see page 255). Bold claims were made for it – that it was the 'most important discovery since those of Prussian blue and artificial ultramarine' – and there is no doubting its considerable commercial impact. As a blue pigment, it shares none of the luxuriant hue of ultramarine; but its importance lies more in the fact that it absorbs red and yellow almost totally, while transmitting or reflecting blue and green – making it the ideal cyan colour for three-colour printing (see Chapter 12).

Manganese blue – barium manganate attached to particles of barium sulphate – also displays a slight greenness of tint. It was patented in 1935 by the German colour cartel IG Farben, and was initially used to colour cement. It has never become a major pigment for artists – these days, the blue market is too tough unless you have something very special to offer.

As indicated at the beginning of this chapter, we need not look far for blue themes in twentieth-century works. I wish to single out Yves Klein because of his uncommon engagement with the technology of colour, which led him to invent a new blue that bore his name.

Klein's early monochromes of the late 1940s and early 1950s left him troubled by the effect of the binding medium on the pigments. He adored the richness of the dry powders – 'what clarity and lustre, what ancient brilliance' – but recognized that this was always diminished once they were mixed with the binder to form a paint:

The affective magic of the colour had vanished. Each grain of powder seemed to have been extinguished individually by the glue or whatever material was supposed to fix it to the other grains as well as to the support.[9]

Klein longed to find a means of retaining the intensity of the pure colour and so realize its full potential to awaken the emotions of the viewer.

He sought the assistance of Edouard Adam, a Parisian chemical manufacturer and retailer of artists' materials. With Adam's help, Klein found his solution in 1955: a fixative resin called Rhodopas M60A, manufactured by the Rhône-Poulenc chemicals company, which could be thinned by mixing with ethanol and ethyl acetate. 'It allowed', he said, 'total freedom to the specks of pigment such as they are found in powder form, perhaps combined with each other but nevertheless autonomous.'[10] To Klein, the matt, velvety texture that resulted possessed a kind of 'pure energy', allowing every nuance of colour to reveal itself as 'a living creature of the same species as the primary colour'. He used the binder to create textured monochrome surfaces in spectacular colours: golden yellows, deep rose pinks. Yet he found that audiences seemed to appreciate his bright canvases largely for their decorative effect, which was not his intention at all. Klein therefore resolved to restrict himself to working in a single colour. It would consequently have to be a truly extraordinary one.

And what could be more extraordinary than Cennino's illustrious ultramarine – albeit now a product of synthetic chemistry, divorced from its mineral source? Yet while Cennino delighted in the grandeur of the material, Klein was attracted by something more abstract – an idea of blueness that would draw the viewer beyond any superficial splendour. For him, the technical achievement involved in realizing this blue was a means to a conceptual end. Thus his patenting of the new colour, International Klein Blue, in

1960 was not so much a commercial act as, on the one hand, a formal validation of the metaphysical idea that his medium represented and, on the other, an insurance against the possibility that others would use it in ways that corrupted the 'authenticity of the pure idea'.

Klein's exhibition in Milan in 1957, 'Proclamation of the Blue Epoch', disclosed his programme in a series of blue monochromes. To emphasize his intention to transcend the superficial, Klein gave each canvas a different price, despite the fact that all were 'identical'. Value, he felt, should reflect the intensity of feeling that had gone into the creation of the work, and not what it 'looked like'. The product was simply a record of that creative energy. This stress on the *making* is an enduring aspect of Klein's contribution to modern art.

The Milan exhibition was a great success. In Paris, where the elite of the avant-garde were prone to bitter, factional controversies, the reception was more mixed. But Klein's bold concept soon won him international acclaim as 'Klein le monochrome'.

These shimmering blue works, mostly identified simply by a numbering scheme prefixed with 'IKB' (Plate 10.5), have to be seen at first hand to be fully appreciated – no reproduction can do them justice. Klein applied the paint with a roller or with sponges, which in 1958 he began to incorporate into the work itself, preserved with a resin and impregnated with the blue pigment.

As Klein's work broadened into new conceptual areas – his Pneumatic Epoch with its focus on the Void, his kinetic sculptures with Jean Tinguely, his body imprints or *anthropométries* – he remained largely true to his blue manifesto. *Hiroshima* (1961) captured blue silhouettes against a deeper blue space, their outstretched limbs recalling the ghostly white shadows of vaporized victims of the atomic bomb. The joyous blue outlines of *Humans Begin to Fly* (1961) mark his conviction that mankind can surmount its physical limitations. His exquisite votive offering (*Ex Voto*) to the shrine of St Rita at the Cascia Convent in Italy, made in 1961, carries his colouristic aims to their logical conclusion by presenting unadulterated pigments, enclosed in clear plastic (Plate 10.6). Here is a prayer accompanied by a primary trinity of medieval descent: ultramarine, gold, and a thoroughly modern deep pink to replace vermilion.

In the IKB-coated world of *Blue Globe* (1957) and the topographic *Planetary Reliefs* (1961) Klein revealed his utopic vision of a planet rendered comfortable and harmonious by a 'permanent miracle' of climate regulation. Nothing served to strengthen this vision more than Yuri Gagarin's words from 1961, a year before Klein's premature death in 1962: 'Seen from space, the earth is blue.'

11. Time as Painter

THE EVER-CHANGING CANVAS

In the history of modern art the use and abuse of colours would furnish a sad chapter, telling of a gross ignorance, and a grosser indifference.

George Field, *Chromatography* (1869)

A colour known as red lead . . . is good only for working on panel, for if you use it on the wall it soon turns black, on exposure to the air, and loses its colour.

Cennino Cennini, *Il Libro dell'Arte* (c. 1390)

'Restoration' is a very poorly chosen term, and, strictly speaking, it signifies something which cannot be done. The genuine restoring of a painting is obviously something which is possible only to its original creator.

Max Doerner, *The Materials of the Artist* (1949)

Titian's *Bacchus and Ariadne* blazes on the wall of London's National Gallery as an unforgettable testament to the Venetians' love of strong colour. But what a different impression we should have had of them before the picture was cleaned in 1967–8! The radiant azurite sky was a muddy brownish-mauve, and the whole image was pervaded by a murk that makes the most 'gravy-brown' Constable look positively radiant (Plate 11.1).

It is small wonder that the unveiling of the cleaned picture provoked outrage. Even a public acclimatized to the garish hues of twentieth-century art were unprepared for the idea that Titian's tones were similarly strident. As far as attitudes towards the Old Masters were concerned, it seemed that little had shifted in public taste since the Victorian age, during which disastrous 'restoration' work transformed one of the most glorious images in art into a gloomy mess, deemed concordant with the sober preferences of a conservative aesthetic.

We can see in the sorry fate of *Bacchus and Ariadne* exactly what 'restoration' meant in those earlier times. Although cleaned to something like its present state in 1806–7, the paint surface was flaking badly, partly as a result of the picture having been rolled up in the sixteenth and seventeenth centuries (one of the hazards of painting on canvas instead of board!). To redress this, the picture was repainted in the most damaged areas, and little by little it was colonized by a re-interpretation in nineteenth- and early-twentieth-century styles. Each repainting was accompanied by a heavy coat of the honey-like varnish beloved by Victorian restorers. So the modern 'cleaning' actually involved stripping away several layers of varnish and paint.

Yet at least cleaning was all that was needed. I have often felt mystified at why van Gogh's *Sun Flowers* commands such high regard – it seems a drab, lacklustre piece, uncharacteristic of the artist. But that is because we are not seeing what the artist painted. Those dirty ochres were once bright; but the pigment (chrome yellow) has degraded over time, and we are left with a shadow of the true painting. Max Doerner believes that we should in this case give thanks to time for making the sunflowers more mysterious. I can't agree, and feel that a van Gogh is almost the last place to look for mystery in art. Be that as it may, this is by no means the only work of the Dutch painter that time has irreparably revised.

We can see, then, that a picture is never finished. No artist has ever painted an image frozen in time; all painting is a perpetual process, every scene is destined to rearrange its tonal contrasts as time does its work on the pigments. When John Ruskin said, 'Every hue throughout your work is altered by every touch that you add in other places,' he might have added, 'and all that happens subsequently'. When the artist has been reduced to the dust of centuries, time – sometimes personified by an over-zealous restorer – still goes on remodelling the colours, bringing darkness here and bleaching there, mocking our attempts to pronounce authoritatively on the colouristic intentions of the image's creator. Even the simple act of cleaning is, as one art restorer has noted, 'an act of critical interpretation'.

So we must ask: is there ever an 'original' version of any work? How much retouching can a painting withstand before it becomes primarily a superimposed copy, however sensitively executed? The Devonshire Hunting Tapestries that hang in august preservative gloom in London's Victoria and Albert Museum are said to be so extensively renovated that not a stitch of the originals remains (yet they are still treated as the genuine item). It is legitimate to ask whether we can ever talk in great detail about the colour practices of, say, the Venetian Renaissance, when our only points of visual reference are 500-year-old patches of pigment. And how much more complex the question of 'true' colour becomes when the artist has applied colours in the knowledge that time will temper them (see page 219)!

This book is, of course, predicated on the assumption that we *can* have a meaningful discussion of colour use in the art of former ages. I think we can have confidence that diligent restoration and careful analysis of pigment samples allow us to reconstruct the intentions and techniques of the artist in considerable detail. Moreover, it is not necessary to see exactly how a work looked when it was painted in order to be able to deduce the artist's attitude to colour and the way it was influenced by his or her materials. Yet in this chapter we shall take a closer look at the work of time in art – for both this and the chapter that follows have as their byword the warning that we should not take too much on trust in our visual appreciation of art. What we see is what we get, but not necessarily what we were *meant* to get. The materials of the artist can be substances of great beauty, but they are treacherous too.

Rescuing the past

Any major gallery must have a team of dedicated conservators if its collection is not to fall quickly into a sorry state. The technical reports produced by these teams make sobering reading. Here you might encounter your favourite pictures, like *Bacchus and Ariadne*, in a barely recognizable form, before the conservators got to work on them. Soon enough you are prowling the galleries with a suspicious eye, asking yourself: is this a *before* or an *after*? Should these skies really be so washed out? These greens really so murky? Many changes are, sadly, irreversible, yet an ability to recognize them allows one to re-evaluate the picture, to sense what beauty must have been present before this ultramarine went black, before that red lake faded. You will soon begin to appreciate that no critical analysis of paintings should be undertaken without a sound knowledge of how colours age.

Restoring a major work is a huge and painstaking undertaking, and many of the less eminent pictures hanging on gallery walls will never find their way to the front of the queue. For every painting like Hans Holbein's *The Ambassadors* in London's National Gallery, recently restored to its original glory, there will be half a dozen lesser canvases consigned forever to brownness.

To appreciate what can befall a famous painting and how that affects our perception of it, consider Cosimo Tura's splendid *Allegorical Figure* (*c.*1459–63) (Plate 11.2). It is one of the earliest Italian works to be painted primarily in oils. The colours are ravishing, produced by a glazing technique that bears the unmistakable mark of the Netherlands. It is generally thought that this picture is a response by the Italian painter to the works of Rogier van der Weyden, who may have met Tura during a visit to Italy in 1450.

No one knows what the subject matter is – it is a deeply inscrutable image, and all the more striking for that. Tura's seated figure gazes out with a mysterious, almost quizzical serenity. But can we recognize her in the description of a commentator in the 1950s as 'a cold-blooded demon'? Such, it seems, was her appearance before cleaning and restoration in the 1980s. Cracks in the paintwork, along with some discoloured and insensitive retouchings, had left the figure with a fierce expression. Moreover, her face, which is delicately modelled with highlights and shadow, was apparently reduced at that time to a flat, 'mask-like smooth' visage. Clearly, the vicissitudes of time had altered the whole tone of the painting.

When the conservators at the Gallery looked into the picture's history to uncover the origins of the damage, they found a sad tale. The painting had originally been owned by George Somes Layard, who bequeathed it to the National Gallery on his death in 1916. In 1866 Layard decided it needed renovating, and sent it with several other works to the Milanese restorer Giuseppe Molteni. It was not a cheap undertaking: Layard complained that the work would cost him as much as he'd paid for the paintings in the first place.

Molteni took the attitude, not atypical for the time, that works which came to him would benefit from alterations to 'improve' them, bringing them more in line with nineteenth-century tastes. This could involve rather extensive repainting. Mercifully, the Tura escaped lightly, perhaps suffering only from Molteni's attempts to reduce the contrasts in the deep shadows of the pink drapery. Yet Molteni seems to have coated the glowing colours with a layer of brown varnish. The brownness was not the result of any shortcomings of varnish manufacture – it was quite intentional. Molteni tinted his varnishes with blackish and red-brown pigments such as Cassel earth. Thus 'tastefully' modified, the picture was returned to its owner.

Then in 1921 the National Gallery sent the picture across London to the Victoria and Albert Museum for woodworm treatment of the wooden panel. Taken from indoors in the middle of winter, the panel may have warped when exposed to the change in temperature and humidity, causing the paint surface to crack. At the V&A it was fumigated with chloroform – which, it was subsequently discovered, attacked and blistered the paint. The damage was particularly severe where green copper resinate had been used, since the organic solvent softened and swelled the resin in the paint.

An attempt to repair the flaking was made in 1939. The panel was sent to a commercial restoration firm, which tried to reattach the loose flakes by pressing them with some heavy implement. Instead, many simply shattered and collapsed, so that the paint was lost. The worst of the damage was then retouched by hand.

The first task of the conservators in the 1980s was to remove all the junk that had accumulated on the panel over the past century or so. The brown varnish and the retouchings were relatively easy to swab away with methylated spirits. Over some damaged areas, such as flaking in the pink robe, a thick black paint had been applied, which was carefully scraped off with a scalpel.

This cleaning process revealed some previously indistinct features of the work, such as the strange puffs of cloud down the right-hand side, and the differences in colour between the pink robe and the paler pink marble. The woman's face was restored to its original, more tender expression. Blisters and flakes of paint were re-attached using glue and a hot spatula.

Yet this cleaned image was a distressing sight, laced with a fine web of cracks so that in places the figure appeared as though seen through a mesh (Figure 11.1). The conservators decided that some of this cracking should be retained – it is, after all, an inevitable aspect of the ageing process, a kind of stamp of authenticity known as craquelure. But if the picture was to be at all fit for display, some retouching of the paint was essential, especially in the area of the face. This was done using pigments matched as closely as possible to those that would have featured in Tura's workshop, bound in a modern medium. The gaps were filled until the cracks were but fine threads. Where the damage was especially bad, the retouchers worked from old photos of the painting taken when it was still in the Layard collection in Venice.

It might come as a disappointment to know that works like this are commonly covered in fine brush-marks of modern origin, rather than representing the unadulterated handiwork of the Renaissance Masters. But clearly, the alternative is either a distorted and discoloured version restructured to suit the anachronistic judgements of another era, or a fragmented surface that offers little hint of the painting's original power and brilliance.

And we can take some comfort from the fact that today's view of gallery maintenance places the emphasis on conservation over restoration. While repainting is sometimes unavoidable, it is generally kept to a minimum,[1] and most effort goes into maintaining the original integrity of a picture rather than reconstructing it in the (vain) attempt to keep it forever as it looked when the paint first dried. That is to say, the conservator seeks not to *complete* the painting, but to create a balanced whole, working creatively with damage and ageing rather than disguising them. In some cases, large

Figure 11.1
After cleaning but before restoration, Tura's *Allegorical Figure*
was covered by a mesh of cracks.

areas of damage are not retouched at all but are simply rendered in
a blank, neutral colour so that the observer can see where they are
without being distracted by them. A little dirt might be left on
bright areas where differential ageing of the pigments would otherwise leave them discordant with more muted surroundings. As Ernst
Gombrich explains of restorers, 'What we want of them is not to
restore individual pigments to their pristine colour, but something
infinitely more tricky and delicate – to preserve [tonal] relationships.'[2]

The restoration of Tura's painting had an unforeseen bonus. To identify areas of repainting the panel was photographed with X-rays. This highlights pigments that absorb X-rays strongly, such as those that contain lead. The X-rays showed the outlines of a throne backed with a row of tall columns resembling organ pipes, revealing that the artist initially had a wholly different programme. The painting was utterly transformed during its execution, something extremely unusual for the fifteenth century. We will probably never know what transpired to change Tura's plans.

Under the skin

Dirty varnishes and cracks are physical impediments to our appreciation of a painting, and as such their effects can usually be more or less eliminated. But chemistry is less relenting. Just as iron rusts, copper corrodes and silver tarnishes, so the chemical compounds that impart colour to paints are liable to react with substances in the air or with light. These chemical reactions can alter their appearance, sometimes drastically. Whereas an iron railing or a copper roof can be scraped clean of a discoloured surface film, a thin layer of pigment on wood or canvas can become transformed throughout by such reactions, and in general there is no easy way to restore it to its original state. To the painter who wishes to create a work that will speak down the centuries, the discolouration of pigments is perhaps the most invidious of dangers.

It has always been thus. The progress of chemistry has enabled a better understanding of the processes that can degrade a colour, but has not necessarily provided better means to prevent them. And as chemistry has supplied ever more colours, so too has it created more possibilities for their deterioration. Moreover, artists are liable to experiment with their materials, but they are no longer chemists and can seldom foresee the consequences of their explorations. Paint companies will now routinely test the permanence of their colours (which until the twentieth century they were by no means sure to do) – yet they cannot always anticipate the ways in which artists will use them.

PLATE 9.1 The Virgin in Jan van Eyck's *The Virgin with Chancellor Rolin* (c. 1437) is robed not in the traditional blue of ultramarine but in crimson, reflecting the great worth of cloth dyed in this colour.

PLATE 9.2 Arthur Hughes's *April Love* (1856) reveals the influence of the 'Mauve Decade'.

PLATE 9.3 A silk dress from c. 1862 dyed with Perkin's mauve, and inset, a bottle of the aniline dye.

PLATE 10.1 Lapis lazuli, the stone from which ultramarine may be laboriously extracted.

PLATE 10.2 Duccio's *The Virgin and Child with Saints* (*c.* 1315) typifies the medieval use of ultramarine for the Virgin's robe.

PLATE 10.3 Titian's Virgin in *Madonna and Child with Saints John the Baptist and Catherine of Alexandria* (*c.* 1530) is robed in a far lighter blue than medieval artists would have deemed suitable, for the transition to oil paints compelled artists to mix ultramarine with lead white.

PLATE 10.4   The rock-like forms of Anish Kapoor's *A Wing at the Heart of Things* (1990) are covered with Prussian blue.

PLATE 10.5   Yves Klein's International Klein Blue, seen here in *IKB 79* (1959), is basically a synthetic ultramarine – but combined with a binder that does not diminish the lustre and intensity of the pigment.

PLATE 10.6   Pigment as art: Yves Klein's *Ex Voto for the Shrine of St Rita* (1961).

PLATE 11.1 Before it was cleaned in the 1960s, Titian's *Bacchus and Ariadne* (*see* Plate 5.7) gave a misleading impression of colour use in Renaissance Venice.

PLATE 11.2 Cosimo Tura's *Allegorical Figure* (*c.* 1459–63), one of the earliest Italian works to be executed (partly) in oils.

PLATE 11.3 A cross-section through a paint layer from Gerard David's *Canon Bernadinus de Salviatis and Three Saints* (after 1501), taken from a part of St Donatian's purplish cloak, shows how the colour is built up from a mixture of red lake and azurite over a reddish underpainting. The black particles are charcoal from the underdrawing.

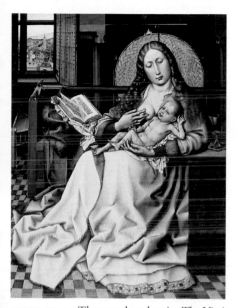

PLATE 11.4 The purple robes in *The Virgin and Child before a Firescreen* (c. 1440) by a follower of Campin have blanched with time as the red lake used by the artist has faded.

PLATE 11.5 The dark foliage and brownish landscape in Antonio del Pollaiuolo's *Apollo and Daphne* (c. 1470–80) were not intended, but are the result of the discoloration of green 'copper resinate'.

PLATE 11.6 Jan van Huysum's *Flowers in a Terracotta Vase* (1736) seems to depict strange blue leaves. They were once green, but the yellow lake has faded.

PLATE 12.1 Jacob Le Blon's three-colour printing process, used to produce this image of a woman's head around 1722, was capable of impressive and subtle modulations of colour.

PLATE 12.2 George Baxter's colour prints, such as *Hollyhocks* (1857), after V. Bartholemew, were made using oil paints instead of inks, giving them unusual vibrancy and longevity.

a   b   c

PLATE 12.3 The effect of different 'cluts' on a digitally recorded image of *View of Delft* by Jan Vermeer. a) shows a well-chosen clut, b) uses a clut that captures the original more poorly, and c) has a wholly inappropriate choice of clut.

PLATE 13.1 The Fauvist use of bright colour is rarely bolder than in André Derain's *The Pool of London* (1906).

PLATE 14.1 Household paints produce strong, bright colours free from the 'painterly' brush marks of traditional oil paints. For works such as *Pottery* (1969), Patrick Caulfield used house paints made by Crown and Dulux. 'I haven't got any brush-strokes, you know,' he said, 'I'm not Rembrandt.'

PLATE 14.2 Does Mark Rothko's Colour Field painting *Ochre and Red on Red* (1954) retain the vestigial traces of landscape?

PLATE 14.3 *VAV* (1960) by Morris Louis was made by pouring highly thinned acrylics down the canvas.

PLATE 14.4 Kenneth Noland's Target paintings, such as *Drought* (1962), use acrylics and PVA emulsions to achieve a flat paint surface with sharp edges.

PLATE 14.5 Frank Stella's *Six Mile Bottom* (1960), painted in aluminium industrial paint, exemplifies the materialist minimalism of the US Hard Edge school.

PLATE 14.6 Beyond minimalism, beyond paint: Stella's *Guadalupe Island* (1979) is part painting, part relief sculpture, made from aluminium honeycomb used in aerospace engineering. Whatever else was in the studio might end up in the picture: 'We had cans of those sequin things and [pigment] powders ... We did throw a lot of ground glass around.'

And so the unreliability of artists' materials has been a constant complaint throughout the ages. We have seen some examples already in earlier chapters. It has been said of Joshua Reynolds, who was particularly given to poorly informed experimentation, that many of his paintings were 'wrecked almost as soon as they left the studio'. The American painter Augustus Wall Callcott described in 1805 how the British artist John Opie 'observed that Painters were as much governed by their tools as their tools were by them, seeming to consider that most of the art was dependent on the materials'. Most probably Opie had Reynolds very much in mind.

Yet how may we know that what now resembles yellow ochre was once the seductively brilliant lemon yellow? That this patch of pale pink left the painter's brush as rosy carmine lake? Knowing how a painting has aged presupposes an ability to identify the pigments used. How is this done?

This question pertains not only to the decay of paintings but to the entire theme of this book – for one might very reasonably ask on what authority I state that Dürer used azurite where Titian would have used ultramarine. An expert can get a very long way indeed with an eye attuned to the differences in hue between greenish azurite and purplish ultramarine. But no historian or conservator will give that much credence without a scientific analysis of the pigments' identities.

Chemists have an impressive battery of methods for detecting the presence of this or that element or ion. Lead compounds dissolved in water release a heavy black deposit of lead sulphide on exposure to hydrogen sulphide gas; soluble sulphate salts precipitate white barium sulphate when mixed with barium chloride. Such tests are all very well if you are analysing a heap of powder. But no one is going to let you scrape away all the yellow from a Monet so that you can tell them what it consists of. Pigment analysis must generally make do with the tiniest fragment of material – removed for instance with the head of a sawn-off hypodermic needle. Occasionally, 'wet' chemical tests can be applied even for work on this scale, sometimes conducted under a microscope. But commonly, more sophisticated methods are needed for definitive identification of a pigment.

Of the many now available, it is possible to make a few generalizations. Spectroscopic techniques are those in which the chemical
components of the sample absorb radiation of some characteristic
wavelength: an elaborate way of saying that one measures the
pigment's colour. But it is a far more precise and quantitative
assessment of colour (and thus of chemical identity) than a mere
description as 'reddish-orange', 'bright green' or whatever: one
determines how much light is absorbed at each wavelength. And
the 'colour' in question might fall outside the visible range – the
absorbed radiation might consist of X-rays or infra-red rays, for
example.

One of the best spectroscopic techniques for detecting particular
elements is called energy-dispersive X-ray analysis (EDX), a method
that measures the characteristic wavelengths *emitted* rather than
absorbed by the sample. In effect the sample glows with X-rays of
a certain 'colour' (that is, a certain wavelength) when stimulated
by a beam of electrons (like that produced inside television sets).
Much the same is true of the technique called laser microspectral
analysis, in which a laser pulse is used to heat a sample suddenly and
vaporize it. The vapour then passes between two charged electrodes,
triggering a spark. The spark acts rather like an electron beam, but
of lower energy than that used in EDX, stimulating emission of
radiation that is typically in the visible range and is diagnostic of the
elements present.

Absorption rather than emission of radiation provides the basis of
Fourier-transform infra-red (FTIR) spectroscopy, which basically
involves looking at the 'colour' of the sample in the infra-red range,
at wavelengths longer than those of visible light. Compounds absorb
infra-red radiation when the bonds between atoms are excited into
resonant vibration by the radiation. The resonant frequencies are
characteristic of the particular chemical bonds present in the
compound.

Looking at small samples under a microscope can provide insights
that spectroscopy cannot. For example, how can one tell if a
nineteenth-century sample of ultramarine is natural or synthetic,
when both are more or less chemically identical? The shape of
the microscopic pigment particles can tell a lot about the way the

material was prepared. Grinding of lapis lazuli typically produces particles with a broad range of sizes, whereas the artificial pigment tends to consist of rounder, more regular and smaller particles. Synthetic modern vermilion prepared by the dry process (see page 87) and then ground has a wide range of particle sizes, whereas wet-process vermilion, which is precipitated from solution as a fine powder, has uniformly sized particles.

Some pigments may be prepared in forms that are identical in chemical composition but slightly different in the way that the atoms are arranged in the crystal. Realgar, the orange sulphide of arsenic, is an example: as well as the normal crystal form, there exists a different form called pararealgar, which is also orange. To tell them apart, one needs to know where the atoms are. This can be deduced from the pattern of X-rays scattered off the pigment particles. The regular stacks of atoms in the crystals reflect the X-rays more strongly at some angles than others, a phenomenon called diffraction. For a jumble of grains in different orientations, this gives rise to a series of concentric rings of reflected X-rays which can be recorded on photographic film. The position and brightness of the rings constitute a record of where the atoms are located in space. By such means, it has been possible to deduce that Paolo Veronese made use (doubtless unwittingly) of both realgar and pararealgar in the orange hues of his *Allegories* (c. 1570s).

The organic dyes that give lake pigments their colours are harder to identify with certainty. It is no good knowing that the dyes contain carbon, hydrogen and oxygen, since that is true of most natural products and will not help us distinguish madder lake (coloured by alizarin and purpurin) from kermes carmine lake or cochineal carmine lake (both coloured by carminic and kermesic acids). There are, however, some wet chemical methods that can be used to distinguish them, even to the extent of differentiating kermes carmine from cochineal carmine. And infra-red spectroscopy reveals the distinctive vibrations of the different organic molecules, provided that the sample is big enough to afford measurable spectra.

The technique of thin-layer chromatography allows the various molecular components in an organic dye to be separated. The components are carried in a solvent through a thin layer of a gel-like substance, and travel at a speed that depends on their size and chemical structure. So gradually the different components separate out into distinct bands on the gel. Two dyes that contain the same component will, at any instant, produce bands matched at the same location. By using so-called high-performance liquid chromatography, it is even possible to distinguish between cochineal lakes in which the dyes have come from different sources: from Old World (Polish) or New World insect species, which produce different proportions of much the same colouring molecules.

Analysing an artist's painting technique is generally a matter of close inspection of how the pigment has been applied to the canvas. Sometimes a great deal can be deduced simply from photographing the painting under strong light skimming across the surface at a low angle: so-called raking light. Like sunlight streaming over the fields just before sunset, this produces exaggerated shadows, highlighting the relief of the paint surface (Figure 11.2). A picture that appears under normal light to be a flat film of paint can then suddenly become a terrain of hills and valleys, showing where the brush has been wielded with long, sweeping gestures or short dabs. The energy of the brushwork leaps into view, almost alarmingly so in van Gogh's wild visions. We can see where modern 'Hard Edge' painters have used masking tape, revealed by the raised ridges this leaves behind in the paint.

Microscopic examination of the paint surface shows us telling details that the eye cannot easily see: where paint was applied wet-on-wet, for example, or where underpainting or drawn or ruled lines have not been fully covered up. We see the grains of sand charmingly stuck to Monet's beach scenes. But still more can be deduced from microscopic cross-sections through the paint layers, which reveal how the Old Masters built up their scenes through meticulous applications of several strata. In a painting by Gerard David from the early sixteenth century, a purplish-red drapery is revealed as a mixture of azurite and red lake over a red underlayer, beneath which black charcoal particles from the original drawing sit on the white ground (Plate 11.3). A plum-red cloak by the sixteenth-century Flemish painter Jan Gossaert is seen to consist of

Figure 11.2

Illuminating a painting by oblique (raking) light reveals the pattern and style of brushwork. Shown here is Camille Pissarro's *Côte des Bœufs at L'Hermitage* (1877).

red lake over dark grey. We find by this means that van Dyck in the seventeenth century sometimes applied double grounds – a brownish-orange and a grey. Over this he would lay down very methodical mixtures: a sky of ultramarine and smalt, over an underlayer of smalt alone, or multiple applications of mixed red pigments. In these hidden layers, the full complexity of the artist's working process starts to unfold.

A history of neglect

Cennino Cennini was no stranger to the fugitive properties of his materials:

> Some lake is made from the shearings of cloth, and it is very attractive to the eye. Beware of this type, for it . . . does not last at all, either with temperas or without temperas, and quickly loses its colour.[3]

He is apparently talking of the insect-based lake made from kermes, which was less stable than madder lake. But it would have been hard for the medieval artists to draw any secure generalizations about their lake pigments, since the resistance to fading depends also on the method of preparation, the inorganic particles on which the dye is bound, and the medium in which the pigment is mixed. All the same, it is broadly true that lake pigments, in which the colouring agents are delicate organic molecules, are more susceptible to fading when exposed to light than are mineral-based pigments.

Such changes can utterly subvert the artist's intentions. It was common in the fourteenth and fifteenth centuries for important figures in a religious scene, particularly Jesus or the Virgin Mary, to be depicted in sumptuous purplish robes (see page 229). These would typically have been coloured with ultramarine mixed or glazed with a red lake. Yet in several paintings of this era the red lake has faded away altogether, with the result that the robes are pale pink in the highlights and midtones (which contain a lot of white lead) and deep bluish-purple in the shadows and folds, where they were darkened with ultramarine.

A particularly striking example is *The Virgin and Child before a Firescreen*, painted by a follower of the French painter Robert Campin of Flémalle around 1440. The Virgin's voluminous robes fill most of the lower half of the painting; yet they are almost as pale as paper, where once they would probably have been a warm mauve (Plate 11.4).

Lake pigments were not alone in presenting medieval and Renaissance painters with hazards of impermanence that might have become evident even during their lifetimes. Vermilion offers a more reliable red, but is not infallible. Like realgar, mercury sulphide adopts two crystalline forms: the red cinnabar that is vermilion, and the black metacinnabar or 'ethiops mineral' (see page 87), which appears first in most methods for synthesizing vermilion. Reversion to metacinnabar may sometimes occur on the canvas, particularly if it is exposed to short-wavelength (blue) light. This process is more common in egg tempera than oil, and is seen in medieval panel paintings such as Nardo di Cione's *Altarpiece: Three Saints (c. 1365)*, where a saint's red-lined gown is patched with dirty brown. The same thing is not unknown in later works in oils.

Max Doerner claims that the darkening of vermilion was 'already known by the ancients', which is why the vermilion wall panels in Pompeii were covered with wax. Glazing it with red lake, which became common practice during the Renaissance, also confers some protection – although whether the Old Masters knew this, or were simply seeking to deepen and enrich the orange tint, is not clear. But Cennino warns against the instability of unprotected vermilion, especially in fresco:

bear in mind that it is not its nature to be exposed to air, but it stands up better on panel than on the wall; because, in the course of time, from exposure to the air, it turns black when it is used and laid on the wall.[4]

Red lead is a still more treacherous colour. Lead's generosity of colours has its drawbacks: for in addition to red, white and yellow, it readily forms a black compound, lead dioxide, when exposed to air. Without the protection of varnish, red lead will therefore darken rapidly, which makes it wholly unsuitable for frescos. This deterioration has been seen on wall paintings in China, Turkestan and Afghanistan, where the red lead has turned chocolate-brown. Such darkening has happened far and wide: in fifteenth-century Indian miniatures, Japanese paintings of the seventeenth and eighteenth centuries, and Swiss wall paintings from the thirteenth to the seventeenth century. Blackening can also be caused by exposure to air polluted by sulphurous fumes, which leads to the formation of black lead sulphide.

Even the revered ultramarine was not immune to decay.

Darkening has taken place in some medieval altarpieces, leaving robes a most inauspicious blue-black. And occasionally pictures fall prey to so-called 'ultramarine sickness', in which the blue becomes mottled with a greyish or yellow-grey discolouration whose cause is not yet fully understood.

In general, however, ultramarine is a wonderfully stable colour whose glory has been little diminished over centuries. Azurite too may age gracefully – but the coarse texture with which the pigment was sometimes applied can cause problems when varnish applied on top of the gritty paint penetrates between the particles, discolouring the pigment layer as it ages and darkens. There are many examples of thick layers of azurite that have darkened almost to black over the years, possibly as a result of the deterioration of the surrounding medium. This is apparent, for example, in the Madonna's robes of Dieric Bouts's *The Virgin and Child* (*c.* 1465) and Gerard David's *The Virgin and Child with Saints and a Donor* (*c.* 1510). The pigment itself is relatively stable unless exposed to acids (such as sulphurous pollution), which wreck the colour by decomposing the copper carbonate to black copper oxide.

Azurite is almost identical in composition to the green mineral malachite, and can become transformed into it over the years. This is especially common in fresco works: medieval Italian churches are full of examples of blues turning to green. Malachite itself, on the other hand, is generally very stable and has lasted well in these murals.

The same cannot be said of the green copper pigment verdigris. Its tendency to darken with age became notorious: Cennino notes that 'it is beautiful to the eye, but it does not last'. Max Doerner says:

Verdigris and other blue and green copper colours . . . had to be used by the Old Masters because of a lack of other pigments. They were well aware of the dangerous nature and incompatibility of these pigments and took the precaution of placing them between coats of varnish. Verdigris was the cause of the blackening of the shadows in the canvases of later Masters, such as Ribera, who used it in oil instead of tempera and without protective varnishes.[5]

And Daniel Thompson says, 'The accidents of time affect no other pigment so generally or so disastrously as verdigris.'

Yet this disrepute may be quite undeserved. Modern tests on verdigris in various media have revealed little sign of darkening, suggesting that there was some aspect of the overall paint formulation that caused the degradation, rather than any inherent defect of verdigris itself. One clear culprit was the practice, common in the late fifteenth century, of mixing verdigris with resins to make the pigment loosely termed 'copper resinate' (see page 129). Light-induced decomposition of the organic resins turns the paint blackish. Paintings of this era are now liberally adorned with deep brown or almost black foliage, giving the appearance of some Magritte-style trick of the light (Plate 11.5). Italian landscape painting of this era is awash with drab brown hills and forests, and Veronese's *Allegory of Love III (Respect)* (c. 1570) is disfigured by green draperies that have turned brown.

Any self-respecting student of fifteenth- and sixteenth-century painting will now be alert to these changes, and will make the appropriate mental translation of the images on gallery walls. But Thompson, writing in the 1920s, commented that darkened verdigris (by which he must largely mean copper resinate) 'misleads art historians daily', inviting them to perceive a medieval penchant for portraying 'mournfully the dreariest days of autumn'.

Not all discolouration is the result of the action of the environment. Some pigments are chemically incompatible with one another, reacting to bring about a change in composition. These adverse reactions contributed to the traditional wariness about mixing pigments. Lacking any understanding of their chemical origins, early painters developed rules of thumb. Verdigris and white lead, said Cennino, are 'mortal enemies in every respect', and Thompson remarks how inconvenient this must have been in the days when 'white lead was so nearly indispensable to the medieval book or panel painter that he could not comfortably rely upon pigments which could not be mixed with it'. But modern tests show no evidence of any harmful effects from a mixture of these two pigments – and indeed, they were often used together. Again, we are left wondering what the early artists were doing differently that caused them difficulties. In any event, warnings like Cennino's would have provided some considerable stimulus for the development of new, safer pigments.

Verdigris was also reputed to be incompatible with orpiment, with which it would otherwise offer an attractive grass-green. This is more readily understood: for in a watery medium (such as egg tempera or size) the copper in verdigris can combine with the sulphur in orpiment to generate black copper sulphide. Orpiment developed a bad reputation for compatibility all round. Heraclius's tenth-century text *De coloribus et artibus Romanorum* warns that 'orpiment does not agree with folium, or with green, or with minium'. (He also takes pains to clarify that this is no reflection on the compatibility of their various colours, but is a matter of the material substances – of the chemistry, had he possessed the word.) In Giovanni Paolo Lomazzo's painting manual *Trattato dell'arte de la pintura* (1584), the author cautions that 'orpiment is an enemy to all save gypsum, ochre, azures, smalt, green azure, green earth, rust of iron, Spanish brown and lake'. To what extent these warnings have a sound basis is not clear, but wise artists tended to heed them: Veronese ensures that orpiment stays isolated in his *Vision of St Helena* (*c.* 1570–80).

Making matters worse

The replacement of egg tempera with oil removed some problems of compatibility by isolating each pigment particle in a coat of oil. But some painters of the seventeenth and eighteenth centuries pushed their luck with elaborate palette mixtures of untested provenance. The introduction of new pigments with no history of reliability did not help. The complex blends used by landscapists such as Claude Lorrain, Gaspard Dughet and Nicolas Poussin could undergo unpredictable changes, particularly since they included new yellow pigments that were less stable than the traditional lead-tin yellow or Naples yellow.

Some painters' manuals sought to limit the damage by recommending a precautionary technique. Roger de Piles's influential *Elémens de peinture pratique* (1684, significantly augmented in 1776 by C. A. Jombert) advocated the use of oil and varnish layers to isolate different colours. But experimentation was on the increase during the Baroque era. The addition of resins to the oil medium to speed up the drying process, in which even the van Eycks dabbled, became common practice for painters such as Velázquez, Rembrandt and Rubens. Resins and balsams could also increase the permanence of the colours, but had a tendency to turn dark or yellow and to induce wrinkling if imprudently applied.

By the eighteenth century there was still not one of the spectral colours with which artists considered themselves adequately supplied in pigments. For blues, azurite and ultramarine were scarce, and smalt, difficult to work with in the first place, had a tendency to fade owing to leaching of cobalt from the pigment particles. (The smalt sky in Velázquez's otherwise radiant *Immaculate Conception* (*c.* 1618) has turned a depressing brown.) Indigo, an organic dye, was not lightfast. The report of the discovery of Prussian blue in 1710 began by saying 'Painters who mix oil with their colours have few that represent blue, and those such that, rightly, they wish for [some] more satisfactory.'

The richest reds were lakes – primarily cochineal and madder – but these might not last. In Joshua Reynolds's portrait of *Anne, Countess of Albemarle* (*c.* 1759-60), the Countess's pallid face was once a healthier pink; the complexion has become deathly as the colour drained from the (probably cochineal) red lake.

Of pure and bright purples there were still none; and for orange, realgar had only ever been used sparingly. Greens were still a particular problem. The Italian Giovanni Angelo Canini commented in the mid-seventeenth century that mixed greens should always be made up 'fresher' than they actually appeared in nature, as they would darken with age. Robert Dossie's *Handmaid to the Arts* (1758) proclaimed that 'The greens we are forced at present to compound from blue and yellow are seldom secure from flying or changing.'

This was largely the result of using fugitive yellow lakes. Foliage would often turn a bizarre and sickly blue colour as the yellow component (sometimes a glaze over blue underpaint) lost its hue under the influence of light. Pieter Lastman's *Juno Discovering Jupiter with Io* (*c.* 1618) has acquired dark blue-green vegetation, while Jan van Huysum's *Flowers in a Terracotta Vase* (1736) has patchy blue leaves (Plate 11.6) owing to the fading of the lake pigment. In 1830 J.-F.-L. Mérimée commented that 'One sees, in several Flemish paintings, leaves of trees have become blue, because the yellow lake, mixed with ultramarine, has disappeared.'

It was hoped that Prussian blue, discovered in the early eighteenth century, would at least satisfy the desire for a blue to replace ultramarine. But already by the middle of the century its tendency to fade had become evident. Dossie warned that the lighter, brighter and most attractive varieties of Prussian blue (which contain white alumina) are 'extremely subject to fly, or to turn to a greyish green'. This propensity to fade is accentuated when the pigment is mixed with a high proportion of white, as it often was for eighteenth-century skies. The skies in several paintings by Gainsborough (such as *Gainsborough's Forest* (*c.* 1748)), Watteau (such as *Récréation italienne* (*c.* 1715–16)) and Canaletto (*Venice: Campo San Vidal and Santa Maria della Carita* (1726–8)) are all pearly and washed out where once they would have been a deeper blue.[6]

In 1834 the painter Franz Fernbach noticed a strange feature of this fading process. He used Prussian blue to decorate parts of an outdoor rain shelter. Returning after having left it to dry in the sun, he was dismayed to see that the colour had already drained away almost completely. But when he went the following morning to review the damage, he saw that the colour was restored in full strength. George Field too noted this ability of Prussian blue to partly regain its colour after fading in the sun and then being removed from the light.

With the influx of new and seductively vibrant pigments in the nineteenth century, the painter's difficulties were exacerbated in proportion to the expansion of choice. Never was there a greater need for professionals like Mérimée and Field to conduct thorough examination of the products with which paint-makers tempted the hapless artist. Many who rushed to use the new colours did so to their cost. The Pre-Raphaelite William Holman Hunt was among those who suffered acutely from hues that shifted or vanished on the canvas, and he became a crusader for proper testing. In a letter to the paint supplier Charles Roberson in 1875 he complained of the instability of a new madder lake, saying, 'I feel that I may do you as well as the profession a service if I induce you to reject the colour as not fulfilling the requirements of the artist for the delicate work for which the original madders are used.' His frustration is palpable in his account of an orange vermilion that turned brown, which he says 'cost me at least ten months of my life' because of the need to rework the painting. Things were much better, said Hunt, 'in the days of Mr Field'.

Field warned against the chrome yellow that was later to dull van Gogh's sunflowers: 'The yellow and orange chromates of lead, withstanding as they do the action of the sunbeam, become by time, foul air, and the influence of other pigments, inferior to the ochres.' He cautioned artists that from a poor choice of colouring materials, there was no prospect of succour: 'Without a strong constitution there is no hope for [painting]; no chemistry can strengthen the sickly frame, restore the faded colour, stop the ravages of consumption: Science stands helpless before dying Art.'[7] All the more reason, then, for the painter and the chemist to collaborate closely: 'Happily there is promise of a healthier state of things. When this comes, Art will be less shy to consult her sister: in the interests of both there should be a closer union.'[8]

But the changes that might overtake the new pigments were hard to anticipate. So much depended on how they were prepared, how mixed and in what medium. Field warned unequivocally against iodine scarlet (see page 185); yet the British painter William Mulready was able to deploy it without catastrophe in *The Widow* (1823), and Holman Hunt's experiment with the colour in his preparatory sketch for *Valentine Rescuing Sylvia from Proteus*, in which he mixed it with copal resin varnish for protection, seems to have stood the test of time. (Whether Hunt trusted it sufficiently to use it in the final painting, however, is not known.) There is a tone of bemused helplessness in the comment of the English painter Samuel Palmer that

painting is a matter of such chemical complexity and intangible subtility that, as I have heard Mr Mulready say more than once, two men shall paint off the same palette with the same vehicle, A's picture shall dry, B's picture shall not dry, A's picture shall stand, B's picture shall fade.[9]

The Impressionists and their successors would surely have bene-fited from the services of someone like Field. As it was, they tended to throw caution to the wind – and pay the price. Some of the new pigments, such as cobalt blue and lemon yellow (strontium chromate), aged very well; others did not at all. Zinc yellow (zinc chromate) goes greenish in oil, which proved disastrous for Georges Seurat's carefully judged pointillism. Discolouration of zinc yellow is apparent in *Bathers at Asnières* (1883–4), while the lawn of *La Grande Jatte* (1884–5) is peppered with brown spots owing to deterioration of a chrome yellow. There can be few more emphatic examples of how the limitations of materials can undermine an artist's delicate colouristic intentions.

It was not until the twentieth century that colour manufacturers began to take seriously their own responsibilities to the artist by testing their products thoroughly before selling them (but see page 257). Meanwhile, there was a growing recognition that the artist had some obligation to understand the materials with which he or she worked – not as a scientist, for that was by now too much to demand, but as a craftsperson who knew how to make the best of them. As Max Doerner said,

The artist cannot be expected to be a chemist; he would only become the victim of a dilettantism more harmful than beneficial . . . [Yet] the laws which govern the materials of the artist are the same for all artists, to whatever schools they may belong. Whoever wishes to employ his mater-ials correctly and to the best advantage must know these laws and follow them, otherwise sooner or later he will pay dearly for his mistakes . . . *Craftsmanship must again be made the solid foundation of art.*[10]

The foundation of the Doerner Institute – officially the State Institute for Technical Tests and Research in the Field of Painting – at the State Art Academy in Munich in 1938 can be seen as a recognition of this necessity. Doerner himself served as an instructor in technical methods at the Royal Bavarian Academy from 1911 until his death in 1939, and he did much to reacquaint the art world with the techniques that left some of the works of the Old Masters in a better state of preservation than those painted in the nineteenth century.

Yet there is something stolid, formal and stifling about the whole business that almost invites rebellion from artists, just as the Impressionists rebelled against the academic strictures of the French Academy. What artist wants to be governed by laws, even under the threat of dire consequences? Experimentation with materials, and the misfortune that often follows, abounded throughout the twentieth century. It seems that every generation of artists must learn its own lessons, just as each must find its own style and its own material means of expression.

12. Capturing Colour

HOW ART APPEARS IN REPRODUCTION

Even the most perfect reproduction of a work of art is lacking in one element: its presence in time and space, its unique existence at the place where it happens to be . . . The presence of the original is the prerequisite to the concept of authenticity.

Walter Benjamin, 'The work of art in the age of mechanical reproduction' (1936)

Our modern painters can't come near it with their colours, and if they attempt a copy make us pay as many guineas as we now give shillings.

Sir James Percival, on Jacob Le Blon's printing process (1721)

For the first time ever, images of art have become ephemeral, ubiquitous, insubstantial, available, valueless, free. They surround us in the same way as language surrounds us.

John Berger, *Ways of Seeing* (1972)

How many Monets and Picassos hang on the walls of even the most modest of suburbs? One can see great works through the windows of almost any street, displayed in framed splendour above the hearth or pinned at ragged corners to the bedroom wall. We can all be collectors now, for good reproductions may be had for the price of an indifferent meal. Between the covers on our bookshelves are whole galleries-worth of masterpieces.

One can hardly complain about this democratization of art. Many artists have wished to see it plucked from the rarefied atmosphere of the gallery and brought into the high street. But purists may complain that a removal of context cheapens the work – that

Michelangelo's outstretched fingers of Man and God become stripped of their cultural significance and transformed into a parodic cartoon when edited on to a greetings card in the visual equivalent of a sound-bite.

There is indeed something a little sad in the way that over-exposure dilutes the impact, like a favourite song that has become tiresome from repetition. Can we really feel the same shock on seeing the original *Guernica*, as its subject matter deserves, when it has been staring back at us for years on the cover of a Sartre novel? In his famous essay of 1936,[1] social historian Walter Benjamin suggests that 'that which withers in the age of mechanical reproduction is the aura of the work of art'. But one can hardly expect the popular dissemination of art to come without a price.

And yet . . . our major galleries are as full as ever they were. If anything, the accessibility of copies serves to whet the appetite for the original. In considerable measure, the impulse to visit the source of the glossy images in art books stems from a desire to bask in the intangible mystique not of the image but of the 'object': these very marks were made by the hand of van Gogh, of Rubens, of Masaccio. The picture becomes a historical artefact, the gallery a museum to human imagination and ingenuity. No one goes to see the Mona Lisa to inspect the beauty of the painting – or if they do, they come away disappointed, having been jostled in a craning throng to catch a glimpse of this underlit and sadly diminutive work.

Benjamin claimed that mass reproduction emancipates art from a 'ritual of authenticity'. He imagined that colour photography and film would bring this about. But it seems that we have merely substituted one ritual for another. People now go to galleries not just to become informed about what artists have done but to worship at the feet of familiar images. An ecclesiastic solemnity presides over our halls of art – we whisper, we act with reverence, we do everything that the Parisians at the boisterous Salons of the nineteenth century did not. 'The work of art', says John Berger, 'is enveloped in an atmosphere of entirely bogus religiosity. Works of art are discussed and presented as though they were holy relics.'[2]

For the serious student of art, there is at least one other good reason to view the original; and if you are an eager collector of art books, you may have noticed it already. How often does *this* Titian look like *that* Titian? In one book *The Assumption* is all golden autumnal light and murky shadow; in another it is the milky glow of spring that bathes the crowd, and the orange-red robe of the Virgin is almost pinkish.[3] For a colouristically complex picture like *Danae*, no two reproductions will look the same. Can there, then, be any reliable discussion of colour based only on reproductions?

Yet much art criticism is necessarily conducted in this way. All written discourses on art must rely on reproductions to make their points.[4] In verbal exposition, such as college teaching, colour slides might instead be the medium through which the object of discussion is displayed. I am fortunate to have on my doorstep two galleries – the Tate and the National – from which many of my examples are drawn, and so I can view the originals relatively easily. But I must rely for most of my research on the images provided by books, seeing all too clearly in perusing several texts on related topics how untrustworthy these images can be. According to John Gage, the limitations of colour reproduction technology are 'themselves part of the history of colour in art'.

How much greater my difficulties would have been if I had been writing this book three decades ago! Even my casual acquaintance with the paintings in the Prado in Madrid tells me that my copy of *The Prado* (1966) gives only a very schematic impression of those works. The same is true of Herbert Read's *Concise History of Modern Painting*, of which I have a 1985 edition. And these are both books by one of the most committed of art publishers, who will commonly spare no expense on illustrations.

So I believe it is essential, in any survey of chemistry's influence on colour in art, to ask how far chemical technology can take us in capturing the image on the page. This is not, as one might expect and hope, a linear tale of gradual improvement in quality; indeed, some fear today that standards may decline as economics of publishing overwhelm considerations of accuracy and longevity.

Moreover, technology today is changing the way visual information is disseminated to an extent not seen since Gutenberg's time. I have done some picture research wholly electronically, and am aware that such a statement is already sounding like that of the scientist who proudly says in the 1950s that 'my calculations were assisted by digital computer'. We now have a completely new way of accessing and displaying information, and it requires no great foresight to predict that many (if not all) of the roles of books will be displaced by the computer in the next few decades. How these changes will affect the quality of art reproduction is in part a question of physics and electronic engineering, but this too is ultimately delimited by the chemistry behind the glowing colours of the monitor screen.

Art for the masses

There was a time when the only way you could possess your own version of a painting was to have a copy painted for you – legally or otherwise. Even in the nineteenth century, many people knew the works of Masters old and new via monochrome engravings. Turner's works, at the height of his fame, would be regularly transcribed in this way, and the results are somewhat like fabulous renditions of architectural wonders in matchsticks: awesomely skilful, but inevitably missing the point. Re-creation of the paintings of Turner, whose language was one of colour, light and texture, in a web of black outlines and cross-hatching holds a fascination in its very folly.

Printing using coloured inks was possible from the moment the printing press was invented, and coloured typography was indeed occasionally used in fifteenth-century manuscripts. Several colours could be laid down on the same page by running it through presses loaded with blocks cut to imprint different areas. This was obviously a cumbersome process, and not to be undertaken lightly. In 1482 Erhard Ratdolt seems to have become the first to master the problem of aligning the different blocks. In the sixteenth and seventeenth centuries, pictures were crudely rendered in two or more colours in this way, and a kind of primitive chiaroscuro could be achieved by overprinting with black hatching or blocked-out shadows (Figure 12.1). Lucas Cranach was one of the first in a long tradition of great painters who have experimented with colour-printing technology:

Figure 12.1

Saturn, a chiaroscuro print by Ugo da Carpi made in 1604 after a drawing
by Pordenone (*c.* 1485–1539).

a tradition that later embraced Henri de Toulouse-Lautrec, Edvard
Munch and Sonia Delaunay. But as a means of *reproduction*, there
could be no pretence that the chiaroscuro technique gave a much
more impressive representation of a colour painting than would a
delicate black-and-white copper-plate engraving.

The earliest attempt at full-colour printing as we now know it
was made in the eighteenth century by the painter Jacob Christoph
Le Blon, born in Frankfurt-am-Main in 1667 to French parents. Le
Blon drew on the idea (expounded by Robert Boyle) that all colours
could be synthesized from three primaries, believed to be red,
yellow and blue. He therefore realized that in principle all colours
should be accessible from these three by superimposing 'separations': a different printing plate for each primary. Each plate laid
down a monochrome partial version of the image, with a density
of ink corresponding to the intensity of that primary in the original.
For example, yellow areas would be reproduced on the 'yellow'

plate but would be left blank on the red and blue plates. Orange features would appear on both the red and the yellow plates, so that the two translucent inks laid on top of one another would generate the secondary colour by subtractive mixing.

How, though, might one prepare the monochrome separations? Le Blon had no choice but to do it by hand and eye. Astonishingly, he set out to hand-engrave each of the plates based on his own visual judgement of how much of each primary was in each part of the image. One might compare it to an attempt to decompose a musical note from an instrument into its separate frequencies: not only to say which frequencies are present, but in what quantities. The surviving examples of Le Blon's works, such as his own composition *Narcissus* with its warm flesh tones and cool green foliage, reveal the engraver's near-miraculous ability to dismember complex colours in this way.

Le Blon's plates were engraved using the method of mezzotinting, invented in the seventeenth century by a German military officer in Amsterdam. The surface of a copper plate is roughened all over using a chisel-like tool called a rocker, whose curved end is incised with a series of parallel lines to raise burrs in the soft copper. This rough surface captures and holds the ink. Gradations in ink density are achieved by smoothing back down the surface to different degrees. A wholly blank area must be polished smooth. The technique takes its name from the fact that it reproduces 'middle' tones of intensity more faithfully than the alternative of line engraving.

For the three-colour method to work, the inks must be good primaries. If, for instance, the red is a little bluish, it will produce only a dirty brownish-orange when overprinted with yellow. But such 'pure' colours were not available in Le Blon's time, and so he was forced to grapple with how the ideal theory of colour mixing propounded by scientists might be realized using the imperfect hues that chemists offered. His quandary stems from much the same considerations that had made early painters cautious about mixing pigments: because they are not 'spectrally pure', their brightness suffers when they are combined.

Le Blon's efforts led him deep into colour theory, and by the 1720s he believed he had discovered the 'laws of colour', which some considered to have been lost since the time of the Old Masters.

Le Blon presented these ideas in *Coloritto; or the Harmony of Colouring in Painting; reduced to mechanical practice under Easy Precepts and Infallible Rules* (1725), wherein he suggested:

The ingenious *Painters*, who shall peruse my Rules, and perform a little in this Way, will soon judge of the knowledge, of Titian, Rubens and Van Dyck, in the *Theoretical* Part of the Coloritto, whether the Common Report or Tradition of their being possess'd of the *Secret*, may be depended upon; and whether any *Masters* besides these *Three*, have had any distinct and regular knowledge of it?[5]

The 'Rules' were basically the now-standard means of preparing the secondary colours from the primaries:

Painting can represent all *visible* Objects with three Colours, *Yellow, Red,* and *Blue*; for all other Colours can be compos'd of these *Three*, which I call *Primitive* . . . and a *Mixture* of those *Three* Original Colours makes a *Black*, and all other Colours whatsoever.[6]

But here Le Blon found himself forced to confront the distinction, then still obscure, between additive and subtractive mixtures as best he could:

I am speaking of *Material* colours, or those used by *Painters*; for a *Mixture* of *all* the primitive *impalpable* Colours, that cannot be felt, will not produce *Black*, but the very contrary *White*; as the great Sir ISAAC NEWTON has demonstrated in his Opticks.[7]

Despite Le Blon's talk of the 'material colours used by painters', he needed inks that were translucent, not opaque paints. Thus his colourants were mostly dyestuffs, and his printing process may have gained some inspiration from the calico-printing industry.

For primary blue, Le Blon used the new Prussian blue, which was in truth a shade too green for the job. He also seems to have experimented with indigo. His yellow was a dark yellow lake. Red was the most difficult of all, and he felt compelled to concoct a mixture of madder lake, carmine and a little cinnabar. In principle, the ideal primaries combine to black; but in practice simple mixtures of these (and any other) primary pigments tend more towards brown. So Le Blon found himself obliged to conduct final retouching of the image – adding black, for example – by hand.

His eagerness to stress the 'easiness' and 'infallibility' of his technique therefore betrays a certain desperation about its shortcomings. Perhaps even more troublesome than the lack of primary inks was the fact that the copper plates did not survive many impressions before their fine detail became blurred. Given the immense industry and patience that went into their making, this was a serious matter.

Yet what the method lacked in practicality, Le Blon made up for in bluster and enthusiasm. After exhibiting some early specimens of the process to eminent persons in Amsterdam in 1704, he began to seek a sponsor. Holland proved fruitless, and he hoped for more luck in Paris in 1705 – but again to no avail. Not until he came to London in about 1719 did he manage to persuade a rich dignitary, Colonel Sir John Guise, to part with the money needed to establish a business. With Guise's backing, Le Blon was able to secure permission from George I to copy some of the pictures in Kensington Palace. The two set up a company called the Picture Office in 1720, and proceeded to generate several thousand copies of twenty-five selected paintings.

But Le Blon was no businessman, and very rapidly the company was in financial trouble. On meeting the entrepreneur, Horace Walpole (son of Sir Robert) was unimpressed, describing him as 'either a dupe or a cheat, I think the former . . . as he was much of an enthusiast, perhaps, like most other enthusiasts, he was both one and t'other'.[8] Guise, meanwhile, swore at and bullied everyone on the company's staff, convinced that this was in the best interests of the business.

Matters deteriorated to the point where a committee was appointed to investigate the dealings of the Picture Office. As a result of the inquiry, Le Blon was removed as director. Yet it seemed that the quality of the prints was actually quite fair (Plate 12.1) – Walpole called them 'very tolerable copies'. In fact, some seem to have been passed off as originals, disguised under heavy layers of varnish. In a time when the public were unaccustomed to seeing full-colour art outside galleries, this seemingly implausible deception becomes far less so. But whatever the merits of the copying process, it was just not profitable enough.

Undeterred, Le Blon established a new company in 1727 with the aim of applying another of his inventions – a method to reconstruct paintings in tapestry form – to the Raphael Cartoons at Hampton Court (which now reside in the Victoria and Albert Museum in London). He believed that in tapestry too, red, yellow and blue threads would, if artfully combined, suffice to create all hues. This venture again came to nothing, and Le Blon was finally forced to flee the country to escape his debts. He made unsuccessful attempts to revitalize the printing technique in Holland and France before dying in 1741 in impoverished circumstances.

Le Blon's method survived his death by only a few decades. In Paris, Jacques Gautier d'Agoty developed a similar process while Le Blon still lived, and argued bitterly with Le Blon over the question of priority. This notwithstanding, Gautier seems to have acquired the rights to the three-colour process after Le Blon's demise, and claimed to have perfected it in the ensuing years. The surviving examples of his efforts scarcely support this claim, although among his innovations was the introduction of a fourth, black plate in lieu of retouching by hand. Gautier's sons continued the trade in the 1770s, and passed the method on to the Italian Carlo Lasinio in the 1780s, who practised it with energy but no great distinction before it disappeared from sight.

Books of colour

Le Blon's invention was an idea ahead of its time, lacking the material means of realization. The alternative colour-printing techniques developed in the eighteenth century had no aspirations towards producing all colours from just three translucent primaries. Instead, they laid on directly whichever colours the printmaker selected, making sure that areas of different colour did not overlap. This meant that the colour range was generally very restricted.

The simplest technique was the old chiaroscuro method, in which blocks were used to imprint flat areas of colour that were subsequently shaded crudely with black. Just one or two colours were typically applied, so the images were not so much 'colour prints' as we would recognize them but merely splashes of dull shades like sepia that served mainly to give the eye some relief from the monochrome page.

The unappealing flat colour-fields of chiaroscuro printing could be avoided using 'half-tone' techniques, which were able to capture nuances of value or tone by varying the density of coloured lines or dots against the white paper. The principle is just the same as that by which a grey scale is obtained in newspaper images: when the dots are small enough, they appear to merge into smooth tonal gradients. The mezzotinting method used by Le Blon is a half-tone process, and was widely used to apply graded local colours rather than Le Blon's ambitious three-colour mixtures.

The basic component of half-tone printing is a metal plate covered with a uniform field of dots, grooves or ridges, which are smoothed to different degrees in different areas. In stipple engraving, the dots are created by piercing a protective film on the plate with a needle and using acid to eat into the exposed metal. The tiny cavities thus produced will retain ink or paint when the plate is coated using a roller and then wiped clean. When the plate is pressed on to paper, the ink soaks into the paper. Like engraving, this is a so-called 'intaglio' printing method: the ink is applied to paper only where material is removed from the surface of the plate to leave an indentation.

Stipple engraving was invented in the seventeenth century by a Dutch goldsmith named Jean Lutma, and was developed into a practical printing method by the Frenchman Jean Charles François, whose efforts were supported in the 1750s by the Académie des Beaux-Arts – a reminder that printing was desired as much for fine art as for commercial purposes. Because a separate plate was usually required for each colour used, most printers could only be bothered (or more probably, could only afford) to use two or three colours. The Englishman William Wynne Ryland, who opened a print shop in London in the 1770s, preferred to employ just one plate, hand-brushed with different colours in different areas.

The method was crude, sure enough – but for a public unaccustomed to seeing any colour at all in art reproductions, the stipple prints were things of beauty. Demand for them boomed, and Ryland would have become rich if he had not run up huge bills indulging his fashionable tastes and the extravagant demands of his mistress. So great were these expenses that they forced Ryland to the desperate extreme of forging a banknote – a capital offence which cost the printer his life in 1783.

Another half-tone technique introduced in the late eighteenth century was aquatinting. The invention is commonly attributed to the French painter and engraver Jean Baptiste Le Prince (1733–81), although he may have acquired the knowledge from elsewhere. The metal plate is covered with specks of resin, which act as a protective mask against acid etching. The grain is very fine, so that the prints can look almost like wash drawings. Aquatints produced by hand-inking a single plate were widely used for book illustrations in the early nineteenth century.

Lithography – literally 'drawing from stone' – was invented in 1796 by John Aloysius Senefelder in Münich, who used it to reproduce coloured drawings by Dürer. A polished slab of a stone such as marble is marked with a greasy crayon, and then dampened with a water-charged roller and loaded with an oil-based paint or ink from another roller. Insoluble in water, the ink is repelled by the damp stone but adheres to the marks left by the crayon. The image is then imprinted on paper.

This technique was generally used in the chiaroscuro fashion of wood-block printing, although unsuccessful experiments were made in the 1830s to develop it as a three-colour process (suitably transparent inks were still not available). But in 1837 the Parisian lithographer Godefroy Engelmann adapted the method into a multi-plate process that became known as chromolithography, which was capable of an impressive range and subtlety of colour. For this work Engelmann was awarded a prize by the ever-supportive Société d'Encouragement pour l'Industrie Nationale.

In England the lithographic technique had humble beginnings:

Thomas De La Rue in London patented a lithographic process in 1832 for printing playing-cards. But some had larger ambitions. The architectural designer Owen Jones teamed up with the printing firm of William Day in 1836 to produce a colour book illustrating the Alhambra palace in Granada, resplendent in gold inks. Jones's illustrated *Grammar of Ornament* (1856) later became a standard text for British designers.

At the Great Exhibition of 1851, at which Jones, Engelmann and others displayed their works of chromolithography, the jurors declared (rather optimistically) that the technique was capable of results equal to a good painting. Automated lithographic machines began to replace hand presses in the 1850s, using zinc metal rollers. In 1852 Day's firm ventured to produce a chromolithographic reproduction of Turner's *A Vessel Burning Blue Lights* – a highly ambitious project at which they apparently acquitted themselves well. Turner's hazy, fluid style demanded that the printers for the first time abandon the convention of outlining in black, depicting the image instead in pure colour.

The desire to apply these new techniques to fine art was shared by the Arundel Society, founded in 1849 by John Ruskin and others. The Society set out to reproduce early Italian frescos for explicitly pedagogical reasons: it wished to stimulate public awareness of the revitalization of art during the Renaissance. Chromolithography was used to reproduce such works as Perugino's *Martyrdom of St Sebastian* and Bellini's *Madonna and Child*. It was a formidable undertaking: each of the chosen paintings had first to be hand-copied by a commissioned artist, before being translated on to separate lithographic plates. Efforts like these gave many people their first inkling of the splendour of the original works; and for the wealthy there was the opportunity to own one's personal version.

Less elevated, perhaps, but equally impressive, was the famous chromolithographic reproduction of a painting by John Everett Millais in the 'Bubbles' advertisement for Pears soap – a feat that gained the artist's somewhat grudging admiration.

Among the books illustrated in colour at that time were those of William Blake, who was himself a printer and engraver as well as a poet and painter. He sometimes painted in the colour by hand –

a supremely laboursome task. But by all accounts he was none too
careful, or perhaps he had little concern for the conventions of
neatness expected at the time. One later commentator says how
Blake's paints were

> applied over all the outline illustrations, and also in smeary patches at the
> sides of, or across the text, much in the same style as one would expect a
> child, in possession of a box of paints, to spoil a book, and tending to
> strengthen the idea that Blake was mentally afflicted.[9]

So important was colour printing by the end of the eighteenth
century that when the Royal Institution was founded in London in
1799 by the scientist Count Rumford, it set up a department to
study the scientific needs of the craft. The departmental head was
a Yorkshireman named William Savage, who set out to remedy the
shortage of coloured inks. These new materials appeared in Savage's
masterpiece, an illustrated book entitled *Practical Hints on Decorative
Printing* (1823), which took him eight years to complete. He used
nothing more sophisticated than the chiaroscuro method with
wooden printing blocks – but they were prepared with such care
and profusion that the results were sometimes exquisite. Some of
the images in this book required up to twenty-nine separate blocks.

The art of wood-block printing was brought to its zenith by
George Baxter (1804–67). He used oil paints rather than inks, and
achieved an unprecedented brilliance and permanence of hue (Plate
12.2). His *Pictorial Album, or Cabinet of Paintings* (1836–7) was the
first full-colour popular book in England – the first coffee-table
book, you might say. It demonstrated just how much could be
achieved with the methods of the time if they were applied with
sufficient diligence; and as a result of Baxter's work, colour printing
began to flourish.

In 1855 the first colour illustrations appeared in a periodical,
the *Illustrated London News*. Combining wood-block and etching
techniques, they were of no great merit but were sufficiently popular
that the newspaper continued regularly producing colour supplements. And in 1861 the renowned London wood engraver Edmund
Evans published the *Art Album*, an attempt to offer works of fine

art in colour to a broad public. Wood-block printing was still deemed adequate for such endeavours in the early twentieth century, when the Knofler brothers in Vienna used it to create fine-art prints. The blunt, uncompromising outlines offered by this method suited the stylistic aims of the German Expressionist painters such as Ernst Ludwig Kirchner and Karl Schmidt-Rottluff, who produced many woodcuts in the pre-war years.

There can be no question now that many of the colour reproductions of the eighteenth and nineteenth centuries, printed from blocks, plates and rollers painstakingly produced by a skilful hand, are works of art in their own right. Yet even by the 1850s an alternative to this hand-tooling was starting to appear. For technologists had discovered how to let light paint its own pictures.

The all-seeing lens

Many technologies blossom not when the technical means are available but when a conceptual advance unlocks their potential. The necessary materials and methods for photography existed for 100 years before they were put to work.

For it was in 1725 that the German anatomist Johann Heinrich Schulze deduced that the darkening of certain silver salts was due to exposure to sunlight. He produced images in this way by covering a glass bottle, containing chalk and silver nitrate solution, with letters cut out from paper. The liquid darkened where exposed to the sun's rays, owing to the formation of silver metal from the soluble silver salt. The tiny particles of silver absorb visible light and so appear dark.[10]

The optical technology behind the camera is even older. The camera obscura, a darkened room within which an outside view is projected on to a screen through a small hole, was described by the Moorish scholar Alhazen around the end of the tenth century. Portable, box-sized versions of the camera obscura fitted with a lens were introduced towards the end of the sixteenth century, and soon became standard items for the natural scientist.

But not until the nineteenth century did anyone think to combine the image-creating properties of the 'camera' with the image-recording potential of light-sensitive silver salts. In 1800 Thomas Wedgwood attempted to imprint images from a camera obscura on to paper coated with silver nitrate. He was able to create negative images of 'masks' such as leaves, insect wings and even paintings – but could not devise a way to preserve the image by avoiding further darkening of the paper when exposed to light. The process interested the chemist Humphry Davy at the Royal Institution, who collaborated with Wedgwood on this primitive form of photography.

The first 'fixed' negative photograph was taken by the Frenchman Joseph Nicéphore Niépce in 1816, who imprinted the view from his window near Chalon-sur-Saône on to paper coated with silver chloride, which he then partially 'fixed' (rendered insensitive to further alteration) with nitric acid. In 1826 he created a true positive photograph by using a camera to expose a thin film of oily bitumen spread on a metal plate. The bitumen hardened where illuminated, and the rest could be washed away with oil and petroleum. As the bitumen protects the metal from attack by acids, this process could be used to make an etched metal plate for printing. This is a primitive form of the technique known as photogravure. Thus photography was allied with printing from the outset.

Four years before his death, Niépce went into partnership with Louis-Jacques-Mandé Daguerre, a Parisian theatre designer. By 1837 Daguerre was able to make permanent photographs on silvered copper plate with an exposure time of about thirty minutes. The slow darkening of the silver salts prohibited the capture of moving objects: Daguerre's street scenes have a ghostly, deserted quality because the strolling pedestrians are smeared out of view. Samuel Morse, an American painter and inventor whom Daguerre invited to view his images, described them thus:

The Boulevard, so constantly filled with the moving throng of pedestrians and carriages, was perfectly solitary, except for an individual who was having his boots brushed. His feet were compelled, of course, to be stationary for some time . . . Consequently his boots and legs were well defined, but he is without body and head, because these were in motion.[11]

In Daguerre's process, the silvered plate was exposed to iodine vapour which formed a thin layer of silver iodide. This was then exposed to light in the camera in the presence of mercury vapour. The mercury settled on the light exposed regions as tiny droplets which formed an amalgam with the silver. The iodide was then dissolved away in a fixing agent (sodium thiosulphate, then called hyposulphite or 'hypo'). The mercury corresponded to the light parts of the image, while the shadows were reproduced in the silver beneath. The developed plate had to be protected with glass to prevent the mercury from being wiped off.

The French government bought the rights to this process from Daguerre and unveiled it in 1839 at a joint meeting of the Académie des Sciences and the Académie des Beaux-Arts. Seeing the results, the artist Paul Delaroche was moved to exclaim 'From today, painting is dead.' (It is reassuring to hear that this claim, common currency today, has a history of falsity.) Photography, in the form of these 'daguerreotypes', was regarded not as a means of documenting life but as a new medium for art.

Thanks to several innovations that shortened the exposure times, by the early 1840s photographic portrait studios began to appear in London and New York. And new kinds of photographic media replaced Daguerre's cumbersome and fragile silver/mercury plates. In 1840 the English inventor William Henry Fox Talbot introduced the calotype process, in which gallic acid was used to develop silver iodide soaked into paper. (The developer promotes the transformation of a light-exposed silver salt into particles of silver metal; the fixer makes the image light-fast by removing unexposed silver salt.) The calotype process produced a negative image, from which positive prints could be generated. In 1844 Fox Talbot published the first photographically illustrated book, *The Pencil of Nature*, with the photos individually pasted in place. It advised the reader that 'The plates in the present work are impressed by the agency of light alone, without any aid whatever from the artist's pencil.'

Like the calotype, Frederick Scott Archer's collodion process, introduced in 1851, was a 'wet' technique in which the photographic paper was prepared on the spot and exposed while wet. Nitrocellulose (the first synthetic polymer) dissolved in ether was mixed with potassium iodide, poured on to a glass plate and sensitized to light with silver nitrate. Once exposed, the plate was developed with gallic acid or iron sulphate and fixed with hypo or potassium cyanide. Thus the photographer was required to carry with him a small chemical laboratory (not to mention a portable dark-room) (Figure 12.2). Photography could never emerge as a mass-market hobby until there was a photographic medium that was portable, robust and easy to develop.

In the mid-1850s Richard Hill Norris found that liquid gelatin could be used to preserve the prepared collodion mixture as an emulsion, which could then be prepared in advance on 'dry' plates. The gelatin softened when wet, so that the developer could do its work. By 1867 the Liverpool Dry Plate and Photographic Company were selling dry plates of a collodion/silver bromide emulsion preserved with tannin.

Fox Talbot introduced a second crucial innovation in 1852. He devised a variant of Niépce's primitive photogravure method, in which a light-sensitized gelatin film hardened in proportion to its exposure to light was used as a mask to make printing plates by acid etching. By exposing the plates through a mesh of black cloth, he could produce stippled images that captured half-tones, rather than consisting of uniformly black and white (exposed and unexposed) areas. This half-tone photogravure was improved in the 1880s by replacing the cloth mesh with two sheets of glass engraved with parallel lines that crossed at right angles.

Fox Talbot's gelatin films were adopted in 1853 by Paul Pretsch of Vienna for his 'collotype' method of photographic printing. As the gelatin hardens, it loses its ability to absorb water. This allows the film to be used in a manner related to lithography: greasy lithographic inks are repelled from the soft regions of the film, which absorb water, and are drawn to the hardened regions. But rather than a sharp division between the two, there is a gradation related to the intensity of exposure and thus the degree of hardening. So collotype printing can capture half-tones without the need for a mesh screen, and does so without the graininess characteristic of the latter. It therefore reproduces images with excellent fidelity, and is still practised today for making high-quality prints. The collotype plates

Figure 12.2

The photographer of the mid-nineteenth century had to carry with him
a small chemical laboratory. The engraving *above* shows a landscape
photographer of around 1859; *below* is the equipment needed to make
daguerreotypes.

wear out after only a few hundred impressions, however, so the technique is expensive and suitable only for short print runs.

In the 1890s, amateur photography began to bloom. George Eastman's photographic company in New York acquired a patent for flexible celluloid-based photographic film in 1889. The film could be neatly packaged in rolls, and Eastman introduced a compact camera – the Kodak – that housed it. The developing could be done only by the Eastman Company, and so the entire camera, with exposed film, had to be sent to the company for making prints. It was returned ready-loaded with a new film. 'You press the button – we do the rest', their advertisements proclaimed.

Was photography an art in itself, or simply a means of reproduction and documentation? Many early photographers were also painters, though often more distinguished behind the lens than the easel. During the 1840s the Scottish landscape painter David Octavius Hill and his technical collaborator Robert Adamson used the calotype process to capture striking portraits that, although intended as reference works for Hill's paintings, brought critical acclaim in their own right. In the 1850s the French artist Gustave Le Gray formed the Société Française de Photographie to promote the new technology as an art form. By the twentieth century similar societies existed in London and New York.

Because of the stark tonal contrasts produced in early photographs, painters using them as a reference source found a new way of depicting the world – one quite at odds with the formalized chiaroscuro practices of the academies. Manet and Degas studied photography in the 1860s, and the immediacy of Manet's *Olympia* (1863), which so outraged traditional sensibilities, exploits a photographic style of lighting. For the painter and art historian Eugène Fromentin, this bold directness threatened a moral decline in painting: 'so clear, so explicit, so formal, so crude'.

In the 1920s, artists such as the surrealist Man Ray and the Hungarian constructivist painter László Moholy-Nagy showed that by manipulating the photographic process one could produce images every bit as imaginative and striking as those that came from brushwork. Yet it was the veracity of 'straight' photography that lent the medium much of its artistic force. In the right hands, it could produce visions that not only were breathtaking, beautiful, disturbing or shocking but had *actually existed* at a point in time. The documentary-style photographs of Henri Cartier-Bresson and Robert Capa straddled this compelling boundary between reportage and art, where photography seemed to possess a force for social change that no painting could ever muster. Walter Benjamin suggests that art in which the 'authentic' no longer has meaning inevitably becomes political. For photography and film, this was surely the case.

My purpose here is not, however, to trace the artistic history of photography, but to look at its influence on the reproduction of paintings. Entrepreneurs wasted no time in using it for that purpose. The brothers Leopoldo, Giuseppe and Romualdo Alinari in Florence, for example, established a photographic workshop in 1852 devoted not only to portraits but to monochrome reproductions of works of art and architecture. Yet it was hard to see how photography could ever satisfy the art lover while all it could offer were tonal sketches in sepia and grey.

Maxwell's tartan ribbon

Colour photography was a surprisingly early invention. Seeing the first photographic images trapped under the glass of daguerreotypes or picked out in dark silver on Fox Talbot's calotype paper, viewers longed for colour to re-create the world their eyes registered. And so painters would hand-tint these early photos. In 1859 the printmaker George Baxter patented the idea of colouring photos using his intricate wood-block technique.

Yet this was simply a more efficient way of adding 'false colour' after the image was developed. How much better it would be to create colour printing plates directly from the photographic exposure. In the late 1850s one Mr Burnett of the Edinburgh Photographic Society made the suggestion, obvious in retrospect, that photogravure or other photographic etching methods could achieve this by the simple expedient of blanking out by hand areas on the printing plate where colour was not wanted. Multi-coloured prints could be constructed from the accumulation of separately coloured patches, in the same way that hand-engraved polychrome prints were then being made. The collotype process became popular for preparing plates for this purpose.

Making plates photographically was certainly easier than engraving them manually. But one still needed a separate plate for every different colour in the image. A three-colour method that generated a full-colour image from just the three primary colours would represent a great economy. To achieve this, one needed first of all a way of exposing photographic plates in a colour-sensitive manner to obtain colour separations in the primary colours.

The physicist James Clerk Maxwell's work on colour optics and additive primaries, along with his knowledge of Thomas Young's three-colour theory of vision, gave him a clear notion of how a colour image might be built up in this way from monochrome separations. In 1857 he wrote:

These three elementary effects, according to [Young's] view, correspond to the three sensations of red, green and violet, and would separately convey to the sensorium the sensation of a red, a green and a violet picture, so that by the superposition of these pictures, the actual variegated world is represented.[12]

He set about making experiments to this end in the late 1850s. In natural outdoor light he and his assistant Thomas Sutton exposed collodion photographic plates before a bow made of tartan ribbon striped with various colours, pinned to black velvet. By placing colour filters between the object and the plate, they obtained negatives that registered light of each of the additive primaries individually. For example, red parts of the ribbon, which absorb blue and green light, would not appear in the exposures taken through blue and green filters.

These filters were glass vessels containing coloured solutions. Someone connected to the world of colour manufacture would surely have used standard dyes; but as a scientist, Maxwell was more familiar with the colours of the academic chemical laboratory: the royal blue of ammoniacal copper sulphate, the green of copper chloride, the red of iron thiosulphate.

To reconstruct the full-colour image from the negative separations, Maxwell projected coloured light through each of them and superimposed the projected images on a screen. He revealed his results in a lecture demonstration in 1861 at the Royal Institution. Despite the resounding success of his demonstration,[13] Maxwell was conscious of its limitations. He knew that the standard photographic emulsion he employed was much less sensitive to red and green light than to blue, so that the reconstructed image lacked veracity:

if the red and green images had been as fully photographed as the blue, [the result] would have been a truly coloured photograph of the riband. By finding photographic material more sensitive to the less refrangible [long-wavelength] rays, the presentation of the colours of objects might be greatly improved.[14]

In fact, the emulsion responded so weakly to red light that it should barely have registered the red separation at all. But modern studies have revealed that, to Maxwell's good fortune, ultra violet light was also reflected from the red parts of his tartan ribbon, and that this instead was able to convert the silver salt to silver metal.

The need to take three separate images of the same scene was naturally a great inconvenience to nineteenth-century colour photographers. In 1893 the enterprising American inventor Frederick Eugene Ives made matters easier with his Kromogram, which could take all three negatives in close succession through red, green and blue-violet filters. By 1900 he had worked out how to do this in a single shot. The colour picture was then reconstructed by viewing through a special projection device of his own invention, called the Kromscop.

More commercially successful as a means of reconstructing the colour image were the Autochrome plates developed by the brothers Auguste and Louis Lumière, the inventors of cinematography, in 1907. These plates were coated with tiny grains of potato starch dyed red, green and blue, over which lay the light-sensitive emulsion. Exposures were taken through the dyed layer, which acted as a colour filter. After development, a positive transparency was prepared from this negative in which small specks of light in the primary colours, transmitted through the starch grains, combined optically to produce a colour image like the pixels of a television screen.

The Lumière brothers devised the principles of the Autochrome system several years before they could put them into practice. They were hindered by the problem Maxwell had identified: the available emulsions were not 'panchromatic', equally sensitive to all wavelengths of visible light. It was not until the invention of new red-sensitive dyes by chemists at the IG Farben dye works in 1905–6 that the absorption of red light by photographic emulsions could be enhanced to produce truly panchromatic plates.

The Autochrome system is, from a historical perspective, an idiosyncratic one. It represents a means of selectively sensitizing the photographic emulsion to light of particular colours by installing a kind of pointillistic screen of coloured filters *in situ* in front of the film. But in 1873 the German scientist Hermann Wilhelm Vogel had already proposed a better way of eliminating the need for Maxwell's liquid light filters. He devised photographic emulsions that were themselves darkened by only one of the three primaries, by adding dyes to the emulsions that absorbed only red, green or blue light. The colour of these dyes must be *complementary* to the colour to which they sensitize the plate: a red dye sensitizes a plate not to red light (which it reflects or transmits) but to green (which it absorbs).

In fact, the ideal sensitizer for green would reflect both red *and* blue light, and so would appear purplish – the colour known as magenta – rather than pure red. Likewise for the blue sensitizer: it reflects red and green light, which combine additively to yellow. And the red sensitizer reflects green and blue, thus having a turquoise appearance which printers call cyan. The ideal sensitizers would, in other words, absorb about one-third of the white-light spectrum and reflect two-thirds: cyan ('white minus red'), yellow ('white minus blue') and magenta ('white minus green').

Vogel employed the compounds naphthol blue or cyanin for the red-sensitive plate, and pinkish eosin for the green plate. Initially he did not consider it essential to add a (yellow-coloured) sensitizer for the blue separation, as the silver bromide in the emulsion is primarily sensitive to blue light anyway. But he later made use of yellow-green fluorescein as a blue sensitizer. All of these, you might notice, are coal-tar dyes, of very recent origin in the 1870s (see Figure 9.1 on page 258).

Vogel was interested in using these separations for preparing three-colour printing plates – which is, after all, the way in which colour photography ultimately supplies reproductions to a mass audience. But his approach of sensitizing emulsions to particular colours using dyes was also adopted for making colour transparencies and positive colour prints – which led to the huge market for amateur colour photography in the 1960s.

The next step in this direction was the invention in 1911 by the German chemist Rudolf Fischer of a film that eliminated the awkward need for three colour separations. In Fischer's film the three dye-sensitized emulsions are not divided among separate plates but are superimposed in layers on a single substrate (Figure 12.3). All

Figure 12.3

Photographic film contains three light-sensitive layers, each sensitized by dyes to one of the three additive primary colours. A yellow filter protects the green- and red-sensitized layers from stray blue light. To form the negative, coloured dyes in yellow, magenta and cyan are substituted for the silver particles formed by the action of light. To make a print, a three-layer film is exposed through the negative, and blue, green and red dyes are added in the exposed areas.

modern photographic film is based on this design. The way in which the film is converted to a true colour negative, from which positive prints may be prepared, is somewhat different today from how Fischer did it; but the principles are much the same.

The objective is to convert an area of darkened emulsion, where silver grains have precipitated, into an area of translucent colour of the appropriate hue. So-called coupling agents are used to deposit in these regions dyes that are complementary to the colour to which the layer is sensitized. For example, where the blue-sensitized layer has darkened, the coupling agent deposits a yellow dye on the silver particles. The precipitated silver particles and unexposed silver salt are then chemically removed from the emulsion, creating a negative transparency.

Photographic companies such as Agfa and Kodak grew rapidly in the early part of the century, benefiting from the demand for colour photography from advertising firms, art galleries and industries. (Agfa, you might recall, began as a Berlin-based dye manufacturer.) In the 1930s the companies introduced Agfacolor and Kodachrome colour film, and in the next decade they commercialized methods for making positive colour prints from the negative transparencies (Figure 12.3).

To alleviate the most egregious shortcomings of the materials, modern photographic film is something of a patchwork. Because conversion of the silver salt to silver is particularly sensitive to high-frequency radiation (that is, to blue light), the red- and green-sensitive layers, which lie beneath the blue, have to be protected from any extraneous blue light passing through the blue layer by an intervening yellow–dyed filter.

More problematic is the fact that the dyes are inevitably imperfect primaries: the cyan dye absorbs a little green and blue, and the magenta some blue. This means that the cyan in the negative potentially imparts a pinkish tinge to the positive, and the magenta is corrupted with yellow. To counteract this, additional pale dyes are added to the cyan and magenta layers in the negative to correct the colour balance.

Ideally the dyes should have a sharp band of absorption within their respective wavelength ranges, with no overlap between them.

In that way, for example, green light would not contaminate the blue separation. But the physics of light absorption does not work this way: there is always a more or less smooth rise and fall in absorption as the wavelength is altered (see Figure 12.4 on page 333). Considerable effort has gone into crafting dyes that have characteristics as close as possible to the ideal – those used in the textile industry aren't designed to meet such narrow constraints. Efforts towards a rational synthesis of colour, initiated by Otto Witt in the nineteenth century (see page 250), have therefore become of central importance to the veracity of colour photography.

Faith in ink

Although James Clerk Maxwell confined himself to additive reconstruction of his three-colour images by projection, it did not take great genius to appreciate that his photographic separations might be used to prepare plates for three-colour printing via the existing techniques of photogravure or photolithography. The idea occurred to several individuals in the early 1860s, making priority a contentious matter. In 1862 the Frenchman Louis Ducos du Hauron proposed that printing plates might be made from photographs exposed through coloured glass. And in 1865 an Englishman named Henry Collen outlined a similar concept in a letter to the *British Journal of Photography*, albeit in ignorance of Maxwell's work. This compelled him to begin with a re-invention of colour photography:

It occurred to me . . . this morning that if substances were discovered sensitive only to the primary colours . . . it would be possible to obtain photographs with the tints as in nature by some such means as the following: – obtain a negative sensitive to the blue rays only . . .[15]

But the credit for putting these ideas into practice must go to Baron Ransonnet in Vienna, who in 1865 set out to use the three-colour principle for photolithography. He collaborated with the Viennese lithographer Johann Haupt to make prints of a Chinese temple, which Ransonnet photographed as a member of the Austrian Imperial East Asian expedition. Haupt found it necessary to add two extra plates, for black and brown, to achieve satisfactory results.

Vogel's dye-sensitized photographic emulsions made the preparation of colour-separation printing plates more direct by eliminating the colour filters. Each plate is then inked in the same colour as the respective sensitizing dye: in general, yellow, magenta and cyan, plus a black separation for emphasis. The plate prepared from the green-sensitive emulsion, for example, is coated with magenta ink.

The key consideration, as Vogel appreciated, is that the inks should absorb light in *precisely* the same way as the dye sensitizers. Unless this is so, the recombination of colours cannot hope to capture faithfully the hues of the original scene. For example, if a reddish ink is used instead of magenta, it absorbs blue light where, in the final print, it ought to be reflecting it.

Ideally, said Vogel, the colourants in the inks should be the very same dyes as those in the sensitizers. It was an implicit injunction to chemical and photographic manufacturers to match their products one to the other. But this was not feasible, since not all dyes make viable inks, both for chemical and for economic reasons. In other words, in the era of photography just as in the period of hand-engraving, the success of three-colour printing hung on a question of materials.

The outcome was inevitably a compromise: one had to make do with whatever inks were available. Frederick Ives (who introduced Fox Talbot's half-tone method to three-colour photographic printing in the late 1870s) proposed in 1888 that Prussian blue (which is greenish), eosin red (which is bluish) and an unspecified 'brilliant yellow' should be used. But photographer E. J. Wall, writing in 1925, commented that 'printing inks that more nearly conform to the strict theoretical requirements . . . would appear to [represent] the field of greatest advance . . . Theoretically perfect inks are still a desideratum.'[16]

Actually, 'theoretically perfect' inks are an impossibility. Just as for the sensitizing dyes in photographic film, the ideal three-colour printing inks would each absorb a third of the visible spectrum in

Figure 12.4

The inks used for colour printing should ideally absorb light in crisply
defined wavelength bands, with no overlap. In practice, this ideal can
never be achieved, and the absorption bands overlap somewhat,
compromising the fidelity of the colour reproduction.

non-overlapping chunks (Figure 12.4). But the physics of the light–
absorption process doesn't permit this: real printing inks have
smooth–edged absorption bands that encroach into one another's
territory. This limits their ability to capture colours accurately when
superimposed.

You can judge for yourself from any colour prints in old books
how effectively (or otherwise) printing inks have coped with these
shortcomings. For those too young to have first-hand recollection,
it is hard to escape the notion that the events of the world in the
years after the Second World War took place in an overcharged

Technicolor glow of ruby-red lips and phthalocyanine-blue skies, just as the First World War was conducted in monochrome.

The extent to which a print is true to the original is always going to be determined by the quality of the inks. They are the chromatic building blocks from which one must try to re-create every colour under the sun, and this can never amount to more than an approximation. Vermilion, for instance, has its own unique hue, its characteristic plucking of the spectrum's many strings. To emulate it using cyan, yellow and magenta – each of which plucks its own blend of harmonics – is analogous to an attempt to reproduce a trumpet sound by mixing, in different proportions, the notes sounded on a piano, a flute and a tuba. One might aim for the same result with a different trio of instruments, and obtain an approximation more or less faithful. Thus one's impression of the rich vermilion of a medieval triptych, as viewed in an illustrated book, is utterly dependent on the printer's choice of inks (among other things). The one thing we can say for sure is that this impression will never be identical to that which you would have from standing before the painting itself.

Eager to dispel such concerns, in 1920 the English art magazine *Colour* bore testimonials from several 'great artists' to the accuracy of their prints. None the less, art historians remained reluctant to accept colour photography – even photographic prints, let alone printed copies in books – as a valid means of recording images until at least the 1950s.

By the 1960s, according to art historian Edgar Wind, colour photographic reproduction of paintings was still so primitive that it was better to rely on black-and-white images. He said:

Since the ordinary photographic plate is sensitive to a larger range of shades than can be recorded in colour, the best black-and-white reproduction of a Titian, Veronese or Renoir is comparable to a conscientious piano transcription of an orchestral score, whereas the colour print, with some exceptions, is like a reduced orchestra with all the instruments out of tune.[17]

To judge from some books of that time, he had a fair point. John

Gage comments that the use of colour slides in art lectures at Cambridge was then the exception rather than the norm.

Digital colour

Principles remain while technologies change. Modern colour printing is almost invariably conducted from an electronic image. There need be no 'copy' that one can hold in the hand and inspect visually between the stage of electronically scanning the original and printing the reproduction in coloured inks – no lithographed plates, no photographic negatives. Even if 'photography' is used, it can be of a kind that converts the reflected light directly into a matrix of magnetically recorded data in a digital camera, rather than leaving an imprint on photographic emulsion. And yet in the end the reproduction is still created as Le Blon did it: by subtractive and optical mixing of three coloured inks, with black added for emphasis. The computer software has to conduct careful deliberations to convert the scanned image data into output instructions that re-create colour values by the half-tone method, mimicking with digital electronics what Fox Talbot did with a sheet of black tulle. The three-colour method, stippled into half-tones, remains the most efficient way of putting accurate colour on the page.

Electronic systems allow a great deal of control over colour reproduction, but this is not the same as saying that they permit perfect accuracy. They *can* be very accurate, but are not routinely so, and digital processing introduces complications of its own.

To convert a coloured image – be it an original painting or a photograph of it – into electronic form, a scanner contains devices that produce an electric current in proportion to the amount of light that falls on them. Coloured filters separate out the light falling on to these devices into the red, blue and green components.

To store the image digitally, it is broken down into a grid of tiny patches, each of which is assigned a single colour. The fineness of this grid ultimately determines the resolution – the degree of detail – that may be recovered in a printed version of the electronically stored image. The finer the grid, the better the resolution – but also the more memory space needed to store the image. In general, the image will be stored on a finer grid than that corresponding to the 'grain size' of the final half-tone print. It is not uncommon, for example, for the scanned image to be broken down into several thousand patches per inch, whereas printing at a resolution of 300 dots per inch is sufficient for all but the highest-quality work.

Before printing, a judgement about the fidelity and balance of the colour in a scanned image will be made by inspecting it on the monitor screen. The electronically stored image is painted in the colours of the glowing phosphor dots of the computer screen.

Each grid point or pixel on the screen contains specks of three different phosphor materials. When they are struck by the beam of electrons fired at the screen from the back of the monitor, the phosphors emit light of a particular colour: one of them glows red, one blue and one green. The electron beam is swept back and forth across the screen so rapidly that the eye registers each shining phosphor dot continuously.

The phosphors therefore embody another system of primaries, which may be slightly different from that of the colour filters of the scanner as well as differing from the yellow/cyan/magenta of the printing inks. The computer must know how to shift its colour reference frame between these different systems. But any method for constructing colours from three primaries, whether additive or subtractive, must inevitably 'lose' some colours. The colour space accessible by additive mixing of three colours can be represented by a triangular field on the CIE diagram (see page 50) that has those three colours at its corners (Figure 12.5a). (But remember that this does not show differing brightnesses, so that a brown is equivalent to a yellow.) Because the full colour space is bounded not by straight borders but by curves, no triangle of primaries can encompass it all. The range of colours that it is possible to obtain from mixing of a certain set of primaries is called the *colour gamut*.

So what should one do with a combination of red, blue and green light recorded by the scanner that the system of primaries in the 'reproduction' – whether the screen phosphors or the printing inks – is not equipped to reproduce? There are two common ways for the computer to handle colours that fall outside the gamut. The simplest is to move them to the nearest boundary of the gamut: to approximate any colour one cannot capture with the nearest colour that one can. This means that two areas of colour that are visually distinct in the original image might become identical in the reproduction. Another alternative that avoids this consequence is to compress the entire colour range of the image evenly, until all the grid points fit within the gamut (Figure 12.5b). This shifts all the colours slightly throughout the image, but maintains a balance that closely approximates that in the original.

The colour gamut of screen phosphors is determined by the materials from which they are made. One might imagine that the ideal phosphors for a full-colour screen would correspond to colours located as far as possible in the 'corners' of the tongue-shaped CIE diagram, to encompass as much colour space as possible.

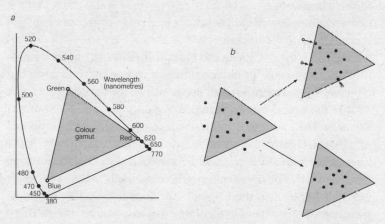

Figure 12.5

(*a*) The colour gamut of phosphors on television screens, displayed on the CIE diagram. (*b*) If scanned colours fall outside the gamut, either the outliers can be shifted to the nearest edge of the gamut, or the entire 'palette' can be compressed. The latter preserves colour relationships, but shifts all the colours across the board. In practice, adjustments made to fit all measured points within the gamut can take these points along quite complex trajectories in colour space.

But in fact it is better not to venture too far into these fully saturated corners, because that would entail using red and blue phosphors that emit at the edges of the visible range. At these extremes, very high light intensity is needed to produce a sensation of appreciable brightness. It is technologically difficult to extract such brightness from phosphors. So for this and other reasons, the phosphors considered 'ideal' have a more restricted gamut (Figure 12.5a). All the same, it is hard to find materials that satisfy this ideal: the canonical green phosphor (zinc cadmium sulphide) cannot reproduce strongly saturated greens.

So even on computer screens, where art is increasingly viewed, manipulated and even created, limitations in materials restrict the colouristic possibilities. As new screen technologies become available, in particular flat-screen systems based on liquid-crystal displays or on light-emitting diodes, new layers of complexity will be added to these limitations. It is by no means obvious at this point that the new technologies will enhance the colour range of on-screen images – possibly quite the opposite.

In general, the red, green and blue phosphors of a monitor screen offer something like 17 million different colour combinations. But typically the palette of a stored image will be much more restricted, so that the image can be stored using only a modest amount of memory. The palette generally contains 256 colours, each composed of a specific combination of red, green and blue to which the hues of the scanned image will be matched via a 'colour look-up table' or 'clut'. The stored image is therefore likely to have a narrower range of colour than the original: one is essentially repainting the picture with a palette of 256 colours that may not be mixed. But if the clut (that is, the digital palette) is well chosen to match the colours of the original, there should be sufficient diversity for the eye to be scarcely able to detect a difference. On the other hand, a poorly matched clut can generate an image with a shifted tonality (Plate 12.3).

Optimizing the clut is a crucial aspect of colour matching. This may be done in different ways on different computer systems, which is one reason why an image's colour range might be altered if it is scanned on one system and viewed or printed on another. Differences between monitors can also alter the balance owing to variations in brightness of the phosphors. For these reasons, an image may be brightened or darkened if transferred between machines: those scanned on IBM PCs tend to look too bright when displayed on AppleMac and Unix systems, whereas the reverse transfer gives darker, muddy images.

To print the scanned image, the computer must convert a grid encoding different intensities of red, blue and green light into instructions for depositing the four (yellow, magenta, cyan, black) inks in a given area in the correct proportions and overlaps to generate the same visual effect as the reflected red, green and blue light from that area of the original. The calculation is complicated by several factors – for example, the properties of the paper, such as its whiteness and graininess, will affect the appearance of any given combination of inks. In practice these calculations would be too time-consuming to perform 'on the spot', as it were, and so they are predetermined for a whole range of different red/blue/green combinations, taking into account the qualities of the printing inks and paper. Then all the computer has to do is look up in a stored table the answers for each patch of the gridded image.

For printing on a large scale, such as for this book, electronically stored images will be physically embodied on printing plates or rollers so that they may then be run off mechanically. To apply ink to paper, most of the processes developed in the nineteenth century are still used. Lithography with rollers patterned into ink-attracting and ink-repelling areas is the most common of these, conducted via the 'offset' technique in which the ink is first transferred from the plates to a rubber blanket that is then pressed against the paper. Intaglio and relief methods (where the inks are respectively held in depressions or carried on raised areas of the plates) continue to find their niches. And rather than using printing plates, it can be cheaper and more convenient for small-scale printing jobs to be conducted by 'direct imaging printing', where the reproduction is created straight from the electronic data using ink-jet systems.

But how good, in the end, are the copies? The gamut on the printed page is still delimited by the extent to which the inks are good primaries; and theoretically perfect inks are still 'a desideratum'.

Because the magentas absorb rather too much blue, and the cyans too much blue and green, it can be hard to reproduce accurately low-saturation (dirty-looking) blues, greens, cyan and magenta. And only in the red-to-yellow range can a three-colour reproduction successfully capture high-saturation colours. The gamut may be further restricted by the paper substrate – newspaper, for example, deadens high-saturation colours, which is why newspapers resort to higher-quality paper for their glossy magazine supplements. The gamut can be extended by using supplementary inks such as strong blues, greens and reds. This adds to the printing costs, and can be contemplated only for the most demanding assignments.

The computer in art

Just as printing methods, such as wood-block and lino-cut, have been used as vehicles for artistic expression in their own right, so too the digital age offers a new way for artists to manipulate line and colour. Computer art is still so new a medium that one cannot yet be sure whether to dismiss it as a fad or hail it as the future of visual art. Yet I cannot imagine that digital technology will fail to be valorized as a means of creative expression once there exists a generation of artists more accustomed to holding a mouse than a paintbrush. No great digital painter has emerged so far to rival those who deal in messy stuff squeezed from tubes, but the electronic visionaries have after all had their paintboxes for barely twenty years.

The use of computers in art began in the 1960s, when digital technology was still so new and mysterious that the graphic art it generated gained kudos by mere association. Monochrome works made by computer were displayed in art galleries; and even if they had no more merit than the tortuous computer music that reached concert halls, well, it was a start. American painter Robert Rausch-enberg was one of the high-profile artists who saw the shape of things to come, and in 1967 he teamed up with physicist Billy Kluver of Bell Laboratories to create an initiative called Experiments in Art and Technology.

Given the absence of colour in these early efforts, it is hardly surprising that the computer art of the 1960s and 1970s focused on

line and volume – on the construction of space. These preoccupations are apparent in the computer-generated works of early pioneers
Frieder Nake and Manfred Mohr. But the danger of an algorithmic
approach to art is apparent in the quest of the German philosopher
Max Bense in the 1960s to identify exact laws that the computer
can explore and use to produce 'aesthetically correct' images. One
is reminded of scientists' attempts to impose strict rules of colour
on painting, and to 'correct' those works that contravene them.

For computer art to broaden and flourish, the three most vital
ingredients were low cost, interactive interfacing, and colour. All
arrived in the 1980s, when Apple introduced the cheap Macintosh
personal computer with its MacPaint interactive graphics software.
(Despite the enticing name, however, this was initially capable of
handling only black and white images.) As colour graphics became
more sophisticated, painters stirred themselves to investigate the
new technology. David Hockney took to using computers for
photocollage works, while Andy Warhol bought an Amiga computer to experiment with colour combinations for his silk-screen
prints.

Because computer technology is now such a fast-moving target,
a snapshot will capture little of lasting relevance. The artist now
has a virtual canvas on which marks can be made that resemble
brush-strokes, pencil or pastel lines, spray-can swashes and so forth
– each in something like 17 million different colours. Canvases can
be revised in an instant, initiated or discarded at no cost. But it is an
open question whether mimicry of manual painting is the best way
to exploit the new medium, when the possibilities for interaction,
animation, collage and cross-referencing are so great. The computer's biggest problem right now is its versatility: too great a range
of options smothers art, as Renaissance colourists knew.

And there are no agreed notions of authenticity and originality
for a work of art that has been created digitally. Is each hard-copy
print an original? If not, where exactly *is* the original? Some
computer artists deal with this problem by making limited-edition
prints – Manfred Mohr made only a single print of his works. Of
course, in a sense the same dilemma is faced by those who create
fine art by photography; but at least there is always an original

negative. As the Internet makes dissemination of digital images ever easier, and since it comes imbued with its culture of free access to all, the issue of 'authenticity' in computer art – and its ramifications for commerce – is likely to become ever more complex.

The liberation of art from ritual that Walter Benjamin foresaw has not yet happened – in part because photography has never really acquired the same artistic status as painting or sculpture. Perhaps it will be the computer, not the camera, that truly provides this emancipation.

Does it matter?

No doubt the majority of artists, living or dead, would be (and often have been) mortified to see what has sometimes become of their work in reproduction. But we should not take it for granted that this will be so. There is a sense in which a carefully wrought reproduction becomes a work of art in itself, its colours chosen so that, even if they do not precisely mimic the original, they harmonize effectively. This is certainly evident in Le Blon's three-colour prints, hand-engraved with truly remarkable skill and sensitivity. A case can be made for the intrinsic artistic validity of the monochrome engravings that, in the nineteenth century, strove to convey the essence of a great painting. Technology takes out much of the hard work, but it needs guidance from the human eye to do justice to an image.

Perhaps this is how the American painter Georgia O'Keeffe felt when some of her works were being prepared for printing by Viking Press in 1976. An artist with a particularly strong feeling for nuances of colour, she nevertheless indicated to the printers that 'It doesn't really matter if the color isn't absolutely right, if the picture feels right when you finish the print.'[18]

13. Mind over Matter

COLOUR AS FORM IN MODERNISM

The new art will really begin when we understand that colour has
an existence of its own, that the infinite combinations of colours
have a poetry and a poetic language much more expressive than
anything before.

Sonia Delaunay

Colours win you over more and more. A certain blue enters your
soul. A certain red has an effect on your blood pressure. A certain
colour tones you up. It's the concentration of timbres. A new era is
opening.

Henri Matisse

Ever since the Middle Ages, painters were constantly reminded of
how inadequate their palette was for capturing the true glory of the
natural world. The colour-maker George Field remarked in
the 1840s that the Old Masters had been forced to 'harmonize much
below nature' because their pigments were not bright enough.
Hermann von Helmholtz concurred:

The representation which the painter has to give of the light and colours
of his object . . . cannot give a copy true in all its details. The altered
scale of brightness which the artist must apply in many cases is opposed
to this.[1]

Even with his modern palette, Cézanne recognized this with palpable anguish: 'I cannot attain the intensity that is unfolded before
my senses. I do not have the magnificent richness of colouring that
animates Nature.' Van Gogh seems to have reconciled himself to

this limitation: 'A painter had better start from the colours on his palette than from the colours in nature.'

Yet ever since Turner began to use the bright new pigments, painting was moving inexorably towards a consensus that the task of the painter was no longer the representation of nature at all. The road to abstraction was prefigured by a liberation from 'naturalistic' colour, heralded by van Gogh, Cézanne and Henri Matisse (1869–1954). 'The truth of the matter', said Matisse, 'was that we kept at the farthest remove from imitative colours.'

The result was an explosion of solid colour and strong primaries. 'I use the simplest colours,' averred Matisse, 'I don't transform them myself, it is the relationships which take charge of them.' The red interiors of *La Desserte* (1908) and *Red Studio* (1911) are almost overwhelming in their uncompromising two-dimensionality, denying the illusion of pictorial volume. The critic John Russell says of *Red Studio*, 'It is a crucial moment in the history of painting: colour is on top, and making the most of it.'

The wild beasts

All use of colour in the twentieth century must be considered in relation to Matisse, just as all use of form relates to Cézanne. Picasso said as much: 'If all the great colourist painters of this century could have composed a banner that comprised each one's favourite colours, the result would certainly have been a Matisse.'[2]

And what are these colours but those of pure joy and pleasure, delighting in the cobalt, chomium and cadmium hues of nineteenth-century chemistry? In 1897 Matisse discarded his previously sombre palette for one that danced with the bright blues, greens and reds of newly invented pigments: a palette much like that of the Impressionists, although he did not exclude earths such as yellow ochre and the sienna pigments. He used cobalt violet, which features only occasionally in Impressionism, and he adopted the new cadmium reds, in light and purplish shades.

Remarkably, cadmium red was essentially the first major material innovation in red pigments since the introduction of carmine lake made from cochineal in the sixteenth century. Mars red (synthetic iron oxide; see page 154) was a refinement of the red ochre known since antiquity; red lake manufacture was improved in the early nineteenth century, but involved no truly new colourants; the aniline reds were never really successful as artists' colours; and synthetic alizarin was the same compound as that which the Egyptians drew from madder root. Every primary and secondary colour except red was given an influential new embodiment in the nineteenth century. Cadmium red is basically cadmium yellow (cadmium sulphide) with some selenium added in place of sulphur. The element selenium, delightfully named for the Moon, was discovered in 1817 – the same year as cadmium – by the Swedish chemist Jons Jacob Berzelius. It has properties similar to sulphur, and often occurs naturally in association with it.

It is not easy to trace the genesis of the pigment, for cadmium sulphide orange can itself approach red closely enough to blur the boundaries. George Field speaks approvingly of a pigment he calls cadmium red in his (posthumous) 1869 edition of *Chromatography*. But as no technical document is known that specifies the sulphide–selenide until a German patent from 1892, we have to suppose that Field's colour, which he describes as 'orange-scarlet', is merely a particularly deep variant of cadmium orange. In any event, the compound that now goes under the name of cadmium red was not available as a commercial product until 1910. The chemicals company Bayer developed a more reliable and economical means of producing it in 1919. By altering the amount of selenium, the colour can be adjusted from orange to dark maroon.

Matisse was much taken with this strong new red, which has excellent stability. He recounts how he attempted, unsuccessfully, to persuade Renoir to adopt a 'cadmium red' in place of the traditional vermilion. Since this was in 1904, however, he was presumably speaking of whatever pigment it was that Field had investigated, whose orange tint would have more closely resembled vermilion than does the deeper modern variety.

Matisse felt, like Cézanne, that it is the relationship between the colours, not the forms, of a painting that gives it its structure: 'Composition is the art of arranging in a decorative manner the various elements at the painter's disposal for the expression of his feeling . . . The chief aim of colour should be to serve expression as well as possible.'[3] This expressiveness, he believed, could not be planned from 'theories' of colour use, but must flow directly from the sensitivity of the artist: 'My choice of colours does not rest on any scientific theory; it is based on observation, on feeling, on the very nature of each experience . . . I merely try to find a colour that will fit my sensation.'[4]

Yet when instinctive colourists speak about their use of colour, we are not wise to look for consistency. Matisse confessed on one occasion that he was 'a good half a scientist', and he had a reputation among his colleagues for adhering to theory. At his art school in Paris, he exposed his pupils to Chevreul, Helmholtz and their interpreter Ogden Rood, through whom Matisse may have developed some interest in materials. Certainly Matisse derived from Rood an understanding that red, blue and green alone could 'create the equivalent of the spectrum' – which of course they can in the additive mixtures that Rood investigated, but not as pigments. Here, none the less, may be the seed of Matisse's *Dance* and *Music*, both painted in 1910, in which these three colours appear in flat juxtaposition, each with a quasi-Aristotelian elemental assignation: blue sky, green earth, red flesh.

At the turn of the century, with Impressionism threatening to become the new establishment, Neo-Impressionism moribund and van Gogh dead, there was plenty of room for a new avant-garde. It appeared first in the movement known as Fauvism, with Matisse the figurehead. The Dutch Fauve painter Kees van Dongen said of this group, 'One can talk about the Impressionist school because they held certain principles. For us there was nothing like that; we merely thought their colours were a bit dull.' Set Monet's water-lilies against Courbet, and you can scarcely credit the accusation. Set them against André Derain's *The Pool of London* (1906) (Plate 13.1) and all becomes clear. Here is colour at full throttle, and it speaks as eloquently of the centrality of bright new pigments as if they had been simply squeezed in sequence from the tubes (which in truth they often were).

Like every other major movement in early-twentieth-century

painting, Fauvism was a direct descendant of Impressionism. Matisse received a classical but open-minded training in Paris under Gustave Moreau in the 1890s, but came under the spell of Impressionism in 1896. The young painter was fortunate to be recognized by that most generous and perceptive of Impressionists, Camille Pissarro, who also fostered Gauguin and Cézanne and advocated the genius of van Gogh.

But Matisse's enthusiasms led him in a different direction. In the works of Cézanne he found not only a resurrection of the idea – buried since the Venetian Old Masters – of colour as constructive medium, but also an emphasis on the importance of harmony and balance of tones, to which some other Fauves paid little heed. From Gauguin, meanwhile, Matisse took an understanding of the impact and emotional force of 'primitive' art, as well as an appreciation of the use of flat rather than modelled colour. (Like van Gogh and Gauguin, he was strongly influenced by the Japanese prints in vogue in France at the end of the nineteenth century.) He laid out his influences plainly enough:

To say that colour has once again become expressive is to sum up its history . . . From Delacroix to van Gogh and chiefly to Gauguin, by way of the Impressionists, who cleared the ground, and Cézanne, who gave the final impulse and introduced coloured volumes, we can follow this rehabilitation of colour's function, this restoration of its emotive power.[5]

But whereas for Gauguin colour had mystical and symbolic implications, for Matisse it was purely the stuff from which pictures are made. Many of his paintings abolish depth from the canvas, building up a two-dimensional tiling of coloured spaces almost like a tapestry. 'What prevents Gauguin from being assimilated to the Fauves', he said, 'is his failure to use colour for constructing space, and his use of it as a means of expressing sentiment.'

André Derain (1880–1954) became acquainted in 1899 with Matisse, to whom he introduced Maurice de Vlaminck (1876–1958) in 1901 at a van Gogh retrospective exhibition in Paris. These three were the core of the loosely-knit Fauve group, and the van Gogh exhibition was the catalyst that ignited their incendiary colours.

Vlaminck went away exclaiming that he loved the Dutchman more than his own father. Matisse remembers Vlaminck from this occasion as 'a young giant who was voicing his enthusiasm in dictatorial tones and declaring that one must paint with pure cobalt, pure vermilion and pure Veronese green [emerald green]'. Derain said of his association with Vlaminck in those days in the Parisian suburb of Chatou, 'We were always drunk with colour, with words that describe colour, and the sun that gives life to colour.'

Derain's palette was even broader than Matisse's, with barely a primary or secondary pigment omitted: all the cadmium colours are there, with barium chromate (lemon yellow) and Mars yellow. The impetuous and egotistic Vlaminck used the modern colours in unmixed form, producing high-keyed and strident works such as *Landscape with Red Trees* (1906–7) that dazzled but ultimately left him unable to develop a mature voice (by 1910 he could do little but emulate Cézanne). Raoul Dufy (1877–1953), also associated with the group, is said to have eschewed all browns, and used the full range of Mars colours (from yellow to violet) as well as the new cerulean blue. There is a strong case to be made that Fauvism, not Impressionism, represents the most glorious fruit of the nineteenth-century advances in pigment technology – the final emancipation of colour from tradition.

Fauvism burst into public view in 1905, when the movement found its name. At the Salon des Indépendants (which the Neo-Impressionists had initiated) in the spring of that year, Matisse exhibited *Luxe, Calme et Volupté*, fresh from his excursion with Paul Signac in Saint-Tropez. It excited much discussion, and inspired others of the Fauves towards the 'Divisionism' into which Seurat's pointillist style had evolved.

But Signac insisted that this style remain bound by rules of colour contrast and complementarity, which ultimately frustrated and alienated the instinctive Matisse. In *Luxe, Calme et Volupté* he is little concerned with scientific exactitude – his stippled colour patches are far too large to 'work' by optical mixing in the way Seurat had intended. Much of the Divisionism practised by Matisse, Derain, Georges Braque and others was simply a separation of colour into unblended dabs (*taches*). Matisse frequently evinces an almost medieval determination to preserve the integrity of pure colour, and he criticized the Neo-Impressionists for undermining it with their optical mixtures.

That summer, Matisse returned with Derain to the south of France, to the small town of Collioure, and here they developed the style that came to be seen as definitive of Fauvism. On seeing a collection of Gauguin's paintings, they realized that the way forward lay not with Divisionism but with flat colour: 'a harmony of intensely coloured surfaces'. Together with the other Fauve painters, they exhibited the results of this excursion at the Salon d'Automne in late 1905. This exhibition was founded in 1903 as a more discriminating alternative to the Salon des Indépendants, whose openness to all-comers meant that the good tended to be buried amongst a surplus of the bad.

The autumnal Salon caused an uproar comparable to that of the first Impressionist exhibition in 1874, prompting scorn of a similar flavour. 'A pot of colours flung in the face of the public,' exclaimed critic Camille Mauclair, lamely repeating the accusation that Ruskin levelled at Whistler in 1877. Others went further, driven almost to a frenzy by this lack of good taste. 'Why put all these maniacs together and show their work to the public', wrote J.-B. Hall, 'if it has no aesthetic value? What is the meaning of this new farce? Who is protecting them?' . . . and so on and so forth until the final snooty punchline: 'What have the daubs of Messrs Matisse, Vlaminck and Derain got to do with art?'

On seeing these dazzling works exhibited in the same room as some traditional Florentine-inspired sculptures, Louis Vauxcelles, the eminent critic of *Gil Blas*, remarked to Matisse, 'Look! Donatello in a cage of wild beasts [*dans la cage aux fauves*]!' And so, like Impressionism before it and Cubism after (again courtesy of the witty Vauxcelles), Fauvism was branded by a derisive joke.

Others were more perceptive. Maurice Denis, a painter with the innovative Nabi group, remarked that 'This is painting above and beyond contingencies, painting for its own sake, the pure act of painting.' It was almost as if he could foresee the inevitable next step into abstraction.

But Fauvism had more shoots than that. Matisse's *Portrait with a*

Green Stripe, a portrait of his wife painted in late 1905, seems to show the way to Expressionism, as well as announcing the redundancy of the colour theories of Impressionism. Here complementaries are sacrificed, and instead there is dissonance: vermilion against violet, green against pink and ochre. With *Blue Nude* (1907), Matisse appears in retrospect to be preparing us for Picasso's astonishing nude figures.

Perhaps it was because Fauvism was simply too fertile that it was so short-lived: by 1908 it had ceased to exist as a coherent movement. In just four years it briefly claimed both Kandinsky and Braque, Picasso's collaborator in the inception of Cubism. Fauvism can perhaps be seen as a kind of catching-up period, an assimilation of the possibilities of the new colours which the Impressionists had only partly glimpsed. After Matisse, there was no looking back.

Experiments in colour

Some early-twentieth-century artists clung to the hope that science, not intuition, would help them navigate the treacherous waters of non-representational colour. In 1906 the Italian artist Gaetano Previati published *Scientific Principles of Divisionism*, which expanded on some of the Neo-Impressionistic views of contrast and optical mixing. It was highly influential on the Italian Futurist painters such as Giacomo Balla and Umberto Boccioni. Boccioni's *The City Rises* (1910) is an image surging with chromatic life, yet giving the impression of a more systematic use of colour than that of Seurat. 'I want the new, the expressive, the formidable,' said the artist, implicitly summarizing the Futurist manifesto.

It may have been a translation of Previati's book that induced the Frenchman Robert Delaunay (1885–1941) to dabble in Divisionism. Delaunay strove to achieve a luminous effect akin to stained glass, which he studied in French churches between 1907 and 1912: a series of paintings executed between 1911 and 1913 was called *Windows*. 'Colour alone', he said, 'is both form and subject' – but it was really coloured light that he was trying to emulate, at first by attempting to suggest transparency through the lustre that Divisionism seemed to promise. Delaunay subsequently abandoned the dots for flat colour patches inspired by Cézanne and the geometric designs of the Cubists. Glowing with fully saturated, vibrant colour, these paintings, such as *Sun Discs* (1912–13), have been called 'fragmented rainbows' – although one might better regard them as mutations of the Newtonian colour wheel. The poet and critic Guillaume Apollinaire called this style Orphism.

Orphism has been dismissed by some as nothing more than Fauvism turned abstract (and Delaunay indeed passed through a Fauvist stage early in his career). But it appears that Delaunay was searching for a colour syntax, whereas the Fauves showed little interest in formulae. He professed, however, to have little patience for scientific principles:

I am mad about the forms of colours but I do not look for a scholastic explanation of them . . . None of the finite sciences has anything to do with my technique of moving towards light. My only science is choosing among the impressions which light in the universe offers to my craftsmanly awareness and which I try to group together by giving them an order . . .[6]

Yet Delaunay studied Chevreul and was probably familiar with the colour theory of Rood (on which Previati had drawn). He made use of complementaries in order to develop his ideas of 'colour movement'. By seemingly paradoxical reasoning, he claimed that complementaries side by side produce 'slow' movements whereas colours close together on the colour wheel, such as orange and yellow or blue and green, produce 'fast' movements. On the basis of these rather vague notions, Delaunay insisted that his works were not truly abstract but grounded in natural rules.

In the USA, Orphism fostered the movement known as Synchromism, whose key proponents were the painters Morgan Russell and Stanton MacDonald Wright. The intersecting planes of the Synchromists were, if anything, even brighter than Delaunay's. And in the 'aesthetic of purity' sought by the Frenchman and his Russian wife Sonia, herself an accomplished painter and poet, one can see the beginnings of the minimalism that was to develop into colour-field painting in the USA.

But Delaunay's weakness was inclusiveness. By embracing the entire spectrum, by failing to make the selection that is essential to all great art, he ran the risk of simply charting the colours of the rainbow rather than constructing them into a convincing work. There are dangers in falling too deeply for the gorgeous modern pigments.

The school without theory

No one can deny that Paul Klee (1879–1940) was a superb and inventive colourist. Jean-Paul Sartre went further: 'Klee is an angel who re-creates the miracles of this world.' Yet it is by no means easy to reduce a Klee composition to any principles of colour theory. He is a conjuror in colour, at one moment working in luminous pastel shades (*Highways and Byways*, 1929), at another in lustrous, subtly modulated reds (*Landscape at Sunset*, 1923), then in bright primaries on a dream-like black background (*Landscape with Yellow Birds*, 1923; *Black Prince*, 1927). *Child with Aunt* (1937) is all shades of autumn; the rose, orange, green and blue of *Glass Façade* (1940) glows as if genuinely backlit. *The Light and So Much Else* (1931) advertises its real subject in the title: light, given a superficially Divisionist treatment but otherwise indebted not one jot to the rigid codes of Neo-Impressionism.

Nothing better captures the sheer exuberance that colour instils than Klee's recollections of the fantastic chromatic visions he found amidst the Arabic culture of Tunisia in 1914, which inspired him to joyous epiphany: 'Colour has taken hold of me; no longer do I have to chase after it. I know that it has hold of me for ever. That is the significance of this blessed moment. Colour and I are one.'[7]

It is no surprise that, with Klee and Kandinsky among the teachers (*Meister*), the Bauhaus school of art, architecture and design in Weimar, Germany, accorded much emphasis to colour in the 1920s. Founded in 1919, the Bauhaus set itself the task – quixotic in retrospect – of both fostering creativity in artists and designers and reconciling their crafts with the demands of the industries that would use them. To some tastes, the school now represents all that is soulless and functional in modern design, with its geometrical forms and its rejection of pure ornament. To others, it symbolizes an avant-garde stripped of pretension, and is one of the central foundations of modernism. To the Nazis it was simply a centre of 'degenerate' art, and they closed the school in 1933.

The Bauhaus arose from an amalgamation of the Weimar Academy of Art and the Weimar School of Applied Arts. Its first director was the architect and designer Walter Gropius, whose vision was to reawaken the manufacturing industries to the importance of art. In the past, the craftsman who made useful artefacts was an artist as well as a technician, trained to make items that were aesthetically pleasing (which is not the same as pointlessly fanciful) as well as functional. With the rise of industrialization, this link had been lost, and mass production had resulted in products that were devoid of any artistic value. 'The artist', said Gropius, 'possesses the ability to breathe soul into the lifeless product of the machine.'

To this end, Gropius set about recruiting skilled and imaginative proponents of both the pure and applied arts, to teach in the Bauhaus workshops and foster a new breed of creative craftspeople. Klee joined in 1921; Kandinsky followed the next year. With these two luminaries on the staff, the school did not find it hard to attract students – but discovered that many wanted to become modern painters and had little interest in a training in the practical crafts.

That was only one of Gropius's problems. Amongst the staff in the school's early years was Johannes Itten, a teacher of painting and a student of the abstract painter and art academic Adolf Hölzel. Colour theory was a strong preoccupation for Hölzel, and he conducted research into the relationship between colour and sound. Itten acquired from his mentor this passion for colour, as well as a penchant for unconventional teaching methods.

Meister Itten was a mystic – a follower of the Mazdaznan belief, rooted in ancient Zoroastrianism. He shaved his head, wore priestly robes, and encouraged the students to do likewise. Itten's outlook drew on the emotional excesses of the nineteenth-century German Romantics and their heirs, the Expressionist painters of the group called *Die Brücke*. He had little time for formal methods, but instead considered 'self-discovery' and experience the raw material of artistic creativity. His students were taught breathing and concentration exercises and were encouraged to empathize with their subject. Before drawing circles they would describe circles with swinging arms; to analyse Grünewald's painting of the crucifixion, they had to weep as Mary Magdalen was weeping.

All of this made Itten a charismatic, controversial and difficult *Meister*. According to one of his students, Paul Citroen, 'There was something demonic about Itten. As a master he was either ardently admired, or just as ardently hated by his opponents, of whom there were many. At all events, it was impossible to ignore him.'[8]

One has a sense that the Bauhaus operated in the early 1920s under conditions of barely controlled anarchy, despite the best efforts of Gropius. This was by no means an inclement environment for such mercurial figures as Klee and Kandinsky; but it hardly made for a coherent theoretical foundation. In no aspect is this more evident than in the Bauhaus attitude to colour.

The Bauhaus inherited from the Weimar School of Applied Arts a tradition of rational experimentation in colour inspired by Neo-Impressionism. Itten himself aspired to a 'grammar of colour', but evinced no clear idea of how to establish such a thing. Kandinsky was responsible for most of the teachings on colour, and the Bauhaus ethos professed that it should be studied from a physical, chemical and psychological point of view. Kandinsky's attempts to conduct 'scientific' consensus experiments in colour psychology (see page 23) were a manifestation of this ethos, which however proved only to undermine his rather dogmatic ideas about the emotional language of colour.

In fact, it seems clear that neither Klee nor Kandinsky, nor Itten, had a strong grasp of contemporary scientific ideas about colour. Klee's lectures made reference to Goethe's views and the use of complementary colours by artists such as Otto Runge and Eugène Delacroix. But he regarded the value of these theories as limited, as far as the artist was concerned – not least because the 'colours' of the scientist were not the same as the pigments of the artist: 'Of course we may use it for a bit, but we hardly have any need for a theory of colours. All the infinite mixtures possible will never produce a Schweinfurt green [emerald green], a Saturn red, a cobalt violet.'[9]

And there is no real sign that anyone at the Bauhaus possessed any knowledge of the chemical basis of colour. For example, Itten's distance from the material aspects of colour leads him to perpetuate the notion that the blue of the Virgin's robe in medieval art has primarily symbolic significance (see page 270). Itten's *Elements of Colour* contains much of interest, but nothing of any note about pigments, the very stuff of colour.

Evidently, none of this is any bar to being a truly great painter, nor an imaginative colourist; but one can only wonder what the students made of it all. One could find fragments of all manner of colour theories floating around the Bauhaus, no matter that some stood in stark contradiction to others. It is no surprise that Josef Albers, a Bauhaus alumnus who later became one of its tutors, sought refuge in a purely empirical approach. He called colour 'the most relative medium in art', liable to change with its context. After the Bauhaus was closed, Albers emigrated to the USA where he taught painting at Black Mountain College in North Carolina. He began his series of paintings called *Homage to the Square* in the 1950s, and pursued them until his death in 1976, by which time his flat-coloured superimposed squares had become emblematic of American minimalism. These images, midway between art and experiment, formed the basis of his influential book *Interaction of Color* (1963), in which he suggests, with echoes of Kandinsky, that certain combinations of primary, secondary and tertiary colours hold particular emotional significance.

It is hardly surprising, given Itten's iconoclasm, that he was not destined to last long at the Bauhaus. His fundamental dispute with Gropius's vision was with the idea of compromise with the world of commerce. He was convinced that true creativity must stem from self-knowledge unfettered by the crude practical demands of industry, and structured his courses accordingly. He demanded that Gropius settle for one or the other: for pure art or for pure practicality. But Gropius insisted that 'I seek unity in the *fusion*, not in the separation of these ways of life.' In 1922 he expressed concern that 'The Bauhaus could become a haven for eccentrics if it were to lose contact with the work and working methods of the outside world.' Itten took the hint, and departed under a cloud with the avowed intention to 'cling to his romantic island'.

Significantly, in 1923 Gropius proposed to replace Itten with a teacher in chemistry, in order to promote a return to the study of colour as a material. (The Bauhaus manifesto of 1923 explicitly classed it as such, alongside wood, metal, glass and so forth.) The school re-opened the workshop in dyeing techniques that had previously been a part of the Weimar School of Applied Arts. After relocating to Dessau in 1925, the Bauhaus re-established its mission as a place of practical training. Klee and Kandinsky continued to teach painting, but more in the spirit of 'resident artists' instilling a sense of aesthetics in the institution than as star teachers of a new breed of modernists.

'Thanks but no thanks'

The apparent rejection, in the Bauhaus of the early 1920s, of the material aspects of colour may have had its origins in something more concrete than the mystical leanings of its *Meister*. Itten's teacher Hölzel was an outspoken opponent of the colour theory of the German chemist Friedrich Wilhelm Ostwald (1853–1932). In 1909 Ostwald was awarded the Nobel prize for his work in physical chemistry, a discipline that he and a handful of others all but invented. An amateur painter who had made his own pigments since childhood, Ostwald developed an intense interest in colour in all its aspects.

Ostwald is scarcely alone among Nobel laureates in acquiring the conviction that his prize conferred invulnerability on any of his subsequent ideas. But few have displayed such single-minded assertiveness and arrogance in propagating them. His espousal of the belief that there were absolute colour principles (his own, of course) in art, violation of which led to art that was 'wrong' and in need of correction, can hardly have endeared him to those of a more instinctive temperament. Coupled with a strong socialist conviction that art should serve the people and not the individual, this was guaranteed to set him on more than one collision course. Max Doerner no doubt spoke for many when he said, 'It seemed somewhat amusing to painters when Professor Ostwald, in analysing Titian, announced that the blue of a mantle was two tones too high or too deep! It was simply Titian's own blue.'[10]

At the Bauhaus, Itten's opposition to Ostwald's theories was shared with equal vigour by Klee. Although the young Klee was one of the few artists to express enthusiasm for Ostwald's handbook *Malerbriefe* (*Letters to a Painter*) in 1904, calling it 'an excellent scientific handling of all technical matters', his later views were scathing:

That which most artists have in common, an aversion to colour as a science, became understandable to me when, a short time ago, I read Ostwald's theory of colours. I gave myself a little time to see if I could succeed in getting something of value from it, but instead only was able to get a few interesting thoughts . . . Scientists often find art to be childish, but in this case, the position is inverted . . . To hold [as Ostwald did] that the possibility of creating harmony using a tone of equal value should become a general rule means renouncing the wealth of the soul. Thanks but no thanks.[11]

But Kandinsky was ambivalent and came to favour Ostwald's views by 1925, while Gropius and the more technologically inclined of the designers viewed them sympathetically all along.

One feature of Ostwald's theory, seemingly odd for a scientist, was to instate green as a 'primary' along with red, yellow and blue. The colour wheel shown in Ostwald's book *The Colour Primer* (1916) awards greens no fewer than nine of the twenty-four divisions. But Ostwald had no quarrel with the notion of green as a 'secondary' mixture of blue and yellow. Rather, he considered green to be *perceptually* autonomous, an acknowledgement of the psychological dimension of colour that owes much to Goethe. Ostwald's scheme was derived from the theories of the Viennese psychologist Ewald Hering, who posited three sets of 'opponent colours' that have a strong resonance with the dualisms of Goethe's theory: black and white, red and green, yellow and blue.

The most important aspect of Ostwald's colour theory, however, was the role that he assigned to the grey component of colours: he introduced the dimension of grey-scale *value* (or brightness) into colour space. Otto Runge's colour sphere (see page 52) had attempted to extend the one-dimensional colour wheel by progressing from black at one pole to white at the other, but it did not find any place for grey as such. Albert Munsell's three-dimensional colour space (see page 53) went further, and Ostwald was much influenced by it when he met Munsell at Harvard in 1905. Ostwald wished to translate this abstract space into a set of principles relevant to the artist – into a means of achieving harmonious colour composition.

He did so by first establishing a grey scale of evenly varying perceptual steps. According to Ostwald, these steps obeyed a mathematical relationship between the progressive ratios of black and white. He then applied this grey scale to each of the hues on his twenty-four-part colour circle, and asserted that colour harmony resulted from the use of colours whose values – their grey components – are balanced. This was the central idea laid out in *The Colour Primer*, which Klee condemned so dismissively. The upshot for painters was a recommendation to temper and harmonize colours with white.

This much would have been a solid enough contribution to colour theory; but Ostwald turned it into the basis for a crusade. His chemical expertise gave him an unusual ability to translate theory into terms relevant to the pigments from which colours were actually made – and his consultancy role with the German paint industry meant that Ostwald was able to impress the theory on to commercial colour products. In 1914 he arranged a 'colour show' of industrial paints and dyes at Cologne on behalf of the Deutsche Werkbund, the German association for art and design, and in 1919 he initiated a series of technical conferences on the topic of colour at Stuttgart that still runs today. His children described their father in his later years as working away in his laboratory with an unkempt beard so full of pigment particles that it shone with all the colours of the rainbow.

In the 1920s, Ostwald's vigorous promotion of his ideas made them pre-eminent among European artists of the time – whether as a basis for practice or an object of vilification. He is said to have become something of a cult figure among the Dutch De Stijl painters such as Piet Mondrian, Theo van Doesburg and J. P. P. Oud. But Mondrian, who was much concerned with the question of primaries, seems to have struggled to comprehend what Ostwald's theory should imply for his own use of colour: should one include green or not? Perhaps there is something to be learned from the prospect of the Dutchman fretting over how to fill his grids according to ill-grasped theoretical principles, while Klee sets his own grids ablaze with unfettered intuition.

14. Art for Art's Sake

NEW MATERIALS, NEW HORIZONS

I think a picture is more like the real world when it's made out of the real world.

Robert Rauschenberg

This was an entirely new conception of colour, and it was put into words, tentatively, by Stella . . . when he said . . . 'I tried to keep the paint as good as it was in the can.' . . . That Stella sought to 'keep' the paint that 'good' suggests that he knew it might be hard to improve on the materials in their raw state, that once the paint had been put to use in art, it might well be less interesting than when it was 'in the can'.

David Batchelor, *Chromophobia* (2000)

For the twentieth-century artist, the medium carries its own message. Collage, explored by the Cubists and brought to a delicious refinement by the surrealist Max Ernst, injected the fabric of the real world into the composition. It spoke directly of the artist's social environment: the newspapers, the cigarette packets, the imitation caning pattern of café furniture, all lending the work an urbanity and immediacy that paint on canvas could only imitate. Georges Braque let sand and sawdust emphasize the solidity, the materiality, of his paints. In the 'ready-mades' of Marcel Duchamp the media do all the work; the artist simply selects. It is not what one sees that matters, but the question posed by its identity as a work-shop product or its placement in a gallery: What is Art?

What is art? We have just lived through the first century in history in which that question has lost its boundaries. The nineteenth-century critic had only to distinguish the good from the bad, the object of attention unambiguously framed, varnished and hung ready for inspection. Today we can pass in the street a billboard, a pile of detritus, a person behaving bizarrely, a graffito, and wonder to ourselves: was that art, or just life?

In letting the medium carry so much of the message, twentieth-century artists were in some respects returning to a secular version of the medieval attitude: materials possess their own intrinsic values and symbolic significance. The substance of art is no longer the passive tool that it became in the intervening centuries, to be arranged and worked until it ceased to be visible beneath the image itself. The very choice of materials may carry a message that is political, subversive, spiritual, shocking. Art is made from animal carcasses, human body fluids, excrement.

And yet few, if any, modern painters have understood their materials in the way that the painters of the Middle Ages or the Renaissance did. And few have seemed to care, or have shown much curiosity about what was actually in their cans (the preferred receptacle for post-war paint). In any case, colours appeared in such bewildering profusion − spurred by the development of new synthetic colourants − that no artist could be expected to keep pace with the march of materials. As a result, painters would mostly take the colours they were given and hope for the best. Even Mark Rothko, one of the foremost of modern colourists and a rare devotee of technical knowledge, occasionally used pigments that did not withstand the ravages of time, so that already some of his paintings have lost their impact.

Such was the fissiparity of art in the twentieth century that few traditional categories survived it. Michelangelo was of course both painter and sculptor, and Alberti painter and architect. But they did these things one at a time. So did Picasso; but by the late twentieth century there are no boundaries: painting is not about the flat canvas, installation may merge image and space, light and tactile experience. The artist's medium is the world: trees and ice, the city and its appurtenances, mountains and sky. So we can hardly be surprised that modern colour too is a multi-faceted gem, no longer uniquely defined by the paintbox, nor even by the rainbow or the Munsell atlas. The question of how artists get their colours thus becomes a matter as much for the philosophy of art as for its related technologies. Colour itself is being re-invented.

Industrial colour

The context of Marshall McLuhan's statement that 'the medium is the message' was the Pop Art of the 1960s, which insisted that there could be no other message *but* the medium. The medium was garish, crude and gloopy in Claes Oldenburg's hamburger sculptures because that was the nature of the fast food it depicted. Andy Warhol's work was repetitive because the advertising it quoted relies on repetition. Art was mass-produced and disposable because the culture in which it was embedded was just the same. In a sense, this art does nothing more than mirror the culture that produces it – it 'says' nothing that has not already been said.

Yet this is worlds away from Yves Klein, Mark Rothko or Jackson Pollock, let alone Matisse and Kandinsky. The pivotal point for the late twentieth century's arch-colourists is that colour itself – which is to say, its material substance – ferries the message to the viewer. The message might be psychological, emotional, spiritual; certainly it is not, for these artists, as stark and blunt as that of Pop Art. But it is conveyed not through the careful depiction of Christ's agonies on the cross, or the watery eyes of a tired old man, or the fragmented, contradictory planes of a woman's face – not, that is to say, through *disegno*. *Colore* speaks for itself, it represents nothing but itself.

This is a radical idea, although we can find its roots at least as far back as Goethe's *Theory of Colours*. Its modern incarnation is often attributed to Kandinsky, who has (rather meaninglessly) been described as the first abstract painter. The tale is told of Kandinsky's epiphany when, on returning from a walk, he glimpsed one of his own early figurative works standing on its side. The removal of all referential objects allowed the full impact of pure colour to work on his senses. He realized that objects – 'signs' – serve only to obstruct this direct communion with colour, preventing access to a deeper layer of reality beneath the physical form of things, 'Modern art can only be born when signs become symbols,' he said.

Could such a conclusion have been reached by a painter less extraordinarily (and neurologically) sensitive to colour than Kandinsky? Was this profound insight or naive Theosophy? It matters little. Abstraction was inevitable; anyone who now looks at the work of Cézanne or Gauguin can see that. Of course, all artists create their own 'ancestors', as Borges said of Kafka. But it is hard to imagine how abstract art could have become so pervasive so quickly if the world of Western art was not already primed for it as the twentieth century dawned – in part because of its new immersion in powerful colour. 'The need for colour, the meaning of that,' says American artist Donald Judd, 'more than anything destroyed the earlier representational painting.'

Yet for the artist who wishes to paint non-representationally, colour is a treacherous ally. For real things are coloured too, and we cannot readily let go of that association. According to art historian Philip Leider,

if you are going to make abstract pictures you have to be sure that your colours don't suggest or take on the quality of non-abstract things, like sky or grass or air or shadow (try black, or if that's too poetic, copper or aluminium).[1]

Thus abstraction makes new demands on colour. In the second half of the twentieth century, some artists did as Leider recommends, making use of paints that were not strictly 'coloured' at all, and not intended for fine art in the first place.

One of them was Frank Stella, who is said to have used industrial paints 'in an industrial way' – applied, that is, as if to a building or a railing. Here the medium of colour comes with its ready-made aesthetic, and it is the one most appropriate to the modern age: anonymous, devoid of charm, mass-produced. Today everything gets assigned a colour, whether it be an office corridor, a battleship or a computer terminal. They are no longer signifiers of worth: an approximation to ultramarine can be bought by the gallon, purple-dyed cloth by the yard.

The work of many of the major artists of the twentieth century's second half, from the American Abstract Expressionists to the Pop

Artists and the British school that includes David Hockney and Peter Blake, can therefore be understood only with reference to the technological and economic context of their materials. This again harks back to the constraints imposed by guilds, contracts and trade patterns in the Middle Ages and the Renaissance, in the sense that the artist's *work*, and not just his or her *practice*, bears an imprint of mundane considerations about cost, availability and properties of materials. The Pre-Raphaelites used the brilliant products of the new chemical technology to depict a world that science had never 'tainted'. But for Jackson Pollock, new types of paint not only demanded new techniques but were essential for the task the painter now faced: 'It seems to me that the modern painter cannot express this age, the airplane, the atom bomb, the radio, in the old forms of the Renaissance or of any other past culture.'[2] Yet for Pollock and many of his contemporaries, the new material forms that enabled innovations in painting style were not so much about colour as about the binding medium for the pigment. Colour was to become subservient not to line or form but to texture and consistency.

New media

From the beginning of the century, synthetic binders were used to create paints with unprecedented qualities. 'Most of the paint I use is a liquid, flowing kind of paint,' said Pollock, whose spattering techniques would not have been possible with anything else.[3] He used enamel gloss paints mass-produced for household and industrial purposes, which were cheap enough to allow him to cover huge canvases and to experiment in ways that would have been prohibited by more costly materials.

American artist Kenneth Noland confesses that financial considerations played a major role in the choice of these mass-market paints by him and his peers. In the 1940s, he said, there was 'no money coming in from painting . . . they couldn't get good art materials and there was a necessity almost to go out and start using housepaint, enamel paint'.

Yet cost was not the only factor. The Mexican mural artist David Alfaro Siqueiros, at whose New York workshops in the 1930s

Pollock and Morris Louis began experimenting with commercial paints, appreciated the durability of these materials. When Peter Blake began using enamel gloss paints in the 1950s, it was partly because of their association with fairground painting, in which he was intensely interested. British painter Patrick Caulfield was also drawn to household paints because of the impersonal sign-painting style they encouraged, with their flat surface unmarked by brush-strokes (Plate 14.1).

For these and other young painters of the 1950s and '60s, there was also a desire to escape from the academic 'painterliness' associated with oils. American painter Helen Frankenthaler took to acrylic emulsions because of their 'lack of sentiment'. British artist John Hoyland says that in those days 'oil paint smacked of garrets and starving artists'. In contrast, new paint media like acrylics 'seemed exciting in the way people got excited about the use of plastics, aluminium . . . and other industrial materials'. It was much the same impulse that led the progressive French painters of the late nineteenth century to abandon the practice of varnishing their works: a rejection of the codified norms of academic painterly practice. Even in the early years of the twentieth century the matt finish so characteristic of the painting of the 1950s was valued by Expressionists such as Ernst Ludwig Kirchner because of its ability to create 'a more intense expression'.

As the transition from egg tempera to oils shows, a new paint binder shifts the boundaries of colour and its application. It alters the optical properties of a pigment, for instance, and also the drying time – with implications for colour blending. Perhaps even more dramatically, those post-war painters who, like Peter Blake, used their commercial paints straight from the can were essentially having their palette determined by the manufacturers, who were producing for a very different market and were at the time often barely aware that artists were using their materials. Frank Stella admits that in his early days his colour range had a kind of inverse relation with the whims of fashion – he used house paints that were sold at a discount because their colour had gone out of style. 'I just took what the regular paint stores had to offer,' he says. In much the same way, the bright impact of graffiti art owes everything to the range of fluorescent colours produced in spray cans. Few, however, have placed their palette so far at the mercy of the paint industry as Robert Rauschenberg, widely personified as the 'father of Pop Art'. He once bought some cheap, unlabelled cans of household paint and painted with whatever colours they turned out to contain.

These new types of paint were an obvious product of the 'age of plastic'; but it is sobering to be reminded that this age began in the first half of the nineteenth century. In 1832 the German-Swiss chemist Christian Friedrich Schönbein discovered that cellulose, a natural polymer that is the main component of plant fibres, can be converted to a semi-synthetic material by reacting cotton fibres with nitric acid. Schönbein's product, which could be moulded and hardened, is commonly called cellulose nitrate or nitrocellulose.

In the late 1860s the brothers John and Isaiah Hyatt in Newark found that a 'plasticizer' such as camphor renders nitrocellulose flexible; their new material, called celluloid, made them rich. But the property of nitrocellulose that elicited the greatest interest was its explosive nature, for which reason it became known also as gun cotton. During the First World War it was manufactured in huge quantities.

At the end of the war there was suddenly a huge surplus of this now redundant substance, and new uses were sought for it. Dissolved in an organic solvent and supplemented with a resin, nitrocellulose provides a varnish – a kind of synthetic lacquer. Coloured with pigments, it is a tough, glossy and quick-drying paint that became known as enamel.[4] These characteristics of enamel paints endeared them to the expanding motor-car industry, and the DuPont chemicals company in the USA began providing enamels to General Motors. As a result, the time needed to paint a car dropped from seven to ten days in the early 1900s to about thirty minutes in the 1920s – a great boost for mass production.

Siqueiros began using the DuPont enamels, called the Duco range, in the 1930s. In the 1950s the British artist Richard Hamilton used nitrocellulose spray paints, notably for *Hers Is a Lush Situation* (1958), whose subject is the motor car. While he admits to some (unwarranted) suspicion at the time that these industrial paints must be better than artists' paints because so much more money had been lavished on them, the primary reason for his choice was symbolic:

I wanted the work to have as close a connection with the source as possible . . . everything was directed not as representing the object but as symbolizing it . . . It's meant to be a car, so I thought it was appropriate to use car colour.[5]

Much the same considerations inform Hamilton's use of nitrocellulose enamel paints in other works concerned with technological artefacts, such as the household appliances depicted in *\$he* (1958–61). The Independent Group in Britain, of which Hamilton was a leading light, explicitly advocated an art that embraced modern developments in science and technology.

Among artists, perhaps the most famous brand-name for enamel paints is Ripolin, made by a French company for household use since the early years of the century. Linseed oil was initially used as the binder, toughened and given a high-gloss finish by addition of resins. Ripolin's reputation is due single-handedly to Picasso, who used the paints extensively since at least 1912, apparently because of their durability. His endorsement of the Ripolin range lent it a certain mystique, motivating several later artists to use the same materials. (There is some suggestion, however, that Picasso tended to use 'Ripolin' as a generic term for commercial paint, much as the British speak of any vacuum cleaner as the 'Hoover' – so he may not in fact have used the Ripolin brand exclusively at all.)

Nitrocellulose has now been replaced as the binder in most industrial and household paints by a new class of synthetic resins called alkyds. These are polyester polymers, and are mixed with oils to make a fast-drying paint medium. The first alkyd resin was produced in 1927, and they were used as binders in commercial paints from the late 1930s in the USA and from the 1950s in Europe. They can accept a greater loading of pigment than nitrocellulose, and so can give more intense, opaque colours. DuPont began to use alkyd resins in place of nitrocellulose in their Duco range from the 1940s, and Ripolin also switched from drying oils to alkyds. Manufacturers of artists' paints, however, have been slow to respond to the enthusiasm for alkyds: Winsor and Newton is one of the few companies to offer alkyd paints for artists, and these were introduced only in the 1980s.

An inconvenience of these synthetic resin-based paints is that, like oils, they must be thinned with organic solvents such as white spirit – a messy and noxious business. It was inevitable that sooner or later someone would devise a paint medium that handled like oils but could be thinned with water. Enter acrylic emulsions, in 1953.

Acrylic plastics, which include hard plastics such as perspex (Plexiglas), have been commercially available since the 1930s. Liquid acrylic polymers do not dissolve in water; but in acrylic emulsions tiny pigment-laden droplets of the polymer are dispersed in water and prevented from coalescing by a soap-like substance called an emulsifier. As the film of paint dries, the water evaporates and the acrylic becomes transformed into a tough but flexible coating. Once it has set, the paint is impervious to water.

The first acrylic emulsions were house paints, but the American paint company Permanent Pigments adopted the same formulation to make a range of artists' paints called Liquitex. Artists such as Andy Warhol and Helen Frankenthaler experimented with them in the 1950s, but the runny consistency did not suit most tastes. Only when Liquitex was reformulated in 1963 with a thicker consistency, more like oil paint, did artists take to it. George Rowney and Sons provided a British version, the Cryla range, in the early 1960s.

As well as being water-thinned, one of the big attractions of acrylic emulsions was the fast drying time: fresh layers can usually be laid on within an hour. This was what prompted David Hockney to switch from oils to acrylics in 1963:

When I worked with oil paints I always had to work on at least three or four pictures at the same time because then you could keep working every day . . . you had to wait for things to dry. Whereas now it's possible to work on one all the time.[6]

Acrylics usually give a very different paint surface from oils: flat and opaque, without brush-marks, the ideal finish for a painter striving for the stark, impersonal style characteristic of the 1960s. And, says Hockney, the paint serves colour well: 'When you use simple and bold colours, acrylic is a fine medium: the colours are very intense and they stay intense, they don't alter much.'[7] Yet acrylics, thinned to translucency with water, can be glazed like oils – with the advantage that the glaze is dry within minutes. Hockney used this traditional technique for *Mr and Mrs Clark and Percy* (1970–71). Yet interestingly, he later felt compelled to revert to oils when he began to work in a more naturalistic style. The medium must suit the message, it seems.

Acrylics were in fact first introduced as a paint medium not as water-dispersed emulsions but as resins, immiscible with water, in which the polymer is dissolved in an organic solvent. In the late 1940s the American paint-makers Leonard Bocour and Sam Golden collaborated with a manufacturer of acrylic resins to devise the Magna range of acrylic 'solution' paints for artists, which they advertised as 'the first new painting medium in 500 years'. Magna paints came in tubes with a consistency similar to oil paints, and could be thinned with turpentine. They could even be mixed with oil colours. The paints had a high loading of pigment, and so could be diluted considerably without losing their intensity of colour, whereas thinned oil paints become translucent. This property was attractive to the American Colour Field artists such as Mark Rothko, Barnett Newman and Kenneth Noland, as well as to Pop Artists like Roy Lichtenstein. Bocour was happy to deal directly with the artists: he collaborated with the painter Morris Louis to develop a customized version of the Magna paints suited to Louis's very individualistic style. Bocour would sometimes test new Magna products by giving them free to his circle of loyal American painters – to the envy of British painters like John Hoyland who, before 1963, had no local access to acrylics.

Roy Lichtenstein has never really used any medium other than acrylic solution paints – which meant that for many years his colour range of bright primaries was delimited by the (rather small) Magna catalogue. When the Magna range was discontinued in the 1980s, Lichtenstein bought up all the remaining stocks he could find. But

Sam Golden's son Mark, now head of Golden Artist Colours, created a similar range of acrylic paints in the late 1980s with a wider range of colours. He too was willing to tailor his products to the specifications requested by Lichtenstein, who comments appreciatively 'Now I have maybe four different light yellows instead of one.'

One drawback of acrylic solution paints is that the dried paint will redissolve in turpentine, and so tends to become mobile when overpainted unless each layer is varnished. Lichtenstein was prepared to go to this trouble ('It gets very sticky if you don't'), but the requirement would scarcely accommodate artists who do not use flat, blocked-out fields of colour.

Acrylics are expensive materials, however, and most household emulsion paints (that is, those that can be thinned with water) are now based instead on polyvinyl acetate (PVA). The principle is the same: PVA is itself a water-insoluble polymer that can be used to form tough plastics and resins, but in emulsions it is dispersed as liquid droplets in water. PVA paints, first marketed in the 1950s, also had the attraction of fast drying times. That, and their ease of handling, was what induced British painter Bridget Riley to use them in the 1960s. The flat finish of PVA complements her precise, illusionistic compositions. Towards the late 1960s, when Riley began to paint her 'Op Art' works increasingly in colour rather than in black, white and grey, she began to seek materials that would give her strong colour intensities. She was not enthusiastic about Rowney's Cryla range of acrylics, considering them too 'pale' and 'greyish', and so found herself compelled to mix her own colours from hand-ground pigment added to PVA. This was an arduous and difficult process, and could result in an uneven paint surface. In the 1970s Riley finally switched to acrylics, which later she sometimes glazed with oils to gain still greater colour density.

For Kenneth Noland, meanwhile, the attraction of PVA was financial: 'You could buy [Elmer's glue, an American PVA glue] by the gallon. I used to put dry pigment in it.' And surely only an age that offers affordable paint 'by the gallon', coupled with a cultural philosophy in which size and space are iconic, could have produced works on the vast scale of the American Abstract Expressionists.

Field and vision

For Mark Rothko (1903–70), immense scale was a way of immersing the viewer in the picture: 'However you paint the larger picture, you are in it. It isn't something you command.'

This is not sheer hubris. Rothko wanted to make works that wrought a transcendent effect, that dealt with spiritual concerns: 'Paintings must be like miracles.' With Barnett Newman and Clyfford Still, Rothko represents, in the words of art critic Robert Hughes, the 'theological side' of Abstract Expressionism.

Rothko and Newman worked with vast fields of unbroken colour, without any figurative reference points at all. In principle at least, there was nothing in these works for the viewer to respond to except raw visual impression, the hue and luminosity of the paint itself. This was Kandinsky's vision taken to its logical extreme: the object had disappeared entirely, and the only thing left was colour. As the strength of the effect was considered proportional to the size of the image, these painters found it necessary to work on a large scale. They have become known as the Colour Field group.

Yet something of the figurative remains if the canvas is not simply monochrome. The eye and brain seem to demand it; they conspire to construct familiar forms from the juxtaposed fields of colour, just as Leider warns. Rothko's *Two Openings in Black over Wine* (1958) becomes a window in a dark room through which one sees the last glimmering of a burgundy dusk. *Ochre and Red on Red* (1954) (Plate 14.2) has echoes of landscape simply by virtue of the horizontal format of the colour fields: we are looking out into the shimmering heat haze of a desert.

According to Rothko, however, these rectangles of luminous colour are not infinite sky or sea, nor even abstractions of them, but 'things'. Typically they do not, after all, fill the canvas as if framed by a window, but stop short of the edge with clear boundaries. This forces the question of whether they are really 'colour-fields' at all. In Newman's work the field is more explicit, typically disrupted by a vertical line which he called a 'zip'. The narrow bands of yellow and blue that frame an almost wholly vermilion-coloured canvas in his *Who's Afraid of Red, Yellow and Blue III* (1966–7) undoubtedly suggest some kind of depth, the red behind the other colours, so that we are seeing not just a blank colour but a scene.[8]

One can theorize endlessly about what drove these painters to seek expression in the anguished minimalism of raw, non-figurative colour. One senses a response to the extremity of the mid-century: to Hiroshima, the Holocaust, the threat of nuclear war and, in the USA in particular, an increasingly reactionary post-war pressure to conform. Pollock's response was that of the wild, virile, self-destructive rebel so compellingly portrayed in the American cinema of the 1950s. Barnett Newman courted later derision with the outrageous, if apparently sincere, claim that his paintings, if seen properly, would spell the end of global capitalism.

Speculation is all the more encouraged, if not indeed required, by the fact that the artists' own pronouncements had this resolutely gnomic quality. Rothko was reluctant to dissect his works with words: 'A painting doesn't need anybody to explain what it is about. If it is any good, it speaks for itself.' Which may be just as well: here is Rothko, for example, on his departure from figurative representation in the mid-1940s: 'It was not that the figure had been removed . . . but the symbols for the figures, and in turn the shapes in the later canvases were substitutes for the figures.'[9]

Perhaps, however, this is not so very different from Kandinsky's statement of the challenge of abstraction. Yet Rothko's solution was quite different. Whereas Kandinsky sought a visual language in colour, for the Colour Field painters colour was (curiously enough) simply a means to an end. Rothko himself disclaimed any strong interest in colour *per se*, but explained that he had no option but to use it as his vehicle: 'Since there is no line, what is there left to paint with?' The idea of arranging colours in some aesthetically or theoretically satisfying way, as 'colourists' would do, horrified Rothko, who destroyed canvases of his own in which he saw this happening. 'If you . . . are moved only by their color relationships,' he exclaimed angrily to one reporter, 'then you miss the point.' And the point was that

I'm not interested in the relationship of color or form or anything else. I'm interested only in expressing basic human emotions – tragedy, ecstasy, doom and so on . . . The people who weep before my pictures are having the same religious experience as I had when I painted them.[10]

It is probably for this reason that Rothko toned down the bright palette of his early Colour Field paintings, preferring to work instead in blacks, browns, greys and deep maroons to avoid the pictures being appreciated simply for their decorative qualities.

The goal of the Colour Field group had nothing to do with a sumptuous display of colour, but was connected to the idea of the sublime, so treasured by the nineteenth-century Romantics. How to describe it? As a sense of vastness, of solitude, silence and infinity – which is precisely why the Colour Field painters found it necessary to expand their works to awesome proportions. Rothko stressed that this vast scale was not an attempt to be 'grandiose and pompous', but quite the opposite: 'because I want to be very intimate and human'. Only through such extremes could the painting act directly on the viewer. One can find the same thing in the high-keyed abstract colour compositions of Sol LeWitt, painted directly on to entire gallery walls so as to merge with the architecture in an all-encompassing experience.

Yet this almost religious intensity of feeling in the Colour Field group did not make for very practical men. Rothko evinces little sign of any system for organizing colour, for all that he is working with nothing else; and Newman and Still display nothing more theoretical than an occasional play of primaries. Fortunately Rothko had an innate sensitivity for colour, but Still has been accused (and I will not deny it) of being a rather poor colourist, something of a drawback for a Colour Field painter. Here indeed is, as John Gage puts it, an art of 'colour without theory'. There is nothing so terrible in that, yet I cannot help but suspect that it is again something of a precondition for a distancing from materials. Rothko himself confessed that he was 'divorced from the conventions of a thousand years of painting' – with consequences that were, in at least one notable instance, disastrous.

Rothko's relationship with his materials is ambivalent. On the one hand, his studio techniques have something of the medieval about them: here he is, half-way up a ladder, employing assistants to help with the brushwork on monumental religious works (such as those commissioned for the Rothko Chapel in Houston), mixing up buckets of paints from dry pigment, boiled rabbit-skin size and egg. His experiments in materials seem to have been partly guided by the practical manuals of Max Doerner and Cennini Cennino. And yet he evinces a wish to escape from the constraints of the paint's physicality: he thinned his paints so much that the unprimed canvases were as much stained as painted, and according to Dore Ashton, a close associate, 'Rothko was always aware that his means fell short of his vision because his means were material.' Nowhere was that vision more compromised than in the huge mural canvases painted as a gift to Harvard University.

The Harvard murals are perhaps one of the most stark reminders of what can happen when untested modern materials find their way to painters with a reckless disregard for technical matters. Rothko gave them to the university in 1962. Within five years they were deteriorating fast; by 1979 they were ruined, and removed from view. Their worth was estimated at around $100,000 at the time of completion; today one suspects Rothko would have sanctioned their destruction. This was partly the result of poor planning and maintenance by the university, but one cannot overlook, in conservator Marjorie Cohn's words, 'Rothko's complete ignorance of, or indifference to, the most basic requirements for permanent painting'.

As always, Rothko chose the colours for the Harvard murals (two panels and a triptych) with great care: he said that they re-enact Christ's Passion, with the dark tones representing His suffering on the Cross and the lighter tones His Resurrection. The predominant colours are dark pink and crimson. But you would never know that now: they have turned light blue.

Rothko made his crimsons from mixtures of synthetic ultramarine, cerulean blue, titanium white, and two modern organic colours: Naphthol Red and Lithol Red. The former, an azo colour (see page 250), has lasted well; the latter is dreadfully fugitive in light, and has faded like the worst of medieval red lakes. It is now not accepted in artists' materials, but was probably widespread in cheap paints of the 1960s. In all probability, Rothko did not even know what the colourants were in his reds. His indifference to materials is often illustrated by his remark to conservator Elizabeth Jones that, while painting the murals, 'when he ran out of paint he had gone downstairs to the Woolworth's and bought more paint – he didn't know what kind it was.'[11] Rothko's son suggests this was merely a mischievous quip – and there seems to be no evidence of household paints in the works. But there is a deeper truth in the jest, if that is all it was.

This is not to imply, however, that Rothko was ignorant of the risks of light-induced fading: he expressed this concern when he saw how the room in which the murals were stationed, a function room of the Holyoke Center at Harvard, received full sunlight. But in general Rothko's insistence on subdued lighting for displaying his works (as is used for the 'Seagram' murals at the Tate Modern in London) was due more to his view that over-bright light washed out the intensity of colours and prevented them from displaying their subtle vibrations. The Harvard authorities, meanwhile, assumed that they could treat the murals as no different from the oil paintings of past presidents that hung on the walls. The Holyoke room was used for meals and social events, adding food stains, rips and graffiti to the damage wrought by the years.

Rothko's experimental technique of applying thinned distemper paints, worked over with thinly brushed oils, raw egg, and synthetic paints, has also left its mark on the Rothko Chapel murals (1965), which are disfigured with whitish streaks and cracking (perhaps due to the swelling of undissolved resin crystals). But at least the synthetic alizarin-based reds used in these dark maroon monochromes have retained their intensity. Elsewhere Rothko uses reliable inorganic reds – cadmium red and iron oxide – and his works executed in acrylics on paper and board have lost little of their glory. That, it seems, may be as much a matter of good fortune as anything else: when Rothko wanted a red, he looked at the hue and not at the composition.

He might have done better to heed the advice of Robert Motherwell (1915–91), in some sense the intellectual leader of the Abstract Expressionists: 'The pure red of which certain abstractionists speak', he said in 1944, 'does not exist . . . Any red is rooted in blood, glass,

wine, hunters' caps and a thousand other concrete phenomena.'
Motherwell thus speaks for the 'dirty' side of the movement, for
the sensualists rather than the transcendentalists. He saw that the
'search for the subject', which all abstractionists must confront, can
be conducted through the physical process of painting itself, which
entails an appreciation of materials: their liquidity or solidity, their
crystallinity and translucency. Commenting on an exhibition of
Pollock's, he said, 'since painting is his thought's medium, the
resolution [of the search for the true subject] must grow out of
the process of painting itself'. This is precisely what Pollock believed:
that the work has 'a life of its own' that would reveal itself through
his handling of materials.

The paintings of Willem de Kooning (1904–97) share with
Pollock's an unmistakable physicality that speaks of the artist's sensitivity to materials. He used a variety of paint media, including oils
and cheap enamels intended for sign painting, and sometimes
enhanced the texture with the addition of plaster of Paris and ground
glass. Some of his works are bright and high-keyed; others have
colours dirty with rubbed charcoal. His predilection for modifying
and reworking the paint surface led him during the 1950s to abandon
alkyd-based paints for the same reason that others favoured them:
their quick drying times.

The golden veil

Kenneth Noland (1924–) and Morris Louis (1912–72) were part of
the group that, in the 1950s, inherited the mantle of the Abstract
Expressionists Pollock, Rothko and Motherwell under the cumbersome label of Post-Painterly Abstractionism. Noland and Louis, like
Rothko, were interested in making colour both luminous and
numinous by achieving a stain-like effect with thin washes. Together
they visited Helen Frankenthaler's studio in 1953, where the forty-
one-year-old Louis appears to have experienced something of an
epiphany. In Frankenthaler's very thin layers of highly diluted oil
paint, which produce a water-colour-like finish in *Mountains and
Sea* (1952), Louis perceived a staining effect that galvanized his art.
But he and Noland were wary of saturating unprimed canvas with

dilute oils, fearing that the paint medium would rot the fibres. So they both welcomed Bocour's acrylic solution paints in the 1940s because of the way that the Magna paints would hold their colour intensity even when thinned to the consistency of water.

Louis created his series of 'Veil' paintings in the late 1950s by pouring highly thinned paint down the canvas. Repeated applications in a range of bright colours created the appearance of translucent, gauzy curtains in which all the colours mixed to a kind of warm golden-brown (Plate 14.3). In these compositions Louis is using paint but is not really painting: the colour impregnates the cloth as if in a dyeing process.

In his 'Unfurled' series of the 1960s, Louis retained the pouring technique but used it with greater control and without superimposing and mixing colours. He combined pouring with a swabbing method to guide the paint into diagonal bands of colour, leaving much of the canvas blank. Now that the colours were on display individually, Louis became more concerned about their quality. His palette of some twenty or so colours was provided directly by Bocour, whom Louis entreated to make the colours afresh each time and to clean the machines carefully between the preparation of each colour. The extreme dilution of the acrylic binder meant, however, that it could be difficult to obtain an even paint surface – there is evidence of clumping of pigment particles in some of these works.

Whereas the images of Rothko and Newman, and to some extent Louis's 'Veils', exude a certain mystery and atmospheric effect, Kenneth Noland and Frank Stella wanted painting to be more straightforward, free from these 'extra' qualities. No miracles, they insist – what you see is what you get. Theirs came to be called the Hard Edge school, exemplified by the stark Target paintings of Noland (Plate 14.4).

In 1969 Noland said: 'I wanted to have color be the origin of the painting. I was trying to neutralize the layout, the shape, the composition, in order to get at the color . . . I wanted to make color the generating force.'[12] There would, in other words, be no *disegno* at all, nor any 'meaning' as such – simply paint for paint's sake. This is a distinctly North American idea (and draw from it what cultural

conclusions you will). Painters from the Old World could never
assimilate it, which may be why John Hoyland found his own
approach to the Hard Edge style ill-received by the Americans he
admired. Whereas the minimalism evident in the works of Stella
and Noland has some kind of precedent in Kasimir Malevich's white
monochrome 'Suprematist' paintings from the 1910s or Yves Klein's
blue monochromes in the 1950s, Malevich and Klein insisted on
a philosophical interpretation: paint as idea. For the American
minimalists, it was just paint.

To Noland, tutored by colour empiricist Josef Albers, even the
paint was to some extent an unfortunate necessity, a cumbersome
layer that represented the only way he knew to get the colour on
to the surface. 'The thing is to get that colour down on the thinnest
conceivable surface, a surface sliced into the air as if by a razor. It's
all colour and surface. That's all.' No wonder he so appreciated the
flatness and high covering strength of the new acrylics.

Yet despite his insistence on the elimination of structure, Noland
was forced to employ some kind of design. His was a minimalism
not of the monochrome but of colour interactions, and with more
than one colour in the picture there had to be borders. His solution
was to use 'neutral' forms devoid (or so he intended) of emotional
content: first the concentric circles of his Target series, then nested
chevrons and parallel stripes. This was nothing new – Albers's
textbook was full of images based on nested squares, and he articulated the intention that motivated Noland: 'For me, color is the
means of my idiom. It's automatic. I'm not paying "homage to a
square". It's only the dish I serve my craziness about color in.'[13]
Within these dishes, marked out with masking tape, Noland served
up chromatic meals of quiet restraint. The colours might be in full
saturation, but the relationships had none of the glory of, say,
Orphism. Often only related colours would be juxtaposed – blue
against green, orange against red and pink, dissonances punctuated
only here and there with a sudden contrast.

Frank Stella's early work in the 1950s was a quite different affair.
It was typically monochrome, a single colour threaded with a linear,
repetitive design (Plate 14.5). He is credited with a materialistic
approach, with placing special emphasis on the materials; yet he did

so simply by cleaving to the idea that the painter does not *need* anything special in the way of materials. As we saw earlier, colour for Stella was (at least initially) at the mercy of commerce: 'I just took what the regular paint stores had to offer.'

On one occasion, what they had to offer was a metallic copper paint used to prevent barnacle growth on boat hulls. Another time it was silvery aluminium paint used for radiators. These metallic paints were, if you like, beyond colour – they had been manufactured not because of their visual effect but because of the other properties that the suspended metal flakes conveyed. By renouncing colour, Stella took it somewhere new.

But by the 1970s, Stella's work had altered radically. He was still as insouciant as ever towards materials, and took to using alkyd household or industrial paints in place of acrylic emulsions, which he saw as 'too sophisticated or something'. These alkyds were manufactured by the Benjamin Moore company, and Stella generally used the primaries and secondaries straight from the tin: 'There was no attempt to adjust the color, it was just a mechanical use of their colors.'

Yet he began to combine these colours in works that were half painting, half sculpture: 'relief paintings' with the appearance of graffiti-daubed found objects, decorated in strong pinks, reds and greens (Plate 14.6). He designed his shapes on paper and then had them cut by a metal-working company from aluminium alloy honeycomb used in the aircraft industry. He covered these objects not only with paint but with a magpie-like assortment of substances: sequins, glitter, ground glass.

What prompted this change? Curiously, Stella's increasing eclecticism of materials was stimulated by a sense that his previous minimalist style was too 'material' – too much enslaved by pure paint. This, he suggested, was the legacy of Kandinsky, who never quite succeeded in converting paint to space, and so ended up 'filling up the landscape with pigment'. Picasso, said Stella,

saw the danger . . . of materiality – the danger that the new, open, atmospheric space of abstraction would be clogged up and weighed down by the mass of its only real ingredient: pigment. Picasso's concern articulated the fear that abstraction, instead of giving us pure painting, would merely give us pure paint – something we could find on store shelves as well as on museum walls.[14]

The problem with Kandinsky, Stella suggests, is a consequence of his failure to accept that he was working not with pure colour (as he might have preferred) but with a physical material that needs to be understood and manipulated to one's will. 'He never seems to push the paint as hard [as Picasso]', Stella laments, 'he never seems to penetrate the surface as successfully.' It is a charge all too plausible when one considers the mystical, anti-materialistic atmosphere at the Bauhaus in the 1920s. Picasso and Malevich, on the other hand, 'in their acceptance of materiality . . . both came to terms with the surface of painting . . . They troweled pigment onto a self-sustaining surface which they had willed into being.'[15] For Stella, then, paint is something that must be overcome.

Many modern colourists have sought to do that by moving beyond paint; and a thorough survey of contemporary artistic colour would have to do the same. The works of Donald Judd and Anish Kapoor, for example, might be properly regarded as sculpture. But Judd deems himself a painter, and traces his roots back to Delacroix and the painterly colour theorists Chevreul and Rood, and most of all to the De Stijl painters. Enamel paint covers some of his minimalist structures of wood and aluminium, but his palette also embraces coloured plastics, metals, and the light of coloured reflections. Kapoor brings a mirrored metal sheen into the domain of colour. The American artist James Turrell composes from a play of coloured light, including the pure blue of day and the spangled firmament of night which show through the openings in his installation works. Other artists work with the gaudy glare of coloured fluorescent lights, or the translucent glow of light-boxes, or the precise rainbow of light-emitting diodes (to which chemists added a blue glow only in the 1990s), making scenes more genuinely radiant than the Impressionists could ever have dreamed of. Each of these media has, of course, its own associated technology with its own histories, stories and limitations. Each replays the dance of cause and effect between scientific innovation and artistic expression.

New colours

But it is time to come back finally to pure paint – for innovation in colour did not cease throughout the twentieth century. There was still plenty of room for improvement.

In the mid-nineteenth century, George Field was able to test virtually all the materials that brought colour to the painter's palette. Today the list of colourants manufactured industrially covers 9,000 pages in nine volumes of the *Colour Index International*, the bible of dyers and colourists. Here these bright, synthetic earths have no fanciful names but are catalogued uncompromisingly by hue, use and a number denoting the chemical composition: CI Vat Red 13 CI No. 70320, CI Food Yellow 4 CI No. 19140. The ambiguities of older terminology are banished, and undoubtedly some of the magic goes with them. About 600 of these materials are pigments, while over 9,000 are dyes, attesting to the might of organic chemistry for tailoring colour to precise ends.

Yet a sociologist might draw some interesting conclusions from the fact that the pigment now produced in far and away the greatest quantities is white. A glance at any street or commercial building interior will remind us that this 'non-colour' is the most widely preferred veneer for our synthetic environment. (Of course, white is also used extensively for moderating the saturation of other pigments to a tone considered, these days, gentler on the eye.) David Batchelor has much fun at the expense of the fashionable minimalist's taste for blank white interiors:

The host was an Anglo-American art collector, and the party was in the collector's house . . . Inside this house was a whole world, a very particular kind of world, a very clean, clear and orderly universe . . . There is a kind of white that is more than white, and this was that kind of white. There is a kind of white that repels everything that is inferior to it, and that is almost everything . . . This white was aggressively white. It did its work on everything around it, and nothing escaped.[16]

Yet this kind of white, the foremost of today's pigments, did not exist before the twentieth century. Lead white was a major

pre-industrial product, and despite the emergence of zinc white as
an artist's colour in the nineteenth century, the lead pigment
remained pre-eminent in an industrial context because it was so
much cheaper and, in oils, more opaque and quicker-drying. In
1900 lead white still commanded virtually all of the market for
white pigment. But between 1916 and 1918, chemicals companies
in Norway and the USA discovered how to manufacture and purify
an opaque white oxide of the metal titanium, an element identified
in 1796 by the German chemist Martin Klaproth.

Titanium dioxide, or titania, has twice the covering power of
lead white and is extremely stable. Once the manufacturing difficulties were resolved, titania quickly became the dominant white
pigment: by 1945 it accounted for 80 per cent of the market. As a
result, the incidence of fatal lead poisoning from preparation of lead
white fell: there were thirty-eight cases in the UK in 1910, none
in 1950. Today most white paint of any sort is 'titanium white'.

But twentieth-century colour makes up in variety for what it
lacks in breadth of application. In the 1950s a completely new class
of pigments was introduced: the richly coloured and highly stable
organic compounds called quinacridones. These are 'true organic
pigments': powdered solids resembling ground minerals but composed solely of organic molecules.

The first true organic pigments, based on salts of azo dyes, in fact
date back to the 1880s. Because these coloured organic compounds
did not have to be attached to inorganic particles to make lake
pigments, it became possible to apply to pigment manufacture
the increasingly rational 'synthesis of colour' that evolved from the
synthetic dye industry. The first azo pigment, tartrazine yellow, was
patented in 1884.

Discovered in 1896, quinacridones took much longer to emerge
as pigments. In 1935 a German chemist named H. Liebermann (not
to be confused with the Liebermann of alizarin synthesis, who died
in 1914) synthesized the first quinacridone suitable for use as a
pigment. Yet it was not until twenty years later that chemists at
DuPont in the USA began to look for ways to make them on a
commercial basis. Quinacridone pigments were marketed from
1958, offering colours from orange-red to violet. They were quickly

adopted by the New York Abstract Expressionists, who welcomed the strong hues. Many artists' paints are now coloured with quinacridones.

Were it not for these organic pigments, one might reasonably fear for the future of red. Cadmium red has become the canonical rich scarlet of the modern age, a colour unmatched by any lake pigments for covering power and light-fastness. Cadmium is a toxic heavy metal – but only mildly so, and the cadmium colours present no great hazard to the painter. All the same, concerns about the health effects of heavy metals in the environment generally, highlighted by the problems caused by lead and mercury pollution, are leading to tighter restrictions on products that incorporate these elements. The complete prohibition of cadmium in paints has been extensively debated. It is not yet clear whether this will happen; but if it does, quinacridones will be the most promising replacements. Indeed, paints labelled as Cadmium Red or Cadmium Orange are now often pigmented with these organic molecules – the name, like others through the centuries, has been transformed from a signifier of composition to one of hue.

We can be confident that new alternatives will continue to appear.[17] In 1983 the first patent was taken out on another class of organic pigments, called diketopyrrolo-pyrroles or DPPs. The light-absorbing organic molecule from which DPPs are derived was discovered in 1974. Initially a very minor reaction product, it was developed into a commercially viable compound by chemist Abdul Iqbal at Ciba-Geigy in Basel. The DPP pigments, which range between red and orange, are still costly; Ciba-Geigy manufactures them primarily for use in the automobile industry. No doubt this larger industrial concern will, according to the age-old pattern, eventually bring the colours to the artists' market. Painters will get their colours for the same reason as always: because chemistry has many other consumers besides.

A tradition of revolution

But will anyone still be painting in ten or twenty years' time? It is not a fashionable art. Painters have become a relative novelty among the candidates for the much-hyped Turner Prize, awarded annually in Britain for young artists. (When I recall that the first Turner prize, in 1984, was awarded to an exponent of sterile, though no doubt impeccably post-modern, photorealist painting, I can reassure myself that it is no litmus test of lasting art.) The names of no new young painters are on everyone's lips (at least, not for longer than a few weeks). We are still blessed with our Frank Auerbachs, our Howard Hodgkins, our Lucian Freuds; but do we have our Klees, our Goyas, our Raphaels?

I must take care that I do not begin to sound like Pliny, lamenting the passing of the Golden Age when Apelles held his brushes. Or perhaps a Pliny in reverse, bemoaning that few now know how best to use strong, brilliant colour rather than the greyish mud, not even Rembrandt-brown, that is spread over many a contemporary canvas. The truth is that we had more than enough greatness in twentieth-century painting, and what does it matter that the final years lost their sparkle? Who now, for example, complains about the fallow time at the end of the seventeenth century, when Vermeer, Velázquez, Rubens and Rembrandt had passed on and none had stepped up to take their place?

And so where will the next great colourists take us, and what will be on their palette? Perhaps conventional pigmentation will indeed take second place, as the metallic flakes and fluorescent splashes of Stella and the Pop Artists become supplemented with new possibilities: pearlescent colours (John Hoyland has used them already), or pigments that change hue as we change our viewing angle. Both are manufactured as automobile pigments. Perhaps artists will use liquid crystals that change colour with temperature, or that offer an iridescent rainbow all at once.

Well, maybe. Certainly, I think all these media will be used – because that is the way of art, to find ways to take advantage of what technology offers. That, I hope, is the one central message of this book: technology opens new doors for artists. And of course technologists cannot then prescribe which ones the artists will go through, or what they will get up to on the other side. 'The painter of the future', said van Gogh, 'is a colourist such as has never been seen before.' I do hope so. The delicious irony is that paint manufacturers, colour theorists and colour-makers, practically inclined craftspeople, have traditionally been conventionally minded folk, offering up gleaming new tools into the hands of visionaries who go and do something crazy with them, break the mould, create a revolution. Long may it last.

Notes

I. THE EYE OF THE BEHOLDER

Epigraphs:

W. Kandinsky, *Über das Geistige in der Kunst* (1912), transl. M. T. H. Sadler as *The Art of Spiritual Harmony* (Constable and Co., London, 1914) and reprinted as *Concerning the Spiritual in Art* (Dover, New York, 1977).

Brassaï, *Conversations avec Picasso* (Paris, 1964), transl. F. Price as *Picasso and Company* (Doubleday, Garden City, NY, 1966).

1. E. H. Gombrich, *Art and Illusion* (Phaidon Press, London, 1977), 5th edn, p. 30.

2. A. Callen, *Techniques of the Impressionists* (New Burlington Books, London, 1987), p. 6.

3. Birren presumably means to refer to cobalt-containing smalt, an inferior blue that he thereby fails to distinguish from the utterly different 'cobalt blue' in the palettes of the Impressionists.

4. B. Riley, in T. Lamb and J. Bourriau (eds), *Colour: Art and Science* (Cambridge University Press, Cambridge, 1995, pp. 31–2. (Minor alterations at the request of the author.)

5. Quoted in A. Blunt, *Artistic Theory in Italy 1450–1600* (Oxford University Press, Oxford, 1962), p. 28.

6. L. B. Alberti, *On Painting*, transl. C. Grayson (Penguin, London, 1991), p. 63.

7. Here Leonardo is indulging in a favourite sport of Renaissance Humanists: to argue for the superiority of one art over another. Leonardo's contemporary Bellini can be found, for example, praising painting over poetry. Renaissance scholars found such debates, called *paragones* by the Italians, in Classical texts, and – because everything Classical was good – they sought to mimic them.

8. Alberti, *On Painting*, p. 61.

9. L. M. Principe, *The Aspiring Adept. Robert Boyle and his Alchemical Quest* (Princeton University Press, Princeton, NJ, 1998), p. 33.

10. Le Corbusier and Amédée Ozenfant, 'Purism' (1920), in R. L. Herbert (ed.), *Modern Artists on Art: Ten Unabridged Essays* (New Brunswick, NJ, 1964).

11. Others have made an elegant case for these connections, notably Martin Kemp in his splendid book *The Science of Art*. But Kemp openly acknowledges that he leaves precisely the gap which I hope to fill: he omits 'any sustained discussion of the way in which the chemistry and manufacture of new pigments affected the parameters of illusionistic imitation in painting', while highlighting the importance of this consideration.

12. J. Kristeva, 'Giotto's Joy', in *Desire in Language*, transl. T. Gora, A. Jardine and L. S. Roudiez (Oxford University Press, Oxford, 1982).

13. Le Corbusier, 'The Decorative Art of Today', in *Essential Le Corbusier: L'Esprit Nouveau Articles*, transl. J. Dunnett (Oxford University Press, Oxford, 1998), p. 135.

14. C. Blanc, quoted in C. A. Riley, *Color Codes* (University Press of New England, Hanover, NH, 1995), p. 6.

15. D. Batchelor, *Chromophobia* (Reaktion Books, London, 2000).

16. Y. Klein, quoted in S. Stich, *Yves Klein*, exhibition catalogue (Hayward Gallery, London, 1995).

17. O. Sacks, *Uncle Tungsten: Memories of a Chemical Boyhood* (Knopf, New York, 2001).

18. P. Levi and T. Regge, *Conversations* (I. B. Tauris & Co., London, 1989), p. 59.

19. M. Platnauer, 'Greek colour perception', *Classical Quarterly*, XV (1921).

20. Alberti, *On Painting*, p. 85.

21. Ibid., p. 84.

22. W. Kandinsky, *Reminiscences* (1913), in K. C. Lindsey and P. Vargo (eds), *Kandinsky: Complete Writings on Art* (G. K. Hall & Co., Boston, 1982), vol. 1, pp. 369–70.

23. Kandinsky, *Concerning the Spiritual in Art*, p. 25.

24. Ibid., pp. 38–41.

25. Riley, in *Colour: Art and Science*, p. 63.

2. PLUCKING THE RAINBOW

Epigraphs:

J. Dubuffet (1973), 'L'Homme du commun à l'avrage' (The Common Man at Work). Quoted in *Colour since Matisse*, an exhibition of French painting, Edinburgh International Festival (Trefoil Books, London, 1985).

C. Blanc, *Grammaire des arts du dessin* (1867), transl. as *Grammar of Painting and Engraving*.

P. Guston, quoted in B. Clearwater, *Mark Rothko: Works on Paper* (Hudson Hills Press, New York, 1984), p. 11.

1. Isaac Newton, *Opticks* (London, 1706), reprinted by Dover (New York, 1952).

2. Ibid.

3. Wolfgang von Goethe, *Die Farbenlehre* (1810), transl. C. L. Eastlake as *Theory of Colours* (1840).

4. H. Maguire, *Earth and Ocean: The Terrestrial World in Byzantine Art* (1987), p. 30.

5. Why a change in *speed* instigates a change in *direction* is subtle. Basically, the light rays take the quickest route from A to B; and the kinked route is, given the speed difference, more rapidly traversed than the straight route.

6. Newton, *Opticks*.

7. Aristotle, *On Colours*, 793b, transl. Hett. See Chapter 3, note 14.

8. Pigments on a painted disc absorb light too, so it may not be clear why Maxwell's spinning discs gave additive rather than subtractive mixing. The answer is that the coloured segments of the disc are not all absorbing at the same place and time. At any location on the disc, just one segment is absorbing at each instant. The part of the white-light spectrum that it removes is replaced a moment later when a differently coloured segment covers that spot. The entire spectrum is thus delivered to the eye: not instantaneously, but in such rapid succession that it makes no difference.

9. G. Field, *Chromatography* (Winsor and Newton, London, 1869).

10. Quoted in F. Birren, *History of Color in Painting* (Van Nostrand Reinhold, New York, 1965).

11. In 1685 the mathematician and painter Philippe de la Hire commented

that 'Painters know hues whose brilliance is much greater by candle-light than by daylight; there is also a number of hues which are very bright by daylight but lose their beauty entirely by candlelight.' From *Dissertation sur les differens accidens de la Vue* (1685).

12. It is not, however, always a straightforward matter to deduce from this spectrum what response the reflected light will induce in the eye and brain.

13. M. Sahlins, 'Colours and Cultures', *Semiotica* 16 (1976), p. 12.

3. THE FORGE OF VULCAN

Epigraphs:

Pliny, *Natural History*; quoted in V. J. Bruno, *Form and Colour in Greek Painting* (Thames and Hudson, London, 1977), p. 68.

R. Davies, *What's Bred in the Bone* (Penguin, London, 1986), p. 292.

T. Bardwell, *The Practice of Painting* (1756).

1. O. Jones, *Athenaeum*, 21 December 1850, p. 1,348.

2. None the less, it had its admirers; the *Illustrated London News* said approvingly that 'the whole produces an effect which is to architectural display what the vista of the grove and the glade of the forest is to the views presented by natural scenery'.

3. The British biologist and science popularizer Lewis Wolpert is not the first to state that 'Technology is not science.' But his book *The Unnatural Nature of Science*, in which this claim appears, contains a useful idea, which makes it all the more important that this fallacy should not hitch a ride on the coat-tails of a truth. Wolpert says, 'The final product of science is an idea . . . the final product of technology is an artefact.' This alone excludes most of chemistry (old and new) from science. Wolpert's argument, however, makes essentially no reference to chemistry – whether through ignorance or for the sake of a tidy thesis, I do not know. Why the 'wrong' ideas of the Greek philosophers (who used them to make nothing useful) should be seen as intrinsically more scientific than the 'wrong' ideas of, say, the medieval alchemists (who were abundant and effective manufacturers) is unexplained.

4. A modern tube of Naples yellow is likely to contain a mixture of more recent pigments, particularly cadmium yellow.

5. A recent illustration of this is the discovery of synthetic laurionite and phosgenite, complex compounds of lead and chlorine, in cosmetic powders from ancient Egypt dating from between 2000 and 1200 BC. They were probably made by reacting lead monoxide with sodium chloride (common salt). See P. Walter *et al.*, 'Making make-up in Ancient Egypt', *Nature*, 397 (1999), pp. 483–4.

6. Pliny, *Natural History*, XXXVI, xvi, 191.

7. Quoted in W. S. Ellis, *Glass* (Avon Books, New York, 1998), pp. 4–5.

8. A sixteenth-century innovation, made possible by the discovery of nitric acid, was the use of gold to make the finest red glass. A mixture of nitric and hydrochloric acids, made by adding sal ammoniac (ammonium chloride) to nitric acid, will dissolve gold: it is the potent *aqua regia* of the alchemists. The metal forms a soluble chloride salt, but can be recovered by evaporating the liquid and heating the residue. In glass-making, gold was precipitated from gold chloride solution as tiny particles, which scatter light strongly to impart a translucent red hue. This kind of chemical processing required considerable knowledge and practical skill, both derived from the use of *aqua regia* to dissolve gold in the refining process of gold mining, where it had to be separated from silver. It is not surprising, in view of the alchemical association of gold with the colour red, that this process acquired considerable significance for alchemists.

9. Pliny, *Natural History*, XXXV, 42.

10. By the Middle Ages any whitish mineral mordant tended to be called alum, regardless of its chemical composition. The Greeks and Romans used primarily a potassium-containing alum mineral found in volcanic regions.

11. Isaiah 1:18.

12. To zoologists the scale insects of the kermes family were previously (and in some cases still are) denoted by the genus *Coccus*.

13. Theophrastus (transl. Hill), quoted in G. Agricola, *De re metallica*, transl. H. C. and L. H. Hoover (Dover, New York, 1950), p. 440. Vitruvius, Dioscorides and Pliny also describe the process.

14. This volume (*De coloribus*) is traditionally attributed to Aristotle, but there is now a widespread belief that its true author was his disciple

Theophrastus. In any event, we can be sure that it gives a fair picture of Aristotle's thought.

15. Quoted in D. Thompson, *The Materials and Techniques of Medieval Painting* (Dover, New York, 1956), p. 125.

4. SECRET RECIPES

Epigraphs:

Theophilus, *On Divers Arts*, transl. J. G. Hawthorne and C. S. Smith (Dover, New York, 1979), pp. 12–13.

G. Duthuit, *The Fauvist Painters* (Wittenborn, Schultz, Inc., New York, 1950).

1. Later revisionist historians of science have portrayed *The Sceptical Chymist* as an anti-alchemical tract. It is now clear that Boyle was instead attempting to separate what he regarded as 'good' alchemy from 'bad'.

2. Paracelsus, 'The Treasure of Treasures for Alchemists'. This appears in *The Water-Stone of the Wise Men: Describing the matter of, and manner how to attain the universal Tincture*, which was published by J. H. Oxon in London, 1659, 'to be sold at the Black Spred Eagle, at the West end of St Pauls'.

3. Albertus Magnus, *Book of Minerals*, transl. D. Wyckoff (Clarendon Press, Oxford, 1967), IV, i, 2, pp. 207–8.

4. D. V. Thompson, *The Materials and Techniques of Medieval Painting* (Dover, New York, 1956), p. 106.

5. Theophilus, *On Divers Arts*, p. 119.

6. Boyle says the process was related to him by a Dutch or Belgian refiner; the discovery must surely have stemmed from the mining practice of separating silver from copper.

7. C. S. Smith and J. G. Hawthorne (ed. and transl.), *Mappae clavicula: A Little Key to the World of Medieval Techniques*. In *Transactions of the American Philosophical Society* (American Philosophical Society, Philadelphia), new ser., 64 (1974), pt. 4, p. 28.

8. M. P. Merrifield (ed. and transl.), *De coloribus et artibus Romanorum*. In *Original Treatises on the Arts of Painting* (1849), reprinted by Dover

(New York, 1967). Heraclius' tract was among those unearthed and translated into English in the 1840s by Mary Merrifield, who was commissioned by the British government to collect Italian manuscripts relating to the early history of the technical aspects of painting. Merrifield was one of those rare Victorian women who succeeded in overcoming the chauvinism of her age to win the respect of the prevailing patriarchy, and her contribution to the technical history of painting is profound. An artist, a scholar of distinction, a mother of at least three children and reputedly 'a forceful character with an agreeable sense of humour', she was the first to translate Cennino's book into English in 1844, as well as bringing a number of other important compilations of medieval recipes to a wide audience.

9. Theophilus, *On Divers Arts*, pp. 11–12.

10. Cennino Cennini, *Il Libro dell'Arte* (c. 1390), transl. D. V. Thompson (*The Craftsman's Handbook*) (Dover, New York, 1960), p. 3.

11. G. B. Armenini, *De veri precetti della pittura* (1587). See W. G. Constable, *The Painter's Workshop* (Oxford University Press, London, 1954), p. 66.

12. Kaspar Scheit, *Die fröhliche Heimfahrt* (*The Joyous Journey Home*) (1552). Quoted in A. Burmester and C. Krekel, 'The relationship between Albrecht Dürer's palette and fifteenth/sixteenth-century pharmacy price lists: the use of azurite and ultramarine', in A. Roy and P. Smith (eds), *Contributions to the IIC Dublin Congress, 7–11 September 1998: Painting Techniques: History, Materials and Studio Practice* (International Institute for Conservation of Historic and Artistic Works, London, 1998), p. 101.

13. Cennino Cennini, *The Craftsman's Handbook*, pp. 84–5.

14. Ibid., pp. 101–2.

15. Heraclius, *De coloribus et artibus Romanorum*.

5. MASTERS OF LIGHT AND SHADOW

Epigraphs:
1 B. Alberti, *On Painting*, transl. C. Grayson (Penguin, London, 1991), p. 85.

1. Alberti, *On Painting*, p. 87.
2. Giorgio Vasari, *Lives of the Artists* (1568), transl. G. Bull (Penguin, London, 1965), p. 284.
3. Ibid., p. 360
4. Theophilus, *On Divers Arts*, transl. J. G. Hawthorne and C. S. Smith (Dover, New York, 1979), pp. 27–8, 32.
5. Giorgio Vasari, introduction to *Lives of the Artists* (1550), transl. L. S. Maclehose as *Vasari on Technique* (Dover, New York, 1960), pp. 226, 230.
6. G. Birelli, *Opera* (Florence, 1601), bk 2, pp. 369–70.
7. C. Merret, *The Art of Glass* (1662), translation of Antonio Neri's *L'Arte Vetraria* (1612).
8. Johann Mathesius, *Sarepta oder Bergpostill* (1562), quoted in G. Agricola, *De re metallica* (1556), transl. H. C. and L. H. Hoover (Dover, New York, 1950), p. 214.
9. Alberti, *On Painting*, p. 85.
10. Quoted in M. Doerner, *The Materials of the Artist* (Harcourt Brace and Co., Orlando, FL, 1949), p. 342.
11. One should be wary, however, of casting Venice and Florence as sixteenth-century rivals. This seems to be largely a nineteenth-century fiction that does not reflect the perceptions of the time. None the less, Vasari is partly to blame. It is ironic that he places the least theoretically inclined of the Florentine masters, Michelangelo, at odds with the Venetian Titian, who shared his intuitive approach to painting. In Vasari's *Lives of the Artists*, Titian receives grudging praise laced with veiled criticisms of those who have not learned to draw well, while Vasari's compatriot Michelangelo is the embodiment of all that is desirable in art.
12. L. Lazzarini, 'Indagini preliminari di laboratorio', in E. L. Ragni and G. Agosti (eds), *Il polittico Averoldi di Tiziano restaurato* (Brescia, 1991), p. 176.
13. The modern painter Frank Auerbach commonly covers his canvases with thick, sculpted impastos of earth colours. But for his version of *Bacchus and Ariadne*, commissioned in 1971 in response to Titian's picture, he was forced to take up an uncharacteristic palette of primary hues. The inspiration for Auerbach's translation is recognizable mainly from its colours rather than its figures. Titian's realgar is reproduced with a strong modern orange.

6. OLD GOLD

Epigraphs:

Quoted in M. Doerner, *The Materials of the Artist* (Harcourt Brace & Co., Orlando, FL, 1949) as 'after Descamps', who attributes the remark to Rubens.

Ibid., p. 371.

1. F. Zuccaro, *Idea de' Pittori, Scultori e Architetti* (1607), bk 2, ch. 6.
2. E. Norgate, *Miniatura or the Art of Limning* (1627–8), quoted in R. D. Harley, *Artists' Pigments c.1600–1835* (Butterworths, London, 1982), 2nd edn.
3. Leonardo da Vinci, *Treatise on Painting*, ed. and transl. A. P. McMahon (Princeton University Press, Princeton, NJ, 1956).
4. Ibid.
5. C. S. Wood, *Albrecht Altdorfer and the Origins of Landscape* (Reaktion Books, London, 1993), p. 63.
6. R. de Piles, *Dialogue sur le Coloris* (1699). Quoted in E. H. Gombrich, *Art and Illusion* (Phaidon, London, 1977), 5th edn, p. 265.
7. Quoted in J. Kirby and D. Saunders, 'Sixteenth- to eighteenth-century green colours in landscape and flower paintings: composition and deterioration', in A. Roy and P. Smith (eds), *Contributions to the Dublin Congress, 7–11 September 1998: Painting Techniques: History, Materials and Studio Practice* (International Institute for Conservation of Historic and Artistic Works, London, 1998), p. 155.
8. H. Peacham, *The Compleat Gentleman* (London, 1622).
9. There has been a recent claim that the colours in this painting are in fact too garish for it to be a work of Rubens at all. The National Gallery emphatically denies this suggestion.

7. THE PRISMATIC METALS

Epigraphs:

W. Cullen (*c.* 1766). See A. L. Donovan, *Philosophical Chemistry in the Scottish Enlightenment* (Edinburgh University Press, Edinburgh, 1975), p. 98.

J. K. Huysmans, 'Turner et Goya', *Certains* (1889).

1. R. Boyle, *The Sceptical Chymist* (1661), quoted in W. H. Brock, *The Fontana History of Chemistry* (Fontana, London, 1992), p. 57.

2. Ibid., p. 61.

3. A. Wurtz, *Dictionnaire de chimie pure et appliquée* (1869), quoted in Brock, *The Fontana History of Chemistry*, p. 87. The colour chemist Jocelyn Field Thorpe retaliated seven decades later with the claim that 'chemistry is an English science, its founder was Cavendish of immortal memory'.

4. Although Lavoisier's new systematic chemistry became dominant in France, its acceptance elsewhere depended on committed advocates. In Germany, no one was more enthusiastic than the apothecarist Martin Heinrich Klaproth, one of the finest analytical chemists of his era and an expert element-hunter. Klaproth was an avid investigator of minerals and his tally of new metallic substances is impressive: cerium, tellurium and titanium were among his discoveries, and his studies of pitchblende led him to the bright yellow compounds of a new heavy element that Klaproth named in honour of William Herschel's discovery of the planet Uranus: uranium. Uranium salts were subsequently to enjoy a brief career as pigments, primarily in orange ceramic glazes. They had been used intermittently in this context since at least the first century AD.

5. Sir Philiberto Vernatti, in *Philosophical Transactions of the Royal Society*, XII, p. 137 (1678).

6. Some texts suggest this was Bernard Courtois, the discoverer of iodine (page 164). But as Bernard Courtois was born in 1777, the idea that he discovered zinc white in 1781 is rather hard to sustain.

7. The origin of the odd name is obscure – some attribute it to Paracelsus, who had a proclivity for strange lexicological invention.

8. Because of impurities in the ore, the product is less pure than that made by the French process, so high-grade zinc white had to be imported to the USA. Indeed, nineteenth-century zinc white came in a number of grades – the best, Zinc White No. 1, was the finest white pigment, while 'stone grey' and 'grey zinc oxide' were poor-quality materials used for primers or industrial paints.

9. F. Stromeyer, 'New details respecting cadmium', *Annals of Philosophy*, transl. from *Annalen der Physik*, 14 (Leipzig, 1819), pp. 269–74.

10. A Viennese chemist called Ignaz Mitis is also credited with the

discovery – he may have made copper aceto-arsenite sometime between 1798 and 1814, and he manufactured it as Mitis green or Vienna green by the later date, if not earlier. It is possible, however, that the discoveries of Mitis and Sattler were more or less simultaneous.

11. Quoted in S. Garfield, *Mauve* (Faber and Faber, London, 2000), p. 105.

12. This surprisingly early date is supported by analysis conducted at the Doerner Institute in Munich; see R. L. Feller (ed.), *Artists' Pigments* (National Gallery of Art, Washington, DC, 1986), vol. 1, p. 213.

13. Chromium oxide has been tentatively identified in Turner's *Somer Hill* (1812), a remarkably early usage that would certainly support Turner's reputation as an avid experimenter with new pigments. See E. West Fitzhugh, *Artists' Pigments* (National Gallery of Art, Washington, DC, 1997), vol. 3, p. 275.

14. Chaptal was himself an industrial chemist, and author of *Chimie appliquée aux arts* (1807), a major influence on the later generations of industrial chemists in the paints and dyes industry.

15. J.-F.-L. Mérimée, *De la peinture à l'huile* (1830), p. ix.

16. G. D. Leslie, *Inner Life of the Royal Academy*, quoted in K. E. Sullivan, *Turner* (Brockhampton Press, London, 1996).

17. There are exceptions. Holman Hunt stated that the lemon yellow used by Turner in *Approach to Venice* (1844) was Field's; yet Ruskin lamented in 1857 that the picture had become 'a miserable wreck of dead colours'. See J. Gage, *George Field and His Circle* (Fitzwilliam Museum, Cambridge, 1989), p. 42.

18. Joyce Townsend (private communication) says that iodine scarlet has been found in Turner's *Téméraire* in the National Gallery, London. If applied without varnish, it is apt to disappear through sublimation.

19. G. Field, *Chromatics* (1845), 2nd edn.

8. THE REIGN OF LIGHT

Epigraphs:

L. C. Perry, 'Reminiscences of Claude Monet from 1889–1909', *American Magazine of Art*, XVIII (1927).

E. Cardon, 'Avant le Salon – L'Exposition des Révoltés', *La Presse*, 29 April 1874.

1. Eugène Delacroix, quoted in F. Birren, *History of Color in Painting* (Van Nostrand Reinhold, New York, 1965), p. 13.

2. Ibid., p. 57.

3. H. von Helmholtz, 'Recent progress in the theory of vision', *Popular Lectures on Scientific Subjects*, II (1901), pp. 121–2.

4. J. Ruskin, *The Art of England*, in *The Works of John Ruskin*, E. Cook and A. Wedderburn (eds) (London, 1908), vol. 23, pp. 272–3.

5. J. Laforgue, *L'Impressionnisme* (review of an exhibition at the Gurlitt Gallery, Berlin, 1883), first published in *Mélanges posthumes. Œuvres complètes* (Paris, 1903), vol. 3; reprinted in *Les Ecrivains devant l'Impressionnisme* (1989). For a translation, see also L. Nochlin, *Impressionism and Post-Impressionism 1874–1904: Sources and Documents*. (Englewood Cliffs, NJ, 1966), pp. 14–20.

6. In his *Leçons de chimie appliqué à la teinture* (1829–30), Chevreul was one of the first scientists to call for a systematic approach to dye chemistry.

7. M.-E. Chevreul, *Les Lois du contraste simultané des couleurs* (*On the Laws of Simultaneous Contrast of Colours*) (Paris, 1839).

8. Underscoring the chemical origins of his interest in colour, he dedicated the book to his friend and colleague, the famous Swedish chemist Jons Jacob Berzelius.

9. H. von Helmholtz, 'Über die Theorie der zusammengesetzten Farben', *Poggendorffs Annalen der Physik und Chemie*, LXXXVII (1852), pp. 45–66; transl. as 'Sur la théorie des couleurs composées', *Cosmos*, II (1852–3), pp. 112–20. Helmholtz elaborated his findings in his *Treatise on Optics* (1867).

10. H. von Helmholtz, 'On the relation of optics to painting', transl. E. Atkinson, in *Popular Lectures on Scientific Subjects* (Longmans, Green and Co., London, 1903), vol. 2, p. 118.

11. All the same, earth pigments do appear in Pissarro's paintings from the 1870s. And Delacroix himself had already called for earth colours to be banished in 1857.

12. Quoted in H. A. Roberts, *Records of the Amicable Society of Blues* (Cambridge University Press, Cambridge, 1924), pp. 53–4.

13. Auguste Renoir, from an interview in 1910. Quoted in J. Rewald, *The History of Impressionism* (Secker & Warburg, London, 1973), 4th edn.

14. Putting this to the test is a disturbing thought. But the American artist Sherry Levine has done almost precisely that. Her *Melt-Down* paintings (1990) are monochromes in the colours obtained by averaging those in famous works, using a computer. *Melt-Down (After Monet I)* is a darkish silver-grey. As a kind of subtractive mixture, this veers towards black rather than white. But the achromacity of the averaged hue testifies to the spectral inclusiveness of Monet's work.

15. Sunlight is of course white, not yellow; but the Impressionists perceived it as golden (see page 214).

16. J. Claretie, *La vie à Paris 1881* (Paris, 1881), p. 266. One commentator, Alfred de Lostalot, suggested that Monet actually had an unusually extended visual range, being able to perceive ultra-violet light.

17. O. Rood, *Modern Chromatics* (1879), pp. 279–80 and 139–40.

18. Ruskin, *Elements*, in *Works*, p. 152.

19. Indeed, it is not clear that Seurat ever studied Rood's text deeply. His knowledge of optical mixing seems to have come largely from Charles Blanc's popularization of Chevreul's theory. See J. Gage, *Colour and Meaning* (Thames and Hudson, London, 1999), p. 213 and n. 10.

20. F. Fénéon, 'Les Impressionnistes', *La Vogue*, 13–20 June 1886.

21. Ibid.

22. P. Signac, quoted in R. L. Herbert, *Neo-Impressionism* (New York, 1968), p. 108. See Gage, *Colour and Meaning*, p. 217.

23. C. Pissarro, letter to Paul Durand-Ruel, 6 November 1886, in L. Venturi, *Les Archives de l'Impressionnisme* (Paris and New York, 1939), vol. 2, p. 24.

24. Paul Gauguin, quoted in L. Bolton, *The History and Techniques of the Great Masters: Gauguin* (Tiger Books International, Richmond, VA, 1988), p. 13. In the same letter to Vollard, written from La Dominique in 1902, Gauguin prefigures the American artists of the 1950s by demanding 'decorators' colours'. 'They cost a third as much,' he says, 'and they are much better.'

25. J.-P. Crespelle, *The Fauves* (Oldbourne Press, London, 1962).

26. V. van Gogh, letter to his brother Theo, June 1888, in *The Letters of Vincent van Gogh*, ed. M. Roskill (Flamingo, London, 2000), p. 268.

27. This carmine lake was probably of the new, synthetic variety, made from artificial alizarin: see page 247.

28. *The Letters of Vincent van Gogh*, p. 252.

9. A PASSION FOR PURPLE

Epigraphs:

R. Browning, 'Popularity' (1855).

All the Year Round (1859), quoted in S. Garfield, *Mauve* (Faber and Faber, London, 2000), p. 66.

1. Pliny, *Natural History*, IX, xxxvi, 126.
2. Aristotle, *Historia Animalium*, bk V, transl. D'A. W. Thompson (Clarendon Press, Oxford, 1910).
3. Pliny, *Natural History*, IX, xxviii, 134-5.
4. Ibid., XXXV, 46.
5. Julius Caesar, *De Bello Gallico*, bk V.
6. R. Hakluyt, *The Principall Navigations Voiages and Discoveries of the English Nation* (1589), reprinted in facsimile (Cambridge University Press, Cambridge, 1965), vol. 2, p. 454.
7. Ibid.
8. W. Cullen (c.1766), quoted in A. L. Donovan, *Philosophical Chemistry in the Scottish Enlightenment* (Edinburgh University Press, Edinburgh, 1975), p. 107.
9. Benzene was nitrated (given a nitro group, containing nitrogen and oxygen) by treatment with concentrated nitric acid. Then the product, nitrobenzene, was 'reduced', which means replacing the oxygen atoms in the nitro group with hydrogens to make the amino group. The molecular structures of these compounds, for those who do not scare easily at chemistry's symbolic formalism, are as follows. The pictures are easier than the words, once you are used to the system. The letters denote atoms of carbon, hydrogen, oxygen and nitrogen; the lines indicate the bonds joining them.

Benzene   Nitrobenzene   Aniline

10. Garfield, *Mauve*, p. 67.

11. There are probably good reasons why the date is somewhat fluid in contemporary accounts – for whether or not Verguin was still employed by Raffard, or by his subsequent employers the Renard Brothers, or by neither, when he made his discovery had some importance for subsequent patent disputes. Industrial espionage was not unknown in this increasingly competitive business.

12. A. W. Hofmann. 'On aniline-blue', *Proceedings of the Royal Society*, 13 (1863), p. 14.

13. The Scottish chemist Archibald Scott Couper proposed the idea of a carbon chain independently of Kekulé, and more explicitly, in 1858. But the publication of his paper was delayed until after Kekulé's had appeared and Couper lost the claim to priority. His ensuing struggles for recognition left him so disenchanted that he eventually gave up chemistry altogether. *Plus ça change* . . .

14. The astute reader will notice that this connects each carbon atom to just three other atoms, not four. The deficit is made up by the ability of carbon to form *multiple* bonds to the same atom. This is illustrated in the diagrams above (note 9), where two parallel lines denote double bonds. It is not, as it might appear, a cheap get-out. Double bonds really are stronger and shorter than single bonds; and one of the two bonds can be broken open, allowing additional atoms to attach themselves to the carbons, without severing the other bond. I must add for completeness that in benzene and other aromatic hydrocarbons the single and double bonds do not really alternate around the rings. Instead, the multiple bonding becomes 'smeared out' among all the carbon–carbon links, so that all these links are equal and can be regarded as though composed of 'one and a half bonds' each.

15. M. Brusatin, *A History of Colors* (Shambala, Boston, 1991), p. 99.

16. The molecular structures look like this:

Anthracene   Alizarin

17. The *modus operandi* in Baeyer's lab was to apply reagents that broke down the organic compounds into fragments or simpler molecules, and to use the resulting information to guide the reverse process of synthesis. To make complex organic molecules, chemists now routinely conduct an analogous 'thought experiment' called retro synthetic analysis.

18. Quoted in *Perkin Centenary London: 100 Years of Synthetic Dyestuffs* (Pergamon, London, 1958), p. 23.

19. The structure of indigo is as follows:

Indigo

20. C. Rawson, 'The cultivation and manufacture of indigo in Bengal', *Journal of the Society of Dyers and Colourists*, (July, 1899), p. 174.

21. Madder has long been a yardstick for the quality of dyes, to the extent that the word 'guarantee' stems from the Italian word for madder, *garanza*.

22. M. Doerner, *The Materials of the Artist* (Harcourt Brace & Co., Orlando, FL, 1949), p. 91.

10. SHADES OF MIDNIGHT

Epigraphs:
V. Nabokov, *Laughter in the Dark* (Random House, New York, 1989).
P. Cézanne, quoted in D. Jarman, *Chroma* (Vintage, London, 1994).

1. W. Kandinsky, *Über das Geistige in der Kunst* (1911), transl. M. T. H. Sadler as *The Art of Spiritual Harmony* (Constable and Co., London, 1914) and reprinted as *Concerning the Spiritual in Art* (Dover, New York, 1977), p. 38.

2. R. Boyle, *Experiments & Considerations Touching Colours* (London, 1664), pp. 219–21.

3. Marco Polo, *Il milione*, ed. D. Ponchiroli (Einaudi, Turin, 1954), ch. 35, p. 40.

4. Cennino Cennini, *Il Libro dell' Arte* (*The Craftsman's Handbook*), transl. D. V. Thompson (Dover, New York, 1960), pp. 37–8.

5. Ibid., p. 38.

6. Ibid., p. 36.

7. J. Itten, *The Elements of Colour* (Van Nostrand Reinhold, New York, 1970), p. 88.

8. P. Hills, *Venetian Colour* (Yale University Press, New Haven, CT, 1999), p. 136.

9. Y. Klein, 'Par la couleur . . .', in *Mon Livre*, unpublished and written in 1957 (Yves Klein Archives). Quoted in N. Charlot, *Yves Klein* (Vilo International, 2000), p. 60.

10. Ibid.

II. TIME AS PAINTER

Epigraphs:

G. Field, *Chromatography* (Winsor and Newton, London, 1869).

Cennino Cennini, *Il Libro dell'Arte*, (*The Craftsman's Handbook*), transl. D. V. Thompson (Dover, New York, 1960), p. 25.

M. Doerner, *The Materials of the Artist* (Harcourt Brace & Co., Orlando, FL, 1949), p. 375.

1. Some specialist paint manufacturers now make 'retouching' paints for conservators, which are colouristically stable, chemically distinguishable from the paints used in the restored works, and capable of being removed with organic solvents. In 2000 the Gamblin Artists Color Company in the USA launched a new range of retouching paints with excellent optical and handling properties, bound in a non-toxic urea-aldehyde resin made by BASF. See L. R. Ember, *Chemical and Engineering News* 79 (30 July 2001), pp. 51–9.

2. E. H. Gombrich, *Art and Illusion* (Phaidon, London, 1977), 5th edn, p. 49

3. Cennino Cennini, *The Craftsman's Handbook*, p. 26

4. Ibid., p. 24.

5. Doerner, *The Materials of the Artist*, p. 83.
6. It should be said in defence of the pigment that modern methods of preparation seem to protect it from impermanence. But this was of no help to the eighteenth-century painter.
7. Field, *Chromatography*, p. 412.
8. Ibid.
9. Quoted in J. Gage, *George Field and His Circle* (Fitzwilliam Museum, Cambridge, 1989), p. 70.
10. Doerner, *The Materials of the Artist*, pp. v–vi.

12. CAPTURING COLOUR

Epigraphs:

W. Benjamin, 'The work of art in the age of mechanical reproduction' (1936), in F. Frascina and J. Harris (eds), *Art in Modern Culture* (Phaidon Press, London, 1992), p. 297.

Sir James Percival, quoted by F. Birren in the introduction to J. C. Le Blon, *Coloritto* (1725), facsimile reprint by Van Nostrand Reinhold (New York, 1980).

J. Berger, *Ways of Seeing* (Penguin, London, 1972), p. 32.

1. Benjamin, 'The work of art in the age of mechanical reproduction'.
2. Berger, *Ways of Seeing*, p. 21.
3. Even as I write this, London's exterior surfaces are adorned with flyposted images of Titian's crimson-robed Madonna, although the 'Renaissance' it advertises has more to do with club culture than with 'high' culture.
4. Jonathan Brown and Carmen Garrido point out that one of the most discussed works of the Western canon, Velázquez's *Las Meninas*, has been interpreted mainly from reproductions. They say, 'No one seems to have been interested in the materiality, or physical structure, of the work, or appreciated it as a pictorial performance . . . However, the [1984] cleaning of the painting . . . allows us to appreciate it as one of the most remarkable artistic tours-de-force in the history of Western culture.' The message (apart from 'Get thee to the Prado') is that by insisting on the conceptual and ignoring the material we

may miss the true beauty of works like this. See J. Brown and C. Garrido, *Velázquez: The Technique of Genius* (Yale University Press, New Haven, CT, 1998).

5. Le Blon, *Coloritto*, Epistle xx.

6. Ibid., p. 28.

7. Ibid., p. 30.

8. Presumably Le Blon did not know of this remark when he dedicated *Coloritto* to Walpole.

9. R. M. Burch, *Colour Printing and Colour Printers* (Sir Isaac Pitman and Sons Ltd, London, 1910), p. 112.

10. When Schulze published his findings, he entitled them *Scotophorus pro Phosphoro Inventus* – a joke on the fact that the experiments had been intended to make phosphorus, inflammable 'bringer of light', but instead produced 'Scotophorus', 'bringer of darkness'.

11. S. F. B. Morse in the *New York Observer*, quoted in J. Carey (ed.), *The Faber Book of Science* (Faber and Faber, London, 1996).

12. J. C. Maxwell, in *Transactions of the Royal Society of Edinburgh*, 21 (1857), p. 275.

13. I am reliably informed that the lecture itself was grim, Maxwell being a notoriously poor speaker.

14. J. C. Maxwell, *British Journal of Photography*, 9 (1861), p. 270.

15. H. Collen, *British Journal of Photography*, 12 (1865), p. 547. Collen proposed that the colour separations be taken according to the subtractive primaries red, blue and yellow, rather than (more properly) the additive primaries used by Maxwell.

16. E. J. Wall, *History of Three-Color Photography* (American Photographic Publishing Co., Boston, MA., 1925), p. 9.

17. E. Wind, *Art and Anarchy* (London, 1963), p. 165.

18. Georgia O'Keeffe, quoted in C. A. Riley, *Color Codes* (University Press of New England, Hanover, NH, 1995), p. 169.

13. MIND OVER MATTER

Epigraphs:

S. Delaunay, quoted in *Colour since Matisse*, an exhibition of French painting, Edinburgh International Festival (Trefoil Books, London, 1985).

H. Matisse (1952), quoted in C. A. Riley, *Color Codes* (University Press of New England, Hanover, NH, 1995).

1. H. von Helmholtz, 'Recent progress in the theory of colour vision', *Popular Lectures on Scientific Subjects*, II (1901), pp. 121–2.
2. J. Flam (ed.), *Matisse: A Retrospective* (Hugh Lauter Levin, New York, 1988), p. 153.
3. Quoted in A. H. Barr Jr, *Matisse: His Art and His Public* (New York, 1951), p. 119.
4. Quoted in Riley, *Color Codes*, p. 134.
5. Quoted in J. Leymarie, *Fauves and Fauvism* (Editions d'Art Albert Skira S.A., Geneva, 1995).
6. R. Delaunay, *Du Cubisme à l'Art Abstrait*, ed. P. Francastel (1957), pp. 182–3.
7. Quoted in H. Read, *A Concise History of Modern Painting* (Thames and Hudson, London, 1974), p. 180.
8. E. Neumann (ed.), *Bauhaus and Bauhaus People* (Van Nostrand Reinhold, New York, 1970), p. 45.
9. P. Cherchi, *Paul Klee teorico* (*Paul Klee, Theoretician*) (De Donato, Bari, 1978), pp. 160–1.
10. M. Doerner, *The Materials of the Artist* (Harcourt Brace & Co., Orlando, FL, 1949), pp. 169–70.
11. Cherchi, *Paul Klee teorico*, pp. 160–1.

14. ART FOR ART'S SAKE

Epigraphs:
R. Rauschenberg, quoted in R. Hughes, *The Shock of the New* (BBC Books, London, 1991).
D. Batchelor, *Chromophobia* (Reaktion Books, London, 2000), pp. 98, 100.

1. P. Leider, 'Literalism and Abstraction: Frank Stella's Retrospective at the Modern' (1970), reprinted in F. Frascina and J. Harris (eds), *Art in Modern Culture* (Phaidon Press, London, 1992), p. 319.

2. Interview with William Wright, reprinted in H. Namuth, *Pollock Painting* (New York, 1950).

3. There is a danger, however, of attributing too much to Pollock's non-traditional materials. He did sometimes use oil paints even in his distinctive 'drip' paintings, albeit apparently squeezed straight from the tube. See S. Lake, 'The challenge of preserving modern art: a technical investigation of paints used in selected works by Willem de Kooning and Jackson Pollock', *MRS Bulletin*, 26(1) (2001), p. 56.

4. Enamel paints are not invariably bound in nitrocellulose – the term simply denotes a tough, high-gloss finish. Some early enamel paints used linseed oil as the main binding medium, toughened with resins. Later, alkyd resins (see later text) provided the binder.

5. Quoted in J. Crook and T. Learner, *The Impact of Modern Paints* (Tate Gallery Publishing, London, 2000), p. 71.

6. *David Hockney: Paintings, Prints and Drawings 1960–1970*, exhibition catalogue (Whitechapel Art Gallery, London, 1970), pp. 11–12.

7. Quoted in Crook and Learner, *The Impact of Modern Paints*, p. 97.

8. I have seen both this work, and some of Rothko's, reproduced upside down: the hazard of abstraction. I don't suppose there are many paintings that give you two scenic views for the price of one. But publishers can be forgiven some confusion when we bear in mind that Rothko himself did not always know which way up a work should go until he had finished it – and even then he sometimes changed his mind.

9. Quoted in D. Anfam, *Abstract Expressionism* (Thames and Hudson, London, 1990), p. 142.

10. S. Rodman, *Conversations with Artists* (New York, 1957), p. 93.

11. E. Jones, memorandum to Agnes Morgan, acting director of the Fogg Museum, 3 November 1970. Quoted in M. B. Cohn (ed.), *Mark Rothko's Harvard Murals* (Harvard University Art Museums, Cambridge, MA, 1988), p. 10.

12. Quoted in Hughes, *The Shock of the New.*

13. Quoted in N. Welliver, 'Albers on Albers', *Art News*, LXIV (1966), pp. 68–9.

14. F. Stella, *Working Space* (Harvard University Press, Cambridge, MA., 1986), p. 71.

15. Ibid., p. 89.

16. Batchelor, *Chromophobia*, p. 10.
17. In 2000 a new class of red and yellow inorganic materials devoid of toxic heavy metals was reported by German chemists M. Jansen and H. P. Letschert: see *Nature*, 404 (2000), pp. 980–82. These are complex compounds containing calcium, lanthanum, tantalum, oxygen and nitrogen. It remains to be seen whether they can be commercialized.

Bibliography

Georgius Agricola, *De re metallica* (1556), transl. H. C. and L. H. Hoover (Dover, New York, 1950).

Leon Battista Alberti, *Della Pittura* (1435). Published as *On Painting*, transl. C. Grayson (Penguin, London, 1991).

C. Aldred, *Egyptian Art* (Thames and Hudson, London, 1980).

D. Anfam, *Abstract Expressionism* (Thames and Hudson, London, 1990).

D. Anfam, *Mark Rothko* (National Gallery of Art, Washington, DC, 1998).

D. Ashton, *About Rothko* (Oxford University Press, New York, 1983).

J. Ayers, *The Artist's Craft* (Phaidon Press, London, 1985).

J. Balfour-Paul, *Indigo* (British Museum Press, London, 1998).

S. J. Barnes, *The Rothko Chapel: An Act of Faith* (University of Texas Press, Austin, 1989).

D. Batchelor, *Chromophobia* (Reaktion Books, London, 2000).

W. Benjamin, 'The work of art in the age of mechanical reproduction' (1936), in F. Frascina and J. Harris (eds), *Art in Modern Culture* (Phaidon Press, London, 1992), p. 297.

J. Berger, *Ways of Seeing* (Penguin, London, 1972).

B. Berlin and P. Kay, *Basic Color Terms* (University of California Press, Berkeley, CA, 1969).

R. S. Berns, *Principles of Color Technology* (John Wiley, New York, 2000).

P. Binski, *Medieval Craftsmen: Painters* (British Museum Press, London, 1991).

F. Birren, *History of Color in Painting* (Van Nostrand Reinhold, New York, 1965).

A. Blunt, *Artistic Theory in Italy 1450–1600* (Oxford University Press, Oxford, 1962).

L. Bolton, *The History and Techniques of the Great Masters: Gauguin* (Tiger Books International, London, 1988).

D. Bomford, C. Brown and A. Roy, *Art in the Making: Rembrandt* (National Gallery Publications, London, 1988).

D. Bomford, J. Dunkerton, D. Gordon and A. Roy, *Art in the Making: Italian Painting before 1400* (National Gallery Publications, London, 1989).

D. Bomford, J. Kirby, J. Leighton and A. Roy, *Art in the Making: Impressionism* (National Gallery Publications, London, 1990).

D. Bomford and A. Roy, *Colour* (National Gallery Company Ltd, London, 2000).

W. H. Brock, *The Fontana History of Chemistry* (Fontana, London, 1992).

J. Brown and C. Garrido, *Velázquez: The Technique of Genius* (Yale University Press, New Haven, CT, 1998).

V. J. Bruno, *Form and Colour in Greek Painting* (Thames and Hudson, London, 1977).

M. Brusatin, *A History of Colors* (Shambala, Boston, MA., 1991).

W. Büchner, R. Schliebs, G. Winter and K. H. Buchel, *Industrial Inorganic Chemistry* (VCH, New York, 1989).

S. Bucklow, 'Paradigms and pigment recipes: Vermilion, synthetic yellows and the nature of the egg', *Zeitschrift für Kunsttechnologie*, 13/1 (1999), p. 140.

R. M. Burch, *Colour Printing and Colour Printers* (Sir Isaac Pitman & Sons, London, 1910).

A. Burmester and C. Krekel, 'The relationship between Albrecht Dürer's palette and fifteenth/sixteenth-century pharmacy price lists: the use of azurite and ultramarine', *Proceedings of the IIC Dublin Congress, 7–11 December 1998* (International Institute for Conservation of Historic and Artistic Works, London).

A. Callen, *Techniques of the Impressionists* (New Burlington Books, London, 1987).

Cennino Cennini, *Il Libro dell'Arte* (c. 1390), transl. D. V. Thompson as *The Craftsman's Handbook* (Dover, New York, 1960).

N. Charlet, *Yves Klein* (Vilo International, Paris, 2000).

M.-E. Chevreul, *The Principles of Harmony and Contrast of Colours* (Henry G. Bohn, London, 1854). Translated from *De la loi du contraste simultané des couleurs* (1839). Reprinted by Van Nostrand Reinhold (New York, 1981).

A. H. Church, *The Chemistry of Paints and Painting* (Seeley and Co., London, 1890).

B. Clearwater, *Mark Rothko: Works on Paper* (Hudson Hills Press, New York, 1984).

C. Cobb and H. Goldwhite, *Creations of Fire* (Plenum, New York, 1995).

M. B. Cohn (ed.), *Mark Rothko's Harvard Murals* (Harvard University Art Museums, Cambridge, MA., 1988).

B. Cole, *The Renaissance Artist at Work* (John Murray, London, 1983).

W. G. Constable, *The Painter's Workshop* (Oxford University Press, London, 1954).

D. Cranmer, 'Ephemeral paintings on "permanent view" – the accelerated aging of Mark Rothko's paintings', *Proceedings of ICOM Committee for Conservation, 8th Triennial Meeting, Sydney* (1987), p. 283.

J.-P. Crespelle, *The Fauves* (Oldbourne Press, London, 1962).

J. Crook and T. Learner, *The Impact of Modern Paints* (Tate Gallery Publishing, London, 2000).

E. Cumming and W. Kaplan, *The Arts and Crafts Movement* (Thames and Hudson, London, 1991).

M. de Keijzer, 'Microchemical identification of modern organic pigments in cross-sections of artists' paintings', *Proceedings of ICOM Committee for Conservation, 8th Triennial Meeting, Sydney* (1987), p. 33.

I. Dickson Gill, *The History and Techniques of the Great Masters: Titian* (Tiger Books International, London, 1989).

M. Doerner, *The Materials of the Artist* (Harcourt Brace & Co., Orlando, FL, 1949). Reprinted 1984.

J. Dunkerton, A. Roy and A. Smith (1987), 'The unmasking of Tura's "Allegorical Figure": a painting and its concealed image', *National Gallery Technical Bulletin*, 11 (1987), p. 5.

G. Duthuit, *The Fauvist Painters* (Wittenborn, Schultz Inc., New York, 1950).

W. Eamon, *Science and the Secrets of Nature* (Princeton University Press, Princeton, NJ, 1994).

D. Elger (ed.), *Donald Judd, Colorist* (Hatje Cantz, Ostfildern-Ruit, 2000).

W. S. Ellis, *Glass* (Avon Books, New York, 1998).

R. L. Feller (ed.), *Artists' Pigments: A Handbook of Their History and Characteristics* (National Gallery of Art, Washington, DC, 1986), vol. 1.

G. Field, *Chromatography* (Winsor and Newton, London, 1869).

E. West Fitzhugh (ed.), *Artists' Pigments: A Handbook of Their History and Characteristics* (National Gallery of Art, Washington, DC, 1997), vol. 3.

P. Fortini Brown, *The Renaissance in Venice* (Weidenfeld and Nicolson, London, 1997).

R. Fox and A. Nieto-Galan (eds), *Natural Dyestuffs and Industrial Culture in Europe, 1750–1880* (Watson Publishing, Canton, MA., 1999).

J. Gage, *Colour in Turner: Poetry and Truth* (Studio Vista, London, 1969).

J. Gage, *George Field and His Circle* (Fitzwilliam Museum, Cambridge, 1989).

J. Gage, *Colour and Culture* (Thames and Hudson, London, 1993).

J. Gage, Review of *Farbe um Bauhaus: Synthese und Synasthesie*, in Kunst Chronik (February 1998), p. 78.

J. Gage, *Colour and Meaning* (Thames and Hudson, London, 1999).

S. Garfield, *Mauve* (Faber and Faber, London, 2000).

H. F. Gaugh, *De Kooning* (Abbeville, New York, 1983).

H. Gernsheim, *A Concise History of Photography* (Dover, New York, 1986).

R. J. Gettens and G. L. Stout, *Painting Materials: A Short Encyclopaedia* (Dover, New York, 1966).

E. H. Gombrich, *Art and Illusion* (Phaidon Press, London, 1977), 5th edn.

E. H. Gombrich, *The Story of Art* (Phaidon Press, London, 1989), 15th edn.

M. Goodwin, *Artist and Colourman* (Reeves and Son Ltd, Harrow, Middx, 1966).

W. Grohmann, *Klee* (Harry N. Abrams, New York, 1985).

S. Hackney, R. Jones and J. Townsend, *Paint and Purpose* (National Gallery Publications, London, 1999).

M. Hall, *Colour and Meaning: Practice and Theory in Renaissance Painting* (Cambridge University Press, Cambridge, 1992).

R. D. Harley, *Artists' Pigments c.1600–1836* (Butterworths, London, 1982), 2nd edn.

A. Heaton (ed.), *The Chemical Industry* (Blackie Academic, Glasgow, 1994).

H. von Helmholtz, 'On the relation of optics to painting', transl. E. Atkinson, in *Popular Lectures on Scientific Subjects* (Longmans, Green and Co., London, 1903), vol. 2.

P. Hills, *Venetian Colour* (Yale University Press, New Haven, CT, 1999).

H. Hodges, *Technology in the Ancient World* (Michael O'Mara Books, London, 1996).

R. Hughes, *The Shock of the New* (BBC Books, London, 1991).

J. Itten, *The Elements of Colour* (Van Nostrand Reinhold, New York, 1970).

D. Jarman, *Chroma* (Vintage, London, 1994).

V. Jirat-Wasiutynski and H. T. Newton Jr, 'Absorbent grounds and the matt aesthetic in post-Impressionist painting', in A. Roy and P. Smith (eds), *Contributions to the IIC Dublin Congress, 7–11 September 1998: Painting Techniques: History, Materials and Studio Practice* (International Institute for Conservation of Historic and Artistic Works, London, 1998), p. 235.

B. Jonson, *The Alchemist* (c. 1610), in *Three Comedies* (Penguin, London, 1966).

W. Kandinsky, *Über das Geistige in der Kunst* (1912), transl. M. T. H. Sadler as *The Art of Spiritual Harmony* (Constable and Co., London, 1914) and reprinted as *Concerning the Spiritual in Art* (Dover, New York, 1977).

M. Kemp, *The Science of Art* (Yale University Press, New Haven, CT, 1990).

J. Kirby, 'Fading and colour change of Prussian blue: occurrences and early reports', *National Gallery Technical Bulletin* (National Gallery Publications, London), 14 (1993), p. 63.

J. Kirby, 'The painter's trade in the seventeenth century: Theory and practice', *National Gallery Technical Bulletin* (National Gallery Publications, London), 20 (1999), p. 5.

J. Kirby, 'The price of quality: factors influencing the cost of pigments during the Renaissance', in G. Neher and R. Shepherd (eds), *Values in Renaissance Art* (Ashgate, London, 2000).

J. Kirby and D. Saunders, 'Sixteenth- to eighteenth-century green colours in landscape and flower paintings: composition and deterioration', in A. Roy and P. Smith (eds), *Contributions to the IIC Dublin Congress, 7–11 September 1998: Painting Techniques: History, Materials and Studio Practice* (International Institute for Conservation of Historic and Artistic Works, London, 1998), p. 155.

J. Kirby and R. White, 'The identification of red lake pigment dyestuffs and a discussion of their use', *National Gallery Technical Bulletin* (National Gallery Publications, London), 17 (1996), p. 56.

T. Lamb and J. Bourriau (eds), *Colour: Art and Science* (Cambridge University Press, Cambridge, 1995).

A. P. Laurie, *The Pigments and Mediums of the Old Masters* (Macmillan, London, 1914).

A. P. Laurie, *The Painter's Methods and Materials* (Seeley Service and Co., London, 1960). Reprinted by Dover (New York, 1967).

J. C. Le Blon, *Coloritto* (1725). Facsimile reprint by Van Nostrand Reinhold (New York, 1980).

H. M. Leicester, *The Historical Background of Chemistry* (Dover, New York, 1971).

J. Leymarie, *Fauves and Fauvism* (Editions d'Art Albert Skira S.A., Geneva, 1995).

A. Lucas, *Ancient Egyptian Materials and Industries* (Arnold and Co., London, 1948), 3rd edn.

E. Lucie-Smith, *Movements in Art Since 1945* (Thames and Hudson, London, 1984).

A. M. Mascheroni (ed.), *Vlaminck* (Park Lane, London, 1993).

M. Menu, 'Cave paintings: structure and analysis', *MRS Bulletin*, 21(12) (December 1996), p. 48.

M. P Merrifield, *Original Treatises on the Arts of Painting* (1849). Reprinted by Dover (New York, 1967).

A. Morrall, *The History and Techniques of the Great Masters: Rembrandt* (Tiger Books International, London, 1988).

A. Morrall, *The History and Techniques of the Great Masters: Rubens* (Tiger Books International, London, 1988).

R. P. Multhauf, *The Origins of Chemistry* (Gordon and Breach, Langhorne, PA, 1993).

K. Nassau (ed.), *Color for Science, Art and Technology* (Elsevier, Amsterdam, 1997).

G. Naylor, *The Bauhaus Reassessed* (Herbert Press, London, 1985).

E. O'Donoghue, R. Romero and J. Dik, 'French eighteenth-century painting techniques', in A. Roy and P. Smith (eds), *Contributions to the IIC Dublin Congress, 7–11 September 1998: Painting Techniques: History, Materials and Studio Practice* (International Institute for Conservation of Historic and Artistic Works, London, 1998), p. 185.

J. Osborne, *Light and Pigments* (John Murray, London, 1980).

N. Penny and M. Spring, 'Veronese's paintings in the National Gallery. Technique and materials: Part I', *National Gallery Technical Bulletin* (National Gallery Publications, London), 16 (1995), p. 5.

N. Penny, A. Roy and M. Spring, 'Veronese's paintings in the National Gallery. Technique and materials: Part II', *National Gallery Technical Bulletin* (National Gallery Publications, London), 17 (1996), p. 33.

Perkin Centenary London: 100 Years of Synthetic Dyestuffs (Pergamon, London, 1958).

A. Powell, *The Origins of Western Art* (Thames and Hudson, London, 1973).

L. M. Principe, *The Aspiring Adept: Robert Boyle and his Alchemical Quest* (Princeton University Press, Princeton, NJ, 1998).

F. Ratliff, *Paul Signac and Color in Neo-Impressionism* (Rockefeller University Press, New York, 1992).

H. Read, *A Concise History of Modern Painting* (Thames and Hudson, London, 1968).

J. Read, 'Alchemy and art', *Proceedings of the Royal Institution*, XXXV (1952), p. 286.

J. Read, *Through Alchemy to Chemistry* (G. Bell & Sons, London, 1957). Reprinted as *From Alchemy to Chemistry* (Dover, New York, 1995).

J. Rewald, *The History of Impressionism* (Secker & Warburg, London, 1973), 4th edn.

D. Rhodes, *Clay and Glazes for the Potter* (Chilton Book Company, Radnor, PA, 1973).

B. Riley, *Mondrian: Nature to Abstraction* (Tate Gallery Publications, London, 1997).

C. A. Riley, *Color Codes* (University Press of New England, Hanover, NH, 1995).

R. Rosenblum, *Ingres* (Thames and Hudson, London, 1990).

H. Rossotti, *Colour* (Princeton University Press, Princeton, NJ, 1983).

A. Roy, 'The materials of van Gogh's "A cornfield with cypresses",' *National Gallery Technical Bulletin* (National Gallery Publications, London), 11 (1987), p. 50.

A. Roy (ed.), *Artists' Pigments: A Handbook of Their History and Characteristics* (Oxford University Press, Oxford, 1993), vol. 2.

A. Roy and P. Smith (eds), *Contributions to the IIC Dublin Congress, 7–11 September 1998: Painting Techniques: History, Materials and Studio Practice* (International Institute for Conservation of Historic and Artistic Works, London, 1998).

N. K. Sandars, *Prehistoric Art in Europe* (Penguin, Harmondsworth, Middx, 1968)

S. Sass, *The Substance of Civilization* (Arcade, New York, 1998).

D. Saunders and J. Kirby, 'Light-induced colour changes in red and yellow lake pigments', *National Gallery Technical Bulletin* (National Gallery Publications, London), 15 (1994), p. 79.

L. Sheldon, 'Methods and materials of the Pre-Raphaelite circle in the 1850s', *Proceedings of the IIC Dublin Congress, 7–11 December 1998* (International Institute for Conservation of Historic and Artistic Works, London, 1998) p. 229.

C. Singer, E. J. Holmyard, A. R. Hall and T. I. Williams (eds), *A History of Technology* (Clarendon Press, Oxford, 1954–8), vols 1–4.

H. Skelton, 'A colour chemist's history of art', *Review of Progress in Coloration* (1999).

A. M. Spalter, *The Computer in the Visual Arts* (Addison Wesley Longman, Inc., Reading, MA., 1999).

J. Steer, *Venetian Painting* (Thames and Hudson, London, 1970).

K. F. Sullivan, *Turner* (Brockhampton Press, London, 1996).

F. S. Taylor, *A History of Industrial Chemistry* (Heinemann, London, 1957).

Theophilus, *De diversis artibus* (*c.* 1122), transl. J. G. Hawthorne and C. S. Smith as *On Divers Arts* (Dover, New York, 1979).

A. Theroux, *The Primary Colors* (Henry Holt and Co., New York, 1994).

A. Theroux, *The Secondary Colors* (Henry Holt and Co., New York, 1996).

A. Thomas, *The Painter's Practice in Renaissance Tuscany* (Cambridge University Press, Cambridge, 1995).

D. V. Thompson, *The Materials and Techniques of Medieval Painting* (Dover, New York, 1956).

J. H. Townsend, 'The materials of J. M. W. Turner: Pigments', *Studies in Conservation*, 38 (1993), p. 231.

A. S. Travis, *The Rainbow Makers* (Associated University Presses, Cranbury, NJ, 1993).

H. Varley (ed.), *Colour* (Marshall Editions, London, 1980).

G. Vasari, Introduction to *Lives of the Artists* (1550). Published as *Vasari on Technique*, transl. L. S. Maclehose (Dover, New York, 1960).

E. J. Wall, *History of Three-Color Photography* (American Photographic Publishing Co., Boston, MA., 1925).

J. Weiss, *Mark Rothko*, Tate Gallery exhibition catalogue (National Gallery of Art, Washington, DC, 1998).

H. Weitemeier, *Yves Klein* (Benedikt Taschen Verlag, Cologne, 1995).

R. White and J. Kirby, 'Rembrandt and his circle: Seventeenth-century

Dutch paint media re-examined', *National Gallery Technical Bulletin* (National Gallery Publications, London), 15 (1994), p. 64.

F. Whitford, *Bauhaus* (Thames and Hudson, London, 1984).

T. I. Williams (ed.), *A History of Technology* (Clarendon Press, Oxford, 1958), vols 5 and 6.

C. S. Wood, *Albrecht Altdorfer and the Origins of Landscape* (Reaktion Books, London, 1993).

H. Zollinger, *Color: A Multidisciplinary Approach* (VCH, Zürich and Wiley-VCH, Weinheim, 1999).

Index

Page numbers in italic denote an illustration.

Absinthe Drinker, The, 261
Abstract Expressionism, 370, 371–5, 383
abstraction, 362–3
  steps towards, 216–21, 344
acetic acid, 70
acrylic paints, 365, 368–70, 377, 378, 379
Adam, Edouard, 1, 2, 12, 280
Adamson, Robert, 324
additive mixing, 42, 44, 47, 122, 183, 197, 312, 336–7
Adoration of the Kings, The, 137, 149, 272; *Plate 6.2*
aerial perspective, 30
Action, 75
Aetius, 126
Agfa, 254, 330
Agricola, Georgius, 89, 113, 133
Agrippa, Cornelius, 94
Albers, Josef, 355, 378
Alberti, Leon Battista, 7–8, 20–21, 119, 120, 121, 122, 136, 151, 361
Alchemist, The, (play), 80
alchemy/alchemists, 12, 80–115
  attraction of arsenic and lead, 88–9
  colour and transformation, 82–3, 84–5
  image of as charlatans, 80–81
  influence of theory on pigment manufacture, 89–91
  knowledge of by educated people and artists, 81–2
  'laborants' and 'adepti', 83
  principal influence on art, 82–3
  role in colour innovation and provision of systematic technology, for manufacturing, 103–15
  special significance of red, 87–8
  and technical handbooks (Books of Secrets), 91–4

and vermilion, 86
Alexander of Aphrodisias, 77
Algerian Women in Their Apartment, 198; *Plate 8.1*
Alhazen, 319
Alinari brothers, 325
alizarin, 247–9, 255, 257, 345, 400 n., 16
alkyds, 367–8, 379
Allegorical Figure, 127, 286–8, 289, 290, *Plate 11.2*
Allegories (Veronese), 293
Allegory on the Blessing of Peace, 160–61
Allegory of Love III (Respect), 299
Altarpiece: Three Saints (Nardo di Cione), 297
Altdorfer, Albrecht, 158
alum, 65, 100, 107
Ambassadors, The, 286
American ('direct') process for making zinc white, 170–71
Ammanati, Bartolommeo, 147
aniline, 237–40, 245, 399 n., 9
aniline blue, 242
aniline dyes, 37, 237–42, 246, 249, 250, 255, 256, 257, 275
aniline purple, 237–40
aniline red, 241–2, 345
aniline violet, 242
aniline yellow, 250
Anne, Countess of Albemarle, 301
Annunciation, The (Titian), 142
Annunciation, with St Emidius, 137; *Plate 5.6*
anthraquinone dyes, 255, 256
Anthroposophist movement, 187
antiquity, 55–79
  blue in, 262–4
  chemistry, 57–67, 68
  dyes, 64–7, 72–3, 223–8

antiquity (*cont.*)
  glass-making, 61–3
  glazes, 63–4
  lake pigments, 72–3
  recipes for colour, 67–73
  see also Egypt, ancient; Greeks/Greece
Apelles, 75, 78, 264
Apollinaire, Guillaume, 351
Apotheosis of Homer, The, 278
apprenticeships, 98–9
April Love, 237; *Plate 9.2*
aquatinting, 316
'Arcanists', 234
Archer, Frederick Scott, 321–2
Arena chapel (Padua), 101, 272; *Plate 4.3*
Aristotle, 19, 28, 39, 73, 74, 166, 167, 224–5, 263
Armenini, G. B., 101
Arnolfini Marriage, 127; *Plate 5.5*
arsenic, 88–9, 173–4
art galleries, 307
Artist and His Model in the Studio at Le Havre, The, 261
Arts and Crafts movement, 8
Arundel Society, 317
arzica, 113
Ashton, Dore, 374
Assumption, The (Titian), 308
At the Theatre, 207
'Attic yellow', 263
aureolin, 179
Autochrome system, 328
Awakening Conscience, The, 188
awo (Japanese colour term), 15
azo dyes, 249–50, 254–5, 258, 374, 382
azurite, 69, 103–5, 113, 130, 131, 135, 137, 160, 266, 272, 298

Babylonians, 64
Bacchus and Ariadne, 5, 141–2, 261, 283–4, 286; *Plates 5.7, 11.1*
Bacon, Roger, 81
Baeyer, Adolf, 247, 252
Balla, Giacomo, 350
Bardwell, Thomas, 159
barite, 171
barium, 173
barium chromate, 177

barium sulphate, 171, 176
Baroque period, 145, 151, 154, 301
BASF, 242, 248, 249, 253, 254, 255
Batchelor, David, 13, 381
Bathers at Asnières, 210, 212, 304
Battle Scene from 'Sinbad the Sailor', 261
Baudelaire, Charles, 192
Bauhaus school, 352–3, 354–6, 357, 380
Baxter, George, 318, 325; *Plate 12.2*
Bayer chemicals company, 242, 250, 254
Beaumont, Sir George, 153
Bellini, Giovanni, 129, 133, 140, 270
Belriguardo chapel, 139
Belshazzar's Feast, 134
Benjamin, Walter, 307, 325
Bense, Max, 341
benzene, 239, 244, 246, 399 n. 9
Berger, John, 307
Berlin Aniline Company, 256
Berlin, Brent, 16, 17, 59
Berthelot, Marcellin, 68
Berthollet, Claude-Louis, 168, 175, 234
beryllium, 175
Berzelius, Jons Jacob, 345
Betrayal of Christ, The, 118; *Plate 5.1*
Bicci, Neri di, 137
bice, 130–31
binding agents, 37–8, 70, 101–2, 280, 364, 365, 367–70
Birelli, G., 129
Birren, Faber, 386 n. 3
  History of Color in Painting, 4
Birth of Venus, The, 111, 134–5
bistre, 153
bitumen, 153
black, 51, 151, 161, 206, 265
Black Prince, 352
blackening, of pigments, 297–8
Blake, Peter, 364, 365
Blake, William, 187, 275, 317–18
Blanc, Charles, 13, 198
Blaue Reiter, Der (The Blue Rider), 261
Blaue Vier, Die (The Blue Four), 261
bleaches, 234
Blind Girl, 25
block printing, 231
blue(s), 11, 49, 161, 178, 260–75
  and antiquity, 262–4

and azurite, 69, 103–5, 113, 130, 131,
    135, 137, 160, 266, 272, 298
blurring of distinction between yellow
    and, 15, 263, 264
cobalt, 4, 33, 178–9, 180, 277, 279, 304
Egyptian, 57–8, 63
and Klein, Yves, 280–82
and light scattering, 30–31
luxury of fine, 272
medieval period, 103–5
mixing with white, 270–71
monastral, 36, 279
Prussian, 11, 34, 157, 159, 273–5, 276,
    301, 302
recognition as a primary, 262–5
Renaissance, 130–34
and smalt, 133–4, 135, 178, 272, 273, 301
in twentieth-century art, 279–82
Virgin Mary robed in, 270, 296, 355
and woad, 228
see also ultramarine
blue bice, 130–31, 133
blue frit, 63, 70, 76
    see also Egyptian blue
blue-glazed ornaments, 62
    see also Egyptian faience
Blue Globe, 282
Blue Horse I, 261
Blue Nude, 250, 261
Blue Room, The, 261
blue verditer, 131–2, 133, 273
Boating on the Seine, 204–5; *Plate 8.5*
Boccioni, Umberto, 350
Böcklin, Arnold, 79
Bocour, Leonard, 369, 377
Bolos of Mendes, 92
Bonnard, Pierre, 218
Books of Secrets, 91–4
Botticelli, Sandro, 111
Böttiger, Paul, 255
Bouts, Dieric, 108, 133, 135, 298
Bowles
    Art of Painting in Water-Colours, 171
Bowood House (Wiltshire), 133
Boyle, Robert, 40, 131
    Experimental History of Colours, 106
    *Experiments & Considerations Touching
        Colours*, 265

Origine of Formes and Qualities, 91
    The Sceptical Chymist, 9, 83, 166–7
Brandt, Georg, 178
brazil, 107, 108, 155
brightness, 52, 53, 121
British Celanese Company, 256
British Dyestuffs Corporation, 254, 256
browns, 51, 151–3
Brueghel, Pieter, 272
Brunelleschi, Filippo, 118–19
Brunck, Heinrich, 253
Brusatin, Manlio, 246
Bucklow, Spike, 90–91
Burial of Christ, The, 123
Butler, Samuel
    Hudibras, 36–7
butterfly wings, 30–31, *31*
Byzantine art, 77, 139
Byzantine churches, 109

cadmium, 172
cadmium orange, 45, 172, 345
cadmium red, 35, 344–5, 383
cadmium sulphide, 35, 172
cadmium yellow, 172–3, 180
caeruleum, 15
calico-printing industry, 236, 312
Callcott, Augustus Wall, 291
Callen, Anthea, 3–4
Calling of St Matthew, The, 123
calotype process, 321, 324
Canal, Martin da, 138–9
Canaletto, Giovanni Antonio, 302
cangiantismo technique, 124, 125, 150
Canini, Giovanni Angelo, 301
canvas, 139–40
Capa, Robert, 325
Caravaggio, Michelangelo Merisi da, 123,
    150, 151, 162
carbon, 245
Carlisle, Anne, 160
carmine lake, 72, 73, 344–5
Caro, Heinrich, 248, 252
carotenoids, 36, 49
Cartier-Bresson, Henri, 325
Casagemas, Carlos, 260
Cassel earth pigment, 152, 162, 287
Caulfield, Patrick, 365; *Plate 14.1*

caustic soda, 65
cave paintings, 58, 59–60
Cavendish, Henry, 167
celluloid, 366
cellulose nitrate, 366
Cennino Cennini, 6, 21, 66, 73, 89, 97,
   105, 108, 112, 151, 296
   egg tempera prescriptions, 102
   fresco techniques, 101
   on gold, 109–10, 111, 112
   Il Libro dell' Arte, 20, 83, 99
   pigment recipes, 90
   shading scheme, 121
   on ultramarine, 267–8, 280
   on vermilion, 86, 87, 297
   on yellow pigments, 113
cerulean blue, 179
Cesariano, Cesare, 264
Cézanne, Paul, 9, 10, 171, 177, 196, 200,
   203, 215–17, 279, 343, 344, 347
chalk, 38, 59, 60,65, 107, 163
Charity (Van Dyck), 162; *Plate 6.5*
Charles I, 160
Chaucer, Geoffrey
   Canterbury Tales, 81
chemical formulae, 244
chemical valency, 245
chemistry, 2, 165–88
   in antiquity, 57–67, 68
   and art, 9–12
   and dyes, 223, 232–4, 237, 243–6, 249
   and elements, 166–8
   fear of, 10–11
   in fifteenth/sixteenth centuries, 116–17
   low status of before eighteenth century, 9
chemists, 6, 13, 57–67, 249
chemotherapy, 250
Chevreul, Michel-Eugène, 41, 197–8, 212,
   265
chiaroscuro printing, 309, *310*, 315, 318
chiaroscuro painting technique, 72, 123,
   149, 151, 153, 162, 196
Child with Aunt, 352
chintz printing, 232, 234
chlorine, 173, 234
chlorophyll, 36, 38
chloros, 17, 178
Cholmeley, William, 155

chromatic painting, 141
chromatography, 293–4
Chromatography (George Field), 44–5, 183,
   185, 345
chrome green, 177
chrome orange, 176
chrome pigments, 175–7
chrome yellow, 11, 175–6, 177, 216, 303
chromium, 32, 33, 34
chromium oxide green, 176, 180
chromolithography, 316, 317
chrysocolla, 70
chrysography, 111
Church, Arthur, 179
Ciba, 242
Cicero, 75
CIE diagram, 50, 51–2, 337–8
cinabrese, 89
cinnabar, 71, 72, 76–7, 85, 86, 89, 102, 108
Cione, Nardo di, 297; *Plate 5.2*
Citröen, Paul, 354
City Rises, The, 350
clut (colour look-up table), 338
coal-tar dyes, 235–6, 237, 238, 239, 241,
   246, 251, 256–8, *259*, 329
cobalt, 32, 133–4, 178–9
cobalt blue, 4, 33, 178–9, 180, 277, 279, 304
cobalt green, 179, 180
cobalt violet, 179, 180
cochineal, 36, 108, 155, 301
collage, 360
Collen, Henry, 331
collodion process, 321–2
collotype process, 322, 326
Colour (magazine), 334
colour(s)
   Berlin and Kay's hierarchy of, 16
   causes of, 28–38
   dependence on circumstances under
      which we look at, 38–9
   and emotions, 23
   in Modernism, 343–59
   and linguistics, 14, 15–17
   measuring, 50–54
   naming, 14–18
   organization of, 21–4
   and perception, 4, 38, 39
colour blindness, 47

Colour Field group, 352, 371–6
colour gamut, 336–9
colour harmony, 20, 56, 121, 123, 124
Colour Index International, 381
colour notation scheme, 52 3
colour space, 51, 52
colour vision, 47–50, 265
colour wheels, 41–2, 42, 43, 45, 50, 52, 198,
    199, 357, 358
colourists, professional, 183, 233, 234
colourmen, 10, 180, 183
complementary colours, 46, 187, 197–200,
    211, 212, 351
*Compositiones ad tingendu (Recipes for
    Colouring)*, 86, 93
computer art, 340–41
computer screens, 337–8
Concise History of Modern Painting (Read),
    308
cone cells, in the eye, 47–9
conservators, 285–6, 288
    see also restoration
Constable, John, 153–4, 181, 183, 184, 275
contrast, of colours, 197–200
Conversion of St Hubert, The, 136
copper, 33, 34, 35
copper blue, 130
copper carbonate, 103
copper resinate, 128, 129–30, 299
copper silicate, 70
Corbichon, Jean, 77
Corot, Camille, 196
Correggio, Antonio, 123, 151
cost
    of colour in Renaissance, 134–8
cotton, 256
Council of Trent, 146
Counter-Reformation, 146, 147, 148
Courbet, Gustave, 153, 196, 208–9
Courtois, Bernard, 169, 170, 185
Crace Calvert, Frederick, 235, 236, 237
cracks
    in paintings, 288, 289, 290
Cranach, Lucas, 136, 309–10
craquelure, 288
crimson, 66–7
Crivelli, Carlo, 137; *Plate 5.6*
crocoite, 175

Crows Flying over a Cornfield, 260
Crucifixion, The (Tintoretto), 134
Cryla range of paints, 368
crystal field, 33–4
Crystal Palace, 55–6
Cubism/Cubists, 349, 350, 351, 360
Cullen, William, 232–3

D'Agoty, Jacques Gautier, 314
Daguerre, Louis-Jacques-Mandé, 320–21
D'Allemagna, Giovanni, 136
Danae, 142–3, 308
d'Anastasy, Johann, 67
Dance, 346
darkening, of pigments, 297 9
David, Gerard, 129, 294, 298
David, Jacques Louis, 193
Davy, Humphry, 178, 185, 320
De clarea (On Brightness), 102
De coloribus et artibus Romanorum
    (Heraclius), 93, 300
de la Chambre, Martin Cureau, 264
De La Rue, Thomas, 317
de Mayerne, Sir Theodore Turquet, 131,
    154
de Montjosieu, Louis
    Commentary on Painting, 264
De re metallica (Agricola), 133
De Stijl, 359
Death of Actaeon, 142
Degas, Edgar, 204, 208, 324
Déjeuner sur l'Herbe, Le, 209
Delacroix, Eugène, 27, 191–4, 198, 207,
    208; *Plate 8.1*
Delaroche, Paul, 321
Delaunay, Robert, 151, 261, 350–51, 352
Delaunay, Sonia, 151, 310
Democritus, 73–4, 75, 262
Demoiselles d'Avignon, 261
Denis, Maurice, 218, 349
Derain, André, 346, 347, 348, 349;
    Plate 13.1
Descartes, René, 26, 39
Descent from the Cross, 134
Desserte, La, 344
Devonshire Hunting Tapestries, 285
Dickens, Charles, 241
Diesbach, 273–4

digital technology, 335–40
diketopyrrolo-pyrroles (DPPs), 383
Dioscorides, 126
Dippel, Johann Konrad, 273
direct imaging printing, 339
discolouration, 290, 297–9, 301–2, 304
disegno
  and *colore*, 8, 10, 120, 124, 145, 181, 190,
    362
distempers, 79, 102
Divisionism, 348–9, 350–51
Doerner Institute, 304
Doerner, Max, 78, 101, 126, 152, 153, 257,
  258, 259, 284, 297, 304–5, 357
Doesburg, Theo van, 359
*Doge Agostino Barbarigo Kneeling before the
  Virgin and Child*, 270
Dongen, Kees van, 346
Dossie, Robert, 132, 133, 301
DPPs (diketopyrrolo-pyrroles), 383
dragonsblood, 76, 77
drugs
  dyes and, 250–51
drying agents, *see* siccatives
Duccio, *Plate 10.2*
Duchamp, Marcel, 360
Dufy, Raoul, 261, 348
Dughet, Gaspard, 300
DuPont, 366, 367, 382
Dürer, Albrecht, 82, 103, 104, 138, 271
dyes, 36, 37, 222–59
  aniline, *see* aniline dyes
  and antiquity, 64–7, 72–3, 223–8
  and artists, 257–8
  azo, 249–50, 255, 258, 374, 382
  and chemistry/chemists, 223, 232–4,
    237, 243–6, 249
  coal-tar, *see* coal-tar dyes
  and colour photography, 328–31
  colourfast, 255–6
  and cotton, 256
  identification of organic, 293–4
  indigo, 227–9, 252–4
  influence of chemical theory, 242–6
  and mordants, 64–5, 110, 232, 237, 256
  and public taste for colour, 230–4
  purple, 236–41
  scarlet, 229–30

synthetic alizarin, 248–9
Tyrian purple, 224–5
used as drugs, 250–51
and wool, 223–30

earth pigments, 32–5, 75, 151–2
  use of by cave painters, 59–60
East India Company, 155, 156
Eastman, George, 324
École des Beaux-Arts (Paris), 190
EDX (energy-dispersive X-ray analysis),
  292
egg tempera, 101–2, 126, 127, 297
Egypt, ancient, 56, 69, 91–2
  and chemistry, 57–8
  and dyes, 72
  glass making, 63
  glazes, 63
  mordanting techniques, 64–5
  painting, 69
  pigments, 69–70
Egyptian blue, 57–8, 63
Egyptian faience, 62, 63
Egyptian frit, *see* Egyptian blue
Ehrlich, Paul, 250–51
Einstein, Albert, 28
El Greco (Domenikos Theotokopoulos),
  134, 147, 150
Elderly Man as St Paul, An, 163
elements, 32–3, 165, 166–8
Elements of Colour (Itten), 355
emerald green, 149, 174, 177
emotions and colour, 23
Empedocles, 75
enamel paints, 364, 365, 366–7, 380
energy-dispersive X-ray analysis (EDX),
  292
Engelmann, Godefroy, 316
Enlightenment, 146
Entombment, The (Bouts), 133
eosin, 249, 257
Equicola, 8
Ernst, Max, 360
Evans, Edmund, 318–19
Expressionism, 219, 350, 365
extenders, 60, 171
Ex Voto for the Shrine of St Rita, 281–2, *Plate
  10.6*

eye, 47–9, *48*

fading, of pigments, 296, 301–2, 375
Faraday, Michael, 12
Fauvism, 218, 246–50, 351
Feast in the Home of Levi, 147, 149
Feininger, Lyonel, 261
Fénéon, Felix, 213, 214, 215
Fernbach, Franz, 302
Field, George, 56, 155–6, 172, 183–5, 188,
    224, 275, 343
    on cadmium red, 345
    Chromatography, 44–5, 183–4, 185, 345
    on chrome yellow, 303
    on Indian yellow, 156
    on Prussian blue, 275, 276, 3023
    and Turner, 185
    and ultramarine, 278
Filarete, A. A., 103
Fine Art academies, 190
Fischer, N. W., 179
Fischer, Rudolf, 329–30
Fisherman at Sea, 181
flavonoids, 36
Flowers in a Terracotta Vase, 159, 302; *Plate
    11.6*
folium, 105–7
Fondaco dei Tedeschi (Venice), 134
fool's gold, 266
Foppa, Vincenzo, 137
Forman, Simon, 80–81
four-colour printing, 234
Fourcroy, Antoine François, 168, 175
Fourier-transform infrared (FTIR)
    spectroscopy, 292
Fox Talbot, William Henry, 321, 322
François, Jean Charles, 315
Frankenthaler, Helen, 365, 368, 376
Frankland, Edward, 245
French Academy, 190, 191, 194, 195–6, 208
French purple, 236–7, 240
fresco painting, 78–9, 100–1, 124, 272, 298
Friedlander, P., 226
Fromentin, Eugène, 324
fuchsine, 241
Futurist painters, 350

Gagarin, Yuri, 282

Gage, John, 3, 53, 308, 334–5, 373
Gainsborough, Thomas, 152, 153, 182, 274,
    302
Gainsborough's Forest, 302
gamboge, 156–7
Gare Saint-Lazare, La, 206–7
Gauguin, Paul, 215, 217–18, 219, 221, 347,
    363
Gay-Lussac, Joseph, 178
Geigy, 242
Gelder, Aert de, 144
Géricault, Théodore, 153
Gesner, Conrad, 167
gesso, 100
giallorino/giallolino, 30, 112–13, 137
gilding, 109–10
Giorgione, 140, 141
Giotto di Bondone, 101, 117–18, 272; *Plates
    4.3, 5.1*
Girl in a Fur Wrap, 161
glair, 102
glas (Celtic colour term), 15, 63
Glass Façade, 352
glass-making, 61–3, 133
glazes/glazing, 62, 63–4, 126–7, 159
Gmelin, Christian, 277
Goethe, Johann Wolfgang von, 22, 25, 30,
    38, 42, 207, 276, 357
    on complementary colours, 45–6
    Theory of Colours, 186–7, 197, 362
gold, 35, 85, 109–12, 136–7
gold leaf, 109–11, 136
Golden, Mark, 370
Golden, Sam, 369
goldsmiths, 97
Gombrich, Ernst, 3, 6, 19–20, 289
Gonzaga Cycle, 134
Gossaert, Jan, 294
Graebe, Carl, 247–8
graffiti art, 365–6
*Grande Jatte, La see Sunday Afternoon on the
    Island of La Grande Jatt*
Great Exhibition (1851), 55–6, 317
Greeks/Greece, 56–7, 64, 73–9, 114
    and blue, 262–3
    chemistry of, 73
    colour awareness, 17
    dislike of pigment mixing, 19, 74

Greeks/Greece (*cont.*)
    four-colour palette, 14, 19, 56, 73–7, 161,
      263, 264
    and light and dark, 15, 17, 39, 40, 74
    manufacture of Tyrian purple, 224
    painting of sculpture, 75
    and pigments, 75
    use of colour, 74–5
green(s), 17, 113–14, 159, 161, 173–7, 301
    chrome, 177
    cobalt, 179, 180
    confusion with red in ancient times,
      14–15, 108
    and copper resinate, 128, 129–30, 299
    dissatisfaction with by artists, 159
    emerald, 149, 174, 177
    mixing of, 159–60
    Ostwald and, 357
    profusion of prescriptions for, 158
    Scheele's, 173–4
    viridian, 176–7, 216
green verditer, 131
grey, 51, 52, 357
Griess, Peter, 250
grinding
    of gold, 111
    of pigments, 32, 98, 202
Groupe des Artistes Indépendants, 210
Gropius, Walter, 353, 354, 355, 356, 357
Guernica, 307
Guignet, C. E., 177
Guildford from the Banks of the Wey, 173
guild, 97, 98, 135
    medieval, 97, 98, 135
    and dyers, 231–2, 234
Guimet, Jean-Baptiste, 277, 278
Guise, Sir John, 313
Guyton de Morveau, Bernard, 168, 169,
    171

Hakluyt, Richard, 155, 228–9
half-tone printing, 315–16
Hals, Frans, 145
Hamilton, Richard, 366–7
Handmaid to the Arts, The (Dossie), 132, 301
Hansa pigments, 258
Hanunoo, 16
Hard Edge school, 377–8

Harley, Rosamond, 131
Harvard murals (Rothko), 374–5
Harvey, Alexander, 237
Haupt, Johann, 331
Hauron, Louis Ducos du, 331
Hay, D. R., 44
Helena Fourment as Venus, 161
Hellenistic culture, 77
Hellot, Jean, 274
Helmholtz, Hermann von, 47, 194, 195,
    198–9, 343
Heraclius, 108, 111, 114
    De coloribus et artibus Romanorum, 93, 300
Hering, Ewald, 220, 357
Hers Is a Lush Situation, 366
Heumann, Karl, 253
Highways and Byways, 352
Hill, David Octavius, 324
Hills, Paul, 270–71
Hillside in Provence, 216–17; *Plate 8.8*
Hiroshima (Klein), 281
Hockney, David, 341, 364, 368, 369
Hoechst, 242, 250, 252, 254
Hoffmann, Roald, 227
Hofmann, August Wilhelm, 235, 237–8,
    242–3, 244, 246, 249
Hogarth, William, 275
Holbein, Hans, 286
Hollyhocks and Other Flowers in a Vase, 159
Hölzel, Adolf, 353, 356
Homage to the Square, 355
Homer, 17
Hoogstraten, Samuel van, 159
Hooke, Robert, 167
Hooker's green, 157
Hopkins, Arthur, 88
Houbraken, Arnold, 163
house paints, 365–6
Hoyland, John, 365, 369, 378, 384
hue, 51–2
Hughes, Arthur, 237; *Plate 9.2*
Humanism, 270
Humans Begin to Fly, 281
Hunt, William Holman, 185, 187, 188, 195,
    302–3; *Plates 7.2, 8.2*
Huygens, Christiaan, 46–7
Huysmans, Joris Karl, 182, 204, 207, 210
Huysum, Jan van, 159, 302; *Plate 11.6*

Hyatt, John and Isaiah, 366

ICI (Imperial Chemical Industries), 254, 256
IG Farben, 254, 258, 279, 328
Il Libro dell' Arte (Cennino Cennini), 20, 83, 99
illuminated manuscripts, 95, 102, 105, 113, 114
Illustrated London News, 318
Immaculate Conception (Velázquez), 301
Imperial Chemical Industries *see* ICI
Impression: Setting Sun (Fog), 200, 209
Impressionists/Impressionism, 3, 18, 27, 133, 177, 182, 187, 189–221, 347, 349
  attitude towards white, 205–6
  and black, 206
  challenging conservatism of French Academy, 191
  change in opinion towards, 210
  concept of contrast in complementary colours, 46, 197–200
  and Delacroix, 194
  devising of own rules, 190
  and exterior light and shade, 196
  importance of new pigments to goals, 200
  not heedful of instability of pigments, 200–1
  and open-air painting, 195–7
  own exhibitions, 209–10
  pigments used, 204, 205; *Plate 8.4*
  and purple, 207
  rejection of by Salon, 208
  ridicule and scorn towards, 191, 208, 209–10
  suppliers of pigments and materials to, 200–4
  technique and use of colour, 204–7
  use of unmixed colours, 205
  see also individual artists
Independent Group (UK), 367
Indian yellow, 155–6
indigo, 36, 65, 76, 105, 226–9, 230, 252–4, 262, 301
  as a dye, 227–9, 231, 232, 255
  in oil, 128–9
  and 'pencil blue' process, 233

source of, 226
as substitute for ultramarine, 135, 272, 273
synthetic, 252–4
infra-red spectroscopy, 293
Ingres, Jean-Auguste-Dominique, 5, 191–2, 193, 194, 198, 278
inks, 331–5, 339–40
intaglio printing methods, 315
International Klein Blue, 280–1
International Style, 116
iodine scarlet, 185, 303
ionamine dyes, 256
Iqbal, Abdul, 383
iris green, 114
iron, 33, 34, 154
iron oxides, 63, 64, 151, 154
Itten, Johannes, 270, 353–4, 355, 356, 357
Ives, Frederick Eugene, 327, 332

Jabir ibn Hayyan, 85, 86, 267
James, Henry, 3
Jawlensky, Alexei von, 261
Jesuits, 147
Jones, Owen, 55–6, 76, 317
Jonson, Ben
  The Alchemist, 80
Judd, Donald, 363, 380
Judgement of Paris, The (Rubens), 161
Jung, Carl, 260–61
Juno Discovering Jupiter with Io, 301–2

Kandinsky, Wassily, 2, 217, 357, 362–3, 372; *Plate 1.2*
  affinity for blue, 260, 261
  and Bauhaus school, 353, 356
  influence of Theosophy, 22
  Concerning the Spiritual in Art, 23
  use of colour, 22–3, 354, 371
Kapoor, Anish, 11, 275, 380; *Plates 1.1, 10.4*
Kay, Paul, 16, 17, 59
Keats, John
  Lamia, 25
Kekulé, Friedrich August, 245–6, 249
Kemp, Martin, 84
kermes, 66, 72, 107, 108, 230, 296
Kirchner, Ernst Ludwig, 319
Klaproth, Martin, 382

Klee, Paul, 27, 261, 352, 353, 354, 356, 357, 359
Klein, Yves, 1–2, 5, 11, 12, 13, 37, 279–82, 362, 378; *Plates 10.5, 10.6*
Kluver, Billy, 340
Kodak, 330
Kolbe, Hermann, 250
Kooning, Willem de, 127–8, 376
Köttig, F. A., 277
Kristeva, Julia, 12
Kunckel, J., 134
Kunstbüchlein, 94

lac, 72
Lacaze-Duthiers, Félix Henri de, 226
Lady in Blue, 261
Laforgue, Jules, 196
lake pigments, 11, 36, 70, 72–3, 107, 113, 135–6, 155, 157, 293, 296
landscape painting, 158–60
Landscape at Sunset, 352
Landscape with Red Trees, 348
Landscape with Yellow Birds, 352
lapis lazuli, 103, 104, 266–8, 293
Large Blue Horses, 261
laser microspectral analysis, 292
Last Judgement, 146–7
Last Supper, The (Bouts), 135
Lastman, Pieter, 301
Laurent, Auguste, 245
Lavacourt under Snow, 205, 207; *Plate 8.6*
Lavoisier, Antoine, 165, 167–8, 244
Lawrence, Thomas, 175, 184
Layard, George Somes, 287
lazurite, 266
Le Blon, Jacob Christoph, 274, 310–13, 315, 335, 342; *Plate 12.1*
Le Corbusier, 9, 10, 12–13
Le Gray, Gustave, 324
Le Prince, Jean Baptiste, 316
lead, 88, 89, 168, 297
lead antimonate, 58, 112, 113
lead carbonate, 70–71
lead glazes, 64
lead oxychloride, 173
lead white *see* white lead
lead-tin yellow, 91, 160
Leclaire, E. C., 170

Leiden papyrus, 67, 68, 69, 85, 91, 92
Leider, Philip, 363
lemon yellow (strontium chromate), 304
Leonardo da Vinci, 7–8, 9, 30, 46, 122–3, 143, 147, 158; *Plate 5.3*
Levi, Primo, 13–14, 254
Levinstein, Ivan, 254
LeWitt, Sol, 373
Liber diversarum artium (*Book of Divers Arts*), 128
Liberal Arts, 7, 8, 9
Lichtenstein, Roy, 369–70
Liebermann, Carl, 247–8
Liebermann, H., 382
Liebig, Justus von, 174
light, 35, 37, 46
    and colour, 28–32, 39
    mixing of, 42, 44
    particle and wave theories, 46–7
light absorption, 28–9, 37, 53
Light and Colour (Goethe's Theory) – The Morning After the Deluge, 186
light scattering, 29–32, 37
Light and So Much Else, The, 352
linear perspective, 118–19
linseed oil, 37
Linstead, R. Patrick, 255
Linton, W., *Ancient and Modern Colours*, 275
Lippi, Filippino, 135, 137, 139
Liquitex, 368
lithography, 316–17, 339
Lithol Red, 374
local colour, 213–14
Lomazzo, Giovanni Paolo, 300
Lord John Stuart and his Brother, Lord Bernard Stuart, 153
Lorrain, Claude, 145, 159, 300
Louis, Morris, 5, 369, 376–7; *Plate 14.3*
Lucca manuscript, 126
Lumière, Auguste and Louis, 327–8
Luther, Martin, 81
Lutma, Jean, 315
Luxe, Calme et Volupté, 348
lye (caustic soda), 65, 66, 73, 107, 267–8
Lyons, John, 18

McLuhan, Marshall, 362
Macquer, Pierre-Joseph, 233

madder red, 36, 73, 108, 155, 184, 232, 234, 247, 249, 301

Madonna (Parmigianino), 148–9

Madonna Alba, 124

Madonna and Child in an Evening Landscape, 134

Madonna and Child with Saints John the Baptist and Catherine of Alexandria, 270; Plate 10.3

Madonna del Granduca, The, 124; Plate 5.4

Madonna with Four Saints, 136

Madonna of the Harpies, 270

Madonna with Saints and Members of the Pesaro Family, 141

magenta, 242

magic, 83 4

Magna paints, 369, 377

Magnus, Albertus, 81, 85, 89

maiolica, 64

malachite, 69, 128, 298

Malevich, Kasimir, 378, 380

Man Ray, 324

Manet, Édouard, 173–4, 208, 210, 324

manganese blue, 27

manganese violet, 180

Mannerism/Mannerists, 125, 146, 148–9, 150–51

Mansfield, Charles, 235

Mappae clavicula (Little Key to Painting), 86, 92–3, 107, 111, 114

Marc, Franz, 261

Marcillat, Guillaume de, 137

Marco Polo, 267

Mars pigments, 11, 154–5, 345

Martyrdom of St Sebastian, The, 122

Masaccio/Masolino, Plate 4.1

massicot, 34, 113

mathematics
and art, 7, 8

Mathesius, Johann, 133–4

Matisse, Henri, 5, 219, 261, 344, 345–6, 347, 348, 349, 350

Mauclair, Camille, 349

Maule, George, 241

mauve, 237, 240–1

Maxwell, James Clerk, 28, 42, 44, 46, 47, 49, 197, 326–7, 331

measuring, of colour, 50–54

Melanthius, 75

Mengs, Anton Raphael, 184

mercury, 85, 86, 89–90, 111

mercury sulphide, 35

Mérimée, J.-F.-L., 155, 180, 202–3, 278

Merret, Christopher, 131

Merrifield, Mary, 112, 391 n. 8

Mesopotamia, 62, 64

Messina, Antonello da, 125

metacinnabar, 35, 297

metallic paints, 379

Meteorology (Aristotle), 263

mezzotinting, 311, 313

Michelangelo, 3, 124–5, 146, 150, 361

microscopic examination of paint surfaces, 294–5

Middle Ages, 20, 32, 72, 91, 93, 102–15, 117, 118, 265, 364
pigments, 102–15
surfaces for painting, 100

Milkmaid, The, 160

Millais, John Everett, 25, 187, 317

miltos, 74

mineral acids, 60

mineral white (permanent white), 171

minimalism, 352, 355

minium, 102

Miracle of St Mark Freeing the Slave, 150

mixing, 27
additive, 42, 44, 47, 122, 183, 197, 312, 336
ancient taboo of and caution towards, 19, 34, 44–5, 74, 120, 299, 311
loss of brilliance in, 74
optical, 140, 211–13, 214, 215
subtractive, 44, 122, 183, 211, 311, 312

Moholy-Nagy, László, 324

Mohr, Manfred, 341

Molteni, Giuseppe, 287

Mona Lisa, 123, 307

monastral blue, 36, 279

Monastral Fast Blue, 255

Mondrian, Piet, 21, 22, 359

Monet, Claude, 164, 172–3, 194, 195, 196, 200, 201, 205, 206–7, 209, 210, 275; Plates 8.3, 8.6

monks, 95, 97

monochrome engravings, 342

Moorish lustre-ware, 64
mordants, 64–5, 110, 232, 237, 256
Moreau, Gustave, 347
Morisot, Berthe, 173, 196
Morris, William, 8
Morse, Samuel, 320–21
mosaic gold, 91, 111–12
Motherwell, Robert, 375–6
Mountains and Sea, 376
Mourning of Christ, The, 118
Mousmé, La, 275
Mr and Mrs Clark and Percy, 369
Mukharji, T. N., 156
Mulready, William, 303
Munch, Edvard, 219, 310
Munsell, Albert, 53, 358
Müntz, J. H., 78
murexide, 236
music
    link with colour, 23
Music, 346
Music in the Tuileries Gardens, 173–4

Nabi Group, 218
Nabokov, Vladimir, 7
Nake, Frieder, 341
Naphthol Red, 374
Napier, James, 237
Naples yellow, 58, 160
National Gallery, 286
natural products, 36, 243
Needham, Joseph, 85
Neo-Impressionists, 27, 215, 348
Newman, Barnett, 369, 371–2, 373
Newton, Isaac, 28, 38, 39, 97, 265
    and alchemy, 81–2
    colour wheel, 41, *42*
    experiments with coloured powders,
        197, 212
    experimentum crucis, 26, 186
    Opticks, 41, 46
    'unweaving the rainbow', 25–6, 41, *42*
Nicholson, Edward Chambers, 241
nickel, 33
Nicomachos, 75
Niépce, Joseph Nicéphore, 320
Nietzsche, Friedrich, 75
Night Café, The, 219–20; *Plate 8.10*

nitrocellulose enamel paints, 366–7
Nixon, Francis, 234
Noland, Kenneth, 364, 369, 370, 376–8;
    Plate 14.4
Norgate, Edward, 152, 157
Norris, Richard Hill, 322

Ochre and Red on Red, 371; *Plate 14.2*
ochre pigments, 33, 59, 70, 74, 163, 216
Odalisque with a Slave, 5, 192, 198
oil painting/paints, 125–9, 140, 300, 365
    advantages, 127–8
    modifying of appearance of pigments,
        38, 128–9
    origins, 102, 125–7, 129
    and ultramarine, 128, 270
O'Keeffe, Georgia, 342
Old Woman, 261
Oldenburg, Claes, 362
Olympia, 209, 324
Ommen, Otmaer, 135
Ophelia, 187–8
Opie, John, 291
optical mixing, 140, 211–13, 214, 215
orange, 23, 44, 45
    cadmium, 45, 172, 345
    chrome, 176
    and realgar *see* realgar
orange vermilion, 184–5
organic chemistry, 242–56
Oriental art, 71
Orphists/Orphism, 151, 351
orpiment, 69, 89, 112, 136, 139, 159, 300
Osborne, Harold, 17
Ostwald, Friedrich Wilhelm, 12, 356–9
Oud, J. P. P., 359
Our English Coasts, 195; *Plate 8.2*
oxygen, 167
Ozenfant, Amédée, 9

painting techniques
    analysis of, 294–5, *295*
Palaeolithic artists, 58–9
Palette with a Landscape, 2, 206
Palmer, Samuel, 303–4
panel painting, 101–2, 110
Pannetier, 176, 177
Papyrus X, 67

Paracelsus, 81, 91
pararealgar, 293
parchment, 100
Parmigianino, 148
patent yellow, 11
patrons, 97–8, 135, 136
Paul IV, Pope, 146, 147
Paxton, Joseph, 55
Peacham, Henry
  The Compleat Gentleman, 159
peacock's colours, 31–2
Pelletier, 132
pencil blue process ('English blue' process), 233
Pencil of Nature, The (Fox Talbot), 321
Perkin, William Henry, 238–41, 244, 248–9
Permanent Pigments (paint company), 368
permanent white, 171
Perrin, Jean, 157
Perugino, Pietro, 122, 271
Peruzzi Chapel (Florence), 101
pharmaceuticals
  and dyes, 250–51
phenol, 235, 246
Philosopher's Stone, 81, 85, 86, 88
Phoenicians, 224, 225
phosphors, 336, 337, 338
photography, 319–31, 332–3, 335
  colour, 325–31
  early, 319–21
  innovations and processes, 321–3
  painters as photographers, 324
photopigments, 49–50
phthalocyanine colours, 255, 279
Physica et mystica, 92
Picasso, Pablo, 1, 260, 261, 275, 344, 350, 361, 367, 379–80
picric acid, 235–6
Piemontese, Alessio, 94
pigments
  ancient recipes, 67–73
  discolouration of and instability, 200–1, 203, 290, 296–9, 300, 302–3, 304, 397–9
  methods in analysing identity of, 291–4
  origin of colour in, 32–8
  suppliers of, 201–2
  synthetic, 165–88

taboo about mixing, 19, 34, 44–5, 74, 120, 299, 311
Piles, Roger de, 158–9
  Elémens de peinture pratique, 300–1
pinks, 157–8
Pino, Paolo, 84
Piombo, Sebastiano del, 140
Pissarro, Camille, 2, 191, 194, 200, 206, 215, 221, 295, 347
Pius IV, Pope, 146, 147
Pius V, Pope, 147
Planetary Reliefs, 282
plant pigments, 36
Platnauer, Maurice, 17
Plato, 73, 74, 263
Pliny, 3, 12, 64–5, 66, 71, 75–6, 89, 112, 126, 228
  on Egyptian mordanting techniques, 64
  four-colour scheme, 14, 19
  and indigo, 226–7
  Natural History, 91–2, 263–4
  and origins of glass, 61
  and Tyrian purple, 223–4, 225
Plutarch, 19, 74
pointillism, 212–15
Pollaiuolo, Antonio del, 121, 122; *Plate 11.5*
Pollock, Jackson, 362, 364, 372, 376
Polygnotos, 75
Pompeii, 14, 56, 78–9
Ponte, Giovanni del, *Plate 4.5*
Pool of London, The, 346; *Plate 13.1*
Pop Art, 362, 366, 384
Pope, Alexander
  The Rape of the Lock, 32
Portrait of a Gentleman, 175
Portrait of Hendrickje Stoffels, 164; *Plate 6.6*
Portrait of Jacob Trip, 163
Portrait of a Man, 142, 161; *Plate 5.8*
Portrait of Margaretha de Geer, 163
Portrait of a Woman and Child, 162
Portrait with a Green Stripe, 349–50
potash, 61, 106, 273
Poussin, Nicolas, 113, 145, 159, 300
Practice of Painting and Perspective Made Easy, The, 159
Pre-Raphaelites, 171, 187–8, 364
Previati, Gaetano
  Scientific Principles of Divisionism 350

Priestley, Joseph, 167
primary colours, 40–42, 56, 263–5
Principe, Lawrence, 9
printing, 309–19
    chiaroscuro, 309, *310*, 315, 318
    and digital processing, 335–9
    half-tone, 315–16
    and inks, 331–5
    and lithography, 316–17, 339
Procion dyes, 256
Prussian blue, 11, 34, 157, 159, 273–5, 276,
    301, 302
Pullar, John, 230
Purkinje, J. E., 49
purple, 106, 222–3, 230, 301
    aniline, 237–40
    dyes, 236–41
    in Impressionist paintings, 207
    Tyrian, 36, 106, 222, 223–6, 227, 236
purpurine, 247
Pynchon, Thomas
    Gravity's Rainbow, 254
PVA (polyvinyl acetate) paints, 370

quicksilver (mercury), 85
quinacridones, 382–3
quinine, 238, 244

Raft of the Medusa, 153
rainbow, 15, 25–6, 29, *30*, 41, 53
raking light, 294, *295*
Rand, John, 202
Ransonnet, Baron, 331–2
Raphael, 123–4, 129, 148; *Plate 5.4*
Raphael Cartoons, 314
Ratdolt, Erhard, 309
Rauschenberg, Robert, 340, 366
realgar, 69–70, 89, 139, 142, 176, 293,
    301
Realists, 18, 196, 208, 209
Récréation italienne, 302
red(s), 17, 44, 107–9, 135–6, 154–5, 272
    brazil as source of, 107
    cadmium, 35, 344–5, 383
    and cinnabar, 71, 72, 76–7, 85, 80, 89,
        102, 108
    and cochineal, 36, 108, 155, 301

confusion with green in ancient times,
    14–15, 108
confusion of medieval terminology with
    regard to, 89
Goethe on, 186
madder, 36, 73, 108, 155, 184, 232, 234,
    247, 249, 301
Mars, 154
and scarlet, 18, 229–30
special significance of to alchemy, 87–8
see also vermilion
red dyes, 65–7, 107–8, 241–2
red lead, 70, 71–2, 89, 135, 297
Red Studio, The, 5, 344
Reeves, William and Thomas, 201
refiner's verditer, 131
refraction, 29, *30*, 37
Regatta at Argenteuil, 200; *Plate 8.3*
Reinhardt, Ad, 17
religious art, 20, 69, 95–7, 146–7
Rembrandt, 134, 151, 153, 154, 157, 161,
    162–4; *Plate 6.6*
Renaissance, 21, 27, 72, 111, 116–43, 145,
    151
    blue pigments, 130–34
    cost of colour, 134–8
    debate about *disegno* and *colore* 120
    emergence of light and shade, 117,
        118–19
    and Humanism, 117–20
    new colours, 129–34
    and oil paints, 125–9
    painting styles, 120–25, 140–43
    Venetian painters, 139–43
Renoir, Pierre Auguste, 195, 202, 204–5,
    207, 209, 278; *Plate 8.5*
repainting, 288, 402 n. 1
reproduction of art, 306–42
    and digital processing, 335–9
    and Le Blon's three-colour printing
        technique, 310–14
    and photography, 319–31, 332, 334, 335
    printing methods *see* printing
resins, 78, 129, 301
    synthetic, 364–70
restoration, 283–5
    of Tura's *Allegorical Figure,* 286 90, 289
Resurrection (Titian), 140

retina, 47, *48*

retinal, in photopigments, 49–50

Reynolds, Joshua, 152, 153, 182, 187, 291, 301

rhodamine dyes, 255

Rhodopas M60A, 280

Riese, Ferdinand, 248

Riley, Bridget, 4, 24, 370

Ripolin, 367

Rohde, Johan, 203

Roman painters, 14, 15, 56, 64, 225, 227

Romanticism, 187

Rood, Ogden, 213–14, 346

   Modern Chromatics, 199 200, *199*, 211

rose-pink, 157–8

Rosetti, Dante Gabriel, 187, 271, 172

Rothko, Mark, 361, 362, 371, 372–3; *Plate 14.2*

   Harvard murals, 374–5

   relationship with his materials, 373–5

Rothko Chapel murals, 374, 375

Roussel, Ker Xavier, 218

Royal Institution, 318

Rubens, Peter Paul, 134, 152, 160–61; *Plate 6.4*

Rumford, Count, 318

Runge, Philipp Otto, 52, 187, 358

Ruskin, John, 8, 181, 184, 195, 212, 284, 317

Russ, Friedrich, 174

Russell, John, 344

Russell, Morgan, 351

Ryhiner, Jean, 234

Ryland, William Wynne, 315–16

Sacks, Oliver, 13

saffron, 113, 154

Sahlins, M., 53

St Francis Renouncing his Heritage, 229

St George and the Dragon, 150; *Plate 6.3*

Saints Peter and Dorothy, 105; *Plate 4.4*

Saladijn de Stœvere, 135, 136

Salon of the French Academy, 190, 208, 209

Salon d'Automne, 349

Salon des Indépendants, 348, 349

Salon des Refusés, 209, 210

Salvarsan, 251

Salviati, Francesco, 125

Samson and Delilah, 161; *Plate 6.4*

San Vitale mosaics, 226

sap green, 114

Sargent, John Singer, 195

Sarto, Andrea del, 270

Sartre, Jean-Paul, 352

Saskia in Arcadian Costume, 163

Sassetta, Stefano de Giovanni, 229

Sattler, Wilhelm, 174

saturation, 52, 53

Savage, William, 318

scarlet, 18, 229–30

   iodine, 185, 303

Scarmiglioni, Guido Antonio, 40

Scheele, Carl Wilhelm, 173, 344

Scheele's green, 173–4

Scheit, Kaspar, 103–4

Schmidt-Rottluff, Karl, 319

Schoenberg, Arnold, 22, 23

Schoenmaekers, M. H. J., 22

Schönbein, Christian Friedrich, 366

Schulz, Gottfried, 87

Schulze, Johann Heinrich, 319

Schürer, Christoph, 133

science

   and art, 6, 7, 9, 11, 25

   division between 'pure' and 'applied', 73

   see also chemistry

Scream, The, 219

Scriabin, Alexander, 22

secco wall painting, 101

secondary colours, 41

Secreta mulierum (The Secrets of Women), 94

Secreti, 94

Segreti Per Colori (Secrets of Colours), 104

selenium, 345

Self-portrait (Rembrandt), 161

Self-portrait with Maulstick, Palette and Brushes, 164

Self-portrait as Zeuxis, 144–5

Senefelder, John Aloysius, 316

Serusier, Paul, 218; *Plate 8.9*

Seurat, Georges, 27, 210–13, 215, 304, 348; *Plate 8.7*

sfumato method, 123, 124

Shane, Eric, 182

She, 367

siccatives, 126, 170

sienna pigments, 151
Signac, Paul, 27, 179, 198, 210–11, 213, 214, 215, 348
sil, 264
silver, 131
'silver-blue', 132
Simpson, George, 241
Simpson, Maule and Nicholson, 250
sinoper, 89
sinople, 14–15
Siqueiros, David Alfaro, 364–5, 366
Sistine Chapel, 124, 146–7
smalt, 133–4, 135, 178, 272, 273, 301
Smith, Cyril Stanley, 92
soap manufacture, 61, 65
Société d'Encouragement pour l'Industrie Nationale, 276, 277, 316
soda (sodium carbonate), 61
Sower, The, 220
Spanish gold, 90
spectroscopic techniques, 292
Stahl, George Ernst, 233, 274
Stella, Frank, 363, 365, 377, 378–80, 384; *Plates 14.5, 14.6*
Stevens, Wallace, 205–6
Still, Clyfford, 371, 373
stipple engraving, 315–16
Stockholm papyrus, 67–8, 69, 91, 92, 225, 228
Stromeyer, Friedrich, 172
strontium chromate yellow, 180
Strozzi chapel, 137, 139
subtractive mixing, 44, 122, 183, 211, 311, 312
sulphur, 85, 86, 89–90
Sun Discs, 351
Sun Flowers, 284
Sun Rising through Vapour, 181
Sunday Afternoon on the Island of La Grande Jatte, 212, 304; *Plate 8.7*
suppliers
    of paints and materials, 200–4
Symonds, Richard, 113
synaesthesia, 22, 23
Synchronism, 351–2
synthetic dyes, 235–58
synthetic fibres, 255–6

Talisman, The, 218; *Plate 8.9*
Tanguy, Julien, 203–4
tapestry, 314
Tarquin and Lucretia, 142
Tassaert, M., 276
tekhlet, 227
tempera methods, 70, 101, 127
    see also egg tempera
Tempest, The, 141
tertiary colours, 52, 184
Thales of Miletos, 68–9
Thénard, Louis-Jacques, 178
Theophilus, 86, 87, 90, 94–5, 99, 102, 106, 111, 113, 126, 266
Theophrastus, 66, 71, 74, 76
Theosophy, 22, 187
Theroux, Alexander, 135, 222
thin-layer chromatography, 293–4
Thompson, Daniel, 76–7, 86–7, 89, 107, 267, 299
three-colour printing, 274, 279, 310–14, 332, 333, 335
Timanthes, 75
tincture of the alchemists, *see* Philosopher's Stone, 87–91
Tintoretto, 129, 134, 139–40, 143, 150; *Plate 6.3*
titanium dioxide (titania), 11, 382
Titian, 3, 5, 56, 128, 134, 139, 140–42, 143, 148, 161, 270; *Plates 5.7, 5.8, 10.3, 11.1*
titration, 106
tonal painting, 142, 143
Toulouse-Lautrec, Henri de, 310
Travis, Anthony, 251
tubes, paints in, 202
Tura, Cosimo, 127, 139, 286; *Plate 11.2*
Turkey red dyeing, 247
Turner, James, 173
Turner, John Mallord William, 12, 180–83, 186, 195, 309; *Plate 7.1*
    and Field, 183, 185
    influence on Impressionists, 194
    reproduction of works by, 309, 317
    sources of pigments, 183
    use of new synthetic pigments, 182–3
    use of synthetic ultramarine, 278
Turner Prize, 384
turnsole, 105, 106

Turrell, James, 380
Two Openings in Black over Wine, 371
Tyrian purple, 36, 106, 222, 223–6, 227, 236

ultramarine, 2, 38, 97, 103, 120, 135, , 265–9, 271–2, 276
   composition, 276
   darkening of and discoloration, 297–8
   difficulty in obtaining, 160
   distinguishing between azurite and, 104
   expense, 130, 137, 160, 271, 278
   indigo as substitute for, 135, 272, 273
   mixing with white, 270
   and oil painting, 128, 270
   synthetic, 275–9
   technique for making, 266–9
   telling difference between natural and synthetic, 292–3
   use of in paintings, 142
Ulysses Deriding Polyphemus, 181; *Plate 7.1*
umber pigments, 151–2, 163
Umbrellas, The, 207, 278
unione, 123–4
Utrecht school, 162

Valentine Rescuing Sylvia from Proteus, 188, 303; *Plate 7.2*
van der Weyden, Rogier, 127, 286
van Dyck, Anthony, 134, 144, 145, 152, 153, 154, 160, 161–2, 294–5; *Plates 6.1, 6.5*
van Eyck, Jan, 125, 126–7, 129; *Plates 5.5, 9.1*
van Gogh, Vincent, 2–3, 171, 203, 206, 218–21, 257, 260, 275, 279, 284, 343–4, 384–5; *Plate 8.10*
Vandyke brown, 152, *see also* Cassel earth
varnishing, 365
Vasari, Giorgio, 124, 125, 128, 140, 145, 148, 150
Vauquelin, Nicolas Louis, 175, 176, 177, 185, 276
Vauxcelles, Louis, 349
'Veil' paintings (Louis), 377
Velázquez, Diego, 152, 159, 301
Venetian painters, 139–43, 149
Venice, 138–9

Venice: Campo San Vidal and Santa Maria della Carita, 302
Venus (Titian), 142
verdigris, 60, 71, 113–14, 128, 129, 298–9, 300
verditers, 11, 131, 132
Verguin, François-Emmanuel, 241
Vermeer, Jan, 160; *Plate 12.3*
vermilion, 23, 38, 67, 85–7, 89–90, 107, 120, 135, 136, 154–5, 293, 296–7, 333–4
   darkening of, 297
   hazards, 35
   manufacture of, 86
   in oil, 128, 129
Vernatti, Philiberto, 100
Veronese, Paolo, 129, 134, 143, 147, 149, 293, 300; *Plate 6.2*
Vessel Burning Blue Lights, A, 317
Vibert, Jean-Georges, 3, 27, 180, 200, 257
Vie, La (Picasso), 261
vinegar, 101, 106
violet, 23, 207
   aniline, 242
   cobalt, 179, 180
   dyes, 236–7
   in Impressionism, 207
Virgin Appearing to St Bernard, The, 122
Virgin of the Canon van der Paele, 127
Virgin with Chancellor Rolin, The, 229; *Plate 9.1*
Virgin and Child, The, 298
Virgin and Child with (?)Leonella D'Este, 111
Virgin and Child before a Firescreen, The, 296; *Plate 11.4*
Virgin and Child with Saints and a Donor, The, 298
Virgin and Child with Saints Peter and Paul, The, 108
viridian, 176–7, 216
vision, colour, 47–50
Vision of St Helena, The, 300
vitriol, 93
Vitruvius, 71, 76, 226, 263
Vivarini, Antonio, 136
Vlaminck, Maurice de, 347–8
Vogel, Hermann Wilhelm, 328–9
Vuillard, Edouard, 218

Wall, E. J., 332

wall paintings, 78, 100–1, *see also* fresco
painting

Walpole, Horace, 313

water mordants, 110

Watteau, Antoine, 274, 302

wax encaustic technique, 77–9

Wedgwood, Thomas, 320

Weiditz, Hans, 82; *Figure 4.1*

weld dye, 113

Wheatfield, with Cypresses, A, 279

white, 11, 50, 52, 265, 381–2
    Impressionists' attitude towards, 205–6
    permanent, 171
    titania, 382
    zinc, 169–71, 172, 180, 382

white lead, 34, 60, 70–72, 89, 105, 137, 169,
    170, 171, 299, 381–2

Who's Afraid of Red, Yellow and Blue III, 371

Widow, The, 303

Wing at the Heart of Things, A, 275; *Plate
10.4*

Winsor and Newton, 174, 179, 202, 275,
    368

Witt, Otto, 250, 331

Wittgenstein, Ludwig, 17

woad, 228, 229, 231

Woman and Child, A, 134

Women in the Garden, 209

wood
    as surface for painting, 100

wood-block printing, 318, 319

Wood, Christopher, 158

Woodward, John, 274

Wright, Stanton MacDonald, 351

Wurtz, Adolphe, 167

yellow, 23, 44, 91, 111–13, 136, 160, 173,
    264, 272, 301
    aniline, 250
    aureolin, 179
    blurring of distinction between blue and,
        15, 263, 264
    cadmium, 172–3, 180
    chrome, 11, 175–6, 177, 216, 303
    gamboge, 156–7
    Indian, 155–6
    instability of new pigments compared to
        earlier, 160
    orpiment, 69, 89, 112, 136, 139, 159,
        300
    'pink', 157, 158
    as shade of treachery and cowardice, 49
    zinc, 177, 304

Young, Thomas, 46–7, 212, 265

Zeuxis, 75

zinc, 169, 172

zinc white, 169–71, 172, 180, 382

zinc yellow, 177, 304

Zosimus of Panopolis, 86, 88

Zuccaro, Federico, 147–8, 149